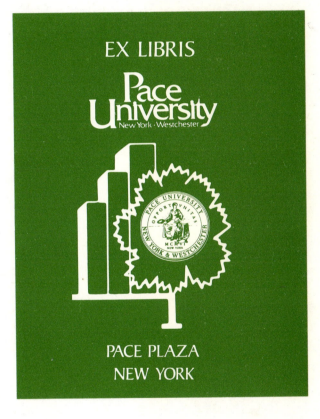

Economic Analysis of the Soviet-Type System

Economic Analysis of the Soviet-Type System

JUDITH THORNTON

University of Washington

CAMBRIDGE UNIVERSITY PRESS

CAMBRIDGE

LONDON · NEW YORK · MELBOURN

Published by the Syndics of the Cambridge University Press
The Pitt Building, Trumpington Street, Cambridge CB2 1RP
Bentley House, 200 Euston Road, London NW1 2DB
32 East 57th Street, New York, NY 10022, USA
296 Beaconsfield Parade, Middle Park, Melbourne 3206, Australia

First published 1976

Typeset in Great Britain
at the University Printing House, Cambridge
(Euan Phillips, University Printer)
Printed in the United States of America

Library of Congress Cataloguing in Publication Data
Main entry under title:
Economic analysis of the Soviet-type system.
Includes index.
1. Communist countries – Economic policy – Addresses, essays, lectures.
2. Marxian economics – Addresses, essays, lectures. I. Thornton, Judith.
HC704.E25   338.947   75–12468
ISBN 0 521 207185

Contents

v

List of Contributors

Edward Ames, State University of New York at Stony Brook
Alan A. Brown, University of Windsor
Earl Brubaker, University of Wisconsin
Elizabeth Clayton, University of Missouri
Edwin G. Dolan, Dartmouth College
Edward A. Hewett, University of Texas at Austin
Holland Hunter, Haverford College
Janos Kornai, Institute of Economics, Hungarian Academy of Sciences
J. Michael Martin, Center for Advanced Studies, General Electric
    Company
B. N. Mikhalevsky
J. M. Montais, Yale University
Egon Neubeger, State University of New York at Stony Brook
Svetozar Pejovich, Ohio University and University of Dallas
Joyce Pickersgill, California State University, Fullerton
John A. Shaw, California State University, Fresno
Judith Thornton, University of Washington
Yasushi Toda, College of Business Administration, University of Florida

Introduction

New approaches to modelling the centrally planned economy

JUDITH THORNTON

This book is concerned with the formal description and economic analysis of centrally planned systems of the Soviet type. The authors bring the tools of contemporary economic analysis to bear on the Soviet-type system to evaluate it in terms that allow comparison with other economic systems. Their papers represent a relatively new approach to the study of Socialist systems – an approach that is long overdue. They represent an attempt to develop a body of analysis grounded both in Eastern European economic institutions and in formal economic theory that can contribute to the theoretical understanding of centrally planned economies and serve as a basis for research in comparative systems.

The contributions are evenly divided between strictly theoretical analyses and economic models that serve as the basis for empirical analysis of the Soviet and East European economies. Some of the papers are concerned with the organization of planned systems – with the behavior of planners, the performance of functional units operating in a planned environment, and the interaction process between planners and functional units. Some of the papers deal with specific planning problems – the planning of foreign trade, monetary policy, resource supply, rationing, or the forecasting of macroeconomic variables. And some of the papers evaluate the consequences of planning processes in the Soviet and East European economies.

The papers provide a representative survey of the main applications and techniques of planning that are pertinent to the centrally planned economy. Taken together, I hope that they provide an introduction to the economic modelling of the Soviet-type system.

With some notable exceptions, the use of the tools of contemporary economic analysis to describe and evaluate the centrally planned economy is a relatively recent development. Empirical work on Soviet growth always drew from standard Western theory of national income and production. In turn, the peculiar problems of the Soviet price system generated useful additions to the theory of national income.

Techniques for measuring national income in sectors that lack marginal cost prices were the subject of discussion by Hicks (1940, 1948), Kuznets (1948), and Samuelson (1950) in the 1940s. Abram Bergson's

1

(1961) adjusted factor cost standard provided the theoretical justification and the empirical procedures for dealing with dual prices that have served as the norm for subsequent studies by Stanley Cohn (1970) and Abraham Becker (1969). The nature of 'index number' bias in a developing economy was first described in Alexander Gerschenkron's study (1951) of Soviet machinery and, then, further explored by G. Warren Nutter (1962) and Richard Moorsteen (1961). Similarly, empirical studies of factor productivity in the United States by John Kendrick (1961) and Edward Denison (1967) were followed quickly by empirical estimates of factor productivity in the Soviet economy (Bergson and Kuznets, 1963).

On empirical subjects other than growth, Western analysis contributed much less, largely because of the view that economic units would have relatively little opportunity to respond to price and income signals in a centrally planned economy, because the maximizing model of the Western firm seemed inappropriate for the Soviet enterprise or collective farm, and because the macroeconomic institutions of the centrally planned economy were thought to make traditional Western macro- and monetary models inapplicable.

Empirical studies of inflation and supply are cases in point. Although both George Garvey (1966) and Raymond Powell (1951) analyzed Soviet monetary policy in traditional Western terms, Joyce Pickersgill (1970) was the first economist to attempt to describe the monetary dynamics of Soviet hyperinflation by modelling the demand and supply for money. Similarly, although the effects of price and income incentives were fully documented in descriptive studies by Naum Jasny (1949), Jerzy Karcz (1944, 1967), and Nancy Nimitz (1964), Elizabeth Clayton's 'Crop Response to Price in the Soviet Union', included here, is the first attempt I know of to estimate the Soviet price elasticity of supply on the private plot. So, in measuring *how well* the Soviet economy performed, traditional Western tools were applied mainly to the study of growth.

Formal Western modelling of *how* the Soviet economy functions is also quite recent. The best early work on the organization of the Soviet economy was descriptive. Herbert Levine's (1959) description of the planning process and Joseph Berliner's (1957) study of the firm detailed the administrative processes and revealed the economic consequences of particular institutional structures and arrangements.

At the same time, the formal models and techniques that have proved most useful to the modelling of the centrally planned economy were first developed and applied in other contexts – input–output, linear programming, and general feedback systems are all cases in point. The applications of these and other mathematical techniques to the problems of the centrally planned economy have led to substantial literatures in four areas: (1) the elaboration of multi-sectoral and multi-level decomposable models of economic structure; (2) the related exploration of algorithms and decentralized procedures for solution of such systems and study of the informational aspects of such procedures; (3) modelling of internal organizational processes and of the strategic or bargaining aspects of the interaction between superior and inferior units in administrative structures; (4) decision-making models of the behavior of decentralized economic units viewed separately from their economic environment. Since the papers included here represent contributions to each of these areas, it will be useful to survey some of the main concerns and issues under discussion in them.

In the Soviet context, the elaboration of multi-sectoral planning models served the purpose, not of forecasting, but of developing procedures for central control and direction of the economic system. If Kantorovich (1960) presented the classic linear programming formulation of an optimal economic plan, then Kornai–Liptak (1963) two-level planning presented a set of administrative procedures for such planning based on an input–output matrix of commodity flows at the aggregate level linked to sectoral linear programming models of alternative technologies at the industry level. Janos Kornai (1970), Michael Manove (1971), and Martin Weitzman (1971) have published multi-sectoral planning models in which the planners' instructions take the form of output quotas and where adjustment occurs through an iterative procedure.

The literature on Lange–Lerner 'trial and error' procedures for decentralized solution of a plan gives the calculation of shadow prices a key role. The Lange procedure postulated constrained maximization by firms in response to parametric planning prices. Alternative procedures proposed by Arrow, Hurwicz and Uzawa (1958) and Malinvaud (1967) combined output targets with shadow prices. In the Malinvaud procedure, the center announces prices and firms respond with quantities; in Kornai–Liptak and Weitzman models, the center announces quantities, and firms respond with costs, although the Kornai–Liptak approach works only for an objective function that is separable among firms. The Soviet planning literature contains a parallel discussion in the 1960s, with Kantorovich (1964, 1965, 1966) exploring the quantity planning algorithm and Novozhilov (1967) and Nemchinov exploring the dual program.

The basic proposition demonstrated was that an efficient allocation of resources could be attained by a suitable set of shadow prices and that decentralized procedures existed for identifying such an allocation. A related concern was whether incentives existed for the requisite exchange of accurate information. Would firms in a planning situation play according to the 'rules of the game'? Would the system generate rewards to bargaining strategies or to the provision of false or incomplete information? Edward Ames (1967) explored some variants of bargaining

3

models in *The Structure of General Equilibrium in a Planned Economy* and he elaborates on these models in this collection. Theodore Groves (1973) raises the same issues in 'Incentives in Teams'. The issues of incentives, information, and bargaining behavior in a centrally planned system are some of the most important questions in the theory of planning, and, since such problems don't arise in the perfectly planned system or its algorithm, they remain the most inadequately treated issues in planning theory.

Finally, there is a substantial recent literature on decentralized units operating in a planned environment. Such units are modelled as constrained maximizers with objective functions that may depend on various variables – revenues, physical outputs, profits, or 'norms'. They optimize subject to technological, physical, and budget constraints. Edward Ames' *Soviet Economic Processes* (1965) described the microeconomic theory of the Soviet output-maximizing enterprise, subsequently elaborated by Richard Portes (1968) and Hayne Leland (1972). Benjamin Ward's 'The Firm in Illyria: Market Syndicalism' (1958) explored the behavior of a worker-managed cooperative. Evsey Domar (1966) and Walter Oi and Elizabeth Clayton (1968) applied the Ward model to the Soviet collective farm, and Michael Martin uses a Ward-type model to study the Soviet reform firm in this volume.

There is a fifth area of theoretical development that should have great potential for the centrally planned economy, the area of macroeconometric forecasting, but, aside from the contributions of Boris Mikhalevsky, one of whose models is presented here, the forecasting models have been relatively weak. A major forecasting effort is under way at the University of Pennsylvania to model the Soviet economy, but at this time, no results are available. Holland Hunter's paper on the Soviet First Five Year Plan in this volume is an interesting effort in what might be called 'retrospective forecasting'.

The papers collected here include contributions to each of the areas just discussed and provide a cross-section of recent developments in these areas. The book is divided into three parts. An introductory part deals with the theory of planning in general; the second part presents theoretical analyses of the Soviet-type economy; and the third part presents quantitative analyses of the Soviet-type economy.

THE THEORY OF PLANNING

The planning models included here deal with two issues – planners' tastes and behavior and the interaction between planners and planned units. From Barone on, the planners' welfare function was viewed as exogenously given or else was derived directly from consumer welfare. Jan Drenowski (1961) raised the issue of the characteristics of 'planners' preferences'. But it was not the models of planned systems, but the Marxian models of capitalism that explored the logical implications of a system in which one group, the workers, consumed their income and another group, the capitalists, invested. Curiously enough, it has been the centrally planned economies that have provided the real world cases in which one group, the planners, invested while another group, the workers, received wages that went largely to consumer goods.

Judith Thornton and J. Michael Montias deal with models where the planners desire to maximize the output of a planned good – investment in the Montias case – subject to a constraint that makes the effective supply of labor input depend on the production of a consumption good. The models have a somewhat Stalinist cast in that the capital good contributes to planners' utility directly as well as indirectly, through its productivity.

The modelling of decentralized procedures for planning generally assumes that firms scrupulously observe the rules of the procedure as laid down. However, the descriptive literature on the Soviet economy details the seemingly endless evasions of firms who have a private interest in infringing the rules and concealing information. Edward Ames' models pursue the implications of cases where firms either cannot or prefer not to fulfil planners directives. In 'The Marshallian Planned Economy', Ames discusses the stability of a planning system in which enterprises, acting as suppliers and demanders, respond to quantitative directives of central planners rather than to prices but where responses are not identical to plans. Although the Ames model is Marshallian in the respect that it is a quantity-adjustment model, the structure is Walrasian, and the conditions for a stable equilibrium of supplying and demanding firms are similar to Walrasian stability conditions. Extending his model to yield a Marshallian adjustment process, Ames presents an alternative form of 'classified planning' in which plan directives are secret to all but planner and recipient.

In 'The Priceless Planned Economy' Ames applies several variants of the classic Cournot duopoly problem to the interaction of a planner and producing units. Just as in the Cournot case, each party adopts assumptions about the behavior of the other party. Equilibrium is reached through a sequence of adjustments. In the example of informationally decentralized planning, the planners set a plan; this causes enterprises to adjust their level of activity, which in turn induces planners to adjust their plans, and so on. By changing the assumptions about information available to each party regarding the other's behavior, it is possible to generate results that parallel the Stackelberg solution or the game theory solution. One interesting possibility that Ames doesn't treat is whether, as in the case of classic duopoly, there exists a collusion solution between the planners and the firms.

THEORETICAL ANALYSES OF THE SOVIET-TYPE SYSTEM

Special problems arise in modelling the centrally planned system. Models must serve the purposes of resource allocation and management; prices may play little informational or allocative role; and adjustment of units may occur in response to a variety of incentives, signals, directives, and constraints. Sometimes, the logic of a planning model may look backwards to the Western theorist – consumer tastes will enter in the constraints and not in the objective function, or final demands will be treated as the balancing item that is cut back to sustain a desired level of raw material deliveries.

The papers by the later B. N. Mikhalevsky and by Edwin Dolan model the Soviet-type economy in opposite ways. To Mikhalevsky, the system is best described by a system of vertically related, hierarchical balances. To Dolan, the interesting aspect is the polycentric character of a network of horizontally related, relatively independent producing units.

Mikhalevsky presents a general systems model for describing complex, dynamic social systems. Section 1 of his paper presents an abstract classification of the structure of dynamic systems and then describes the modelling and planning of such systems. Section 2 describes the structure of a five-level planning model used to simulate medium-range variants for planning in the Soviet Union.

The model consists of a series of hierarchical, successively more disaggregated balances used to investigate the effects of alternative policies on investment, growth, income distribution, technical progress, employment, and prices. According to Mikhalevsky, the system is much better suited to answering the question, 'what happens if...' than the question, 'how can some given aim be attained in an optimal way and what type of control is best for this'. Information generated on the most aggregative level becomes input to solution of the balance on the next level, and so forth. Section 3 summarizes the results of some simulations of Soviet medium-range growth. Table 2 presents the predicted rates of technical progress.

Joyce Pickersgill's paper on financial planning and Edward Hewett's paper on foreign trade planning are also examples of contrasting approaches. Along with the papers on production functions and supply in part III, the Pickersgill paper analyzes the Soviet system in terms that invite direct comparison with Western systems. She describes the determinants of the supply and demand for money in the Soviet Union and then extends Phillip Cagan's (1956) model of hyperinflation to deal with the pre-war Soviet case of an economy subject to partial rationing. Her findings support the existence of a stable demand function for money in the Soviet Union.

Edward Hewett's model describes an Eastern European-type economy in which central planning and fixed coefficient balancing are combined with a high dependence on foreign trade. He presents a multi-sectoral programming model that is concerned with the decision as to what goods to export and import. The main constraints of the model are an input–output technological matrix, capacity constraints on gross output, a foreign exchange constraint, and demand constraints for net export. Investment demand is not explored. Like actual foreign trade planning in some Eastern European countries, the Hewett model is designed to achieve trade balance. It is not intended to allow decisions as to the optimal foreign trade program of the sort that are possible, for example, in Michael Bruno's (1966) programming models for Israel. For Eastern European planning, Hewett introduces a distinction between 'hard-core' and residual exports and imports. Hard-core trade is defined to be trade that is large relative to domestic output and such trade is assumed in the model to vary proportionally to output.

Modelling of the Soviet-type system is clearly inadequate if it fails to deal with allocation in markets subject to rationing. Command economies have been characterized on the production side by a combination of prices and fixed coefficient rationing to enterprises and, on the consumption side, by a combination of retail prices and rationing of commodities to consumers. John Shaw treats the problem of utility maximization by consumers who face a combination of prices, budget constraints, and explicit rations. He uses a non-linear programming formulation to express the inequalities that arise when rationing constraints are not binding. Aside from the familiar result that rationing prevents the achievement of Pareto optimality, another proposition shows up. If the planners set each individual's ration so as to exhaust available supplies, then all individuals must consume their full ration or leave unused inventories of the commodities. If, at the pre-rationing prices, the rationing constraint is not binding on all individuals, then the relative prices of rationed commodities will have to fall after the imposition of rationing in order to prevent unsold inventories of them.

Janos Kornai's 'Pressure and Suction on the Market' presents a more general theory of markets that are not cleared by prices and describes the expected adjustments that are likely to be observed in such markets. The reader will not be surprised to find that conditions of unsatisfied demand are characterized by queuing, administrative rationing, reduction in quality and service or that conditions of unsatisfied suppliers are likely to generate the corresponding phenomena on the opposite side of the market. Kornai defines 'forced substitution' as the deviation of consumer's achieved purchases from the mix that would have been desired at observed nominal prices. I find Kornai's indexes of pressure and suction on markets useful as indexes of the potential market power an administrative allocator could exercise by virtue of being in a position to decide who gets what.

7

The third group of papers present models of three main types of Socialist economic units – the Soviet firm, the market socialist firm, and the Soviet cooperative farm. They explore how decentralized units will respond to alternative success indicators, property rights, price signals, and institutional constraints.

The theory of the Socialist firm owes much to Edward Ames' (1965) analysis of the output-maximizing enterprise and Benjamin Ward's (1958) modelling of the profit-sharing labor-managed firm. Subsequently, Evsey Domar (1966) and Walter Oi and Elizabeth Clayton (1968) extended a Ward-type model to the Soviet collective farm. In 'Price, Appropriability and the Soviet Agricultural Incentives', Elizabeth Clayton explores the kinds of responses to change in governmental prices and quotas that are predicted by the Clayton–Oi model and shows how these responses are affected by constraints on the producing unit. An empirical test of the model is provided in the third section of this book. In 'Crop Response to Price in the Soviet Union', Elizabeth Clayton uses Soviet agricultural data from the period 1953 to 1959 to test the predictions of her model of collective farm behavior. The empirical results show the expected responses to price and income changes in the case of private agriculture and show how output quotas and fixed input constraints distort the response to price change in state farm and collective agriculture.

Similar distortions in the behavior of decentralized units show up in Svetozar Pejovich's paper on the investment behavior of the profit-sharing syndicalist firm. In this type of enterprise, workers may take profits in the form of current income by paying out a larger wages bill or in the form of expected future income streams by reinvesting profits. Thus, the savings alternatives of workers consist of reinvesting in the firm or of saving out of wages in the form of savings accounts. But, since workers can neither share in firm profits after they leave the firm nor sell their claims to future earnings of the enterprise, they will require a substantially higher rate of return at the margin on capital reinvested in the firm than on private savings. Given these peculiar institutions, the response of firms to availability of bank credit turns out to be perverse. When bank credit becomes available to the firm, each additional dollar the firm borrows from the bank increases total investment of the firm by less than a dollar. Pejovich shows that informal evidence on Yugoslavia in the sixties supports his predictions about the response of profit-sharing firms to the expansion of bank credit. Both Pejovich and Jaroslav Vanek have discussed the possible investment distortion under worker management (Vanek and Miovic, 1970; Vanek, 1971). But, if we view the market socialist firm as facing the alternatives of financing a given investment through a bank loan repaid at the end of a fixed period or of 'borrowing' from the workers and repaying over the same period in the form of higher wages equal to a self-liquidating annuity, then it is clear that the present values to the firm of the two alternatives are identical and they differ only in their cash flow characteristics.

Other sorts of distortions in firm behavior can be predicted in the case of Soviet firms if these firms follow the rules laid down in the economic reform in the Soviet Union. At first, the Soviet economic reform was described by many economists as an attempt to move toward profit-maximizing incentives for the Soviet firm. In his paper, J. Michael Martin builds a decision-making model of the Soviet reform firm based on the complex accounting rules laid down in the Soviet reform and predicts the behavior of enterprises operating subject to these rules. He shows that the enterprise that has profit-rate on capital in its objective function tends to choose a consistently lower capital–labor ratio for every level of output. The output response of this sort of firm depends in a predictable way on whether growth of profit, growth of output, and the level of wages bill appear explicitly in the objective function of the firm.

All of the models of various types of Socialist decision-making units detail distortions that arise when an economic unit is not rent-maximizing and when units are not constrained to operate at the least-cost, zero-profit rate of output and input. But serious questions remain in attempting to aggregate over such units to derive market equilibrium. Clearly, aggregate equilibrium will depend on how rents are capitalized in the Socialist enterprise. In most of the cases studied, the efficiency effects and distortions caused by non-profit-maximizing incentives disappear at the margin in the zero-profit case. But, after appropriate capitalization, all firms may be viewed as symmetrical to the marginal case. So, studies of such decentralized decision-making units should be understood to describe the adjustment process in Socialist markets and not to characterize market equilibrium.

QUALITATIVE ANALYSIS OF THE SOVIET-TYPE ECONOMY

While the papers in part II focus primarily on theoretical analysis, many provide empirical tests of their formal models. Conversely, in part III, the papers are primarily empirical, but the authors have applied formal theoretical analysis to generate their empirical results, to evaluate the consequences of planning processes in the Soviet and East European economies.

Elizabeth Clayton's investigation of supply elasticities in Soviet agriculture supports the deductions of her model of collective farm behavior. Two studies apply familiar Western production function models to data for the Soviet Union and Eastern Europe. Both of these studies apply estimation procedures used elsewhere to allow direct comparison of the findings presented here with the results of earlier empirical studies of other economists. Earl Brubaker extends the work of Beckman and Sato (1969) on the specification of technical progress. Brubaker explains the effects of alternative specification of technical progress on relative factor prices and quantities. Then he presents a statistical analysis of the relationship between relative factor prices and quantities for data on the Soviet nonagricultural non-residential sector. Brubaker's results parallel those of Beckman and Sato; they are inconclusive. And, since the results derived from specification of technical progress are, in turn, dependent on the assumed form of the production function, the empirical tests in both the Soviet and in earlier Western cases yield only tentative conclusions.

The interdependency of specification of technical progress and of the form of the production function comes out clearly comparing the Brubaker approach to the Brown–Neuberger approach. Brown and Neuberger use data on output and inputs in Hungary to explore the specification of the Hungarian production function. They start off from a recent study in which Martin Weitzman finds that a CES production function with an elasticity of substitution substantially lower than one is implied by Soviet data. They argue that the elasticity of substitution between factors is still lower in Hungary, that it approaches a Leontief-type L-shaped isoquant. Their interpretation of the data implies an extraordinary measure of inefficiency in the Hungarian economy, since the observed capital–labor ratio there shows substantial shifts. There is room for considerable argument here and the approach is likely to be the subject of further controversy.

I think that the methodology of Yasushi Toda's estimate of costs under disequilibrium prices raises similar question. His findings are dependent on the specification of a model in which we assume that the wage of labor diverges from labor productivity in the same direction and at an equal pace to the divergence between product price and cost. Finding ways to deal with disequilibrium prices is a most important issue in analyzing the performance of the Soviet economy, and Toda's contribution will provide a provocative start to this discussion.

An altogether different and intriguing empirical paper by Holland Hunter uses a multi-sectoral programming model to test the feasibility of the Soviet first five-year plan. Hunter takes Soviet initial conditions at the start of the five-year plan as described by input–output relations and capital stocks. He then solves a dynamic program for alternative consumption–investment paths and terminal stocks to explore the feasible alternatives that faced the planners. His simulations demonstrate that the Soviet first five-year plan targets were far beyond the realistic capacity of the economy, even given enormous reductions in interim consumption. This is a novel and highly successful application of the sort of model that has been applied by Eckaus and Parikh (1968) to the case of India and by Bruno (1966) to the case of Israel. It remains to compare small variants of the variables in order to learn more about the rates of trade-off between major variables that faced the Soviet planners. There is a substantial literature on predicting the feasibility of Communist medium-range plans. Hopefully, the Hunter approach will now replace for most purposes the rules of thumb and economic intuitions of the old-fashioned economic predictions.

The papers collected here provide the student of comparative economic systems with examples of models developed for analyzing the functioning of Soviet-type economies. The models are applied to Eastern European institutions and developments making possible analytical comparisons between economies organized on different principles. The economist who wants an introduction to the problems of macro- and microeconomic modelling of the Eastern European economies will find papers on many important new developments collected here.

REFERENCES

Ames, Edward (1965). *Soviet Economic Processes*. Irwin.
Ames, Edward (1967). The structure of general equilibrium in a planned economy. Purdue Working Paper.
Arrow, K., L. Hurwicz and H. Uzawa (1958). *Studies in Linear and Non-linear Programming*. Stanford: Stanford University Press.
Becker, Abraham (1969). *Societ National Income, 1958–64*. University of California Press.
Beckman, M. J. and R. Sato (1969). Aggregate production functions and types of technical progress: a statistical analysis. *American Economic Review*, **59**, 88–101.
Bergson, Abram (1961). *The Real National Income of Soviet Russia Since 1928*. Cambridge, Mass.: Harvard University Press.
Bergson, Abram and Simon Kuznets (1963). *Economic Trends in the Soviet Union*. Cambridge, Mass.: Harvard University Press.
Berliner, Joseph (1957). *Factory and Manager in the USSR*. Cambridge, Mass.: Harvard University Press.
Bruno, Michael (1966). A programming model for Israel. In *Theory and Design of Economic Development*, ed. Irma Adelman and E. Thornbecke. Baltimore: Johns Hopkins.
Cagan, Phillip (1956). The monetary dynamics of hyperinflation. In *Studies in the Quantity Theory of Money*, ed. Milton Friedman, pp. 25–120. Chicago: Chicago University Press.
Cohn, Stanley H. (1970). *Economic Development in the Soviet Union*. Heath and Co.
Denison, Edward (1967). *Why Growth Rates Differ*. Brookings Institute.
Domar, Evsey (1966). The Soviet collective farm as a producer cooperative. *American Economic Review*, **56**, 734–57.
Drenowski, Jan (1961). The economic theory of socialism, a suggestion for reconsideration. *Journal of Political Economy*, **64**, 341–54.
Eckaus, Richard S. and Kiret Parikh (1968). *Planning for Growth*. MIT Press.
Garvy, George (1966). *Money, Banking and Credit in Eastern Europe*. Federal Reserve Bank of New York.

Judith Thornton

Gershenkron, Alexander (1951). *A Dollar Index of Soviet Machinery Output, 1927–28 to 1937.* Rand R-197, 6 April 1951.

Groves, Theodore (1973). Incentives in teams. *Econometrica.*

Hicks, J. R. (1940). The valuation of the social income. *Economica,* **7**, 105–24.

Hicks, J. R. (1948). The valuation of the social income. *Economica,* **15**, 163–72.

Jasny, Naum (1949). The socialized agriculture of the USSR. Food Research Institute.

Kantorovich, L. V. (1960). *Ekonomichiski raschot nailushehvo izpolzovania resursov.* Academy of Sciences (*The Best Use of Economic Resources*).

Kantorovich, L. V. (1964). Dinamicheskaya model' optional'nogo planirovaniya. In *Planirovanie i ekonomko-matematicheskie metody.*

Kantorovich, L. V. (1965). Optimal'nye modeli perspektivogo planirovaniya. In *Primenenie matematiki v ekonomicheskikh issledovaniyakh,* vol. 3, ed. Nemchinov.

Kantorovich, L. V. (1966). Matematicheskie problemy optimal'nogo planirovaniya. In *Matematicheskie modeli i metody optimal'nogo planirovaniya,* ed. L. V. Kantorovich.

Karcz, Jerzy (1964). Quantitative analysis of the collective farm market. *American Economic Review,* **54**, 315–34.

Karcz, Jerzy (1967). Thoughts on the grain problem. *Soviet Studies,* **18**, 399–434.

Kendrick, John (1961). *Productivity Trends in the United States.* National Bureau for Economic Research.

Kornai, J. (1970). *Mathematical Planning of Structural Decisions.* North-Holland.

Kornai, J. and F. Liptak (1963). Two-level planning. *Econometrica,* **33**, 141–69.

Kuznets, Simon (1948). On the valuation of social income. *Economica,* **15**, 1–16.

Leland, Hayne (1972). The dynamics of a revenue maximizing firm. *International Economic Review,* **13**, 376–85.

Levine, Herbert (1959). The centralized planning of supply in Soviet industry. In *Comparisons of the United States and Soviet Economics,* Joint Economic Committee, US Congress, pp. 151–76. Washington.

Malinvaud, E. (1967). Decentralized procedures for planning. In *Activity Analysis in the Theory of Growth and Planning,* ed. E. Malinvaied and M. A. L. Bacharach, pp. 170–208. New York: St Martin's Press.

Manove, Michael (1971). A model of Soviet type economic planning. *American Economic Review,* **61**, 390–406.

Moorsteen, Richard (1961). On measuring production potential and relative efficiency. *Quarterly Journal of Economics,* **75**, 451–67.

Nimitz, Nancy (1964). *Soviet government grain procurements, depositions and stocks.* Rand.

Novozhilov, V. V. (1967). *Problemy izmereniya zatrat i rezul'tatov pri optimal'nom planirovanii.*

Nutter, G. Warren (1962). *The Growth of Industrial Production in the Soviet Union.* Princeton University Press.

Oi, W. Y. and E. M. Clayton (1968). A peasant's view of a Soviet collective farm. *American Economic Review,* **58**, 37–59.

Pickersgill, Joyce (1970). A long run demand function for money in the Soviet economy. *Journal of Money, Credit and Banking,* February.

Portes, Richard (1968). Input demand functions for the profit-constrained sales maximizer. *Economica,* 233–48.

Powell Raymond (1951). Soviet monetary policy. Ph.D. dissertation. Berkeley.

Samuelson, P. A. (1950). Evaluation of real national income. *Oxford Economic Papers,* **2**, 1–29.

US Congress Joint Economic Committee (1966). *New Directions in the Soviet Economy.* Washington.

Vanek, Jaroslav (1971). Some fundamental considerations on financing and the right of property under labor management. Cornell University Working Paper.

Vanek, Jaroslav and Peter Miovic (1970). Explorations into the 'realistic' behavior of a Yugoslav farm. Cornell University Working Paper.

Ward, Benjamin (1958). The firm in Illyria: market syndicalism. *American Economic Review*, **48**, 455–89.

Weitzman, Martin (1971). Material balances under uncertainty. *Quarterly Journal of Economics*, **75**, 262–82.

I. Theory of Planning

1. The Theory of Planned Economics

On Maximizing Subject to a Planners' Feasibility Function

JUDITH THORNTON[1]

The key characteristic of a planned economy is the substitution of planners' preferences for private tastes in the determination of the output mix and resulting input mix of an economy. In most models, this substitution is described by means of an adjustment of the output mix of the economy to a new equilibrium where the marginal rate of transformation between any two commodities in production is equated to the marginal rate of substitution between the commodities in planners' tastes.

But models that view the planning process in terms of the simple imposition of a new set of preferences on a fixed resource capacity are abstracting from an important part of the problem. Not only does the output of goods depend on the supply of productive factors, but factor supplies, in turn, depend on real factor payments. The substitution of planners' preferences for consumers' preferences in an economy generally will result in the production of a different mix of goods than would have been produced in response to consumer demands, a mix yielding a different level of real consumer satisfaction. And, except in the special case where factors are supplied inelastically with respect to the mix of goods produced, the productive capacity of the economy will not be independent of the output mix.

This effect is easily integrated into a model of planners' choice. Nevertheless, most attempts to describe equilibrium in a planned economy assume either that productive capacity is fixed or that the size of productive capacity can be influenced solely by the saving and investment decisions of the planners. Benjamin Ward's 'The Planners' Choice Variables' (1960) is one of the few models that attempt to treat the effect of a variable supply of productive factors on the planners' choices. Ward treats the case of maximization of a planners' welfare function that depends on the output of a planned good subject to a labor supply function that depends on the output of a consumption good.

Following Ward's special case, the model considered here describes the maximization of a general class of planners' welfare functions subject to production functions and an input supply function. First, we describe the short-run planners' optimum for an autarkic economy and for an economy with foreign trade. Then we extend the single-period analysis

17

to treat the long-run maximizing behavior that results from the same model.

We demonstrate that in the case of a variable input supply when the arguments of the input supply function and the planners' welfare function differ, the relevant static resource constraint for the planners is not a production possibilities curve, but the planners' feasibility constraint developed here.

The necessary conditions for maximization subject to the planners' feasibility function differ from the usual conditions for efficiency. At equilibrium, the marginal rate of product substitution on the planners' welfare function is not equal to the marginal rate of transformation, or ratio of marginal costs, on a production possibilities curve. The two rates differ by an amount that reflects the marginal input supply. From the point of view of the planners, a variable input supply may be treated as a special kind of external effect. The variable input effect shows up in both the static and dynamic models as an external benefit to the planners from the production of consumer goods or, alternatively, as a reduction in the true social cost of consumer goods to the planners.

THE PLANNERS' FEASIBILITY FUNCTION

Assume that the planners maximize a welfare function, (1), subject to short-run production functions, (2) and (3), and an input supply condition, (4)

$$W = w(C, M); \frac{\partial W}{\partial C} > 0, \frac{\partial W}{\partial M} > 0, \frac{\partial^2 W}{\partial C^2} < 0, \frac{\partial^2 W}{\partial M^2} < 0 \qquad (1)$$

$$C = c(V_1); \frac{dC}{dV_1} > 0, \frac{d^2C}{dV_1^2} \leqslant 0 \qquad (2)$$

$$M = m(V_2); \frac{dM}{dV_2} > 0, \frac{d^2M}{dV_2^2} \leqslant 0 \qquad (3)$$

$$V_1 + V_2 = V = v(C), \frac{dV}{dC} > 0, \frac{d^2V}{dC^2} < 0, V_1 \geqslant 0, V_2 \geqslant 0, \qquad (4)$$

where C is the output of consumer goods, M is the output of state goods, or monuments, and V is the total quantity of labor supplied consisting of V_1 allocated to the production of consumer goods and V_2 allocated to the production of monuments.

Writing (2) in inverse form, the three constraints can be combined into a single expression, which we call the planners' feasibility function:

$$M = m(V_2) = m(V - V_1) - m[v(C) - c^{-1}(C)]. \qquad (5)$$

The planners' feasibility function completely describes the mixes of the two commodities that are feasible given the production functions and

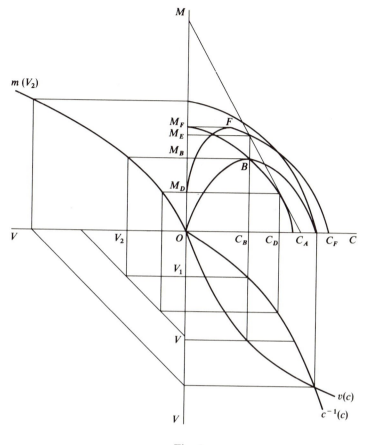

Fig. 1

factor supply conditions. Each possible output of C projected by the planners generates a total labor supply, $v(C)$, and costs the planners a quantity of labor, $c^{-1}(C)$, which cannot exceed the total labor supply. The remainder of the labor force, if any, is available for the production of M.

The feasibility constraint is demonstrated in fig. 1. Combinations of state and consumer goods are measured in the first quadrant, production functions for M and C in the second and fourth quadrants. A given quantity of the variable input, labor, is represented as a factor constraint in the third quadrant, and any point on the factor constraint represents an allocation of the total variable factor between the two outputs. The labor supply equation, $v(C)$, appears in the fourth quadrant.

Each level of C generates a total labor supply that is allocated between V_1 required to produce that level of output of consumer goods and V_2, the input available for production of state goods. The maximum possible output of monuments in this case occurs at that level of C where the positive difference between the total labor supply function and the total labor cost of consumer goods is maximized, at point B. The reader can verify by similar construction that each alternative output of C calls forth a residual labor supply that can be used to produce some quantity of monuments. These combinations trace the planners' feasibility frontier in the absence of foreign trade, OBC_A. The feasibility function describes the locus of points on the various production possibilities frontiers corresponding to each labor supply. The slope of the feasibility function at any point, (6), differs from the slope of the production possibilities curve through that point, (7), by a term that represents the effect of variable labor supply. (The slope of the production possibilities curve is simply the ratio of the marginal labor costs of the two goods.)

$$dM = -\frac{\frac{\partial c^{-1}(C)}{\partial C}}{\frac{\partial m^{-1}(M)}{\partial M}} + \frac{\frac{\partial v(C)}{\partial C}}{\frac{\partial m^{-1}(M)}{\partial M}} \tag{6}$$

$$\frac{dM}{dC} = -\frac{\frac{\partial c^{-1}(C)}{\partial C}}{\frac{\partial m^{-1}(M)}{\partial M}}; v(C) = \bar{V} \tag{7}$$

Maximizing the planners' welfare function, (1), subject to the planners' feasibility constraint, (5), yields the Lagrangian expression:

$$L = w(C, M) + \lambda(M - m[v(C) - c^{-1}(C)]). \tag{8}$$

Solving, we have:

$$\frac{\partial L}{\partial C} = \frac{\partial w}{\partial C} - \lambda \frac{\partial m(V_2)}{\partial V_2}\left[\frac{\partial v(V)}{\partial C} - \frac{\partial c^{-1}(C)}{\partial C}\right] = 0 \tag{9a}$$

$$\lambda = \frac{\partial w}{\partial C} \Big/ \frac{\partial m(V_2)}{\partial V_2}\left[\frac{\partial v(C)}{\partial C} - \frac{\partial c^{-1}(C)}{\partial C}\right]$$

$$\frac{\partial L}{\partial M} = \frac{\partial w}{\partial M} + \lambda = 0 \tag{9b}$$

$$\lambda = -\frac{\partial w}{\partial M}.$$

Combining (9a) and (9b) yields:

$$-\frac{\frac{\partial w}{\partial C}}{\frac{\partial w}{\partial M}} = -\frac{\frac{\partial c^{-1}(C)}{\partial C}}{\frac{\partial m^{-1}(M)}{\partial M}} + \frac{\frac{\partial v(C)}{\partial C}}{\frac{\partial m^{-1}(M)}{\partial M}}. \tag{10}$$

The left-hand side of (10) measures the slope of the planners' welfare function and the right-hand side the slope of the feasibility function. So long as $(\partial v(C)/\partial C)/(\partial m^{-1}(M)/\partial M) \neq 0$, the planners' marginal rate of substitution between C and M will not equal the marginal rate of transformation in production, measured as the ratio of marginal costs. The true marginal cost to the planners of a unit of consumer goods equals the marginal labor cost reduced by the amount of additional labor force called forth by that unit of consumer goods; consumer goods are an indirect input in the production of monuments.

In the absence of foreign trade, the planners' optimum will lie on the feasibility frontier at or between C_A and B in fig. 1. When $\partial w/\partial M = 0$, only C will be produced and welfare will be maximized at C_A where the total labor cost of consumer goods equals the total labor supplied in response to that quantity of consumer goods.

When $\partial w/\partial C = 0$ the necessary condition for a maximum is simply

$$\frac{\partial v(C)}{\partial C} - \frac{\partial c^{-1}(C)}{\partial C} = 0 \tag{11}$$

and the planners maximize the output of monuments at B where the marginal labor generated by an additional unit of consumer goods just equals the marginal labor cost of that unit.

In this latter case, the planners are acting as monopoly suppliers of consumer goods. The marginal labor cost of consumer goods is dV_1/dC. The marginal and average labor revenue generated are dV/dC and V/C. The relationship between marginal and average revenue yields:

$$\frac{dV}{dC} = \frac{V}{C} + C\frac{d(V/C)}{dC} = \frac{V}{C}\left(1 + \frac{C}{(V/C)} \cdot \frac{d(V/C)}{dC}\right) = \frac{V}{C}\left(1 - \frac{1}{\eta}\right), \tag{12}$$

when

$$\eta = -\frac{dC}{d(V/C)} \cdot \frac{(V/C)}{C}.$$

So the maximizing condition in (11) can be written:

$$\frac{V}{C}\left(1 - \frac{1}{\eta}\right) - \frac{dV_1}{dC} = 0, \tag{11'}$$

which is monopoly equilibrium.

THE PLANNERS' FEASIBILITY FUNCTION WITH TRADE

The opportunity to engage in foreign trade expands the planners' possible output mixes but does not change the necessary conditions for a maximum. With foreign trade, our earlier model becomes:

$$W = w(C_d + C_f, M_d + M_f); \tag{13}$$

$$C_d = c(V_1); \tag{14}$$

$$M_d = m(V_2); \tag{15}$$

$$V_1 + V_2 = V = v(C_d + C_f); \tag{16}$$

$$p_c C_f + M_f = 0; \; p_m = 1 \tag{17}$$

where the price of monuments in foreign trade is taken as unity, and the subscripts d and f refer to domestic and foreign production. (A negative value for foreign imports implies export of domestic production.) We assume the functions take the same form as before.

For foreign trade to be in balance, a positive value of imports of one commodity must be offset by a negative value, or exports, of the other commodity. The feasibility function now takes the form:

$$M_d + M_f = m[v(C_d + C_f) - c^{-1}(C_d)] - p_c C_f. \tag{18}$$

The feasibility function with trade can be generated in fig. 1 as follows. Assume we can control the level of consumption of C, then any level of consumption of consumer goods, say $C_d + C_f = C_B$, would generate a labor supply, V. If this labor force were allocated between the production of C and M so as to maximize the value of output at foreign trade prices, the economy would produce mix C_D and M_D of the two goods. Then, the difference between domestic production of C and domestic consumption would be sold (or bought) in foreign trade. In fig. 1, $C_D - C_B$ is sold in order to acquire $M_E - M_D$ of the planners' good. When the planned economy is competitive in foreign trade, meaning that foreign trade prices are given, and when domestic production possibilities from given resources demonstrate the normal diminishing marginal rates of transformation, the feasibility function with trade OFC_F will lie on or outside of the function without trade. Each new set of foreign trade prices will generate a new feasibility constraint for the planners.

Maximizing the planners' welfare function, (13), subject to the feasibility constraint, (18), yields the necessary conditions for a maximum from which we can show that the planners marginal rate of substitution in equilibrium will diverge from both the ratio of domestic marginal costs and the world price ratio:[2]

$$-\frac{\dfrac{\partial w}{\partial (C_d + C_f)}}{\dfrac{\partial w \cdot}{\partial (M_d + M_f)}} = -\frac{\dfrac{\partial c^{-1}}{\partial C_d}}{\dfrac{\partial m^{-1}}{\partial M_d}} + \frac{\dfrac{\partial v}{\partial (C_d + C_f)}}{\dfrac{\partial m^{-1}}{\partial M_d}}, \tag{19}$$

$$-\frac{\dfrac{\partial w}{\partial (C_d + C_f)}}{\dfrac{\partial w}{\partial (M_d + M_f)}} = -\frac{p_c}{p_m} + \frac{\dfrac{\partial v}{\partial (C_d + C_f)}}{\dfrac{\partial m^{-1}}{\partial M_d}}, \tag{20}$$

$$\frac{p_c}{p_m} = \frac{\partial c^{-1}}{\partial C_d} \Big/ \frac{\partial m^{-1}}{\partial M_d}. \tag{21}$$

The planners' feasibility function

From (21) we see that the planners will allocate domestic resources between the two commodities so that the ratio of the marginal labor costs of the two goods equals the foreign trade price ratio; that is, they will always choose to produce that mix of goods that maximizes the value at foreign trade prices of the total output produced by each labor supply. But the labor supply at equilibrium is determined, not by the mix produced, but by the mix of goods consumed in the economy. From (19) and (20) we see that at an optimum consumption mix, the planners' marginal rate of substitution between C and M still differs from both the ratio of domestic marginal costs and from the foreign trade price ratio by a term that measures the labor supply effect.

When $\partial w/\partial M = 0$ for the planners, only C will be consumed in the economy. The mix of C and M produced is still determined by the condition

$$\frac{p_c}{p_m} = \frac{\partial c^{-1}}{\partial C_d} \bigg/ \frac{\partial m^{-1}}{\partial M_d},$$

but all M produced domestically will be sold in foreign trade. As long as the labor supply effect is positive, the planners can call forth a larger total labor force, and the economy can enjoy a larger consumption of C by taking advantage of foreign trade than they could under autarky.

When $\partial w/\partial C = 0$ the necessary conditions for a maximum are:

$$\frac{\partial v}{\partial (C_d + C_f)} - p_c = 0 \tag{22}$$

$$\frac{\partial v}{\partial (C_d + C_f)} - \frac{\partial c^{-1}}{\partial C_d} = 0 \tag{23}$$

$\left(\text{since in equilibrium } \dfrac{\partial m^{-1}}{\partial M_d} = p_M = 1\right).$

With trade, the output of monuments is maximized at M_F in fig. 1. At this point, an optimum amount of consumer goods is supplied through domestic production and foreign trade so that the marginal labor generated by an additional unit of consumer goods consumed in the society just equals the price of those consumer goods in terms of units of M in foreign trade. The quantity of goods traded equals the difference between the optimum consumption mix and the domestic production mix that maximizes the value of production at foreign trade prices. So the marginal labor generated by an additional unit of consumer goods consumed equals both the foreign trade price and the domestic marginal cost of consumer goods in terms of units of M.

LONG RUN MAXIMIZATION SUBJECT TO A FEASIBILITY FUNCTION

In the one-period models, we assumed that the planners had only a single input whose quantity could be varied and that the planners' good, monuments, contributed to planners' utility but not to production. Next, we relax these assumptions and treat M, the planners' good, as the current output of machinery which can be added to the productive capital stock, K.

Assume that the planners maximize a welfare function:

$$W = \int_0^\infty U(C, K)\, e^{-\rho t}\, dt;\ \frac{\partial U}{\partial C} > 0,\ \frac{\partial U}{\partial K} > 0,\ \frac{\partial^2 U}{\partial C^2} < 0,\ \frac{\partial^2 U}{\partial K^2} < 0 \quad (24)$$

subject to the following constraints:

$$C(t) = C(K_c(t), V_c(t));\ \frac{\partial C}{\partial K} > 0,\ \frac{\partial C}{\partial V} > 0,\ \frac{\partial^2 C}{\partial K^2} < 0,\ \frac{\partial^2 C}{\partial V^2} < 0 \quad (25)$$

$$\dot{K} = M(t) - \mu K = M(K_m(t), V_m(t)) - \mu K;$$

$$\frac{\partial M}{\partial K} > 0,\ \frac{\partial M}{\partial V} > 0,\ \frac{\partial^2 M}{\partial K^2} < 0,\ \frac{\partial^2 M}{\partial V^2} < 0 \quad (26)$$

$$V_c(t) + V_m(t) = V(C(t)) \quad (27)$$

$$K_c(t) + K_m(t) = K(t) \quad (28)$$

$$K(0) = k \quad (29)$$

where μ represents the depreciation rate on capital stock, and the planners' welfare function and the labor supply function retain the previous form. The welfare function seems peculiarly Stalinist since, when $\partial U/\partial K > 0$ the capital stock contributes directly to planners' utility in addition to its indirect contribution to the rate of output. Equations (25) and (26) contain the production functions for consumer goods and capital goods. Growth of the capital stock equals the current output of machinery less depreciation on the existing capital stock. From (27), the quantity of labor available at each point in time still depends on the level of consumption provided by the planners, as in the static case. The labor supply function is stable through time, implying a stable population. (The labor supply condition differs from the familiar case in many growth models in which labor is supplied inelastically at each point in time but in which the labor supply function is assumed to shift through time. For example, see Shell (1967) and Chase (1967).) As before, the planners are assumed to control resource allocation either directly or indirectly through the prices they set for decentralized socialist firms.

The planners' feasibility function

If we define $V_c(t) = F(C(t), K_c(t))$ as the minimum quantity of labor required to produce output $C(t)$ with the capital stock $K_c(t)$, the feasibility function at any point in time takes the form:

$$\dot{K} = M(t) - \mu K(t) = M\langle K(t) - K_c(t), V[C(t)] - \{F[C(t), K_c(t)]\}\rangle - \mu K(t).$$
$$(30)$$

We write the Lagrangian as $\int_0^\infty H\,dt$ where:

$$H = \langle U(C, K) + \lambda\{M[K - K_c, V(C) - F(C, K_c)] - \mu K - \dot{K}\}\rangle e^{-\rho t} \quad (31)$$

and λ is a Lagrange multiplier. The necessary conditions show the same labor supply effect that we encountered in the static model. Along the optimal consumption path at any time, the marginal labor cost of consumer goods to the planners is lower than the marginal labor cost in production by an amount equalling the extra labor called forth by consumer goods. Since this is a two sector model, the allocation of capital between K_c and K_m at each point in time is also a decision variable, but this is simply governed by the usual value of marginal product condition.[3]

$$\frac{\partial H}{\partial C} = e^{-\rho t}\frac{\partial U}{\partial C} + e^{-\rho t}\lambda\frac{\partial M}{\partial V}\left(\frac{\partial V}{\partial C} - \frac{\partial F}{\partial C}\right) = 0;$$

$$\frac{\partial U}{\partial C} = \lambda\frac{\partial M}{\partial V}\left(\frac{\partial F}{\partial C} - \frac{\partial V}{\partial C}\right); \quad\quad (32a)$$

$$\frac{\partial H}{\partial K_c} = -e^{-\rho t}\lambda\frac{\partial M}{\partial K_M} - e^{-\rho t}\lambda\frac{\partial M}{\partial V}\frac{\partial V_c}{\partial K_c} = 0;$$

$$\lambda\frac{\partial M}{\partial K_M} = \lambda\frac{\partial M}{\partial V}\frac{\partial V_c}{\partial K_c}; \quad\quad (32b)$$

$$\frac{d}{dt}\left(\frac{\partial H}{\partial \dot{K}}\right) = \frac{\partial H}{\partial K}; \quad\quad (32c)$$

$$\dot{K} = M(K_M, V_M) - \mu K.$$

From (32a) we have

$$\frac{d}{dt}(\lambda e^{-\rho t}) = \left(\frac{\partial U}{\partial K} + \lambda\frac{\partial M}{\partial K} - \mu\lambda\right)e^{-\rho t};$$

$$-[\dot{\lambda} - \rho\lambda] = \frac{\partial U}{\partial K} + \lambda\frac{\partial M}{\partial K} + \mu\lambda; \quad\quad (33)$$

$$\dot{\lambda} = \rho\lambda - \frac{\partial U}{\partial K} - \lambda\frac{\partial M}{\partial K} + \mu\lambda.$$

Equation (33) says that the rate at which the value of adding to capital stock from current output is changing consists of the time discount and

depreciation rates less the marginal contributions of capital to planners' utility and to output.

Assuming convexity of the welfare, labor supply, and production functions, a unique optimum path exists, and along the optimal path, K will tend to a steady state value. (The model tends to a steady state value because of the assumption of zero population growth.) At that value, $\dot{K} = 0$ and the output of the machinery industry is just equal to depreciation of the existing capital stock:

$$M(K_m, V_m) = \mu K. \tag{34}$$

With no change in net capital stock, $\dot{\lambda} = 0$ and the marginal value of adding to capital stock from current output, λ, is constant and equal to:[4]

$$\lambda = \frac{\partial U/\partial K}{\rho + \mu - \dfrac{\partial M}{\partial K}}. \tag{35}$$

(Notice that for $\lambda > 0$, we must have $\rho + \mu > \partial M/\partial K$.)

Setting $\dot{K}, \dot{\lambda} = 0$ and taking into consideration the necessary conditions in (32) allows us to describe the steady state.

$$\lambda = \frac{\partial U/\partial C}{\dfrac{\partial M}{\partial V}\left(\dfrac{\partial F}{\partial C} - \dfrac{\partial V}{\partial C}\right)} = \frac{\partial U/\partial K}{\rho + \mu - \dfrac{\partial M}{\partial K}}; \tag{36a}$$

$$-\frac{\dfrac{\partial U}{\partial C}}{\dfrac{\partial U}{\partial K}} = \frac{\dfrac{\partial M}{\partial V}\left(\dfrac{\partial V}{\partial C} - \dfrac{\partial F}{\partial C}\right)}{\rho + \mu - \dfrac{\partial M}{\partial K}}. \tag{36b}$$

The dynamic equilibrium in (36) proves to be exactly symmetrical with the static equilibrium in (10) because, with $\dot{K} = 0$ and $\dot{\lambda} = 0$, nothing is changing.

$$\frac{\dfrac{\partial w}{\partial C}}{\dfrac{\partial w}{\partial M}} = -\frac{\dfrac{\partial c^{-1}}{\partial C}}{\dfrac{\partial m^{-1}}{\partial M}} + \frac{\dfrac{\partial v}{\partial C}}{\dfrac{\partial m^{-1}}{\partial M}}; \tag{10a}'$$

$$-\frac{\dfrac{\partial w}{\partial C}}{\dfrac{\partial w}{\partial M}} = \frac{\partial m}{\partial V_2}\left(\frac{\partial v}{\partial C} - \frac{\partial c^{-1}}{\partial C}\right). \tag{10b}'$$

Even more important, equation (36) demonstrates that the model treats consumer goods and capital goods in a symmetrical manner. Consumer goods figure both as a direct argument in utility and, indirectly, as an input to production via their effect on labor. And similarly, capital goods

may figure both as a direct argument in utility and as an input to production. In (36b) $(\partial M/\partial V)/(\partial F/\partial C)$ reflects the labor costs of consumer goods, in terms of machinery, and $(\partial M/\partial V)/(\partial V/\partial C)$ reflects the indirect marginal product of consumer goods in expanding the output of M. Similarly for capital, the discount rates $\rho + \mu$ measure the cost of maintaining the capital stock in terms of current goods and $\partial M/\partial K$ reflects the marginal product of capital in expanding the output of M.

When $\partial U/\partial K = 0$, the marginal value of expanding the capital stock, λ, falls to 0 and, at the optimum, the planners produce capital goods just to the point where the marginal product of capital equals the sum of the depreciation and time discount rates.

$$\rho + \mu - \frac{\partial M}{\partial K} = 0. \tag{37}$$

When $\partial U/\partial C = 0$ the planners maximize the size of the capital stock. At each point in time, they produce consumer goods just to the point where the marginal labor generated by an additional unit of consumer goods equals the marginal labor required to produce that unit of consumer goods with the existing capital stock. In this case, the necessary condition corresponds to the maximum at B in fig. 1 in the static model.

$$\lambda \frac{\partial M}{\partial V} \left(\frac{\partial V}{\partial C} - \frac{\partial F}{\partial C} \right) = 0. \tag{38}$$

CONCLUSIONS

In many cases where the mix of output is determined by planners' rather than consumers' tastes, the feasibility function provides a useful substitute for the production possibilities function. The welfare functions of consumers cannot be measured directly by the planners, but consumer tastes underlie the labor supply function observed by the planners. Although consumer welfare is not a direct argument in the planners' welfare function, the production of consumer goods paid to the labor force may be.

The labor supply function implies simply that in the relevant range, higher real wages (consumer goods per worker) call forth larger quantities of workers. After a point, the labor supply curve may be backward bending, but the planners would never be observed to operate in this region. A variable supply of labor need not be justified solely by the labor–leisure choice. In an underdeveloped country, the planners may be drawing their labor force out of a subsistence agricultural sector, or, in a subsistence economy, increased consumption per worker may increase worker productivity, and, thus, the quantity of available labor services.

The planners will never produce in the range to the left of B in fig. 1 where the marginal labor called forth by an additional unit of consumer goods exceeds the marginal labor required to produce that unit with the existing capital stock, because expanding the rate of output of consumer goods would allow the planners to have more of both goods. From one point of view, consumer goods are a primary good used by the planners to produce an intermediate good, labor, which is then turned into more primary and final goods. From another point of view, the labor supply effect is a production externality, and the true marginal cost of consumer goods to the planners is their marginal cost in production less the value of the marginal labor supply.[5]

The distinction between consumption and capital goods is blurred. Capital stock may contribute to planners' utility directly in addition to its indirect contribution to the rate of output. And consumer goods, in turn, contribute not only to planners' utility but also to the rate of total output via the labor supply they produce.

Finally, when the supply of labor is variable, the simple market socialist rule that a maximizing planner should choose a mix of output such that his marginal rate of substitution between C and M equals the ratio of their marginal costs must be modified to take into account the labor supply effect. At every point in time, the planners maximize their welfare subject not to fixed inputs but to the range of possibilities described by the planners' feasibility constraint.

NOTES

1 I have profited from the advice of my colleagues Frank Mills, Michael Hadjimicha-lakis, and Richard Parks; I am, of course, responsible for any remaining errors.

2 $L = w(C_d + C_f, M_d + M_f) + \lambda \{M_d + M_f - m[v(C_d + C_f) - c^{-1}(C_d)] + p_c C_f\};$

$$0 = \frac{\partial L}{\partial C_d} = \frac{\partial w}{\partial C_d} - \lambda \frac{\partial m(V_2)}{\partial V_2} \left[\frac{\partial v(C_d + C_f)}{\partial (C_d + C_f)} - \frac{\partial c^{-1}}{\partial C_d} \right]; \quad \text{(a)}$$

$$0 = \frac{\partial L}{\partial C_f} = \frac{\partial w}{\partial C_f} - \lambda \frac{\partial m(V_2)}{\partial V_2} \left[\frac{\partial v(C_d + C_f)}{\partial (C_d + C_f)} \right] + \lambda p_c; \quad \text{(b)}$$

$$0 = \frac{\partial L}{\partial M_d} = \frac{\partial w}{\partial M_d} + \lambda; \quad \text{(c)}$$

$$0 = \frac{\partial L}{\partial M_f} = \frac{\partial w}{\partial M_f} + \lambda. \quad \text{(d)}$$

3 In order to show the equilibrium conditions in all markets, it is convenient to use the expanded form of the constraints and to rewrite (31) as:

$$H = \{U(C, K) + \lambda_1[C(K_c, V_c) - C] + \lambda_2[M(K_m, V_m) - \dot{K} - \mu K]$$
$$+ \lambda_3[V(C) - V_c - V_m] + \lambda_4(K - K_c - K_m)\} e^{-\rho t}.$$

The necessary conditions at each point in time show both the familiar conditions for efficient resource allocation and the labor supply effect of consumer goods. The planners' marginal utility from consumer goods differs from their marginal cost by the value of the additional labor called forth.

$$0 = \frac{\partial H}{\partial C} = \frac{\partial U}{\partial C} - \lambda_1 + \lambda_3 \frac{\partial V}{\partial C}, \qquad MU = P_c - \left(VMP_v \cdot \frac{\partial V}{\partial C} \right); \tag{a}$$

$$0 = \frac{\partial H}{\partial K_c} = \lambda_1 \frac{\partial C}{\partial K_c} = \lambda_4, \qquad P_c MPP_k = P_k; \tag{b}$$

$$0 = \frac{\partial H}{\partial K_m} = \lambda_2 \frac{\partial M}{\partial K_m} - \lambda_4, \qquad P_m MPP_k = P_k; \tag{c}$$

$$0 = \frac{\partial H}{\partial V_c} = \lambda_1 \frac{\partial C}{\partial V_c} - \lambda_3, \qquad P_c MPP_v = P_v; \tag{d}$$

$$0 = \frac{\partial H}{\partial V_m} = \lambda_2 \frac{\partial M}{\partial V_m} - \lambda_3, \qquad P_m MPP_v = P_v. \tag{e}$$

4 If $\dot{\lambda} = 0$, then:

$$\rho\lambda = \frac{\partial U}{\partial K} + \lambda \frac{\partial M}{\partial K} - \mu\lambda;$$

$$\lambda = \frac{\partial U / \partial K}{\rho + \mu - \partial M / \partial K}.$$

The expanded form of the same model has two prices for capital – the price of capital stock, λ_4, and the price of machinery λ_2.

$$\frac{d}{dt}\left(\frac{\partial H}{\partial \dot{K}}\right) = \frac{\partial H}{\partial K};$$

$$\frac{d}{dt}\left(\lambda_2 e^{-\rho t}\right) = \left(\frac{\partial U}{dK} + \lambda_4 - \lambda_2 \mu\right) e^{-\rho t}.$$

$$-[\dot{\lambda}_2 - \rho\lambda_2] = \frac{\partial U}{\partial K} + \lambda_4 - \lambda_2 \mu;$$

$$\dot{\lambda}_2 = \rho\lambda_2 - \frac{\partial U}{\partial K} - \lambda_4 + \lambda_2 \mu.$$

If $\dot{\lambda} = 0$,

$$\rho\lambda_2 = \frac{\partial U}{\partial K} + \lambda_4 - \lambda_2 \mu;$$

$$\lambda_2 = \frac{\partial U / \partial K + \lambda_4}{\rho + \mu}.$$

5 Note the similarity between the analysis and the analysis of a consumption externality by Dolbear (1967).

REFERENCES

Chase, Elizabeth S. (1967). Leisure and consumption. In *Essays on the Theory of Optimal Economic Growth*, ed. Karl Shell, pp. 175–80. MIT Press.

Dolbear, F. T., Jr (1967). On the theory of optimum externality. *American Economic Review*, **57**, 90–103.

Shell, Karl (1967). Optimal programs of capital accumulation for an economy in which there is exogenous technical change. In *Essays on the Theory of Optimal Economic Growth*, ed. Karl Shell, pp. 1–30. MIT Press.

Ward, Benjamin (1960). The planners' choice variables. In *Value and Plan*, ed. Benjamin Ward, pp. 132–61. Berkeley: University of California Press.

Principles of Resource Allocation and Real-Wage Determination for an Economy Maximizing Capital Formation

JOHN M. MONTIAS

INTRODUCTION

Present-day governments in most developed countries, and in many parts of the underdeveloped world as well, have perfected means of totalitarian control over their populations that enable them, when the occasion arises, to mobilize the entire nation in the pursuance of a single goal, such as an all-out war effort or an industrialization campaign. The Soviet government in the 1930s and the Chinese Communists in the 1950s pressed forward industrial-expansion programs that called for heavy sacrifices on the part of the population, which was enlisted *en masse* to help carry out their rulers' objectives. An essential restraint on the planners waging this kind of campaign is that the amount of consumer goods they make available to the population must not fall below the level where the drop in the productivity of labor caused by the lack of food or other commodities would jeopardize the industrialization drive itself. This danger point may be warded off by appealing to the patriotism of the population and by coercive measures, but it must eventually set a limit to the austerity measures decreed by the government.

In this article I want to look into the logical implications of a model where the authorities in control – or 'planners' – are bent on maximizing the net output of one or more sectors turning out producer goods, subject to various constraints including the availability of labor, whose efficiency is taken to be dependent upon its consumption of wage goods produced in the remaining sectors.[1]

After experimenting with the alternative of introducing an explicit function relating labor productivity to the consumption of wage goods per laborer, I found that it was both more convenient and more realistic to introduce wage goods directly into the production function of each sector. This approach permits continuous substitution along a given production isoquant of the wage-goods input for factors of production other than labor – an essential feature of the present model.[2] Whatever its convenience, it may be noted that there is nothing new in the idea of introducing the wage fund as an input in the production function: it was inherent in most classical analyses up to and including Marx.

TWO-SECTOR MODEL IN A CLOSED ECONOMY

In the following analysis of a two-sector model operating in a closed economy, we shall assume that the transformation of inputs into outputs in both sectors takes place instantaneously. In general, only the conditions for static efficiency will be investigated; it is taken for granted that these conditions, if they apply to every period separately, must also apply to a multi-period system; but only a few observations will be made on the growth of the sectors in the long run.

The production function for sector I, producing wage goods (called 'food' for short), will be chosen as a particular form of (1):

$$X = \phi(X_x, L_x, K_x, Y_x), \tag{1}$$

where X is total food output, X_x is the consumption of food by the sector during this same period, L_x and K_x are the labor and capital (including land) employed in the sector, and Y_x is the amount of the producer goods delivered by sector II currently consumed in making X. In general, the subscripts used refer to the sector to which an input has been assigned.

The production function in sector II making producer goods is a particular form of (2):

$$Y = F(X_y, L_y, K_y, Y_y), \tag{2}$$

where Y is the production of the sector, X_y is the amount of input of sector I consumed in producing Y, L_y is the labor and K_y is the capital employed in the sector. Finally, Y_y is the input of producer goods consumed within the sector.

The constraints and allocation equations that must be satisfied for the economy as a whole are the following:

$$\left.\begin{aligned}
X_x + X_y &= X \\
L_x + L_y &= \bar{L} \\
K_x + K_y &= \bar{K} \\
Y_x + Y_y + Y_I &= Y
\end{aligned}\right\}, \tag{3}$$

where $\bar{L}$ and $\bar{K}$ represent, respectively, the total labor force and the total capital supply available in any given period. Note, however, that in any given period $\bar{L}$ and $\bar{K}$ are exogenous variables, whereas X and Y are endogenously determined. Our last variable is Y_I, which stands for that portion of the output of the second sector that is neither allocated to the first (Y_x) nor consumed within the sector (Y_y). Y_I represents the output of capital goods that contribute to the increase in the stock of capital.

The problem the planners must solve is to maximize Y_I representing the volume of investment goods available for subsequent periods, subject to the above constraints.

On the other hand, Y_y and Y_x are materials produced in the second sector that are immediately consumed (in sectors II and I respectively).

It is assumed that the planners can allocate all factors of production between the sectors as they see fit. (This implies, for instance, that they may disregard the preferences of labor between the sectors without incurring any loss of efficiency.) The labor force is measured in terms of work-hours, according to the legally prescribed length of the working day and the number of able-bodied participants in the labor force.

Some assumptions will now be made regarding the nature of the production functions used in this analysis. (1) First, I posit a lower bound on the real wage in both sectors below which no production is possible, either because a revolution would occur or because the laborers would be too weak to come to work. (2) The marginal conditions require that the production function should be continuously differentiable and homogeneous of the first degree: They should exhibit constant returns to scale with respect to their inputs and increasing marginal rates of substitution for all inputs throughout. Thus food can be substituted for labor on the same production isoquant of sectors I or II, but successive increments of food input will permit the planners to economize increasingly small amounts of labor as food is substituted for labor (as the food-wage of laborers in the sector is raised). In other words, the increments in labor productivity associated with increments in the food consumed by laborers become increasingly small as they get better fed (though these productivity increments may be quite high at low levels of consumption). (3) At a later point in this paper, I subject the functions to two further restrictions: The elasticity of substitution between any two factors in a production function is assumed constant for all levels of output and all combinations of inputs; and, for most purposes of the analysis, the elasticities of substitution are taken to be the same for all pairs of factors entering in the same function. These constant elasticities, however, may take on any values.

Given the second assumption, it is easy to show, as well as intuitively obvious, that the following conditions are necessary for allocative efficiency, irrespective of the specific form of the production functions and of the objective function posited:

$$\frac{\partial Y}{\partial L_y} = \frac{\partial Y}{\partial X_y} \cdot \frac{\partial X_y}{\partial L_x}; \tag{4}$$

$$\frac{\partial Y}{\partial K_y} = \frac{\partial Y}{\partial X_y} \cdot \frac{\partial X_y}{\partial K_x}; \tag{5}$$

$$\frac{\partial Y}{\partial X_y} \frac{\partial Y_y}{\partial X_x} = 1. \tag{6}$$

If both (4) and (5) are met simultaneously, then:

$$\frac{\partial X}{\partial L_y} \bigg/ \frac{\partial Y}{\partial K_y} = \frac{\partial X_y}{\partial L_x} \bigg/ \frac{\partial X_y}{\partial K_x}. \tag{7}$$

Equations (4) and (5) state that the marginal allotment of an exogenous factor must have the same effect on the output of the capital good Y as a result of its employment in the food sector and of the allocation of the resulting increment in food X to the making of Y as if it has been allotted directly to the Y sector. After dividing the left-hand side of these two equations by $\partial Y/\partial X_y$, it is also apparent that the marginal product of labor or capital in making X must equal the marginal rate of substitution of either of these factors for food in making Y.

Equation (6) may be interpreted as follows: the output of the producer-goods sector used for current consumption in the food sector (Y_x) must be pushed to the point where the last unit will have a marginal effect on food output just sufficient to release a unit of Y when this increment of X is delivered to the Y-sector.

Equation (7) states the familiar principle of rational allocation that the ratio of the marginal products of any two factors must be equal in alternative uses (as long as the planners take into account only the productivity of factors in competing uses, disregarding their preferences, or those of consumers, for alternative employments).

It may be observed that in equations (4), (5) and (6), the variable Y may be replaced by Y_I or by any other function of the arguments in equation (2).

The marginal condition for the allocation of labor between the food sector and the producer-goods sector is illustrated in fig. 2.

In fig. 1, the total labor force $\bar{L}$ is represented by the segment O–O'. If OA units of labor are allotted to the producer-goods sector, whose food–labor isoquants are shown on the right-hand side, $O'A$ units will be left to employ in the food sector. The isoquants showing the production of Y for varying combinations of L_y and X_y are seen to increase in the north-west direction.

The other inputs into Y that are not shown in the diagram are assumed to be given; for the family of functions we shall be dealing with, the level of these inputs will only affect the numbering of the isoquants, not their slopes at any point, which are exclusively determined by the two inputs singled out here (see equation (15) below).

The concave functions relating the gross and net output of food to the input of labor in the second sector are shown on the left side of the figure. With a labor allotment of $O'A$,the sector can produce AQ units of food and deliver AP units to the first sector, the remainder PQ being retained for consumption in the food sector. The wage of laborers in the food sector equals PQ/FP or the slope of line FQ. The wage of laborers in the producer-goods sector is AP/OA or the slope of the ray OP from the origin. As can readily be ascertained from the diagram, wages in the two sectors are not necessarily equal.

It is evident that point P represents a feasible allocation, given the

33

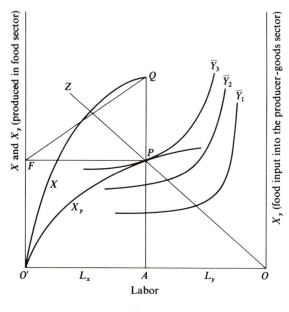

Fig. 1

labor force $\bar{L}$, since enough food is produced, in addition to the internal consumption of the food sector, to supply the producer-goods sector requirements at P. It is also an efficient allocation, since the net-food-output curve touches the highest possible Y-isoquant. At point P, in accord with the marginal condition stated in equation (4), the slope of the net-food-output curve X_y is equal to the marginal rate of substitution of food for labor, which is of course represented by the slope of the highest attainable isoquant at that point.

In view of what was already said about the effect of changes in resources other than labor on the numbering of the food–labor isoquants, it should be obvious that an upward shift in curve X_y – due, say, to a transfer of capital from the second to the first sector – will not necessarily raise the net output of Y, even though it will allow the curve X_y to become tangent to a geometrically higher isoquant than before. For this reallocation may so reduce the output index assigned to each isoquant that the 'higher' Y-isoquant to which the X_y curve will be tangent will correspond to a lower output than at the old equilibrium point.

How is the relation of curve X_y to curve X determined? This depends on the production function for food. Suppose we restrict ourselves to functions exhibiting constant elasticities of substitution between inputs for the likely range of variation in input proportions. Three cases may be distinguished.

(1) The elasticity of substitution relating any pair of inputs (say X_x and Y_x) is equal to the elasticity relating any other pair entering the function (e.g., L_x and K_x). We then have a function of the Arrow, Chenery, Minhas and Solow (1961) type (abbreviated henceforth as ACMS function):

$$X = A_x(\omega_1 X_x^{-\beta} + \omega_2 L_x^{-\beta} + \omega_3 K_x^{-\beta} + \omega_4 Y_x^{-\beta})^{-1/\beta}, \qquad (8)$$

where A_x is a shift variable, which may increase through time with technical progress or may vary in a more limited planning period with the weather or other chance variables, and the constants ω_1 to ω_4 may be interpreted as the partial elasticities of output with respect to the corresponding inputs when the elasticity of substitution is equal to unity. The constant β is related to the elasticity of substitution σ by the formula:

$$\sigma = \frac{1}{1+\beta}.$$

To maximize the net output of food available to the capital-goods sector (X_y), we differentiate the expression for X_y with respect to X_x and set the result equal to zero:

$$\frac{\partial X_y}{\partial X_x} = \frac{\partial(X - X_x)}{\partial X_x} = \frac{\partial X}{\partial X_x} - 1 = 0.$$

From (8) and the above expression we obtain after simplification:

$$X_x = \omega_1^{1/(\beta+1)}\left(A^{\beta/(\beta+1)} - \omega_1^{1/(\beta+1)}\right)^{1/\beta}\left(\omega_2 L_x^{-\beta} + \omega_3 K_4^{-\beta} + \omega_4 Y_x^{-\beta}\right)^{-1/\beta}$$

$$= \left(\frac{\omega_1}{A_x^\beta}\right)^{1/(\beta+1)} X. \quad (9)$$

The terms in the first parentheses of the expanded expression show the crucial condition necessary to make this maximization economically meaningful.[3] The average real wage in the food sector is obviously equal to

$$\frac{\omega_1^{1/(\beta+1)}}{A_x^{\beta/(\beta+1)}} \cdot \frac{X}{L_x}, \qquad (10)$$

or a constant multiplied by the sector's labor productivity.

Since the numerator is a concave function exhibiting decreasing returns when K_x and Y_x are held constant, the real-wage ratio must decline as the labor input in the food sector increases. This decline, however, should proceed at a diminishing rate. (It cannot, of course, drop below the point where, according to our earlier assumption, the entire production function would collapse.)

Considering that X_y must equal

$$\left(1 - \frac{\omega_1^{1/(\beta+1)}}{A_x^{\beta/(\beta+1)}}\right) X, \qquad (11)$$

we can see that the optimal proportion of 'marketed' output X_y to total output X depends exclusively on the elasticity of substitution and on the parameters A_x and ω_1. This last parameter may be interpreted as the partial elasticity of X with respect to the food input X_x when the elasticity of substitution is equal to unity. The higher this elasticity coefficient, the more food will be retained in the sector. The effect of A_x on the optimal marketed share depends on the sign of β; that is, on whether the elasticity of substitution is smaller or greater than one. If it is smaller than one ($\beta > 0$), then the marketed share should vary proportionately with A_x. If A_x is interpreted as a random parameter associated with weather conditions, then we may conclude that when β is positive the state should collect a greater share of a good than of a bad harvest (assuming the plan period to be long enough to take in the lagged effects of varying X_x on the following year's production). An elasticity of substitution greater than one ($\beta > 0$) would cause the planners – if they were really intent on maximizing net output over the whole planning period – to collect a greater share of poor than of good harvests. Finally, if the elasticity of substitution happened to equal one, the marketed share should be constant, irrespective of the state of the harvest.

(2) Suppose, instead of (8), that the production function were of the following type:

$$X = A_x X_x^{\alpha} (\omega_2 L_x^{-\beta} + \omega_3 K_x^{-\beta} + \omega_4 Y_x^{-\beta})^{-(1-\alpha)/\beta},$$

where α is a positive constant smaller than one.

In this production function, all factor inputs except X_x are related by the same elasticity of substitution $1/(1+\beta)$, while the elasticity of substitution of all these factors with respect to X_x equals unity.

In this case, as may be verified by differentiating the expression for X_y, the optimal 'marketed' share would be $1 - \alpha$, and it would be invariant with the random parameter A_x.

(3) The third and last form a constant-elasticity function can possibly assume requires that X_x and some other input(s) be enclosed in the same ACMS function, which would be related to the remaining input(s) by a unit elasticity of substitution (see Uzawa, 1961, p. 10). (This overall function may be conceived as a geometrical average of two or more ACMS functions, with weights adding up to one.) Where X_x and L_x are the enclosed inputs, we have, for example:

$$X = A_x (\omega_1 X_x^{-\beta} + \omega_2 L_x^{-\beta})^{-\alpha/\beta} (\omega_3 K_x^{-\gamma} + \omega_4 X_2^{-\gamma})^{-(1-\alpha)/\gamma}, \qquad (12)$$

where $0 \leqslant \alpha \leqslant 1$.

Even for this complicated-looking function, we obtain a relatively simple expression for the share of marketed output in the sector (see mathematical appendix):

$$\frac{X_y}{X} = 1 - \frac{X_x}{X} = 1 - \left(\frac{\alpha \omega_1}{A_x^\beta}\right)^{1/(\beta+1)} \left(\frac{M}{N}\right)^{\beta(1-\alpha)/(\beta+1)}, \qquad (13)$$

where M is the first ACMS function $(\omega_1 X_x^{-\beta} + \omega_2 L_x^{-\beta})^{-1/\beta}$ and N the second $(\omega_3 K_x^{-\gamma} + \omega_4 Y_x^{-\gamma})^{-1/\gamma}$. Just as in the first case, we find that depending on whether β is above or below zero (whether the elasticity of substitution pertaining to the first function is smaller or larger than one), a larger A_x will increase or reduce the 'marketed' share. The second parenthetical expression shows that the share X will vary with the ratio of the two functions: if the elasticity of substitution is greater than unity ($\beta < 1$), then a larger share will be marketed – less will be retained in the sector – if production is relatively food-and-labor intensive than if it is capital-and-materials intensive. We may also observe that the closer α, the exponent of the food-and-labor function, is to one, the larger should be the share of output retained in the sector.

In fig. 1 the relation between the two curves X and X_y as functions of L_x has been assumed constant, in accord with cases (1) and (2) above. If L_x and X_x were enclosed in the same ACMS function as in case (3), then the curves would open out more than they do in the diagram, provided the elasticity of substitution between these two inputs were greater than one, since *pari passu* with the injection of labor into the food sector, the ratio of M to N would increase.[4]

By the same technique we have used to determine the relation between food deliveries and food output for any constant-elasticity function, we can eliminate Y_y, the internal consumption of the capital-goods sector.

We are now ready to proceed with our analysis of the input–output relations between the sectors, starting from the marginal conditions stated in equations (4) and (5). We shall confine ourselves to the examination of ACMS functions where all inputs are related to each other by the same elasticity of substitution. Accordingly, the X_y function is taken to be given by equation (6) and the Y function, after the elimination of the internal requirements of the sector, by the following expression:

$$Y_m = Y - Y_y = (A_y^{\delta/(\delta+1)} - \alpha_1^{1/(\delta+1)})^{(\delta+1)/\delta} (\alpha_2 L_y^{-\delta} + \alpha_3 K_y^{-\delta} + \alpha_4 X_y^{-\delta})^{-1/\delta}, \qquad (14)$$

where Y_m (equals $Y_I + Y_x$) is the net output of the sector plus the deliveries of the Y-sector to the found sector, and δ is related to the elasticity of substitution σ_y by the formula $\sigma_y = 1/(1+\delta)$.

The marginal rate of substitution between labor and food in producing Y_m is easily derived from (14):

$$\frac{\partial Y_m}{\partial L_y} \bigg/ \frac{\partial Y_m}{\partial X_y} = \frac{\alpha_2}{\alpha_4} \frac{X_y^{\delta+1}}{L_y^{\delta+1}}. \qquad (15)$$

This marginal rate should be set equal to the marginal product of labor in terms of net output X_y, which may be computed from equation (8) and (9):

$$\frac{\partial X_y}{\partial L_x} = \left(\frac{X_y}{L_x}\right)^{\beta+1} \omega_2 (A_x^{\beta/(\beta+1)} - \omega_1^{1/(\beta+1)})^{-(\beta+1)}. \tag{16}$$

The equality then reads:

$$\frac{\alpha_2 X_y^{\delta+1}}{\alpha_4 L_y^{\delta+1}} = \frac{X_y^{\beta+1} \omega_2}{(A_x^{\beta/(\beta+1)} - \omega_1^{1/(\beta+1)})^{\beta+1} L_x^{\beta+1}} \tag{17}$$

or:

$$L_x = \frac{L_y^{(\delta+1)/(\beta+1)} (\omega_2 \alpha_4)^{1/(\beta+1)} X_y^{(\beta-\delta)/(\beta+1)}}{\alpha_2^{1/(\beta+1)} (A_x^{\beta/(\beta+1)} - \omega_1^{1/(\beta+1)})}.$$

It is evident that when the elasticities of substitution are equal in both sectors $(\beta = \delta)$, the X_y term falls out, and the ratio of L_x to L_y will be equal to a constant

$$\frac{(\omega_2 \alpha_4)^{1/(\beta+1)}}{\alpha_2^{1/(\beta+1)} (A_x^{\beta/(\beta+1)} - \omega_1^{1/(\beta+1)})}.$$

The labor allocation, in other words, will be invariant with respect to the supply of any exogenous factor. As capital accumulates, the (efficient) labor allocation of the initial period should remain fixed, at least in the absence of technical progress. If technical progress takes place in the food sector – note that since A_y does not appear in (17), technical progress in the producer-goods sector does not affect this efficiency condition – as long as the elasticity of substitution is greater than unity $(\beta < 0)$, the proportion of L_x to L_y will increase during the development process: It will be advantageous to allot relatively more labor to the food sector and increase real wages in the producer-goods industry. If the elasticity should be smaller than one, laborers should gradually be transferred from sector I to sector II. (Alternatively, more laborers accruing from the natural increase in the labor force should be hired in section II than in sector I.)[5]

If the common elasticity of substitution should be unity then β and δ would both equal zero and:

$$L_x = \frac{\omega_2 \alpha_4}{\alpha_2 (1 - \omega_1)} L_y. \tag{18}$$

This last result, which may be applied to any family of Cobb–Douglas production functions, tells us that the allotment of labor to the food sector is proportional to α_4, the partial elasticity of Y with respect to the input of food, and to ω_2 the partial elasticity of X with respect to labor, while it varies inversely with α_2 the partial elasticity of Y with respect to labor. The effect of an increase in ω_1, the partial elasticity of food production with respect to food input, is also to increase the optimal proportion of L_x to L_y (via a decrease in the value of the denominator). For such functions, as long as technical progress remained neutral, the same allocation of labor would theoretically be maintained for any number of planning periods. Similarly, the accumulation of capital due to the accrual of Y_I in each period would have no effect on efficient allocation. Whatever the rate of technical progress or of capital accumulation, the real wage would rise at the same rate in both sectors.

Similar equations may be written for the allocation of capital or, for that matter, of any other exogenous factor entering a constant elasticity-of-substitution function of the ACMS type.[6]

The invariance of the labor allocation in the absence of (neutral) technical progress will hold true for any production function in the producer-goods industry where the marginal rate of substitution of labor for food is of the form given by equation (15). These functions include all constant-elasticity functions where X_y and L_y are enclosed in the same ACMS function.[7]

Using the equations (9) and (10) to express X_x in terms of X_y, we can find the optimal real-wage relation between the sectors:

$$\frac{X_y^{\delta+1}}{L_y^{\delta+1}} = W_y^{\delta+1} = \frac{\alpha_4\omega_2 X_x^{\beta+1}}{\alpha_2\omega_1 L_x^{\beta+1}} = \frac{\alpha_4\omega_2}{\alpha_2\omega_1} W_x^{\beta+1}. \tag{19}$$

Here, the optimal wage relation *is* dependent on the allocation of exogenous factors other than labor (unless $\beta = \delta$), for these factors influence X_x and X_y which in turn have a differential effect on the right- and left-hand sides of (19), depending on the elasticities of substitution in each sector.

From equations (4), (5) and (7) above, we may infer that when the allocation for each of several exogenous factors taken separately is efficient relative to the intermediate product X_y, then the allocation of these factors is also efficient with respect to each other. This suggests that when the production functions in *any two sectors* have approximately the same elasticities, resources can be allotted sequentially: The planners should be able to experiment with the effects of changes in the allocation of any one exogenous factor on the net output of producer goods without undue worry about the need to reshuffle the remaining factors *pari passu*.

The rather curious conclusions we have drawn from algebraic reasoning call for further explanation in economic terms. Fig. 2, which is a straightforward elaboration of fig. 1 above, may help to show why the allocation of an exogenous factor such as labor should be independent of the allocation of other factors if the production functions in the two sectors have the same elasticity. This figure, as we shall see, can also serve to predict in which direction the equilibrium will be shifted if the production functions have different elasticities.

Fig. 2 shows two net-food-output curves as functions of the labor allotment to the food sector L_x, the lower curve X_y^1 corresponding to a smaller allotment of capital and the higher curve X_y^1 to a larger allotment of capital parcelled out of this sector. The two curves are tangent to a

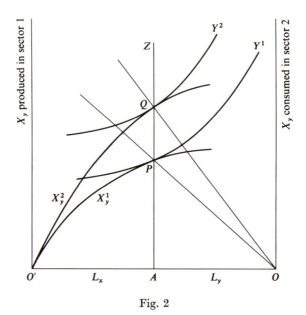

Fig. 2

Y-isoquant at points lying on the vertical line drawn from *A*, that is, at points corresponding to an identical allocation of labor.

We note first that the slope of each successively higher isoquant on the vertical line *AZ* should be greater than the last, since the marginal rate of substitution of food for labor in producing *Y* should rise with increases in the food-to-labor ratio. The elasticity of substitution between food and labor tells us in what proportion the slope should increase between points such as *P* and *Q* on isoquants Y^1 and Y^2 relative to the percentage rise in the food-to-labor ratio (i.e., in the real wage of laborers in the producer-goods sector). If the elasticity of substitution were smaller than one, for instance, the relative increase in slope from points *P* to *Q* would be greater than $(QA/AO)/(PA/AO)$ (or QA/PA).

Consider now the curves X_y^1 and X_y^2. The increase in capital available to the food sector not only causes a rise in X_y but also in the slope of the curve at any point. The relative increase in the slope of X_y, according to equation (16), must equal $\beta + 1$, or $1/\sigma$, times the relative increase in the ratio X_y to L_x. But if σ is also the elasticity of substitution of food for labor in producing *Y*, then, by the definition of σ, the relative increase in the slope of the *Y*-isoquant must also be equal to the relative increase in the ratio of X_y to L_y times $1/\sigma$. At a labor allocation corresponding to point *A*, the relative increases in the ratios X_y to L_x and X_y to L_y from *P* to *Q* must be equal. Hence the change in slopes of the X_y line and of the *Y*-isoquant from *P* to *Q* must be the same, and if these lines were tangent at *P*, they must be tangent at *Q*.

What if the elasticities of substitution in the two sectors should differ, as we may normally expect them to? Suppose for example that this elasticity were greater in the food sector than in the producer-goods sector. Then the slope of Y^2 at Q would be steeper than the slope of X_y^2 at that point, and the optimal allocation of labor would shift to the left of A: given a constant labor force, laborers should be transferred from the food into the producer-goods sector. Now, since the optimal level of food consumption in the food sector (X_x) is a constant multiple of the amount of food delivered to the producer-goods sector (X_y), the proportional increases in X_x and X_y due to the injection of K_x in the food sector must be the same (cf. equations (9) and (10)). But the new X_y must now be shared among a larger number of laborers and the new X_x among a smaller number. We conclude that if the elasticity of substitution is greater in the food than in the producer-goods sector, the accumulation of capital with a constant labor force should cause *relative* wages in the producer-goods sector to decline compared to wages in the food sector. (We are of course talking about the optimal wage in each sector that will maximize Y_I.)

So far, I have glossed over my initial assumption about a minimum consumption level, below which production would collapse. Turning back to fig. 2, we may suppose that AP/OA represents such a level. If this is the case, of course, the portion of isoquant Y^1 to the left of OP no longer lies 'in the ball park'. We may reason from our earlier analysis that a drop in A_x should prompt a transfer of workers from the producer-goods to the food sector if the elasticity of substitution in the former sector is smaller than one. If X_y should drop below P, however, the 'back-to-the-farm movement' would have to become much more pronounced than on the way down from Q to P, before the economy reached this impasse. In principle, the retreat would have to follow line OP, a path which, in the absence of our minimum livelihood assumption, would only be taken under extraordinary elasticity conditions.

The conclusions we have reached on the effect of reallocations of one exogenous factor on the optimal apportionment of another may be applied to the classical case of underemployment of labor in agriculture. Suppose that, previous to the initiation of a development program, there had been a misallocation of labor, too much labor being employed in agriculture relative to industry, whereas the allocation of capital had been deemed satisfactory (i.e., had met the relevant marginal conditions). What changes should be made in the allocation of capital as labor is gradually transferred to the producer-goods sector? The answer, of course, depends on the form of the functions and on the relative elasticities of substitution, but we know that if the functions may be approximated by an ACMS formula and if the elasticities of substitution are equal in the two sectors, the allocation of capital should remain unchanged.

While these restrictions on the production functions may seem rather stringent, it may be appropriate at this point to remind the reader that the empirical calculations based on ACMS functions *implicitly* assume these conditions when they leave out intermediate goods from the production functions they posit. Unless the elasticity of substitution among factors happens to be equal in all sectors of the economy, aggregated output cannot be expressed as a function of exogenous factors exclusively.[8] This may be shown in the two-sector case by substituting the expression for X_y obtained in equation 14. We are left with an equation for Y_m (equals $Y - Y_y$) of the following type:

$$Y_m = k[\alpha_2 L_y^{-\delta} + \alpha_3 K_y^{-\delta} + \alpha_4 (A_x^{\beta/(\beta+1)} - \omega_1^{1/(\beta+1)})^{(\beta+1)/\beta}$$
$$\times (\omega_2 L_x^{-\beta} + \omega_3 K_x^{-\beta} + \omega_4 Y_x^{-\beta})^{\delta/\beta}]^{-1/\delta}, \quad (20)$$

where $k = (A_y^{\delta/(\delta+1)} - \alpha_1^{1/(\delta+1)})^{(\delta+1)/\delta}$.

Taking the partial derivative of Y_I (equals $Y_m - Y_x$) with respect to Y_x and setting the result equal to zero yields after rearrangement of terms:

$$Y_x^{\beta+1} = k\omega_4 T^{-(\delta+1)/\delta} V^{(\delta-\beta)/\beta},$$

where T is the whole expression in brackets and V is the second expression in parentheses in (20).

If β equals δ, then:

$$Y_x = (k\omega_4)^{1/(\beta+1)} T^{-1/\delta} = dY_m,$$

where d is another constant. Hence Y_x is a constant proportion of Y_m.

But, unless the elasticities of substitution are equal, Y_x will not be a constant proportion of Y_m (and Y) and it will not be possible to net out the intermediate product.

EXTENSIONS TO AN OPEN ECONOMY AND TO ANY NUMBER OF SECTORS

Our results may also be applied to an economy open to international trade, provided that this economy faces infinitely elastic conditions for both its imports and its exports demand. For if P_i is the constant price obtained abroad for a unit of intermediate good i, and P_j the constant price for importing a unit of good j, then supplies X_j of good j can be 'generated' according to the function:

$$X_j = (P_i/P_j) A_i (\omega_1 L_i^{-\beta} + \omega_2 K_i^{-\beta})^{-1/\beta},$$

where L_i and K_i are the exogenous-factor inputs used in the production of the export good X_i. It is obvious that X_j can be introduced as an input in the production of the priority sector without altering the allocation principles developed so far.

This possibility of exchange enlarges the scope of our two-sector model in a significant way, since we can now envisage that food may be consumed domestically (to maintain a satisfactory labor productivity) or traded for inputs directly necessary for the industrialization process. Such trade, one may recall, has been a conspicuous feature of the industrialization process of Russia and China during their maximum-austerity period.

By now we have digressed quite far from our primary purpose, which was to investigate a model of an austerity economy where the real wage in terms of food in each sector was to be determined by efficiency considerations rather than by the preferences of the individuals concerned. In the two-sector case, we may illustrate diagrammatically the essential differences that arise between a situation where unskilled laborers are free to distribute themselves among alternative employments according to their preferences and where planners have the power to assign them to one or the other sector with an eye only to their productivity.

In fig. 3 the net outputs of food and producer goods are represented in the positive (northeastern) quadrant by the abscissa and ordinate respectively, while the labor inputs into the two sectors are shown in the south-western quadrant. The output of food measured along the positive abscissa corresponds to X_y in the model in the first and second sections of this paper: it is the amount of food that can be supplied to the producer-goods sector after satisfying the internal requirements of the food sector. For every given supply of capital (K_x) and food consumed in the food sector (X_x), we can trace out the functional relation between food produced (gross or net) and labor employed in the sector. One such curve has been drawn for net output X_y and one for total output X in the southeastern quadrant, both of which correspond to the optimal consumption of food in the sector. At T, for instance, OS units of labor are employed in the food sector to produce ST units of net food output and SV units of total food output. The real wage in the food sector equals the food retained in the sector X_x, represented by the segment TV, divided by OS, the labor employed. Since OS equals DT, the real wage is inversely proportional to the slope of line DV.

In the southwestern quadrant the line EF shows the distribution of the labor force between two sectors in the case analyzed in previous sections where labor can be assigned at will to either sector, regardless of its preferences (OE and OF are therefore equal). Thus if OS labor hours are consumed in the first sector, there will be MS or OR hours left to employ in the second. To represent the ratio of real wages in the two sectors more graphically, I have measured a segment OC along the ordinate equal to OR and joined points C and D by a line, the slope of which is inversely proportional to the real wage in the producer goods sector. It is clear that the ratio of the slopes of CD and DV equals the ratio of real wages in the food and producer-goods sectors. This ratio has also been drawn in

43

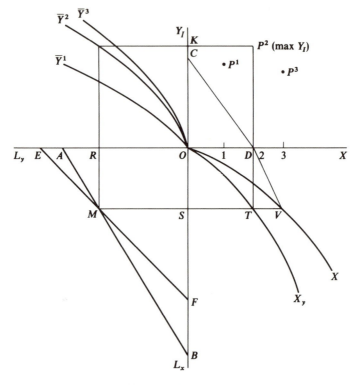

Fig. 3

the southwestern quadrant, where it appears as the slope of line AB going through M.

The northwestern quadrant exhibits various functional relations between the net output of producer goods and L_y, each higher line corresponding to a larger food consumption in the sector. It can easily be checked that the allocation of labor at M, which yields ST units of X_y and OK units of Y_I, is optimal if the planners are maximizing Y_I. The allocation-generating curve $\bar{Y}^1$ makes insufficient allowance for food input into the producer-goods sector while the allocation-generating curve $\bar{Y}^3$ assigns so much labor in the production of food that not enough is left to turn out the maximum volume of Y_I. The three points just referred to are marked $P_2(\max Y_I)$, P_1 and P_3 respectively in the northeast quadrant.

It is worth noting that relative wages in the two sectors are not directly linked to the observable physical marginal products of the two sectors; neither is the opportunity cost of the production possibilities curve at P^2 equal to the ratio of marginal costs in the two sectors as conventionally measured. Even though physical marginal products and wages are positive in both sectors, the marginal cost of producing Y_I appears to be infinite compared to the marginal cost of producing X_y. These apparent violations of elementary economic notions only arise, of course, when we ignore the interdependencies in the system. Indeed, the true marginal product of labor in producing Y_I, taking into consideration all indirect effects, should be zero at M.

Suppose, on the other hand, the laborers were free to choose among alternative employments according to their relative preferences (while still observing the legal requirements prescribing the extent of all individuals' participation in the labor force), what spontaneous allocation should we expect to come about? For laborers to distribute themselves between the two sectors in the optimal way, the community's indifference curve between the two types of employment would have to be tangent to AB at M. The location of the curve would of course depend on the absolute as well as on the relative size of the real wage paid out in each sector. For the particular case we have drawn where the real wages at the optimal point are higher in the producer-goods than in the food sector, the optimal allocation could be sustained only if laborers preferred to work an extra hour in the food sector than in the producer-goods sector (at least in the neighborhood of the allocation corresponding to point M). If the opposite were the case – if the ratio of the marginal disutilities of the two employments at M were smaller than the slope of EF – setting relative real wages in the ratio AB would cause laborers to shift from the food sector to the producer-goods sector, as compared to the compulsory allocation at M. As a result, unless enough additional voluntary work hours were supplied to the producer-goods sector to compensate for this effect, the drop in real wages in this sector would be detrimental enough to the average efficiency of laborers to cause a reduction in Y_I. If this threatened to be the case, the authorities would be well advised to regulate and control the migration from country to the city, in such a way as to maintain optimal wage levels in both sectors.

CONCLUSIONS

1. Wherever a sector, such as agriculture, may be treated as maximizing its surplus over internal requirements for delivery to other sectors, the allocation of output between internal uses and external deliveries can be determined for any production function exhibiting constant elasticities of substitution between any pair of inputs. If the sector is an aggregate of consumer goods industries, then the optimal level of real wages for the sector in question also emerges from this analysis. In general, as we should expect, real wages should increase proportionately with labor productivity; but deviations from this trend may be optimal if elasticities between pairs of inputs differ. The technique used in the text can also be

applied to the study of incentive schemes and profit-sharing arrangements, where something is known about the effect on output or profits of
increasing employees' earnings.

2. In the analysis of the interrelation between two or more sectors,
simple, easily interpretable results were obtained where the production
function postulated in each sector had a unique elasticity of substitution
between all inputs.

It turned out that the relation between the elasticities of substitution
in any two sectors was crucial in determining how the allocation of an
exogenous factor such as labor would be affected by the increased
availability of capital or any other factor. If the elasticities happened to
be equal, the allocation of every exogenous factor should be invariant
with respect to the supply of all other factors. It is also true that *unless*
the elasticities happened to be equal the 'netting out' of intermediate
products in the construction of aggregate production functions where
total output depends exclusively on exogenous factors will not be justified.

3. Where there is a unique elasticity of substitution in each sector,
there will be a linear logarithmic relation between the optimal real wages
in the food and producer-goods sector as long as food is an input in both
functions. If the elasticities are equal, then optimal real wages in the two
sectors will be strictly proportional, irrespective of the supply of exogenous factors other than labor.

4. If the relative attractiveness of the two sectors differs and laborers
are allowed to choose their place of employment, then relative wages
may differ from their optimal relation. Preventing the spontaneous
migration out of rural areas may be justified, for instance, if real wages
are not high enough in the city to allow the new migrants to attain the
optimal level of productivity.

APPENDIX

Let the production function for X be of the following type:

$$X = A_x(\omega_1 X_x^{-\beta} + \omega_2 L_x^{-\beta})^{-\alpha/\beta} (\omega_3 K_x^{-\gamma} + \omega_4 Y_x^{-\gamma})^{-(1-\alpha)/\gamma}. \tag{1}$$

We denote the first ACMS function by M and the second by N, so that we may write:

$$X = A_x M^\alpha N^{1-\alpha}. \tag{2}$$

Differentiating X with respect to X_x yields:

$$\frac{\partial X}{\partial X_x} = \frac{N^{1-\alpha} A_x \alpha \omega_1 M^\alpha X_x^{-\beta-1}}{\omega_1 X_x^{-\beta} + \omega_2 L_x^{-\beta}} = 1,$$

and using (1):

$$X_x^{\beta+1} = \frac{\alpha \omega_1 X}{\omega_1 X_x^{-\beta} + \omega_2 L_x^{-\beta}}.$$

We note from (1) and (2) that:

$$\omega_1 X_x^{-\beta} + \omega_2 L_x^{-\beta} = (A_x N^{1-\alpha}/X)^{\beta/\alpha}.$$

Hence:
$$X_x^{\beta+1} = X^{1+\beta/\alpha}\alpha\omega_1(A_x N^{1-\alpha})^{-\beta/\alpha},$$

and
$$X_x = X^{(\alpha+\beta)/\alpha(\beta+1)}(\alpha\omega_1)^{1/(\beta+1)}(A_x N^{1-\alpha})^{-\beta/\alpha(\beta+1)}.$$

The proportion of food retained in the sector equals:

$$\frac{X_x}{X} = X^{\beta(1-\alpha)/\alpha(\beta+1)}(\alpha\omega_1)^{1/(\beta+1)}(A_x N^{1-\alpha})^{-\beta/\alpha(\beta+1)}$$

$$= (\alpha\omega_1)^{1/(\beta+1)}\left(\frac{X^{1-\alpha}}{A_x N^{1-\alpha}}\right)^{\beta/\alpha(\beta+1)}.$$

But the expression in parentheses above can be rewritten:

$$\frac{X^{1-\alpha}}{A_x N^{1-\alpha}} = \frac{A_x^{1-\alpha}(\omega_1 X_x^{-\beta}+\omega_2 L_x^{-\beta})^{-\alpha(1-\alpha)/\beta} N^{(1-\alpha)^2}}{A_x N^{1-\alpha}}$$

$$= \frac{(\omega_1 X_x^{-\beta}+\omega_2 L_x^{-\beta})^{-\alpha(1-\alpha)/\beta}}{A_x^{\alpha}(\omega_3 K_x^{-\gamma}+\omega_4 Y_x^{-\gamma})^{-(1-\alpha)\alpha/\gamma}}$$

$$= \left(\frac{M}{NA_x^{1/(1-\alpha)}}\right)^{\alpha(1-\alpha)}.$$

Therefore:
$$\frac{X_x}{X} = (\alpha\omega_1)^{1/(\beta+1)}\left(\frac{M}{NA_x^{1/(1-\alpha)}}\right)^{\beta(1-\alpha)/(\beta+1)}$$

$$= (\alpha\omega_1/A_x^{\beta})^{1/(\beta+1)} \cdot (M/N)^{\beta(1-\alpha)/(\beta+1)}.$$

NOTES

1 For evidence and arguments to justify this approach, see Leibenstein (1957, pp. 62–6).

2 For every production function selected, there is an implicit relation between labor productivity and the consumption of wage goods per laborer. Thus the choice of specific functions where wage goods are introduced directly as an input rather than *via* their effect on the efficiency of labor imposes restriction on this latter relation. For example, the assumption we shall make about the homogeneity of first degree of all our production functions rules out a functional relation of the following type between labor productivity and real wages:

$$P/L = W^\beta K^\gamma,$$

where P is total output, L is the labor input, W is the real wage of laborers, K is a capital input, and β and γ are positive constants smaller than unity. As the real wage W equals the total consumption of wage goods F divided by the labor supply L, we may write the production function for the sector as:

$$P = L^{1-\beta}K^\gamma F^\beta.$$

Since the exponents add up to more than unity, the production function exhibits increasing returns to scale. This violates the assumption of first-degree homogeneity.

3 If the elasticity of substitution $1/(1+\beta)$ is smaller than 1, A_x must be large enough for $A_x^{1/(\beta+1)}$ to exceed $\omega_1^{1/(\beta+1)}$; otherwise X_x will turn out to be negative – a nonsense result. If, however, the elasticity of substitution should be greater than one, then A_x must not exceed a number which would make the value of the difference in the first parentheses negative. What would happen in this case, as can easily be verified, is that the value of the derivative of X with respect to X_x would always exceed X_x; hence

the quantity of net output X_y would be unbounded; with given L_x, K_x and Y_x, it would always be possible to generate more X_y by feeding laborers more food.

4 If X_x were enclosed with capital or some other input(s) but labor, then, on the contrary, the two curves would fan out less than they do in fig. 1 (for $\beta < 1$).

5 This effect can be interpreted in the following economic terms: As it becomes easier to produce an intermediate good such as food and as the substitution of food for other inputs in the producer-goods sector precipitates a marked decline in its marginal productivity (due to a low elasticity of substitution among inputs), it becomes more advantageous to assign labor directly to the producer-goods sector than to use it in a roundabout way to increase the supply of intermediate-good inputs to this sector.

6 If ω_i denotes the exponent of exogenous factor E_i entering into Cobb–Douglas functions for X and Y respectively, then: $E_{ix} = \dfrac{\alpha_4 \omega_i}{\alpha_i (1 - \omega_1)} E_{iy}$, where E_{ix} is the allotment of E_i to the first sector and E_{iy} to the second $(E_{ix} + E_{iy} = E_i)$, while α_4 and ω_1 are the partial elasticity coefficients of food to output already defined.

7 On the other hand if K_y, or some other exogenous factor, were enclosed with X_y in the same ACMS function, then the allocation of that exogenous factor would be invariant to the allocation of all other factors.

8 For an example of an aggregated ACMS function for the United States economy that omits material inputs, see Kendrick and Sato (1963, p. 984 and *passim*).

REFERENCES

Arrow, K. T., H. B. Chenery, B. S. Minhas and R. M. Solow (1961). Capital–labor substitution and economic efficiency. *Review of Economics and Statistics*, **63**, 225–50.

Leibenstein, Harvey (1957). *Economic Backwardness and Economic Growth: Studies in the Theory of Economic Development*. New York and London.

Kendrick, J. W. and Ryuzo Sato (1963). Factor prices, productivity and growth. *American Economic Review*, **53**.

Uzawa, Hirofumi (1961). *Production Functions and Constant Elasticities of Substitution*. Technical Report No. 104, Institute for Mathematical Studies in the Social Sciences.

2. Planners and Firms

The Marshallian Planned Economy

EDWARD AMES[1]

In planned economies, we all know, the price mechanism need not serve to allocate resources and production. Plans have that function even if institutional arrangements include money, money payments and prices. In what follows, we consider a planned economy in which there are n kinds of goods and services, and in which there is a plan for each kind. By this, we mean that a central planning agency issues an instruction to the economy which says, 'You must produce and/or use quantity π_i of commodity i $(i = 1, ..., n)$.' We assume that the plans influence economic activity in a fundamental way, and we propose to theorize about the workings of this economy. We do not propose to discuss whether the plans are good, bad, or indifferent. For a theory of planned economies should not have to assume that planners are wise, or virtuous, or fools, or scoundrels. Planners, like businessmen, or feudal lords, or slaveowners, may have quite varied intellectual and moral endowments, and a concentration on these may interfere with our understanding of how planned economies work.

More important, we must not assume that the economy does exactly what the plan provides. For everyone who has ever talked or written about the workings of planned economies agrees that the most important practical problem the governments of such economies face is to attempt to secure a reasonable degree of compliance with the plan by suppliers and users alike. Our question, then, is the following: given an economy in which economic activity is fundamentally influenced by plans (even if economic performance may differ from the plan), what can we say about the way in which economic performance is influenced by plans?[2] And what plans will be laid?

A natural way for a tradition-respecting economist to analyse a planned economy is to hypothesize commodities $1, 2, ..., n$; to construct n demand functions

$$D_i(p_1, p_2, ..., p_n) \quad (i = 1, 2, ..., n)$$

and n supply functions

$$S_i(p_1, p_2, ..., p_n) \quad (i = 1, 2, ..., n)$$

and then to establish n equilibrium conditions

$$D_i = S_i \quad (i = 1, 2, ..., n).$$

This system obviously looks like the familiar general equilibrium system, *but* $(p_1, p_2, ..., p_n)$ has suddenly become a vector of production plans, and not a vector of prices. The analytical question suddenly becomes, 'Is there a general plan which will simultaneously equalize all quantities supplied and demanded?' And the broader question raised by this little exercise is, is it useful to analyze the equilibrium properties of planned economies by making direct use of concepts which form a part of the familiar reasoning pertaining to competitive economies?

The following discussion will show that *if* we follow through the project just outlined, we can gain understanding of planned economies. It requires some exercise of the imagination to start this enterprise, because of the mental image most of us have formed of planning in the USSR. Nothing in the first paragraph suggests the picture of Stalin telling the Russians in 1929 to overtake the United States in five years – was Stalin, in any reasonable interpretation of his word, making an effort to find a set of plans which would equate quantities demanded and supplied?

A part of this difficulty recalls the seventeenth century theological problem of freedom of the will. If planners are indeed free to select any plan they will to, how is it that plans can be treated as endogenous variables in a theoretical system? Conversely, if plans are a solution to a set of equations (and hence endogenous) how can planners be considered free to choose what they will do? The answer to this is standard economics (as it was theology). If we could read the soul of the planner, so that we could tell his preferences, we would see that he makes his choice (given the constraints) in precisely the way that will maximize his welfare. He is bound once he has chosen his preference function, but he is presumably free to select that. And we judge him partly on his arithmetic (can he solve a system of first-order or second-order equilibrium conditions?), partly on his preferences (do they agree with our own?), and partly on his efficiency (given his resources, is he as happy as he might be and are his subjects unnecessarily badly off?). Just so the greedy monopolist, seeking to maximize his profit, is constrained to set marginal cost equal to marginal revenue, as if he were a simple, but pure competitor. So let us see how central planners may be forced to select some particular plan, given their tastes and the environment in which they work. And let us try to keep on as similiar ground as possible, eschewing whenever possible mathematics and complexity in favor of the simpler graphical technique of Alfred Marshall.

The theoretical literature on planned economies relies on the concepts of a *center*, from which plans emanate, and a *periphery* of enterprises to which plans are addressed (see Camacho, 1970). Much of the discussion treats the center as an atom, a computer into which some objective function and some collection of constraints is fed and out of which a solution to a programming problem is printed. The periphery, in turn, is treated as a collection of homogeneous atoms, each responding to a set of messages from the center. Writers on planning theory tend to assume that enterprises will do what they are told. Writers on planning practice and enterprise management stress the discrepancies between plans and actuality, and seek to explain them by the incentive structure of the organism.[3] The more sociologically oriented economist regards both the center and the periphery as collections of more or less hierarchically ordered subunits (e.g. Montias, 1970). In either case, however, the economic process is viewed as consisting of three sets of entities: messages from center to periphery; messages from periphery to center; and actions taken at the periphery, once the two sets of messages have reached (approximate) agreement.

This center–periphery characterization is much like the account of economic life in Walras' *Elements of Pure Economics*. Walras' economic process acts as if there were a hypothetical 'auctioneer', who sends out messages consisting of vectors of prices. Consider him as 'the center' of the economy. An enterprise at the periphery receives the price vector, and sends back a vector of the quantities of goods it would buy or sell if that price vector existed in the market. The auctioneer tallies the messages from the periphery, computes excess demand, and uses this data as a means of computing a new price message, designed to reduce the excess demands which have been shown to exist. Just so the central planning authority may be thought to send out a vector, essentially a draft plan. Enterprises interpret this vector as asking, 'What would you do if this were the national plan?' Each answers by sending a vector, interpretable as the sentence, 'Given your latest draft, here are the quantities I would use or make.' On receipt of messages from the periphery, the center decides whether to accept the draft plan as final, or to prepare and circulate a new draft (see Portes, 1971).

One of the early planning models (the Barone–Lange–Taylor tradition) is indeed formally indistinguishable from the purely competitive model (Barone, 1935). But the interpretation given the symbols in the model is different. Walras would say 'when one sees positive excess demand, one lowers the price'. The pronoun 'one' (the French pronoun *on*) gives the auctioneer a purely abstract role. (The market acts as if the auctioneer existed.) In competitive theory nobody knows for sure whether there can exist a market in which for each commodity transactions take place at a single price which, however, is not an equilibrium price. Interpret the auctioneer as a rudimentary central planner in the Barone–Lange manner, however, and the process becomes conceptually much simpler. The mind does not boggle over a planner who uses his power to fix prices so as to control the economy.

These two processes – one for a competitive, the other for a planned process – have several features in common: they determine an outcome for the entire economy at one fell swoop (so that they are truly general equilibrium models). Moreover, they are at least potentially anonymous and operational and therefore decentralized in one of Hurwicz's senses (see Hurwicz, 1959). That is, the price messages, the plan messages, and the response-to-plan messages could all be formulated in such a way that no message-receiver need know the name of a message-sender; no message-sender need write an address on his message; and so that the numbers in a vector describe real actions such as outputs, consumptions, money payments, etc.

The members of the periphery, in this economy, may have neither direct personal nor business contacts. Once a price (or plan) has been fixed, a member of the periphery either places a quantity of goods he supplied upon a certain shelf, or he goes to the shelf and removes from it a quantity of goods. In equilibrium, he surely can find what he wants. He need never communicate directly with any other member of the periphery, and the events pertaining to any individual commodity or commodity group need never be isolated for special consideration. Ordinary experience suggests, as Dorothy Shays put it, that 'We are such neighborly people, friendly and sweet/Except when we happen to meet.' In the purely competitive economy, one never meets one's neighbors face to face, and social relations will therefore be friendly and sweet. Lange's planned economy would also be friendly and sweet. Empirical economies differ in certain respects from this norm, for they do involve some pairwise contacts among individuals, and hence disharmony.

Suppose that each enterprise makes only one product. The periphery may then be partitioned into (non-overlapping) industries. Two enterprises make the same product if the center considers that a given sum of the outputs of the two has a fixed utility to the state, regardless of the shares of the two enterprises in the sum.[4] The produces of the given product will be referred to as suppliers; other enterprises as demanders.

Now suppose the center is able to communicate directly with individual enterprises. It sends the message, 'If we sent you the plan $(p_1, p_2, ..., p_n) = \mathbf{p}$ prescribing your purchases and sales of goods 1, 2, ..., n, what would you do?' In this case, we suppose that the enterprise replies, 'If you told us to do $\mathbf{p}$, we would actually do $(p'_1, p'_2, ..., p'_n) = \mathbf{p}'$.' To justify this assumption, it would be necessary to construct a model explaining the behavior of individuals and enterprises, and stating why and how their behavior is influenced by plans.[5] Since there are many possible ways in which the influence could be exerted, there is no reason to select a particular model for this paper. Rather, we shall proceed in a Marshallian spirit, and consider merely the conditions which must be met in an arbitrary economy in which the economic activity of the periphery (the enterprises and consumers) is indeed determined by plans generated by a center (the central planners). These conditions will be expressed in a rather formal fashion at first. Then a more intuitive explanation of their economic content will be given.

For any industry (collection of economic units selling the same product) and any plan for the total amount to be bought or sold, there is clearly an infinity of ways of allocating the plan among individual enterprises. Rather than consider individual enterprise as having their own plans, it is convenient to consider plans at the industry level. And so it is necessary to argue that for any industry plan there will be a unique allocation of planned supply and another of planned demand among enterprises. This argument runs as follows:

The product in question is either one which the center wants for its own use, or else it is not. If it is, then the center will wish to encourage suppliers, and to discourage other demanders of the product. If it is not, then either the commodity is, in the center's opinion a social 'good', or else it is a social 'bad'. In the former case, the center will wish to encourage both demanders and suppliers, or it will wish to discourage both demanders and suppliers. In all of these cases, the center will select an allocation among enterprises of a given total planned demand or supply, such that the quantity actually supplied will be either maximized or minimized, as the case may be. This means that the planner will send instructions to individual enterprises in such a way that the marginal response of all buyers (or all sellers) with respect to a change in the enterprise plan for purchases (or sales) will be equal, for each possible industry plan.

If the response functions of the individual enterprises are well-behaved, there will then be a unique best way of allocating a given industry-wide plan for demand or supply among enterprises, and hence a unique response by demanders and suppliers to an industry-wide plan. It is thus possible to construct aggregate schedules showing the quantities of a commodity that will be demanded or supplied, for each given industry-wide plan, other plans in the economy being given. These schedules will show quantities as functions of plans.

Fig. 1 shows the configuration of such partial equilibrium demand and supply schedules. If quantities demanded (or supplied) are invariant with respect to changes in plan, the schedule will be a vertical line. If the quantities demanded (or supplied) are not totally inelastic with respect to changes in plan, the line will be sloped.[6] We assert that both demand and supply functions will have positive slopes (elasticities) with respect to changes in plan. We also assert that both demand and supply functions will intersect from below a 45° line from the origin. That is, if the plan is sufficiently small, the quantity demanded (or supplied) will exceed the plan. If the plan is sufficiently large, the quantity demanded (or supplied) will be less than the plan. The rationale for these assertions is as follows:

(*a*) The supply function will slope upward over at least part of its

Edward Ames

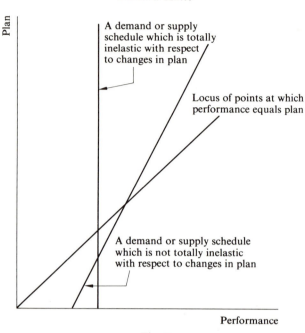

Fig. 1

range and will nowhere slope down.[7] In a reasonable planned economy there will be a reward to economic units for increasing output if the plan is increased. If the plan is sufficiently large (other plans remaining constant), quantities supplied may become perfectly inelastic, but over lower ranges of the plan, some positive response to increases in the plan is to be expected. For sufficiently small plans, quantities supplied will exceed plan, since the planned resources available to suppliers are, by hypothesis, held constant, and the incentive structure will force sellers to use them in a way which causes quantity supplied to exceed plan.

(*b*) The demand function will slope upward over at least part of its range, and will nowhere slope downward. In a reasonable planned economy demanders will reduce their purchases if the plan decreases. They may be happy to reduce their purchases (if these had been made grudgingly at the larger plan). They may reduce their purchases willingly in response to the workings of the incentive system. They may reduce their purchases grudgingly in response to the workings of a control system. If the plan is sufficiently large, the quantities demanded may become totally inelastic with respect to changes in plan, because of *ceteris paribus* limitations. (Thus the quantity of labor demanded by an industry may become totally inelastic, given the plans for supply of raw materials to the industry.) But over part of the range of plans, the demand function will have positive slope (elasticity). If all other plans are given

54

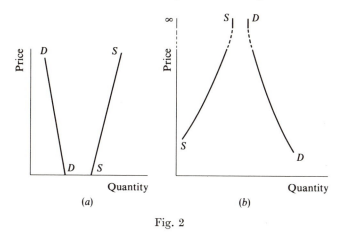

Fig. 2

(e.g. plans for raw materials) the quantity demanded (e.g. of labor by an industry) will exceed the plan, if that plan is sufficiently small.

To repeat: we have not specified what microeconomic system exists which leads enterprises to respond to changes in plan. We have merely assumed some such system exists, and have asserted that if it exists, supply and demand schedules (in a partial equilibrium sense) will have the general shape indicated in fig. 1. A set of institutions which cause enterprises to have negative elasticities of demand or supply with respect to changes in plan will be incompatible with successful operations of the system. We are considering only viable planning systems. We consider next the concept of an equilibrium.

In a competitive Marshallian market, there may be no equilibrium price, i.e. no price which equates supply and demand. Fig. 2 (a) shows a market in which price will fall to zero, but in which quantity supplied will still exceed quantity demanded. Fig. 2 (b) shows a market in which at all finite prices quantity demanded will exceed quantity supplied. Marshallian price theory, therefore, applies only to markets in which an equilibrium price exists.

So also in Marshallian planned economies, there may be no plan which will equate quantities demanded and supplied. But if such a plan exists, it will be called an equilibrium plan. Consider, first, the case where none of the commodity in question is purchased or sold by the center, and suppose, as before, that the plans for all other commodities are fixed. In this case, a given quantity of goods will be purchased if and only if (a) the plan is such that demanders will wish at least this quantity, and also (b) the plan is such that sellers wish to dispose of at most this quantity.

Suppose the plan is selected in such a way that the quantity demanded is different from the quantity supplied. Then either there will be an unsold surplus, or an unsatisfied shortage. If the situation is to exist,

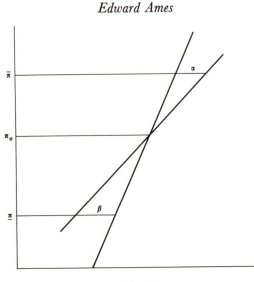

Fig. 3

it must be that someone not on the periphery is absorbing the surplus, or making up the shortage. Otherwise it is impossible that the hypothesized state of affairs can exist. But the only economic unit not on the periphery is the center. The plan will, therefore, be such as to equate quantities demanded and quantities supplied, unless the center desires to acquire or dispose of stocks of goods. These situations are illustrated in fig. 3. At plan $\bar{\pi}$ the center must acquire α; at plan $\underline{\pi}$ it must dispose of β. Otherwise these situations could not exist. It is true that the acquisition or disposal may be voluntary, or it may be involuntary. Under conditions of perfect information, we rule out the latter. If we insist on the latter, uncertainty is introduced into our model. It is dangerous to allow uncertainty into a theory until one has worked out the case of complete information, and we shall not allow it now.[8]

It is straightforward to extend this discussion to cover the cases in which the center wishes to acquire or dispose of some stock of the commodity. For the effect of such a decision is merely to shift, respectively, the demand or the supply function by the amount of the stock being bought or sold.

Furthermore, a *stable* equilibrium is one like that depicted in fig. 4: at the equilibrium plan, the supply function is more elastic than the demand function. If the equilibrium is stable, and if the plan is slightly greater than equilibrium, there will be an excess supply. The center will then reduce its plan, and reduce the excess supply. If the plan is slightly less than equilibrium, then there will be an excess demand, which the the center can reduce by increasing the plan.[9]

Observe that at equilibrium, the actual quantities exchanged may be

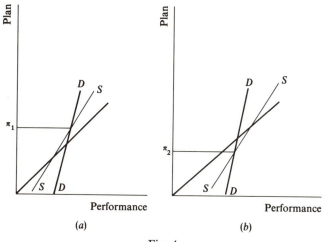

Fig. 4

either less than plan (as in fig. 4(*a*)) or greater than plan (as in fig. 4(*b*)). Thus we assert that an equilibrium plan is not, in general, one which will be exactly carried out. There is a literature on this phenomenon, which is a part of the *incentives problem* of students of East European economies. But it is convenient to discuss the incentives problem later, in the context of general economic equilibrium.

The promise to supplement the formalism of the foregoing discussion by a more intuitive explanation must now be honored. Readers of early drafts of the preceding discussion of Marshallian equilibrium have suggested that it is necessary to give an intuitively appealing interpretation to several questions, specifically:

(*a*) Exactly what *ceteris paribus* assumptions are needed to justify a partial equilibrium analysis of planned economies?

(*b*) Why, indeed, might one expect the demand and supply functions to be positively sloped, under partial equilibrium conditions?

(*c*) Why might the stability conditions – that plan elasticity of supply be greater than plan elasticity of demand – have any plausible economic content?

Enough has been written about partial equilibrium in competitive market to make it clear that this concept, while intuitively appealing, has been fraught with technical difficulties. But it seems that there are several essential ingredients to a partial equilibrium analysis. These pertain to an empirical assumption and a bookkeeping observation. The empirical assumption is well stated by Friedman (1949). In the case of any commodity to which partial equilibrium analysis is applicable, it is possible to list a small group of 'closely related commodities', which are affected by conditions in the given market, and a much larger group of commodities which are, for practical purposes, unrelated to the given commodity. The second principle is a 'double-entry bookkeeping principle' justified in competitive price system by Walras' Law: shifts in demand or supply schedules must always affect at least two schedules. Thus an increase in one demand schedule must be accompanied by a decrease in another demand schedule, or by an increase in a supply schedule, these changes occurring in the small group of 'related' commodities. An excess demand in one market is also accompanied by excess supply in a closely related market.

These considerations mean that in partial equilibrium price theory, one assumes that prices and quantities in all markets other than closely related markets can remain unaffected by a disequilibrium in any given market. Likewise, in a planned economy, a *ceteris paribus* assumption means that all plans and performances in industries which are not closely related to a given industry remain unaffected by disequilibrium and shifts in schedules in that industry. On this basis, then, some of the standard 'textbook problems' of partial equilibrium competitive price theory have analogs in partial equilibrium planning theory. As a first example, consider the pair of interrelated demand functions for butter and margarine. A shift in tastes results in an increase in the quantity of butter and a decrease in the quantity of margarine that consumers will wish to buy at any level of the plans. If the two commodities are in stable equilibrium (fig. 5), then plan for butter will rise and the plan for margarine will fall. But sellers will also respond to changes in plans, and the amount by which plans must change depends on the elasticity of supply with respect to changes in plan in each of the two markets. The diagrams of fig. 3 will be readily followed by anyone who has had a course in price theory.

Or suppose a technological change increases the amount of steel supplied and decreases the amount of labor demanded at any plan. If the equilibria are stable, consider (fig. 6) the amounts by which plans must change to maintain equilibria. Again the familiar conclusion. The more elastic the functions in question (the greater the response of the appropriate groups of buyers and sellers, to a given change in plan) the greater will be the changes in performance, and the smaller will be the changes in plan needed to restore equilibrium.

Examples of this sort could be multiplied. They indicate the way in which one would proceed, in constructing a theory of the planned economy comparable to the theory of a competitive economy. Such exercises, because of space limitations, must be left to the reader.

These simple examples show that this Marshallian analysis 'works' in much the same way as Marshallian price theory, *given the shapes of the curves assumed above*. What may one say about these shapes, speaking behaviorally? Consider several examples.

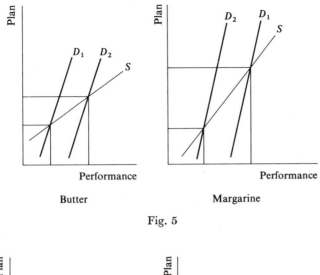

Fig. 5

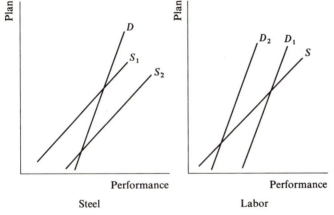

Fig. 6

Suppose a planned economy in which consumers know the plans for a durable commodity, such as automobiles, in which automobiles are actually distributed among applicants by a Quartermaster Corps in accordance with an elaborate series of forms. Is there any plausible justification for a sloping demand function? Suppose that the plan is published, and consumers see that this year there is an increase in the plan for automobiles. Then the consumer will reason as follows: this year there is a higher probability that if I apply for an automobile I will be able to buy one than there was last year. Some consumers who decided last year that it was not worth the bother to apply for a car will decide this year that the chances of success are now high enough to justify the bother of applying. The larger plan then induces a larger number of applications

– a smaller plan would reduce the number of applications. Here 'transactions cost' of a special sort is involved.

Suppose a planned economy in which producers receive plans both for production for input utilization (the latter being 'closely related' commodities). At any given moment, producers select quantities of production and factor utilization. These decisions reflect the rewards and punishments they get for performance, and for deviations from planned targets, the technology of their production processes, and their native endowments of energy and sloth. Suppose now that output plans increase, the plans for factor utilization remaining constant. In the output market, then, there will be some response to the change in plan. Specifically, output will increase somewhat. There will also be some response in the 'closely related markets', unless the effect of the increase in the output plan is merely to decrease the wastefulness and sloth of producers.

The theorist describes the output response when he traces a supply function in the given market. He recognizes that changes go on in a few 'closely related' industries, but he assumes that in most industries of the economy, the induced changes are small enough safely to be ignored. Indeed, if pressed, he will reduce his study of indirect effects to a series of cases like that of butter–margarine or steel–labor. He cannot do this with precision unless he knows the detailed form of the objective function and the constraints facing the firm. But whatever these forms may be, they should be of the kind indicated above.

The stability condition states that in the vicinity of equilibrium an increase in plan produces an increase in excess supply. If this condition does not hold, when planners see an excess demand, they will reduce the plan; and when they see an excess supply they will increase the plan. Both these forms of behavior seem implausible. But if planners react plausibly in seeking equilibrium, then it must be the case that at equilibrium supply schedules are more plan-elastic than demand schedules. That is to say, planners are able to influence supply more effectively than they can influence demand.

We might justify this stability condition by a rough-and-ready appeal to recent Soviet history. Since 1954, state and cooperative retail prices have been effectively stable, and there has been no rationing. Except in cases such as the automobile case given above, the quantities demanded may well have been extremely plan-inelastic. On the other hand, enterprises have been rewarded in response to plan fulfillment. This system of rewards is imperfect, but it makes for greater plan-elasticity of supply than of demand. That is all our stability theory requires.

Again, in Soviet labor markets, there exist relatively direct controls over supply: these include those of the educational system, on-the-job training, the laws against absenteeism and parasitism, and the 'moral suasion' of the Communist Party apparatus. In contrast, the demand for labor tends to be plan-inelastic, because labor regulations are strong and the rewards for cutting of labor costs fairly weak. Consequently a *prima facie* case exists for claiming that the stability conditions have been met in Soviet labor markets.

In Soviet capital goods markets, output is allocated to enterprises, but the cost is mainly born by the Ministry of Finance. Consequently, demand is but little affected by changes in plan. In contrast, the enterprises producing capital goods are rewarded on the basis of plan fulfillment, and it is plausible that their response to changes in plan should be substantially greater than those of demanders.

This impressionistic argument is not a formal demonstration. Much more elaborate techniques would be needed to convince skeptics. At this point, however, all that is needed is an argument which shows that the formal elements of the analysis correspond to intuitively appealing interpretations of 'facts' which are referred to in all general discussions of Soviet reality.

Marshallian methods are appealing because they make possible (*inter alia*) discussions of the effects of public policies upon particular sectors of the economy. Some examples of such policies have already been considered. Thus, if the center does not wish to purchase or sell any of its stocks of the given product, it must set the plan at π_0 (fig. 3); if it wishes to acquire an inventory equal to α, it must increase the plan by more than α, since an increase in the plan will induce an increase in quantities demanded by the periphery. If the center wishes to dispose of an inventory equal to β, it must reduce the plan by more than β, since quantities demanded by the periphery will also fall. This proposition strengthens the remarks made about fig. 4. In connection with that figure it was observed that an equilibrium plan was not necessarily one in which performance was exactly equal to plans. Here we assert that if the center wishes to change its net purchases, the absolute value of the change in plan will exceed the absolute value of the desired net purchases.

In teaching the theory of the market economy, it is customary to show the effects of an excise tax on a competitive market. It is shown that an excise tax is analytically equivalent to the existence of a difference between the price paid by buyers (P_B) and the price received by sellers (P_S). Equilibrium is found when the quantities demanded and supplied are equal, and when the difference between the two prices is equal to the tax (fig. 7(a)).

In a planned economy, there is an analog to a tax. This analog exists when there is a discrepancy between the plan given to demanders and the plan given to suppliers of a commodity. This requires (in Hurwicz's terminology) centralization. Messages sent by the center must contain an address, and it is not the case that everyone can read everyone else's mail. Such a system can create situations which otherwise would not exist.

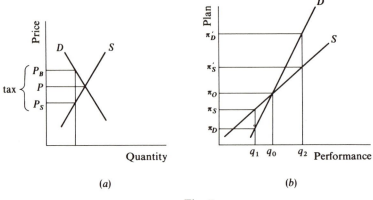

Fig. 7

Suppose (fig. 7(*b*)) the center wishes to reduce the consumption of the commodity from q_0 to q_1, without any 'open market operations' of its own. (The center, for instance, would have to sell from inventory if it reduced the plan below π_0, and it may not have an inventory to sell.) In this case, if it transmits the plan π_S to sellers and the plan π_D to buyers, it will equate quantities demanded and supplied at q_1. Suppose, on the other hand, the center wished to increase the quantity to q_2, without being forced to make 'open market purchases'. In this case it transmits the plan π'_D to buyers and the plan π'_S to sellers.

The manipulations just described have the effect of producing an equilibrium other than that given in fig. 3. The new equilibrium exists because of changed assumptions about the planning process and the flow of information within the economy. It will be useful to consider the two systems in further detail; and some nomenclature will be useful. We therefore shall speak of *unclassified* and *classified* planning processes.

(a) In an *unclassified* planning process, the plans sent to demanders are the same as the plans set to suppliers, and all may be considered as being public knowledge.

(b) In a *classified* planning process, the plans sent to demanders may differ from the plans sent to suppliers. Both of these plans may differ from the internal plan, or outcome desired by the center.

Fig. 3 is a graphical representation of a partial equilibrium in an unclassified planning process. Fig. 7(*b*) is a graphical representation of a partial equilibrium in a classified planning process. We have seen that the changeover from an unclassified to a classified planning process has the effect of altering the equilibrium in a planned economy. It alters it, moreover, without the intervention of the center as a residual buyer or seller. To make the manipulation successful, it is necessary to destroy the anonymity of the information system. It is now useful to consider the industry in a classified planning system in terms of planning cost, or, as Hayek (1945) would put it, information cost.

One of the advantages claimed for decentralized systems is that the computational costs of running the system are small. In the Barone–Lange system, at any iteration of the plan the center has only the cost of calculating excess demands associated with the price vector $\mathbf{p}_t$, and the cost of calculating the next price vector $\mathbf{p}_{t+1}$. Given the data for its periphery, it needs only to select a function $\mathbf{p}_{t+1} = F(\mathbf{p}_t, \mathbf{x}_t)$ which converges to an equilibrium $\bar{\mathbf{p}} = F(\bar{\mathbf{p}}, 0)$ as rapidly as possible; once this function has been selected analytically, the costs of planning are minimized.[10]

How is the unclassified Marshallian planned economy related to the Barone–Lange economy? The center, here, sends out a message, π, to the periphery; this message must be interpreted by buyers and sellers. In an industry where there are m identical enterprises, the enterprise reads π as saying 'you should sell π/m units'. If the enterprises are not identical, each enterprise is given a coefficient ϕ; then enterprise i interprets π as saying 'You should sell $\phi_i \pi$ units'. To construct the coefficients $\{\phi_i | \Sigma\phi_i = 1\}$, the center may have some centralized information (i.e., some information about the supply functions of individual enterprises), but this information need not be calculated at each step of the process. It is true that there may be loss of efficiency if the ϕ_i are selected 'in a wrong way'. There is, however, an increase in computational costs if the ϕ_i are recalculated too often.

The information system under discussion thus has the following parts. There is a code box attached to each enterprise, so that when the center sends out the plan π, the enterprise receives a decoded message $\phi_i \pi$. The decoding costs are assumed to be negligible, but the costs of changing the code are significant. The center incurs two kinds of cost: the cost of measuring excess demand (of tabulating the messages received from the periphery); and the cost of calculating and transmitting the next iteration of the plan. A scheme of these computations is given in fig. 8(a).

The calculations required in the classified system are more complicated. The center must first compute a desired value for q_1. Given q_1, it must then compute separately two plans, π_D and π_S, and have a means of determining whether these will bring about a performance of q_1. To do so, it must alter the decoders of suppliers, so that these will respond to π_S but not to π_D, but it need not alter the decoding programs. It must alter the decoders of demanders, so that these will respond to π_D but not to π_S, but it need not alter the decoding programs. Within the center, it must be possible to distinguish the messages of demanders from the messages of suppliers. Two 'tatonnement processes' then occur. The first is designed to determine a plan $\bar{\pi}_D$ which will bring about a quantity demanded equal to q_1; the second to determine a plan $\bar{\pi}_S$ which will bring about a

63

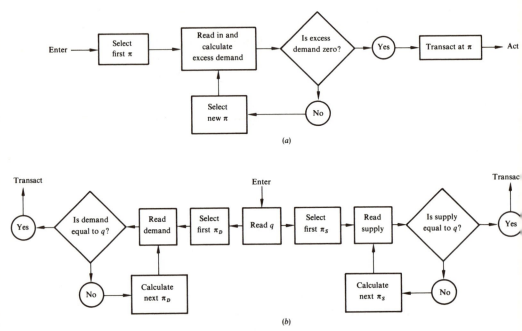

Fig. 8. (a) Program associated with fig. 4; (b) Program associated with fig. 7 (b).

quantity supplied equal to q_1. The total computation is more than doubled: two tatonnement processes are needed rather than one; and also a computation of a 'best value' of q_1 is needed. Finally there is a once-and-for-all change needed in the peripheral decoding machines and in the central read-in equipment.

There may be another cost, less easy to evaluate, but not necessarily negligible. The enterprise on the periphery, at a certain moment, receives an order to execute a particular plan. So far, the model says that the enterprise goes to a shelf, finds the exact amount of goods it needs, and takes them away; or it goes to a shelf, leaves the amount of goods it has said it would leave, and returns, having spoken to nobody. If the enterprise had talked to another enterprise, in an unclassified planned economy it would turn out that all enterprises had read the same messages into their decoders, and all would have been able to agree that if the center wants anything, it wants what it says it wants. And everyone would be right.

Suppose, however, that the planning process is classified. If a supplier talks to a demander, it will turn out that the suppliers think the center wants π_S to happen; the demanders think that the center wants π_D to happen; and both groups would be wrong, since the center actually wants q_1 to happen. Confusion is apt to result. It becomes important that members of the periphery do not speak to each other and that the center should not make public its true intentions.

It is tempting to see in this simple discussion an explanation of the secrecy which has surrounded so many empirical planning processes; a secrecy pertaining to the contents of the plan used by the center, and stringent security measures concerning the public discussion of enterprise plans. It has been customary in discussions of official secrecy to postulate (a) that military security was involved; (b) that the facts were so bad that planners dared not release them; or (c) that an unreasonable bureaucratic paranoia prevailed. But if the center has a preference ordering on the space of possible outcomes, and if it uses its planning mechanism to achieve particular ends, then the success of the planning process may necessarily depend on the closing of channels of communication which might otherwise exist. If this is a tenable conclusion, certain patterns of silence may be inherent in some forms of economic planning.[11]

To go from equilibrium on a single planned industry to equilibrium in a planned economy is to go from Marshallian to Walrasian analysis on a single jump. This transition may be undertaken with ease if the procedures of Quirk and Saponsnik (1968, especially ch. 3) are followed. Suppose only that the quantity of each commodity which enterprises desire to buy or to sell depends on all the individual targets set forth in the plan. Then, given any plan $\pi = (\pi_1, \pi_2, ..., \pi_n)$ there will be vectors of quantities demanded, $\mathbf{q}^D = (q_1^D, q_2^D, ..., q_n^D)$ and of quantities supplied, $\mathbf{q}^S = (q_1^S, q_2^S, ..., q_n^S)$, and functions f and g such that $\mathbf{q}^D = f(\pi)$ and $\mathbf{q}^S = g(\pi)$. In this case, $f^{-1}(\mathbf{q}^D)$ defines the set of plans which will result in a particular vector of demand $\mathbf{q}^D$. Suppose that f^{-1} is single valued. (It is impossible to alter a plan π without altering at least one of the quantities demanded.) Now proceed as follows: select a particular demand vector $\bar{\mathbf{q}}^D$. This vector would be generated by the plan $f^{-1}(\bar{\mathbf{q}}^D) = \bar{\pi}$. If $\bar{\pi}$ were indeed the plan chosen, then the quantity supplied would be $\bar{\mathbf{q}}^S = g(\pi) = g[f^{-1}(\bar{\mathbf{q}}^D)]$.

Consider the function $g[f^{-1}(-)]$. If there is a vector $\bar{\mathbf{q}}$ such that $\bar{\mathbf{q}} = g[f^{-1}(\bar{\mathbf{q}})]$ then $\bar{\mathbf{q}}$ will be a general equilibrium vector, and $f^{-1}(\bar{\mathbf{q}})$ will be the equilibrium plan. Conversely if there is a general equilibrium, $\bar{\mathbf{q}}$, it will satisfy the condition $\bar{\mathbf{q}} = g[f^{-1}(\bar{\mathbf{q}})]$.

In mathematical jargon, there is a general economic equilibrium if and only if $g(f^{-1}(-))$ has a *fixed point*. There are various mathematical theorems establishing that for very general categories of functions f and g, $g(f^{-1}(-))$ will indeed have a fixed point. These theorems are precisely the ones needed to prove the existence of a general economic equilibrium in a competitive economy; only very recently has it become possible to demonstrate the existence of a competitive general equilibrium without invoking such theorems. A very nice feature of the present approach to planned economies is precisely the fact that it uses so much familiar analysis even though its institutional context is quite different. Ockham's Razor comes immediately into action to cut away objections.

The mathematical side of the proof that there is a general equilibrium will not be undertaken here. The proof would depend on our knowing more about the supply and demand functions than we so far have stated. But one side of the proof is of general interest, for it resembles fig. 4. In that diagram, if the plan is sufficiently small, the quantity demanded will exceed the quantity supplied. If the plan is sufficiently *large*, the quantity supplied will exceed the quantity demanded. And so (the mathematician would reason) if there curves are continuous and bounded there must be an intermediate plan where the demand and supply curves intersect. The fixed point theorem follows this reasoning in a many-dimensional space.

Is it plausible, thinking of general economic equilibrium, that an analogous reasoning should be valid? Part of the foregoing is certainly plausible. Imagine, for instance, that planners tell everyone not to buy anything or to sell anything, so that all plans are zero. To enterprises, this may present no problem; to people, however, this plan is equivalent to the order 'Drop dead'. It is plausible, then, that for a plan sufficiently close to zero, there might be excess demand for all products other than personal services, and an excess supply of personal services.

Now imagine a plan which tells everyone to buy and sell enormous (but finite) amounts of everything. It is plausible that such a plan would make people work longer hours than they would like, and, in the circumstances, to provide more goods than people would turn out to want. Thus there would be excess demand for personal services and excess supply of goods.

So if we can find two plans, such that there is (a) excess demand for goods and excess supply of services in one case, and (b) excess supply of goods and excess demand for services in the other, then it should be the case that somewhere in between (a) and (b) there is a plan (c) with neither excess demand nor excess supply for either goods or services.

To apply the theorem in a partial equilibrium case, we need only appeal to 'laws' of diminishing marginal utility, which mean, that given consumption of all other goods, there is a maximum amount of any good which consumers will use, even if that good is a free good. This condition creates a bound on demand; and an analogous bound exists for supply. So excess demand is also bounded. In this case, if the functions are continuous, there is a fixed point. In general equilibrium, there is an analogy: no amount of goods supplied will induce people to provide more more than a certain amount of services. Thus the ability of a planned economy to expand is bounded ultimately by the supply of services by its population. If this is true, we should be able to prove there exists general equilibrium, given continuity of the supply and demand functions.

It is worth repeating that no proof has been given that general equilibrium exists in a planned economy. Rather, we have looked at the economic meaning of some very general conditions which would be sufficient to guarantee that there is a general equilibrium.[12]

In this discussion, it was necessary to use an argument that there would be excess demands in some markets and excess supplies in others. This argument, then, resembles that of Walras' Law, in which the sum of the values of the excess demands in a competitive economy is shown to be zero, whatever the prices which may be considered.

In order that Walras' Law be pronounceable (let alone provable) it is necessary that some valuation system exist, so that 'money' incomes and expenditures are defined, and that the members of the periphery have budget constraints. (Readers will note that we have so far not mentioned the word *price* in connection with planned economies. Some planned economies might get along without any prices at all. The argument of this paper is potentially applicable to them.)

If the institutional structure of a planned economy is specified more sharply than we have specified it here, then stronger and sharper propositions about it may be proved. Thus in an earlier paper (Ames, 1969), the author showed that Walras' Law would hold in a planned economy with money. The law says that if the rules which assign money values to commodity transactions are fixed, then whatever these rules may be, for every plan selected, the total money value of all excess demands (supplies) will be zero. The argument runs as follows: each enterprise has a budget, which includes as revenues any subsidies and credit it can obtain from other sources, as well as that from the sale of its products. A plan provides for the revenue and expenditures of each enterprise. In a monetary economy, an enterprise cannot wish to have above-plan (below-plan) revenue without simultaneously wishing to have above-plan (below-plan) expenditures, and conversely. For each enterprise, then, the money valuation of the deviation of its activities from plan must be zero, since both plans and intentions exhaust the income of the enterprise. Consequently, the money value of the deviations from plan of all enterprises combined must be zero, regardless of what the plan is, and regardless of the particular way in which transactions are assigned money values.

Let us return, now, to the main context of this paper, in which as few institutional restrictions as possible are placed on the planned economies under consideration. Suppose we can show that there is a general economic equilibrium in such an economy, so that quantities demanded and supplied will be equal, if some particular plan is selected. Now let us ask, will the performance of the economy, in equilibrium, be that described in the plan?

The easy answer to this question is *No*. Look at fig. 4. There is no *a priori* reason why general economic equilibrium should involve equality between plan and performance. Going back to our statement of the fixed point theorem on general equilibrium, recall that an equilibrium exists if and only if:

$$\mathbf{q}^S = g(f^{-1}(\mathbf{q}^D)) = \mathbf{q}^D.$$

In order that equilibrium plans be exactly carried out, however, the conditions (in an unclassified economy) are that

$$\pi = g(\pi) = f(\pi).$$

That is, π must be a fixed point of both g and f, as well as of gf^{-1}. Clearly, if π is a fixed point of both g and f, it will also be an equilibrium; but the converse is not necessarily true.[13]

This conjecture about the existence of a general economic equilibrium in a planned economy, if verified, would make it possible to discuss three topics in the literature about empirical planned economies, the problem of *policy*, the problem of *incentives*, and the problem of *administrative structure*.

The existence of a general equilibrium given above was predicated on the assumption that the center was neither a demander nor a supplier of goods and services. Moreover, it did not assert that there was a unique equilibrium. It has been noted, in connection with the partial equilibrium system, that the effect of demand or supply by the center could be regarded as a shift in demand and supply functions. In effect, such activity merely replaces $f(\pi)$ by $f(\pi) + \mathbf{D}_c$, where $\mathbf{D}_c$ is a vector of quantities demanded by the center; and $g(\pi)$ by $g(\pi) + \mathbf{S}_c$, where $\mathbf{S}_c$ is a vector of quantities demanded by the center. Thus

$$\mathbf{q}^D - \mathbf{D}_c = f(\pi)$$

$$\pi = f^{-1}(\mathbf{q}^D - \mathbf{D}_c)$$

$$\mathbf{q}^S = g(\pi) + \mathbf{S}_c = g[f^{-1}(\mathbf{q}^D - \mathbf{D}_c)] + \mathbf{S}_c$$

and there is an equilibrium if and only if

$$\mathbf{q}^S - \mathbf{S}_c = g(f^{-1}(\mathbf{q}^D - \mathbf{D}_c)).$$

But $\mathbf{q}^S - \mathbf{S}_c$ is the vector of demand by the periphery, and $\mathbf{q}^D - \mathbf{D}_c$ is the vector of demand by the periphery. Thus this last condition is not fundamentally different from the first statement of general equilibrium. The interesting questions of public policy arise from the way in which $\mathbf{D}_c$ and $\mathbf{S}_c$ are interrelated with each other and with the demand and supply vectors of the periphery. Does the center merely requisition goods, or does it have a budget? Does the center produce only 'public goods' which the periphery cannot refuse to use (like anti-ballistic missiles and concentration camps)? Are there vectors essentially like exports and imports? And so on. To discussed these questions concretely it is necessary to introduce more specifications about the economy than have here been used. A general remark, however, is in order. If the center is free to select more

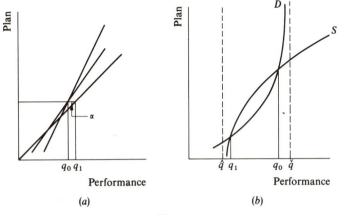

Fig. 9

than one pair $(\mathbf{D}_c, \mathbf{S}_c)$, or if there is more than one equilibrium for a given pair, then the usual problems of public policy in planned economies can be discussed. For then the center can select some particular equilibrium as maximizing some objective function of its own. There is nothing in the foregoing argument to suggest that there is a single equilibrium, even if $g(f^{-1}(-))$ has a single fixed point.

The incentives problem arises particularly in discussions of Eastern Europe.[14] In a partial equilibrium context, it is associated with deviations of performance from plan. Thus in fig. $9(a)$ the discrepancy between performance and plan, at equilibrium is measured by the horizontal line segment α. In general equilibrium, performance is given by the fixed point $\bar{\mathbf{q}} = f(g^{-1}(\bar{\mathbf{q}}))$, while the plan producing that outcome is given by $\boldsymbol{\pi} = g^{-1}(\bar{\mathbf{q}})$. Thus if there is some metric M on the space in question, $M(\bar{\mathbf{q}} - \bar{\boldsymbol{\pi}})$ will be a measure of the discrepancy between performance and plan.

There are various reasons why the deviation of performance from plan, at equilibrium, may be of concern to the planners. It is convenient to discuss the problem in a partial equilibrium context, although a general equilibrium analog exists. To introduce the discussion readers will be reminded that the industry demand and supply functions are added up from enterprise demand and supply functions. These, in turn, are solutions to optimization problems facing the individual enterprises. One way to shift the functions is to alter the objective functions of enterprises. If authorities wish to reduce $M(\bar{\mathbf{q}} - \bar{\boldsymbol{\pi}})$, the discrepancy between performance and plan, they need only discover what objective functions will make this function arbitrarily close to zero. In the limit, one would have $f(\boldsymbol{\pi}) \equiv \mathbf{q}^S \equiv \mathbf{q}^D \equiv g(\boldsymbol{\pi}) \equiv \boldsymbol{\pi}$. In this case, every plan would be an equilibrium plan. In partial equlibrium, both demand and supply functions would coincide with the 45° ray from the origin. Whatever plan was adopted would be exactly executed.

Let demand and supply functions be those given by fig. 9(b). Here there is a single stable equilibrium, leading to output q_0; q_1 is an unstable equilibrium. A feature of this industry is that the demand function has an upper bound of $\check{q}$, and the supply function has a lower bound of $\hat{q}$. If the authorities can alter the supply functions, but not demand functions, there is nothing which they can do to expand actual performance above $\check{q}$; if they can control demand functions, but not supply functions, there is nothing they can do to reduce actual performance below $\hat{q}$. These limits would exist even if imports or centralized inventory depletion takes place in the first case; and even if exports or centralized inventory acquisition takes place in the second place. Thus performance is constrained by the existence of a bound on performance.[15]

A general equilibrium analog would exist if there is no plan which will lead to certain quantities being demanded (or supplied). While such 'inaccessible regions' of the performance space may be the result of technological considerations, they may also be the result of the choice of objective functions, or of internal accounting constraints placed upon enterprises. It is natural, then, for a planned economy, in certain conditions, to alter the conditions under which enterprises work, as a means of making possible the attainment of certain performance vectors, which could otherwise never be attained because they are not images of any plan, under either the demand function f or the demand function g, as the case may be.

Suppose, however, that both demand and supply functions have values everywhere in some connected region R of the space, and that planners are concerned with obtaining performance within that range. Let us assume that $\bar{q}$ is an equilibrium performance in R, and that $\bar{\pi}$ is a plan which brings about this equilibrium. Finally, suppose that the authorities, by manipulating imports, exports and their own inventories, can bring about all possible performances in a neighborhood of $\bar{q}$. It is natural to inquire why they might be dissatisfied by a discrepancy between plans and performances. After all, if performance is one which the planners want, why should they care if it diverges from the plan? Is the insistence that incentives must be altered to secure conformity with plan reasonable, or is it merely an aesthetic preference?

To select plans which bring about a desired performance (even though this differs from the plan), the center must carry out two computations: it must calculate what it wants, and it must then calculate what plan will bring about the desired result. There is a cost to this additional computation (and to acquisition of the information needed to make it). On the other hand, there is a cost attached to finding out the particular objective functions which will lead demand and supply functions to be in an equilibrium at which plans are exactly fulfilled. *A priori* there is no telling which costs will be higher. At the same time, a more subtle reason exists to explain why it may be desirable to create an 'incentive structure' which leads to the adoption of equilibrium plans which are approximately equal to performance.

In a planned economy with given enterprise utility functions, suppose the center opts for plans which minimize the discrepancy between plan and performance. Then it allows its behavior to be guided by existing institutional practices, and gives up its ability to direct the allocation of resources.

Now suppose that the center has preferences on the performance space, and does not want to alter utility functions so as to increase conformity to plan. In this case it selects that plan which produces the most desirable outcome, even though the outcome is no longer a replica of the plan.

To operate on this latter basis, the center must stop considering published plans either as forecasts of a future state of affairs, or as descriptions of a desired state of affairs. Rather, they are instructions which will bring about some desired result, known to differ from the instructions.

A criticism is often made of published plans: that they are not feasible, and that they will not be realized. If the plan is not a description of some future reality, but a set of instructions, which are expected to be disobeyed in a predictable way, this criticism is beside the point.

Another criticism of planned economies is that things do not work out as the plan said they would. Imagine, in this context, a 'perverse' industry in which suppliers, given a plan π, always produce π^{-a} ($a > 0$). In this industry, a planner, wishing to increase output, would always decrease his plan. It would be foolish to criticise the plans because performance was different from plan. In the 'real world' behavior is not so perverse as in this example, but it may be sufficiently perverse to create a real, and important discrepancy between plans and the real objectives of the center.

It may be possible to design institutions so that the forecasting and control functions generate the same collections of numbers. But a simpler problem in social designing may be the following: sets of numbers, called plans, would be distributed to enterprises; these numbers would be used by the enterprises to determine their production and consumption. The plans would then produce forecasted outputs which were satisfactory to the planners.

This argument, once again, supposes that even in an unclassified planning system, the center may have good reason to keep its desires hidden. For if these desires are different from the published plans, enterprises will know that the things they are told to do are not quite (perhaps not at all) descriptions of the state of affairs the center wishes to bring about. Confusion is bound to result, and the credibility and power of the center are apt to be weakened. The center may prefer credibility and power, and hence it will also prefer secrecy.

This survey of the theory of planned economies, from the Marshallian point of view, has made clear certain fundamental similarities between the equilibrium and stability conditions of competitive economies and those of planned economies. These similarities suggest that a far more precise analysis of economic planning is possible than has hitherto been attempted; and that price theory can be used as a guide to beginners in this work. On the other hand, Hayek's suggestion that market economies may be informationally very efficient seems to be borne out. For one cannot go far into a discussion of planned economies without considering the meaning of flows of messages within such economies. We have illustrated these informational problems by comparing classified with unclassified planned industries, and by discussing explicitly questions of secrecy and publicity. These turn out to be economic questions in planned economies, rather than political questions, as is generally assumed.

It is pleasant to find new ways of using familiar ideas. In part, our satisfaction derives from the unexpected strength and versatility of our accustomed tools. In part it derives from the fact that apparently strange phenomena turn out to be similar to phenomena we think we already understand. Students of the natural sciences are disturbed when atoms and galaxies fail to follow the same laws. Perhaps economists should be more disturbed than they are at claims that planned economies are different from competitive economies. If this paper is right, planned economies are really very much like competitive economies–providing that it is understood that plans really do take the place of prices in determining resource allocation. If this is really the case, then Marshall, Walras and Hayek can give us the start we need to develop a workable theory of planned economies.

NOTES

1 If obscurity and error remain in this paper, the fault certainly does not lie with my colleagues Estelle James and Egon Neuberger. They, indeed, forced clarity and precision into many points in my draft, and I give them my thanks.
2 Many topics in this paper are discussed more formally in Ames (1969). There are, however, two differences between that paper and this one. That paper is more specialized in that it assumes the existence of money, while this one does not. It is more general, however, in that it assumes the existence of an adjustment mechanism, such that at least some situations in which quantities demanded differ from quantities supplied can exist.
3 The exact meaning of the expression *incentive structure* is considered later in the paper.
4 If the center considers each enterprise to be recognizably different from each other enterprise, the number of goods equals the number of enterprises. This is a special form of monopoly.

5 So far as I know, the only such construction in the literature is given in Ames (1965). Even such an excellent book as Ward (1967) does not explain why enterprises behavior depends on plans.

6 We use the standard definition for elasticity, $\partial \log q / \partial \log p$, where q is the quantity (demanded or supplied) and p the (industry-wide) plan.

7 Hunter (1961) suggests a downward-sloping supply function. His argument, however, is based on dynamic considerations: if 'we' increase our output today, 'they' will merely increase the plan tomorrow.

8 In an unstable equilibrium, an increase in plan would increase the (absolute value) of excess demand. If there are countably many equilibria for a given commodity, these will be alternately stable and unstable.

9 This adjustment mechanism is Walrasian, not Marshallian. The Marshallian price adjustment process considers a non-equilibrium quantity, and notes that buyers and sellers would require different prices for this quantity to represent an equilibrium. Reasoning comparable to that in the Marshallian adjustment process occurs below in the discussion of classified planning systems.

10 It would appear that the literature on dynamic price adjustment processes would apply to this problem, with only a renaming of symbols. This literature makes sense only in tatonnement market processes. These correspond to iterative planning processes like those described here.

11 My colleague, Egon Neuberger, has pointed out another possible situation. The center, here, tells the enterprises, 'We will tell you to do certain things, and even reward you for doing them. Our instructions may seem bizarre to you, and we urge you not to try to understand them. We know more than you about economic interrelations, and we know that our way of procedure, however strange it may seem, will produce better results than any procedure which you might consider intelligible.' Such an economy would work in the manner of psycho-social experiments, in which it is important that the subjects of the experiment do not know the purpose of the experiments, since such knowledge would affect the outcome. It would, however, be difficult to prevent leakage of information in cases where the subjects of the experiment are not college sophomores, and in which the stakes exceed the standard $2.00-per-hour-for-five-hours reward for participation.

12 As noted above, the proof would depend on the selection of an appropriate theory of behavior for individual economic units.

13 Ames (1969) argues that there exists a plan which will be exactly fulfilled. This argument now appears to be incorrect. It depends on the assertion that the class of vectors $(\mathbf{q}_1/\pi_1, \mathbf{q}_2/\pi_2, ..., \mathbf{q}_n/\pi_n)$ are a function of π. For π in the neighborhood of zero this class will be outside the unit n-sphere. It is correctly said that for an 'intermediate' π, the vector must be on the boundary of the sphere. But this is not the same as showing that the plan is exactly fulfilled. For that to be the case, there must be a plan whose image is the vertex $(1, 1, ..., 1)$ of the unit n-cube. I retract the claim.

14 See, for example, Montias (1962) especially chapter 9; Novel (1961) especially chapter 6; James and Neuberger (1970); Hoffman 1967. Most western economic discussions of Eastern Europe discuss this question, at least in passing. A more formal attempt to discuss the issue is given in Groves (1973).

15 The incentive problem is thus different from the unbiasedness question (see Hurwicz, 1959). Writers on competitive market economies have shown that such economies are unbiased: every Pareto optimum can be attained by a competitive price equilibrium, given an appropriate initial allocation of resources (property). It is not clear that any concept of initial allocation of resources is generally appropriate for planned economies, for it is not clear what property means in this context.

But given any initial allocation of resources, suitably defined, the final allocation of resources depends on the 'utility functions' of enterprises. These are subject to selection by the center, at least within some limits.

REFERENCES

Ames, E. (1965). *Soviet Economic Processes*. Homewood, Ill.: Irwin.

Ames, E. (1969). The structure of general equilibrium in a planned economy. In *Jahrbuch der Wirtschaft Osteuropas*, Band I. Munich: Guenter Olzog.

Barone, E. (1935). The ministry of production in the collectivist state. Reprinted in *Collectivist Economic Planning*, ed. F. A. Hayek. London: Routledge.

Camacho, A. (1970). Centralization and decentralization of decision-making mechanism: a general model. Evanston, Ill.: Northwestern University Graduate School of Management. Mimeographed.

Friedman, M. (1949). The Marshallian demand curve. *Journal of Political Economy*, **57**, 463–95.

Groves, T. (1973). Incentives in teams. *Econometrica*.

Hayek, F. A. (1945). The use of knowledge in society. *American Economic Review*, **35**, 519–30.

Hoffman, C. (1967). *Work Incentives, Practices and Policies in the People's Republic of China 1963–65*. Albany: SUNY.

Hunter, H. (1961). Optimum tautness in development planning. *Economic Development and Cultural Change*, July.

Hurwicz, L. (1959). Optimality and informational efficiency in resource allocation processes. In *Mathematical Methods in the Social Sciences*, ed. K. J. Arrow, S. Karlin and P. Suppes. Stanford, California.

James, E. and E. Neuberger (1970). The Yugoslav self-managed enterprise: a systematic approach. Research Conference on Economic Reform in Eastern Europe, 16–18 November 1970, University of Michigan. Mimeographed.

Montias, J. M. (1962). *Central Planning in Poland*. New Haven: Yale.

Montias, J. M. (1970). A framework for theoretical analysis of economic reforms in Soviet-type economies. Research Conference on Economic Reform in Eastern Europe, 16–18 November 1970, the University of Michigan. Mimeographed.

Nove, A. (1961). *The Soviet Economy*. New York: Praeger.

Portes, R. D. (1971). Decentralized planning procedures and centrally planned economies. *American Economic Review, Papers and Proceedings*, **61**, 422–9.

Quirk, J. and R. Saposnik (1968). *Introduction to General Equilibrium Theory and Welfare Economics*. New York: McGraw-Hill.

Ward, B. (1967). *The Socialist Economy, A Study of Organizational Alternatives*. New York: Random House.

A Priceless Planned Economy

EDWARD AMES[1]

Economists have generally recognized that the ordinary theory of constrained maxima needs changing if it is to deal with organizations having functional components. Various approaches to the theory of collective decisions have been taken in recent years, of which voting theory and team theory are examples. In voting theory, a group of individuals having different utility functions is endowed with a social preference ordering by the specification of a voting procedure. While this ordering is specific to the voting mechanism considered, it permits application to groups of a maximization technique, which, given Arrow's impossibility theorem, would otherwise be unavailable.

In team theory, the organization consists of individuals with identical tastes. They are forced, by communications problems, to make independent decisions, even though the outcome of these decisions reflects interdependencies within the organization. Whereas the voting theory problem deals with the nature of the social preference ordering, the team theory problem deals with externality and imperfect information.

In what follows, a different approach to group decisions will be undertaken. The fundamental proposition on which it relies is that the utility of a given action to a member of the group is influenced by messages he has received from others in the group. This proposition is unlike the situation in other models. Usually, it is stated that the utility of an action to an individual depends solely on that action and on the actions of other members of the group. If a member of the group has power over other members, this power exists because he can do things which influence the payoff of actions taken by other members. In the present hypothesis, the power of an individual lies in the fact that messages he sends to others alter the attactiveness to them of each of the actions in their choice set.

The cases studied here use the standard model of a group $\{0, 1, ..., n\}$ of individuals. Individual 0 is referred to as the *planner* (the *center* is a common alternative in economic literature); the others are referred to as *enterprises* (the *periphery* is a common alternative). In the general situation, each individual has a utility function. The planner is regarded as sending plans to the enterprises, and receiving information about the production and use of goods by the enterprises. (The planner neither produces nor consumes goods.) Each enterprise receives a plan from the planner and selects a rate of production and use of goods.

Each enterprise produces one good. At any period, it has an activity vector of non-negative numbers $(x_1^i, x_2^i, ..., x_n^i) = \mathbf{x}^i$, where $\mathbf{x}_i^i$ is its output rate and $\mathbf{x}_j^i$ ($j \neq i$) its rate of use of j's output. It selects $\mathbf{x}^i$ on the basis of a plan vector of non-negative numbers $(\pi_1^i, \pi_2^i, ..., \pi_n^i) = \boldsymbol{\pi}^i$ received from the planner. The planner receives a vector $(x^1, x^2, ..., x^n) = \mathbf{x}$ (in an n^2-dimensional space) and selects a plan $(\pi^1, \pi^2, ..., \pi^n) = \boldsymbol{\pi}$ (in an n^2-dimensional space) for transmission to the enterprises. Each enterprise receives only it own plan. There are neither prices nor money in the system.

These units each have utility functions. For enterprise i,

$$\mathbf{U}_i = \mathbf{U}_i(\mathbf{x}^i|\boldsymbol{\pi}^i).$$

The enterprise, given $\boldsymbol{\pi}_i$, selects that $\mathbf{x}_i$ which maximizes $\mathbf{U}_i$. For the planner, $\mathbf{U}_0 = \mathbf{U}_0(\boldsymbol{\pi}|\mathbf{x})$. The planner selects that plan $\boldsymbol{\pi}$ which maximizes $\mathbf{U}_0$, given the activities $\mathbf{x}$ of the enterprises.

While still operating non-technically, we may compare this model to the Barone–Lange tradition of planning models. There, the planner is essentially a Walrasian auctioneer, seeking plans which will clear markets. The planner sends a price vector to the enterprises, but we may regard this message as a coding of an activity vector, just as enterprises regard it. The enterprise, given a message $\boldsymbol{\pi}^i$, selects an activity $\mathbf{x}^i$. Let us imagine that some other message, $\hat{\boldsymbol{\pi}}^i$, had been sent. Then the enterprise might well select a different activity, say $\hat{\mathbf{x}}^i$. The Barone–Lange tradition does not ask whether it is possible that

$$\mathbf{U}_i(\mathbf{x}^i|\boldsymbol{\pi}^i) > \mathbf{U}^i(\hat{\mathbf{x}}^i|\boldsymbol{\pi}^i) \quad \text{and} \quad \mathbf{U}_i(\hat{\mathbf{x}}^i|\hat{\boldsymbol{\pi}}^i) > \mathbf{U}_i(\mathbf{x}^i|\hat{\boldsymbol{\pi}}^i).$$

That question has no meaning. If in one case $\mathbf{x}^i$ is selected and in another case $\hat{\mathbf{x}}^i$ is selected, this difference reflects a difference in the constraints facing the enterprise, and hence in the choice set. In what follows, however, the pair of inequalities just given do have a meaning.

It will be useful to start our exposition with an economy consisting of a planner and a single enterprise which produces a single commodity. A plan π consists of an instruction to produce at the rate given by the number π; an activity x consists of a decision to produce at the rate given by the number x. In this economy, the enterprise has the special utility function[2]

$$U = e^{-x}x^{f(\pi)}. \tag{1}$$

When the enterprise receives the signal π, it selects that x which maximizes U. It performs the calculation

$$\frac{\partial U}{\partial x} = \left(-1 + \frac{f(\pi)}{x}\right)U = 0 \tag{2}$$

and sees that the optimal rate of production is $x = f(\pi)$. It may be that the enterprise is happiest doing exactly what it has been told to do. In this case, $f(\pi) \equiv \pi$; we do not claim this is the case.

The extremum given by (2) is in fact an optimum, for

$$\frac{\partial^2 U}{\partial x^2} = \frac{-f(\pi)}{x^2} U + \left(-1 + \frac{f(\pi)}{x}\right)^2 U. \tag{3}$$

If (2) is satisfied, the second right term of (3) vanishes. The first right term is certainly negative, and (2) therefore characterizes an optimum.

The enterprise is not indifferent to the plan given it. Assume that it behaves optimally, setting $x = f(\pi)$. If it does so, its utility is given by

$$\bar{U} = e^{-f(\pi)} f(\pi)^{f(\pi)}. \tag{4}$$

and the derivative of this function with respect to π is easily shown to be

$$\frac{\partial \bar{U}}{\partial \pi} = \frac{\partial f}{\partial \pi} \log f(\pi) \, \bar{U}. \tag{5}$$

The sign of this expression is not independent of the unit of measure of x, for the sign of $\log f(\pi)$ depends on the (accidental) question of whether f is greater or less than 1. It is assumed that the unit of measure is small, so that over the relevant range $f > 1$. In this case the sign of $\partial \bar{U}/\partial \pi$ is the same as the sign of $\partial f/\partial \pi$. Economically this means that an increase in the plan increases the (equilibrium) welfare of the enterprise if and only if the enterprise responds to an increase in the plan by increasing its output or use of the good in question.

Now we consider the economy of three units, $\{0, 1, 2\}$, a planner (0) and two enterprises $(1, 2)$. The enterprise utility functions are of the form (1), but their behavior functions are not assumed to be the same. This simple economy is generalizable in a number of respects but it is a useful basis of departure. The planner's behavior is central to the working of the system, and several cases will be considered.

Case 1

The planner has a stock $\bar{x}$ of a good to allocate, in amounts x_1 and x_2, to the enterprises. He does so by giving them plans, π_1 and π_2. The planner's utility function, $U_0(x_1, x_2)$, subject to the constraint $x_1 + x_2 \leqslant \bar{x}$, is assumed to be maximized when $x_i = \bar{x}_i$ $(i = 1, 2)$.

It has been noted that

$$U_i = e^{-x_i} x_i^{f_i(\pi_i)} \quad (i = 1, 2)$$

is maximized when $\qquad x_i = f_i(\pi_i).$

Since $\qquad U_0(\bar{x}_1, \bar{x}_2) \geqslant U_0(x_1, x_2) \quad$ when $\quad x_1 + x_2 \leqslant \bar{x}$

it is merely necessary to calculate

$$\bar{\pi}_i = f_1^{-1}(\bar{x}_i).$$

In this case $\qquad U_0(f_1^{-1}(\bar{\pi}_1), f_2^{-2}(\bar{\pi}_2)) \geqslant U_0(x_1, x_2).$

To make this calculation, it is necessary for the planner to know the functions f_1, f_2. In this sense, the system is *informationally centralized*, as Hurwicz (1959) defines the term. But the system is not *centralized* in Camacho's sense, for no restrictions are placed by the choice of plan upon the set of quantities from which the enterprises may select (Camacho, 1970).

This system produces Pareto optima if and only if the outcome maximizes the planner's utility function. Consider an arbitrary pair of plans, $\hat{\pi}_1, \hat{\pi}_2$. Corresponding to these plans there exist quantities demanded, $\hat{x}_i = f_i(\hat{\pi}_i)$ $(i = 1, 2)$. Any reallocation of consumption between 1 and 2, given these plans, will make both enterprises worse off. Thus if $\hat{\pi}_i = \bar{\pi}_i$, so that the $\bar{x}_i$ are optimal to the planner, every reallocation of goods will make all the agents $(0, 1, 2)$ worse off.

There is no reason, moreover, why $\bar{x}_i$ should equal $\bar{\pi}_i$; there is also no reason why the plans should be 'feasible' in the sense that $\bar{\pi}_1 + \bar{\pi}_2 \leqslant \bar{x}$. To show that this is the case, let us consider the following special 'demand functions' characterizing enterprise behavior:

$$f_i \equiv C_i^{(n_i-1)/n_i} \pi_i^{1/n_i}.$$

It is a feature of these functions that

(a) $f_i = \pi_i$ if and only if $\pi_i = C_i$,

(b) $\partial \log f_i / \partial \log \pi_i = 1/n_i$, so that the 'elasticity of demand with respect to changes in plan' is the constant $1/n_i$.

Given these 'demand functions', the optimal plans turn out to be

$$\bar{\pi}_i = \bar{x}_i / c_i^{n_i-1}.$$

Consequently, if $\qquad \bar{x}_1 + \bar{x}_2 = \bar{\pi}_1 c_1^{n_1-1} + \bar{\pi}_2 c_2^{n_2-1} = \bar{x},$

then in general $\bar{\pi}_1 + \bar{\pi}_2 \neq x$. In particular, if $c_i^{n_i-1} < 1$, then $\bar{\pi}_1 + \bar{\pi}_2 > \bar{x}$, and the plan will be 'unfeasible', even though it leads to optimal results.

This last result puts an evident constraint on the information flow in this economy. For if enterprises can exchange information on their plans, and if they know the stock available to the planner, they will see that the planner cannot possibly 'really' want them to do what the plan tells them to do. It appears to be necessary, therefore, for the planner to prevent communication between enterprises, and perhaps also to conceal information concerning $\bar{x}$.

It also appears certain that the planner should have no illusion that the plan $(\bar{\pi}_1, \bar{\pi}_2)$ that he selects is a forecast of the result $(\bar{x}_1, \bar{x}_2)$ which he wishes to obtain.

This case assumed that the planner's utility depended on the outcome of the process. He selected the plan which produced that outcome. In the following case, the planner has a utility function in which the 'best plan' depends upon what the enterprises are doing.

Case 2

The enterprises have the same utility functions as before. Now, however, the planner has a utility function $U_0(\pi_1, \pi_2 | x_1, x_2)$. On observing a particular vector (x_1, x_2) his strategy is to select the plans $g_1(x_1, x_2) = \pi_1$, and $g_2(x_1, x_2) = \pi_2$. The exact nature of these functions will not detain us at the moment. We note that

$$U_0 = e^{-\pi_1 - \pi_2} \pi_1^{g_1(x_1, x_2)} \pi_2^{g_2(x_1, x_2)}.$$

It is readily verified that if

$$\frac{\partial U_0}{\partial \pi_i} = \left(-1 + \frac{g_i(x_1, x_2)}{\pi_i} \right) U_0 = 0$$

then this condition defines a maximum for U_0.

In this case, we can ask whether there is an equilibrium. That is, whether there is a vector (π_1, π_2, x_1, x_2) which would lead to the simultaneous stabilization of all four of the variables. A property of such an equilibrium would be that

(a) For the planners

$$(\pi_1, \pi_2) = [g_1(x_1, x_2), g_2(x_1, x_2)] = G(x_1, x_2)$$

(b) For the enterprises

$$(x_1, x_2) = [f_1(\pi_1), f_2(\pi_2)] = F(\pi_1, \pi_2).$$

If the planner does not know the functions f_1 and f_2, and if the enterprises do not know the functions g_1 and g_2, the system is *informationally decentralized*. We can then interpret the functions F and G as iterative bidding schemes, so that

$$(\pi_1, \pi_2)_{t+1} = G(x_1, x_2)_t$$
$$(x_1, x_2)_{t+1} = F(\pi_1, \pi_2)_t.$$

Then we can inquire whether this bidding scheme will converge to some limit. Alternatively, we can observe that an equilibrium will exist if the functions $G \circ F$ and $F \circ G$ have fixed points. The fixed point of the first is an equilibrium pair of plans, that of the second is an equilibrium pair of activities.

Suppose such an equilibrium exists. Given an equilibrium pair $(\bar{x}_1, \bar{x}_2)$, no change in $(\bar{\pi}_1, \bar{\pi}_2)$ can make the planner better off. Given an equilibrium pair (π_1, π_2), no change in (x_1, x_2) can make the enterprises better off. What of a simultaneous change in all four? Consider the differential forms

$$dU_0 = \frac{\partial u_0}{\partial \pi_1} d\pi_1 + \frac{\partial u_0}{\partial \pi_2} d\pi_2 + \frac{\partial u_0}{\partial x_1} dx_1 + \frac{\partial u_0}{\partial x_2} dx_2,$$

$$dU_1 = \frac{\partial u_1}{\partial \pi_1} d\pi_1 \qquad\qquad + \frac{\partial u_1}{\partial x_1} dx_1,$$

$$dU_2 = \qquad\qquad \frac{\partial u_2}{\partial \pi_2} d\pi_2 \qquad\qquad + \frac{\partial u_2}{\partial x_2} dx_2.$$

If enterprises have adjusted optimally to plans and planners have adjusted optimally to outputs, these expressions simplify, at the equilibrium point, to

$$dU_0 = \frac{\partial u_0}{\partial x_1} dx_1 + \frac{\partial u_0}{\partial x_2} dx_2,$$

$$dU_1 = \frac{\partial u_1}{\partial \pi_1} d\pi_1,$$

$$dU_2 = \frac{\partial u_2}{\partial \pi_2} d\pi_2.$$

If the utility functions are those assumed above, the explicit statement of these forms is

$$\frac{du_0}{u_0} = \left(\sum_1^2 \log \pi_i \frac{\partial g_i}{\partial x_1} \right) dx_1 + \left(\sum_1^2 \log \pi_i \frac{\partial g_i}{\partial x_2} \right) dx_2,$$

$$\frac{du_1}{u_1} = \log x_1 \frac{\partial f_1}{\partial \pi_1} d\pi_1,$$

$$\frac{du_2}{u_2} = \log x_2 \frac{\partial f_2}{\partial \pi_2} d\pi_2.$$

Thus, unless the equilibrium is one which produces a maximum for the f_i, there exists a change in plans which would improve the welfare of the enterprises. Unless a somewhat more complicated condition on the g_i is satisfied (one case of which is maximization of the g_i), there is a change in outcomes which would increase the planner's welfare.

In this sense, there exists the possibility of an equilibrium which is not Pareto optimal. In part this departure from optimality reflects the fact that the welfare of the enterprises depends not only on the goods they produce, but also on the messages they receive. (This is a feature of the model which causes it to differ from the usual models.) In part it reflects the informational decentralization of the system.

There are two ways to centralize information. Either the planners may have information about the functions f_1 and f_2, or the enterprises may have information about the functions g_1 and g_2. These two cases will be studied in Cases 3 and 4.

Case 3

The utility functions of planners and enterprises are as in Case 2, but the planner knows the enterprises' behavior functions, f_1 and f_2. Thus the planner's problem is to substitute f_1 and f_2 in

$$U_0 = e^{-\pi_1 - \pi_2} \pi_1^{g_1(x_1, x_2)} \pi_2^{g_2(x_1, x_2)}$$

so as to obtain $\bar{U}_0 = e^{-\pi_1 - \pi_2} \pi_1^{g_1[f_1(\pi_1) f_2(\pi_2)]} \pi_2^{g_2[f_1(\pi_1) f_2(\pi_2)]}$,

and find the values of π_1 and π_2 which maximize this function. The first- and second-order conditions to be satisfied are

$$0 = \frac{\partial U}{\partial \pi_1} = \left[-1 + \frac{g_1}{\pi_1} + \frac{\partial f_1}{\partial \pi_1} \left(\frac{\partial g_1}{\partial f_1} \log \pi_1 + \frac{\partial g_2}{\partial f_2} \log \pi_2 \right) \right] U_0,$$

$$0 = \frac{\partial U}{\partial \pi_2} = \left[-1 + \frac{g_2}{\pi_2} + \frac{\partial f_2}{\partial \pi_2} \left(\frac{\partial g_1}{\partial f_1} \log \pi_1 + \frac{\partial g_2}{\partial f_2} \log \pi_2 \right) \right] U_0,$$

$$0 > \frac{\partial^2 U}{\partial \pi_1^2} = \left[-\frac{g_1}{\pi_1^2} + \frac{2}{\pi_1} \frac{\partial g_1}{\partial f_1} \frac{\partial f_1}{\partial \pi_1} + \frac{\partial^2 f_1}{\partial \pi_1^2} \left(\frac{\partial g_1}{\partial f_1} \log \pi_1 + \frac{\partial g_2}{\partial f_1} \log \pi_2 \right) \right] U_0,$$

$$0 > \frac{\partial^2 U}{\partial \pi_2^2} = \left[-\frac{g_2}{\pi_2^2} + \frac{2}{\pi_2} \frac{\partial g_1}{\partial f_1} \frac{\partial f_2}{\partial \pi_2} + \frac{\partial^2 f_2}{\partial \pi_2^2} \left(\frac{\partial g_1}{\partial f_2} \log \pi_1 + \frac{\partial g_2}{\partial f_2} \log \pi_2 \right) \right] U_0,$$

$$0 < \frac{\partial^2 U}{\partial \pi_1^2} \frac{\partial^2 U}{\partial \pi_2^2} - \left(\frac{\partial^2 U}{\partial \pi_1 \partial \pi_2} \right)^2,$$

where

$$\frac{\partial^2 U}{\partial \pi_1 \partial \pi_2} = \left[\frac{1}{\pi_1} \frac{\partial g_1}{\partial f_2} \frac{\partial f_2}{\partial \pi_i} + \frac{1}{\pi_2} \frac{\partial g_2}{\partial f_1} \frac{\partial f_1}{\partial \pi_1} + \frac{\partial f_1}{\partial \pi_1} \frac{\partial f_2}{\partial \pi_2} \right.$$
$$\left. \times \left(\frac{\partial^2 g_1}{\partial f_1 \partial f_2} \log \pi_1 + \frac{\partial^2 g_2}{\partial f_1 \partial f_2} \log \pi_2 \right) \right] U_0.$$

By hypothesis, the optimal behavior for the planner is $\pi_i = g_i$. This means that in the first-order conditions

$$\frac{\partial f_i}{\partial \pi_i} \left(\frac{\partial g_i}{\partial f_i} \log \pi_1 + \frac{\partial g_2}{\partial f_i} \log \pi_i \right) = 0.$$

The first way to obtain this is to select extremal values for g_1 and g_2, so that $\partial g_j / \partial f_i = 0$. If this can be done, the first two second-order conditions reduce to

$$0 > \frac{\partial^2 u_0}{\partial \pi_i^2} = -\frac{g^i}{\pi_i^2} u_0$$

and these are clearly satisfied. The last condition is

$$\frac{g_1}{\pi_1^2} \frac{g^2}{\pi_2^2} > \left[\frac{\partial f_1}{\partial \pi_1} \frac{\partial f_2}{\partial \pi_2} \left(\frac{\partial^2 g_1}{\partial f_1 \partial f_2} \log \pi_1 + \frac{\partial^2 g_2}{\partial f_1 \partial f_2} \log \pi_2 \right) \right]^2.$$

This is trickier. It suffices, however, that

$$-\frac{g_i}{\pi_i^2} < \frac{\partial f_1}{\partial \pi_1}\frac{\partial f_2}{\partial \pi_2}\left(\frac{\partial^2 g_1}{\partial f_1 \partial f_2}\log \pi_1 + \frac{\partial^2 g_2}{\partial f_1 \partial f_2}\log \pi_2\right) < 0$$

for this to be met. In particular, if the g_i are maximized, the contents of the square brackets are negative. If the f_i are not too responsive to plan changes, so that $\left|\dfrac{\partial f_i}{\partial \pi_j}\right|$ is not too great, and if the signs of both of these partial derivatives are the same, then the last second-order condition will be met.

Thus one rule for the planner is, 'Take the pair $(\bar{x}_1, \bar{x}_2)$ which maximizes g_1 and g_2.'

It may be impossible to apply this rule. First, the functions g_i may have no maximum. This would be the case if they are monotone increasing functions of x_1, x_2. It may be that they have maxima, but these are associated with different pairs of values for the x_i. Finally, it may be the case that there is a pair $(\hat{x}_1, \hat{x}_2)$ which simultaneously maximizes g_1 and g_2, but $\hat{x}_i$ is not in the range of f_i. (Nothing on earth could persuade enterprise i to do $\hat{x}_i$.)

If the planner cannot apply the rule, 'Maximize the g_i', he may still be able to apply the rule, 'Take extremal values of the f_i'. In this case, he sets $\partial f_i/\partial \pi_i = 0$, and guarantees (in the first-order conditions) that $g_i = \pi_i$. Then, if $\partial g_i/\partial f_j \geqslant 0$ (or $\leqslant 0$) he selects a maximal (or a minimal) value of f_i; this guarantees that the first two second-order inequalities are met. The third is now reduced to

$$\frac{g_1}{\pi_1^2}\frac{g_2}{\pi_2^2} \geqslant 0$$

and is thus automatically satisfied.

From the viewpoint of Pareto optimality the system now has the properties, in the neighborhood of equilibrium:

$$dU_0 = \frac{\partial U_0}{\partial \pi_1}d\pi_1 + \frac{\partial U_0}{\partial \pi_2}d\pi_2,$$

$$dU_1 = \frac{\partial U_1}{\partial \pi_1}d\pi_1 + \frac{\partial U_1}{\partial x_1}dx_1,$$

$$dU_2 = \frac{\partial U_2}{\partial \pi_2}d\pi_2 + \frac{\partial U_2}{\partial x_2}dx_2.$$

The planner has selected the plans which were best for him; each enterprise has selected the output which was best for him, given the plans.

Thus, using results already known,

$$dU_0 \equiv 0,$$

$$dU_1 = \frac{\partial U_1}{\partial \pi_1} d\pi_1 = \frac{\partial f_1}{\partial \pi_1} \log f_1 U_1 d\pi_1,$$

$$dU_2 = \frac{\partial U_2}{\partial \pi_2} d\pi_2 = \frac{\partial f_2}{\partial \pi_2} \log f_2 U_2 d\pi_2.$$

If the planner did not reach his optimum by maximizing the f_i, the outcome is not Pareto optimal. There is a displacement $(d\pi_1, d\pi_2)$ which would have made the enterprises better off.

It continues to be the case, however, that no reallocation of goods in the economy would make anyone better off, assuming the plans to be unchanged.

Case 4

In the last example, the planners knew the behavior of the enterprises, and from it they computed the plan which was best for him. Suppose that the opposite situation holds true: the enterprises know the behavior of the planner, but he does not know theirs. In this case, what behaviour will the enterprises adopt if they want to induce the planner to select the plan which is most advantageous to them? (This view of planning is 'West European', while Case 3 was 'East European'.)

In this case, the enterprise utility functions are, to begin with

$$U_i = e^{-x_i} x_i^{f_i(\pi_i)} \quad (i = 1, 2).$$

But if the enterprises know the planner's behavior, they become

$$U_i = e^{-x_i} x_i^{f_i[g_i(x_1, x_2)]}.$$

The first-order equilibrium conditions become:

$$\frac{\partial U_i}{\partial x_i} = \left(-1 + \frac{f_i}{x_i} + \frac{\partial f_i}{\partial g_i} \frac{\partial g_i}{\partial x_i} \log x_i \right) U_i$$

$$\frac{\partial U_i}{\partial x_j} = \frac{\partial f_i}{\partial g_i} \frac{\partial g_i}{\partial x_j} \log x_i U_i.$$

A sufficient condition that $x_i = f_i$ is that $\frac{\partial f_i}{\partial g_i} \frac{\partial g_i}{\partial x_i} = 0$. If the second first-order condition is to be met, $\frac{\partial f_i}{\partial g_i} \frac{\partial g_i}{\partial x_j} = 0$. These two conditions will always be met if $\partial f_i/\partial g_j = 0$. This means that the plan selected is one which maximizes f_i, the performance of the enterprises.

The second-order conditions are that the matrix $\left(\frac{\partial^2 U_i}{\partial x_j \partial x_k} \right)$ be negative definite. This matrix turns out to be the sum of the matrices

$$\frac{\partial f_i}{\partial g_i} \log x_i \begin{pmatrix} \dfrac{\partial^2 g_i}{\partial x_1^2} & \dfrac{\partial^2 g_i}{\partial x_1 \partial x_2} \\[2ex] \dfrac{\partial^2 g_i}{\partial x_2 \partial x_1} & \dfrac{\partial^2 g_i}{\partial x_2^2} \end{pmatrix} + \begin{pmatrix} -\dfrac{f_i}{x_1^2}\delta_{1i} & 0 \\[2ex] 0 & -\dfrac{f_i}{x_2^2}\delta_{2i} \end{pmatrix}.$$

If $\mathbf{M}$ and $\mathbf{N}$ are negative definite matrices, so is $(\mathbf{M}+\mathbf{N})$. If $\partial f_i/\partial g_i = 0$, this sum is certainly negative definite. (This is the case where the f_i are maximized.) Otherwise, let g_i be maximized. In this case the matrix $\left(\dfrac{\partial^2 g_i}{\partial x_j \, \partial x_k}\right)$ is negative definite, and the sum will be negative definite if $\partial f_i/\partial g_i$ is positive. (This means that f_i is less than maximized.)

The rule for the enterprises, then, turns out to be the following: If possible, maximize the f_i. Otherwise, maximize the g_i.

Suppose this rule is followed. The Pareto optimality of the system is studied locally, as before, in terms of the system.

$$dU_0 = \frac{\partial U_0}{\partial \pi_1} d\pi_1 + \frac{\partial U_0}{\partial \pi_2} d\pi_2 + \frac{\partial U_0}{\partial x_1} dx_1 + \frac{\partial U_0}{\partial x_2} dx_2,$$

$$dU_1 = \frac{\partial U_0}{\partial \pi_1} d\pi_1 \qquad\qquad + \frac{\partial U_1}{\partial x_1} dx_1,$$

$$dU_2 = \qquad\qquad \frac{\partial U_2}{\partial \pi_2} d\pi_2 \qquad\qquad + \frac{\partial U_2}{\partial x_2} dx_2.$$

If the planners have been required to set their plans at the level which maximizes f_1 and f_2, then this system reduces to:

$$dU_0 = \frac{\partial U_0}{\partial x_1} dx_1 + \frac{\partial U_0}{\partial x_2} dx_2$$

$$= \left(\frac{\partial g_1}{\partial x_1} \log \pi_1 + \frac{\partial g_2}{\partial x_1} \log \pi_2\, dx_1 + \frac{\partial g_1}{\partial x_2} \log \pi_1 + \frac{\partial g_2}{\partial x_2} \log \pi_2\right) dx_2,$$

$$dU_1 = 0,$$

$$dU_2 = 0.$$

Thus there is a readjustment $(dx_1\, dx_2)$ of output which would leave the planners better off.

If this solution is impossible, then the enterprises would have to seek the solution which maximized g_1 and g_2.

Thus the fourth case has something in common with the third. But if the information is centralized with the planner, the plan would maximize g_1 and g_2 rather than f_1 and f_2. If the information is centralized with the enterprises, f_1 and f_2 would be maximized rather than g_1 and g_2.

An extension of this approach to the many-enterprise analog of Case 1 will now be given, to indicate briefly some of the results which may be expected from the elaboration of this way of thought. The economy consists of $\{0, 1, ..., n\}$ units. The ith enterprise receives a plan,

$$\boldsymbol{\pi}^i = (\pi_1^i, \pi_2^i, ..., \pi_n^i)$$

and decides on an activity level $\mathbf{x}^i = (x_1^i, x_2^i, ..., x_n^i)$. The ith component is taken to be an output. The others are inputs. The utility functions:

$$U_i = \prod_{j=1}^n e^{-x_j^i} x_j^{i f_j^i(\pi^i_1... \pi^i_n)}$$

yield optimal behavior patterns of

$$X_j^i = f_j^i(\pi_1^i, ..., \pi_n^i).$$

The market, in this economy is cleared when

$$f_i^i = \sum_{j \neq 1} f_i^j.$$

Thus there are n excess demand functions,

$$Z_i = f_i^i - \sum_{j \neq i} f_i^j.$$

Each excess demand function is a function of all the plans:

$$\mathbf{Z}_i = Z_i(\pi_1^1, ..., \pi_s^r, ..., \pi_n^n).$$

Thus there are n functions, with n^2 plans as arguments. There are problems of describing the limitations which equilibrium places on the plans, but we shall not consider them here.

Suppose a plan clears all markets. Then the equilibrium conditions $x_j^i = f_i^i$ determine an optimum for each enterprise; if the plan is optimal for the planner (as in Case 1) it is a Pareto optimum for the economy. Let us observe now that the marginal rates of substitution have the form

$$\frac{\partial U/\partial x_i}{\partial U/\partial x_j} = \frac{-1 + \dfrac{f_i}{x_i}}{-1 + \dfrac{f_j}{x_j}} = \frac{0}{0}$$

at equilibrium. But the limit values are given by

$$\lim_{\substack{x_i \to f_i \\ x_j \to f_j}} \frac{\partial U/\partial x_i}{\partial U/\partial x_j} = \left.\frac{\partial^2 U/\partial x_i^2}{\partial^2 U/\partial x_j^2}\right|_{\substack{x_i=f_i \\ x_j=f_j}} = \frac{f_i/f_i^2}{f_j/f_j^2} = \frac{f_j}{f_i}.$$

Thus two individuals in this economy would *not* have the same marginal rates of substitution, unless, by chance, they had exactly the same consumption patterns.

This economy has seemed 'queer' both to the author and to those with whom he has discussed it. In part the queerness exists because of the absence of any of the usual restrictions, such as production functions, prices, budgets, and so forth. It is natural to inquire what would happen, in such an economy, if enterprises are given plans, as before, but are also subject to a budget constraint. Since all quantities have been assumed non-negative, the prices would (by convention) be positive for outputs and negative for inputs. In this case, the ith enterprise is given a plan π^i, and it seeks an activity x^i which maximizes $U_i(x^i|\pi^i)$ subject to the budget constraint $\Sigma p_j x_j^i \geqslant 0$. Using the usual methods,

$$G_i = U_i - \lambda \Sigma p_i x_j^i$$

$$= \prod_{j=1}^{n} e^{-x_j^i} x_j^i f^i{}_j{}_{(\pi^i)},$$

$$\frac{\partial G_i}{\partial x_j} = \left(-1 + \frac{f_j}{x_j}\right) U_i - \lambda p_j = 0,$$

$$\frac{\partial G}{\partial \lambda} = \Sigma p_j x_j^i = 0.$$

Now, indeed, things become more familiar. The marginal rates of substitution

$$\frac{\partial u_i / \partial x_j}{\partial u_i / \partial x_k} = \frac{(f_j - x_j)/x_j}{(f_k - x_k)/x_k} = \frac{p_j}{p_k}$$

will be the same for all individuals. Moreover, prices have a very precise interpretation:

f_j is the use of j which i would make, if there were no budget restraint;

$f_j - x_j$ is the amount by which his consumption is altered;

$(f_j - x_j)/x_j$ is the proportion by which his consumption would be altered by the removal of the budget constraint.

Thus

$$\frac{p_j}{p_k} = \frac{(f_j - x_j)/x_j}{(f_k - x_k)/x_k}$$

tells us that the higher a price is, the greater the percentage by which the enterprise's use of a product has been restricted by the budget constraint. In this respect, at least, the addition of familiar institutional restrictions to the model produces more familiar results.

A variety of interesting possibilities still remains to be explored in this type of system. Indeed, one of the reasons for presenting the fundamental hypothesis, in the simple form used here, is that it may suggest other applications to readers interested in economies which do not rely entirely (or mainly) on price mechanisms.

A priceless planned economy

APPENDIX

The usual formulation of the problem would take a utility function $U(x_1, ..., x_n)$ and a set of constraints $z_1(\pi_1, x_1), ..., z_n(\pi_n, x_n)$, $z_i \leqslant 0$. Then the problem is to maximize $U + \Sigma \lambda_i z_i$. The first-order conditions,

$$U_i + \lambda_i \frac{\partial z_i}{\partial x_i} = 0 \tag{1}$$

$$z_i = 0$$

yield a system of differential forms

$$\left. \begin{aligned} \sum_j u_{ij} dx_j + \lambda_i \frac{\partial^2 z_i}{\partial x_i^2} dx_i + \lambda_i \frac{\partial^2 z_i}{\partial x_i \partial \pi_i} d\pi_i + \frac{\partial z_i}{\partial x_i} d\lambda &= 0, \\ \frac{\partial z_j}{\partial x_j} dx_j + \frac{\partial z_j}{\partial x_j} d\pi_j &= 0, \end{aligned} \right\} \tag{2}$$

which can be solved, so as to give

$$\left. \begin{aligned} dx_j &= \sum_k w_{jk} d\pi_k, \\ d\lambda_j &= \sum_k w'_{jk} d\pi_k. \end{aligned} \right\} \tag{3}$$

Then the demand functions are the functions $x_j(\pi_1, ..., \pi_n)$ associated with these differential forms.

In the present problem, we start with functions $f_j(\pi_1, ..., \pi_n)$ describing consumer behavior.

These yield the forms

$$df_j = \Sigma \frac{\partial f_j}{\partial \pi_k} d\pi_k. \tag{4}$$

It may turn out that the inverse of the matrix $(\partial f_j / \partial \pi_k)$ can be associated with the matrix of a system such as (2). To make this association, one would have to find suitable functions z_i to go with it. In that case, one would be able to identify the functions $u(x | \pi, f)$ of the sort given in this paper with a problem $G = u(x) + \Sigma \lambda_i z_i$, in the sense that both produce the same behaviour patterns. But not all behavioral patterns $f_1, ..., f_n$ will permit this association. To take a simple example, the matrix (u_{ij}) of (2) is certainly symmetric, and it would ordinarily follow that in (3), (w_{jk}) would also be symmetric. Hence also $\partial x_i / \partial \pi_j = \partial x_j / \partial \pi_i$. But no constraint $\partial f_i / \partial \pi_j = \partial f_j / \partial \pi_i$ need be assumed for the utility functions presented here.

It may be useful to present briefly an analogous model in the theory of demand in competitive markets. Here, we make the consumer's utility depend on prices, and select, in particular, the function

$$u \equiv u(x, p) \equiv e^{-\mu \Sigma p_i x_i} \prod_{i=1}^{n} x_i^{p_i f_i(p, \cdots p_n)}. \tag{5}$$

The constrained maximization problem is

$$G = U + \lambda \Sigma p_i x_i. \tag{5a}$$

At a maximum

$$\frac{\partial G}{\partial x_i} = \left(-\mu p_i + \frac{p_i f_i}{x_i} \right) U + \lambda p_i = 0,$$

the p_i cancel out, and

$$\frac{f_i}{x_i} = \frac{\mu U - \lambda}{U}. \tag{6}$$

Thus consumption (x_i) is a given multiple of f_i for all commodities. We now show that this multiple may be taken to be 1. We have

$$\frac{\partial G}{\partial \lambda} = 0 = \Sigma p_i x_i. \tag{7}$$

Likewise,

$$\frac{\partial G}{\partial \mu} = -\Sigma p_i x_i U, \tag{8}$$

and if G is selected so as to maximize λ, then G will be independent of U. We may thus assume that

$$\mu = \frac{U+\lambda}{U}. \tag{9}$$

If, now, this value of μ is substituted into the first-order condition,

$$\frac{\partial G}{\partial x_i} = \left(-\frac{U+\lambda}{U} p_i + \frac{p_i f_i}{x_i}\right) U + \lambda p_i$$

$$= \left(-1 + \frac{f_i}{x_i}\right) U = 0,$$

and it follows that $\quad \dfrac{\partial^2 G}{\partial x_i} = \left(-1 + \dfrac{f_i}{x_i}\right)^2 U - \dfrac{f_i}{x_i^2} U = -\dfrac{f_i}{x_i^2} U < 0,$

so that the extremum is indeed an optimum.

If, then, it is the case that utility is maximized when $x_i = f_i$, we can write immediately the differential forms associated with these functions:

$$dx_i = \Sigma \frac{\partial f_i}{\partial p_j} dp_j \quad \text{or} \quad dx_i = f_{ij} dp_j. \tag{10}$$

On the other hand, the usual demand theory defines the problem as the maximization of

$$H = V(x_1, ..., x_n) + \lambda \Sigma p_i x_i, \tag{11}$$

and gives first-order conditions $\quad V_i + \lambda p_i = 0,$

$$\Sigma p_j x_j = 0.$$

From these, we obtain $\quad \Sigma V_{ij} dx_j + p_i d\lambda + \lambda dp_i = 0,$

$$\Sigma p_j dx_j = 0.$$

The matrix of this system is the bordered Hessian

$$\mathbf{K} = \begin{pmatrix} V_{11}, ..., V_{1n} & p_1 \\ ... & ... & ... \\ V_{n1}, ..., V_{nn} & p_n \\ p_1, ..., p_n & 0 \end{pmatrix}$$

and the demand functions are obtained by integrating the forms

$$dx_i = \Sigma w_{ij} d_{pj}, \tag{12}$$

where the w_{ij} are elements of $\mathbf{K}^{-1}$. Thus the matrix of (10) is associated with that of (12). If it turns out that

$$(g_{ij}) = (f_{ij})^{-1}$$

is associated with the form

$$\Sigma\Sigma g_{ij} dx_i dx_j$$

88

and that there is a function G from which this form may be derived, then the utility function (5) produces behavior identical with that of a consumer having a utility function V as in (11). But not every problem of the form (5a) is behaviorally equivalent to some problem of the form (11). In this sense, the function (5) is more general than the usual utility function, as indeed might be expected.

NOTES

1 Two people have directly helped bring this paper into being. In 1967, at the Berkeley Conference on Economic Systems, Benjamin Ward suggested the need for what I have called the 'fundamental proposition', and criticized earlier work of mine in which plans affected behavior only by affecting the constraints faced by enterprises. At that time, neither Ward nor I knew how to deal with the suggestion. Alain Cotta asked me to present an early version at his seminar on economic power in 1971, and pointed out the possibility of a broader application of the methodology – cases 3 and 4 are the result. In a more general way, Holland Hunter's well-known paper on 'optimal tautness' is clearly an ancestor of this one. The optimum is reached when $f' = 0$, as perhaps he suggested.
2 Functions like (1), are used, with embellishments, throughout this paper. Since they are rather different from ordinarily used utility functions, the appendix discusses them more fully.

REFERENCES

Camacho, A. (1970). Centralization and Decentralization of Decision-making models: a general model. Northwestern University Graduate School of Management.
Hurwicz, L. (1959). Optimality and informational efficiency in resource allocation processes. In *Mathematical Methods in the Social Sciences*, ed. K. J. Arrow, S. Karlin and P. Suppes. Stanford, California.

II. Theoretical Analysis of the Soviet-Type System

I. Aggregate Planning

The Basic Characteristics of a multi-level System for Medium-range Planning

[In this paper B. N. Mikhalevsky outlines the general theoretical aspects of constructing decomposable, hierarchical models of dynamic systems and discusses the particular problems of macroeconomic modelling of dynamic economic systems. In the second section, he describes the structure of a five-level planning model developed for use in medium-range planning of the Soviet economy, and finally he presents the results of some preliminary economic forecasts prepared on the basis of this model.

In translating his paper, I have supplemented his systems analysis terminology with explanations and definitions in terms that are more familiar to the economist. JUDITH THORNTON]

> The Red Queen shook her head. 'You may call it ''nonsense'' if you like', she said, 'but I've heard nonsense, compared with which that would be as sensible as a dictionary!'
>
> Lewis Carroll, *Through the Looking Glass*

This paper presents the general outlines of a decomposable multi-level model for medium-range planning with some numerical estimates for a ten year planning horizon. It is a direct application of systems method: it is based on a critical analysis of equilibrium models of a mechanical–organic type, on qualitative and formalized description of the developing (*razvivaiushchaiasia*) system, and on the application of man–machine technology to medium-range forecasting and planning.[1]

DEFINITION OF THE DEVELOPING SYSTEM[2]

> 'Speak English!' said the Eaglet. 'I don't know the meaning of half those long words, and, what's more, I don't believe you do either!' And the Eaglet bent down its head to hide a smile; some of the other birds tittered audibly.
>
> Lewis Carroll, *Alice's Adventures in Wonderland*

A developing system is characterized by the following necessary and sufficient conditions (see Mikhalevsky, 1972).

1. It possesses boundaries and is open [non-isolated] to some degree.

2. There exists an open 'whole' [or system] (*tselostnost'*) described by a specific, qualitatively specified state and having an identified component

as a minimal unit. Social systems form the most highly developed special class of open systems that are characterized by psychic forms of energy and intelligence and that combine classificational, relational, and relevantial ways of organizing information.[3] On the basis of an infinitely increasing maximum total program and a finite minimum for components and parts, a social system can generate infinite informational variety and corresponding finite material–energetic variety, given a restricted number of potential states at any point in time. Thus, an open system of this sort is, at the same time, superadditive, incomplete, and, therefore, not fully deterministic but still stochastically ultra-stable. Through differentiation–integration processes, the system can evolve a qualitatively new and more complex totality from relatively autonomous and self-determining parts.

3. Within the system, there will be negentropically increasing multi-valued and multi-goal informational and material–energetic potential. [In this context, negentropy or 'negative entropy' refers to increasing order or energy in the system.] That is, there will be increasing degrees of freedom both of the constraint space defining the environment (feasible inputs) and of the constraint space defining feasible internal programs (feasible internal states). The basis of this process consists of: progressive organization of information (primarily through institutionalization of the results of intellectual development); a corresponding, differentiated development of technology, energetic capacity, and generalized work capacity;[4] a relatively slower development of teleogenesis [goal-formation] and teleology [goal-direction] in the value space with simultaneous generation of variety in the objectives and norms space.

4. The system has a meta-organization structure [a structure reflecting its organizing principles], and that structure is decomposable. Decomposability of structure refers to arrangement in a relatively centralized hierarchical–cooperative totality[5] consisting of a finite number of echelons,[6] levels and subsystems that are qualitatively different and increasingly complex in potential and state. Thus, decomposability is an informational and material–energetic organizing principle for situations of high complexity.[7]

5. The system has an incompletely deterministic and increasingly complex realization space of its potential and structure which corresponds to the system's informational meta-organization in the form of a hierarchy of values, goals, and norms. Content of the realization space embraces actual processes of change in the system and consequent specific forms of change – for example, change in development, growth, or behavior.

Change in the system is an infinite, and, consequently, unfinished multi-valued historical sequence resulting from various types of disturbances in the historical constraints on the system. This sequence results from the infinite possibilities of the informational meta-organization combined with entropic [energy- or order-reducing] forces of various types and strengths, and insufficient actual potential energy. The sequence is constrained by structural and functional constraints; it generates values, goals, and norms; it affects both the potential capacity of the system and the accelerating rate of realization of multi-final states in the realization space.

As a result of the predominance of irreversible morphogenetic [form-creating] processes,[8] this sequence of disturbances of constraints gives rise to either an infinite historical multi-valued process of alternating equilibrium and disequilibrium states or to a finite process of change of state within the boundaries of a given equilibrium position. In either case and on all levels of the system, irreversible changes that are predominantly progressive and secondarily regressive coexist simultaneously with other changes that are cyclic or reversibly regressive.

Irreversible progressive and regressive changes generate an incompletely deterministic sequence of disequilibrium transitions to a new asymmetrical state having a different amount of entropy [organization].

By multi-valued changes in the system we mean an irreversible, infinite, and incompletely deterministic historical sequence of multi-final changes. Multi-valued changes occur as a result of a strong relaxation of both environmental and internal constraints combined with a high level and rapid increase of potential and of generalized work. These changes make it possible to counteract the strong entropic forces acting internally and in the environment. This assumes a high and continuously increasing degree of variety and organization, a large and expanding region of freedom, a relatively decreasing role of ecological regulation, a high and progressing level of technology and of normative order. Within the normative order, the value subspace related to biological and social survival contracts and the value subspace arising from feedback and higher forms of pragmatic understanding expands. This latter subspace becomes a powerful source of variety in the system and, to a considerable extent, replaces absolute authority as the instrument for correcting the normative order.

Corresponding to these processes, there occurs in the realization space the following: (a) relatively low and decreasing degree of closure; (b) a high and rising degree of differentiation–integration of the system – of its structure and function – with a corresponding rise in stability; (c) occurrence of compressed historical sequences of change leading to increased organization. Thus, in the realization space, there occur qualitative, quantitative, intensive and extensive changes, generally of an oscillatory type. Development of the system is cumulative and continuous in that the information meta-organization is subject to irreversible, multi-valued changes of a predominantly disequilibrium type that lead to a general rise in the level of organization of the system. This process is made up of progressive, regressive, and cyclical processes, but with a predominance of the first.

Combinations of these three types of processes give rise to both normal and hypertrophic [unbalanced] development. Normal development occurs when the contradictions between potential and the value system are weak, when entropic forces are moderate, and the level of potential is sufficiently high. In this case, informational and material–energetic insufficiency is not too pronounced.

Normal development is characterized by the following:

1. Moderate relative lead in speed and institutionalization of multivalued, primarily progressive development and growth of a sufficiently large number of leading sectors (echelons, levels, subsystems, and components) throughout the whole structure combined with a small proportional share of single valued regressive–cyclical development and growth of the low priority parts of the structure and system.

2. Increasing predominance of negentropic processes of multivalued development over predominantly single-valued processes of growth; the maintenance for a long period of time of high rates of growth of generalized potential and moderate rates of actual development and growth.

3. The existence and development of a decomposable, multifunctional structure that is moderately centralized, allows rapid institutionalization of change, and provides for extensive autonomy and self-determination of its parts. This constitutes an additional source of increased adaptability and control, i.e. an additional source of negentropy.

4. A consequence of the above is a general predominance of a multivalued, progressive (i.e., negentropic) type of disequilibrium development offering extensive possibilities for resolution of conflicts adaptively or on the basis of priorities.

Hypertrophic [unbalanced] disequilibrium development occurs when there are sharp contradictions between potential and the value system in combination with strong and extended entropic forces occurring in a case where the level of potential is moderate or low. This leads to a clear information and material–energetic insufficiency.

The hypertrophic type of development is characterized by the following features:

1. A strong relative lead in the speed and institutionalization of multivalued, predominantly progressive development and growth of a fairly narrow priority part of the structure.

2. This multi-valued development proceeds at the expense of lower rates of progressive development and a widening region of regressive–cyclical development in the low priority part of the system; this causes a gradual rise in the entropy of the system.

3. A high share of growth processes compared to developmental processes.

4. Transformation of a moderately centralized, decomposable structure to a slowly changing (rigid) structure whose parts have little autonomy or self-determination leading to a corresponding decrease in adaptivity and ease of control of the whole system. These processes are associated with a further rise in entropy which, after a fairly extended period, will begin to outweigh the negentropic effect of increased centralization.

5. By comparison with the normal type of development, there will be a temporary acceleration of rates of increase of potential, of development, and of growth followed by a decrease of these rates. This decrease occurs because of the continued sharp contradiction between potential and the value system combined with strong entropic influences – factors that prevent any real decrease in informational and material–energetic insufficiency even at high levels of potential. The consequences are a persistent, increasing gap between actual and potential rates of development and growth, decreasing rates of institutionalization of multi-dimensional development and growth in low and extended priority sectors associated with increasing entropy and a weakening of negentropic processes, increasing inconsistency between the institutions of a rigid, centralized structure, on the one hand, and enlarged potential, on the other, which potential would allow the development of an adaptive, multi-functional structure having essentially more autonomy and self-determination of its parts.

6. As a consequence, there is a progressive increase of the above conflict combined with restricted possibilities for adaptive or priority resolution of conflict.

Along with all of the negentropic mechanisms previously mentioned, such systems contain, as an additional negentropic instrument, a complex self-organizing process of dual combined control which is an element of the decomposable structure, taking the form of social control based on authority.

Dual control of the system originates from the relationship between information potential and generalized work and informational and material–energetic insufficiency. Secondly, it is provided by the corresponding system of normative order, structure, and functions. Dual control generates values, objectives, and norms. It functions as a teleological [goal-directed] decomposable totality of cognitive and constraint activities of various sorts (including planning, regulating, and directing).[9] It operates on the basis of man–machine processing of information, increasing the degree of organization and, thus, the negentropy of the system. This additional negentropic effect transfers a part of the increasing diversity of the system to the sphere of combined control and provides for development of a mechanism for such control.

In order to achieve combined control, the following system of activities is required.

Development of planning

Planning is the cognitive element in dual control which synthesizes the solutions of the model, comparing desired and [feasible] possibilities in the range of probable future outcomes. This synthesis is made in the sphere of values, norms, and goals. It is based on symbolic logic, requires continuous feedback from both environmental and internal spaces of the system, and serves as the basis for subsequent multi-level man–machine control of the system. Planning increases the negentropic effect of dual control in a number of ways: (a) It improves processes for value formation, goal formation, and goal direction by increasing the accuracy of the projected hierarchies of long-range, medium-range, and short-range goals and norms. (b) It allows multi-level man–machine processing of information. (c) It provides a better system of organization for continuous feedback from the system and its environment, facilitating more accurate adjustment and greater planning flexibility over various time horizons.

Use of combined control

Combined control includes both regulation and direction. For purposes of increased organization, combined control has certain advantages: (a) Regulation of a subsystem provides direction for the whole system, so an increase in both variability and in stability can be achieved at the same time. (b) Simultaneous dual control of discrete changes in the state of the system and of qualitative–quantitative changes in the internal system and its environment become possible. (c) It becomes possible to have simultaneous control over both present and future time periods.

Application of combined control of a decomposable structure for coordination of objectives and norms

In this case, the rise in negentropy can be achieved in the following way: (a) By repeated decreases in the entropy of output of each previous level of the system. This process allows direction of parts of the system having high energetic and low informational levels by means of control systems having high informational and low energetic levels. This is equivalent to an increase in efficiency of central control, including the incentive–sanction system. (b) By development, within the framework of centralized direction, of decentralized dual control on the basis of increased relative autonomy and self-determination for branches, levels, subsystems, and components. The subsystems carry out the whole vertical cycle of decision-making and control at their level while, at the same time, being influenced by the central dual combined control and its system of values, goals, norms, incentive–sanctions, and analogous local mechanisms. (c) By perfecting the mechanism for generalized control of the whole system, in part by means of the system of incentives and sanctions.

Dual combined control takes the form of social control grounded on authority.

A developing system is a restricted form that simultaneously satisfies the five conditions given at the beginning of the paper. Thus, the concept of a developing system imposes certain requirements on the modeling and planning of the economic process:

1. Specification of a rationalized and operational process for working out the system of values, objectives, and norms of socio-economic change based on complex analysis of natural–demographic, technological, social, psychological, and cultural–contextual factors.

2. Inclusion in the model of the full system of individual and social motivation.

3. Adequate description of the processes of goal-formation and goal-direction and of the growing complexity of the socio-economic system.

4. Application of the decomposition principle to the specification of multi-level teleogenetic [goal-formation] processes of change and development in an open socio-economic system with multi-stage dual control. By multi-stage control we mean a system that combines hierarchical, centralized control with decentralized direction and provides for a more or less strict definition of their relative spheres and functions.

Now we may look at the consequences of this specification for the planning mechanism. The primary consequences arise from treating the economy as a subsystem in the broader dynamic processes of an open social system (see fig. 1). From that point of view, the economic system receives input from the natural–demographic environment, from the biological and personality subsystems of man, from technological subsystems of the given social organization and from other social systems, from the social order of the given system, from the rates and interrelationships of production, and from distribution and consumption. Outputs of the economic system and of associated parts of the social system appear as activity rates of the economic subsystems.

The economic subsystem is interconnected on the same hierarchical level with the political subsystem and with other economic subsystems. Moving down the network, it is connected with lower levels of the system, including the technological subsystem, the biological and personality subsystems of man, and the environmental system. Moving up the network, the economic subsystem connects with higher levels –

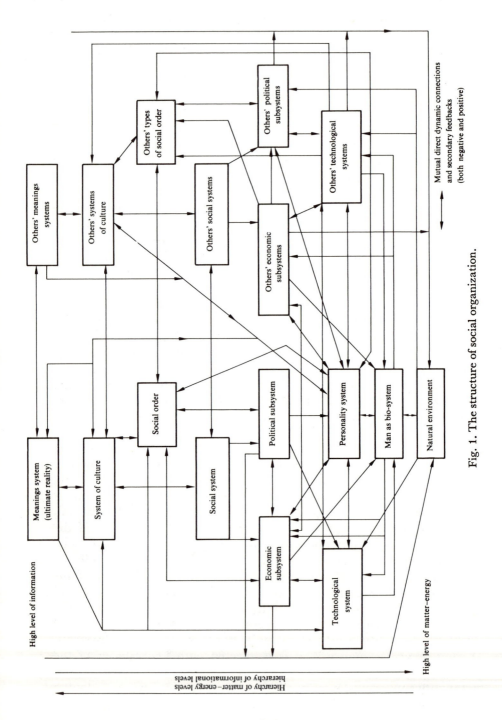

Fig. 1. The structure of social organization.

with the social order, the cultural subsystem, and the conceptual, or meaning, system.

So, in the systems analysis framework, the criteria and mechanisms of production and distribution of resources, products and income and also the dynamics of decision-making must be formulated within the context of the whole social organization. Thus, they are essentially different from the postulates of a mechanical–organic concept of economic welfare (see Mikhalevsky, 1971). As a result, economic plans with various time horizons must be based on a long-run socio-economic program that takes into consideration the gradual development of a multi-structural external environment that is subject to rising entropy along with an internal structure displaying concrete socio-economic organization. The inter-relations between the social organization and the systems of long- and medium-range planning are described in fig. 2.

A macroeconomic plan must always be a combination of the prevailing central plan, of the plans of relatively autonomous organizations, and of the plans of basic economic and social units. Coordination of these three types of planning, subject to the leading role of the central plan, is facili-tated by mechanisms for specifying objectives and functions, where the control mechanism with its system of incentives and sanctions is viewed as one type of function. Similarly, the central plan always embodies some sort of system of decompositional planning and corresponding multi-level coordination process. These properties can be seen from fig. 2.

Next, we turn to the modeling and planning of dynamic economic processes within a systems analysis framework. An example that is familiar in the literature is a macroeconomic system of the capitalist type, an example of a single-level open dynamic system.

The structure of objectives of an open, dynamic macroeconomic model interacts with a corresponding system of values and norms at higher levels of the system, at lower levels, and on the same level. This structure provides for a balancing of at least the aims listed below: (*a*) Some sort of improvement in the international position of that country or system of countries. These aspirations take two forms simultaneously – a tendency for predominant countries or systems to maintain and extend their dominance by means of increases in their technical–economic, military, and political power, and a tendency for countries or systems with lesser potential to move toward equal status as a result of nationalism, uni-fication, modernization, development and industrialization. (*b*) A system of conflicting internal economic objectives which are determined by the international situation and by the history and structure of the system. A model and plan of the internal economic objectives facing a system involves balancing various social goals of the system, on the one hand, and balancing these goals with the real feasible economic mechanism on the other.

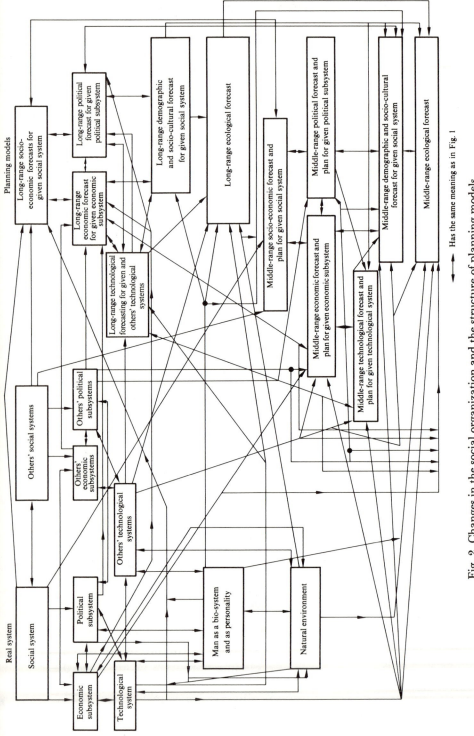

Fig. 2. Changes in the social organization and the structure of planning models.

Real system

Planning models

Social system

Others' social systems

Political subsystem

Others' political subsystems

Economic subsystem

Others' economic subsystems

Technological system

Others' technological systems

Man as a bio-system and as personality

Natural environment

Long-range socio-economic forecasts for given social system

Long-range political forecast for given political subsystem

Long-range economic forecast for given economic subsystem

Long-range technological forecasting for given and others' technological systems

Long-range demographic and socio-cultural forecast for given social system

Long-range ecological forecast

Middle-range socio-economic forecast and plan for given social system

Middle-range economic forecast and plan for given economic subsystem

Middle-range technological forecast and plan for given technological system

Middle-range political forecast and plan for given political subsystem

Middle-range demographic and socio-cultural forecast for given social system

Middle-range ecological forecast

⟶ Has the same meaning as in Fig. 1

102

Within the system of economic objectives, the plan has to provide for a compromise among at least the following seven objectives:

1. The pace of modernization, development and industrialization, as measured by rates of socio-political transformation, development or adoption of new technology, economic growth, and the share of resources going to capital investment.

2. The level and share of military and other governmental expense.

3. The level or rate of reduction of unemployment or the cost of maintaining full employment.

4. The level and rate of growth in the standard of living of various social groups.

5. Maintenance of a stable balance of payments.

6. Maintenance of an efficient and sufficiently stable price system and monetary system.

7. Maintenance of a desired income distribution among various social and income classes.

Planning a compromise between these general social objectives of the capitalist-type system and the functioning of the real underlying mechanisms of economic growth and social stability is achieved by combining central objectives with a relative autonomy of social and economic units, by means of mechanisms of social, administrative, and moral incentive and sanction on these units.

From a macroeconomic point of view, the system of goals described above corresponds to the abstract modeling and planning of the optimal combination of stable, traditional economic and social structures and of types and tempos of multi-dimensional disequilibrium development having concomitant, primarily progressive sorts of changes.[10]

A macroeconomic strategy of this type has the following characteristics:

1. Growth of productive and financial potential based on increasing rates of utilization of all resources, a high rate of investment, and priority distribution of resources. It is an example of normal or hypertrophic disequilibrium development providing both the cumulative mechanisms of modernization, industrialization, economic growth, and technical progress along with means to offset the negative consequences of development. However, this assumes that there is an elite capable of working out such a program – capable of reducing rates of increase of population, achieving social mobilization, preventing a too-rapid disruption of traditional economic and socio-political structures, and maintaining independence in spite of the dominance of other countries and systems having high informational, psychological, technical, economic, social and military potential.

2. Such a strategy of economic development assumes significant and

changing imbalances in the internal structure of final demand and between demand and supply of resources. It assumes significant pressure on the standard of living of the population and on the whole incentive system.

3. Such a structure of production and resource stocks is associated with a moving, disequilibrium system of prices for resources and products, with weakly differentiated rates of return to resources, a system of financial and economic incentives that includes budgetary, tax, financial and credit instruments, progressively differentiated income taxes, and a substantial role for central regulation.

Thus, some type of normal, or even hypertrophic, disequilibrium development turns out to be the price a system has to pay in order to improve its international position, accelerate economic development, and achieve the full benefits of technological progress and expansion of technical, economic potential.

However, it is extremely important to emphasize that disequilibrium development of the economy is advantageous and makes sense only within narrowly determined limits. Beyond these limits, it becomes pointless or, at least, leads to a rapid breakdown of the whole economic mechanism as a result of the obvious discrepancy between ends and means.

So the planning model must balance stable economic structure and balanced growth with a strategy of disequilibrium development. It must provide a continuously fluctuating, adaptive historical process of social and economic development that exhibits growing complexity of structure, diversification, and increased multi-functionalism together with an irregular alternation between states of structural disequilibrium and moving equilibrium.

Thus, a model of economic dynamics and corresponding planning model may be constructed only within the general framework of multi-dimensional disequilibrium development of a decomposable system of social organization like the one described in figs. 1 and 2.

The type of planning described here raises heavy demands in all respects, so, in practice, we observe only partial examples. Among the most practicable are discrete, stochastic models based on historical data and embodying an implicit decision mechanism. In cases where the economic mechanism is known and can be clearly specified, models of adaptive change can be closed or even estimated as fully determined models of economic growth. (One example is the multi-input production function model.) In other cases, such models are expressed as a stochastic system of simultaneous equations, offering more or less detail and allowing point or interval estimation of some of the most important economic variables. As a rule, stochastic models of adaptive change are specified with distributed lags. Although they lack an explicit decision function, the principle of dual combined control appears fairly explicitly.

The next section of the paper describes a decomposable heurorithmic (man–machine) model of this sort for centralized medium-range planning.

THE STRUCTURE OF MEDIUM-RANGE PLANNING SYSTEMS

'You needn't say "exactly",' the Queen remarked. 'I can believe it without that. Now I'll give *you* something to believe. I'm just one hundred and one, five months and a day.'

'I can't believe *that*!' said Alice.

'Can't you?' the Queen said in a pitying tone. 'Try again: draw a long breath, and shut your eyes.'

Lewis Carroll, Through the Looking Glass

A model of a medium-range planning system and its implementation mechanisms is given in simplified form in fig. 3. Figs. 2 and 3 represent a real developing economic system, and provide an explicit specification of production, distribution, financial and organizational characteristics of the economy.

The model represents an open system in total and on each level. The superstructure of the system is shown in fig. 2. This shows that the boundaries of the medium-range planning system are closed conditionally by fixing the values of certain exogenous parameters and variables. These values are revised continuously by introducing moving, mutually consistent control parameters. Fig. 3 shows that an analogous process occurs in the subsystems of every level.

At the top, the system forms a single conceptual whole with the informational system. The structure is made up of a coordinated set of heterogenous, relatively autonomous blocs, which, taken together, approximate a real macroeconomic system carrying out processes of differentiation, integration, and simple production. On each level, the elementary bloc is characterized by a partially ordered triple relationship of input–internal state–output or by a dual relationship of input and output and also by the interaction between its structure and the historical process. Thus, each bloc is an elementary goal-forming and goal-directed system.

The system has a decompositional structure, allowing both separability and decomposition (both classificational and functional decomposition). In total, the system is a special case of a hierarchical–cooperative system – a multi-level system with horizontal and vertical links on each level and a two-way system of vertical links between different levels. There are no firm rules for determining the number of levels of a decomposable system, so the number of levels is determined informally, mainly on the basis of classificational–functional heterogeneity and differences in the time parameters for planning and control on different levels. The separability of the system serves two functions. It is possible to formalize alternative

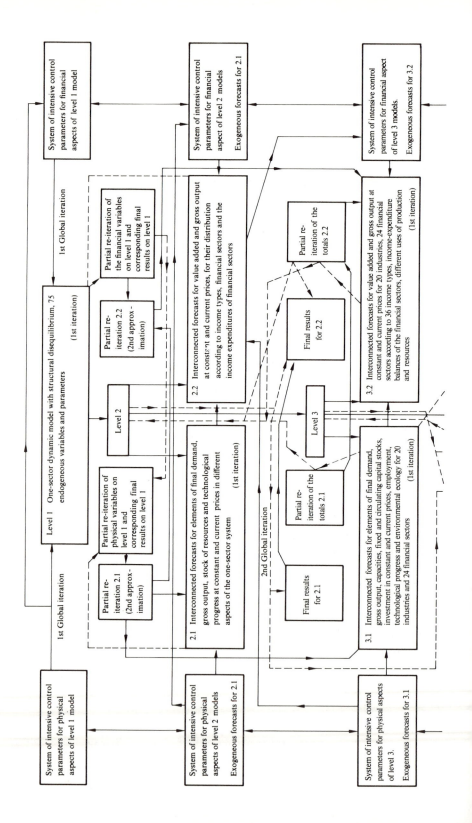

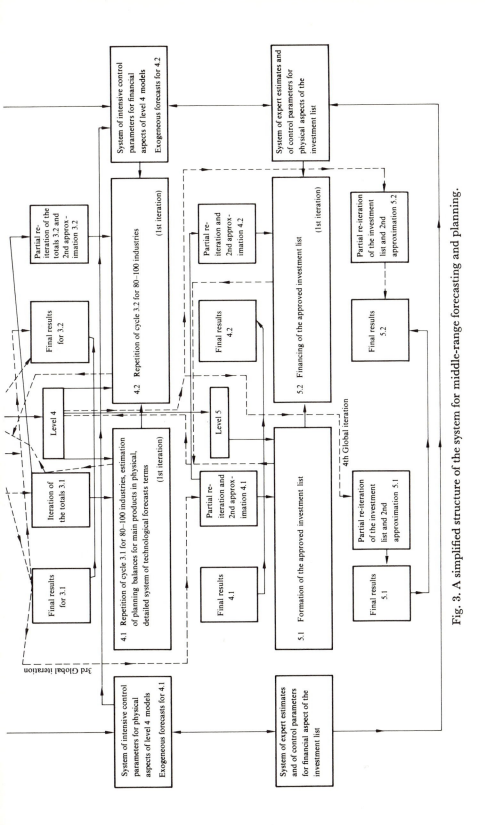

Fig. 3. A simplified structure of the system for middle-range forecasting and planning.

medium-range planning hypotheses and to test them empirically at different levels of aggregation within the overall framework of the long-range plan. It is also possible to use the principle of 'in succession and in parts' to introduce relatively independent partial changes in the plan.

The system describes the disequilibrium development of an open macroeconomic system in general, and by specifying the functional relationships it can also describe the system's behavior. Such specification refers to both the process of increasing potential of the real system and to the system's actual dynamics in the realization space.

The aggregate socio-economic model shown in fig. 2 describes the long-run, coordinated processes of modernization and development of society and industrialization of the economy. The corresponding relationships in the medium-range model in fig. 3 are the social and (mainly) economic goals specified for a limited time on the basis of a medium-range criterion. This medium-range criterion summarizes balancing of economic goals – rates of economic growth, shares of capital investment, personal and governmental consumption in national income, active and passive monetary balances (including the share of saving), income distribution among resources (assumed to be exogenous), types and rates of technical progress, level of employment, price and income stability, financing of basic elements of consumption, and growth of resources. It follows that, even on the first level, the criterion cannot be formulated explicitly, since this is impossible in the case of such complicated processes. But the criterion covers all of the basic economic processes and does provide for their coordinated development in cases where partial optimization is achieved through choice of the optimal share of accumulation. Then this criterion and the system of disequilibrium development are expressed in lower levels of the model as a detailed set of basic and derived indices of the medium-range material and financial plans. This process generates the detailed list of planned investments on the last level.

The system is much better suited to answering the question, 'what happens if...' than the question, 'how can some given aim be attained in an optimal way and what type of control is best for this'. The limits of the model result from the intermediate character of the criterion, the predominantly evolutionary characteristics of the macroeconomic system, the limited planning horizon and marked inertia of the system. These limits sharply reduce the possibilities for controlling medium-range planning.

Nevertheless, elements of choice and control are present in the medium-range planning model. They include the following:

1. At level 1, the key variable subject to optimal choice is a basic parameter in the process of economic growth – the share of accumulation in final output. This control variable influences the whole lower level

system by determining the volume and structure of accumulation and the growth of fixed and working capital.

2. The whole iterative process of informal coordination of various aspects of the medium-range plan on all five levels includes elements of choice and control. This flexibility is achieved by requiring strict correspondence between different exogenous and endogenous variables on the basis of some combined criteria. (For example, the size and structure of fixed capital stock is coordinated with rates and shares of capital investment and also with the capital–labor ratio, labor productivity, and employment – i.e., with all implicit criteria.)

3. On all five levels, forecasts of financial parameters introduce another element of control.

4. On level 5, the whole complex of controls is supplemented by a partial procedure of explicit optimization of the choice of investment projects. This procedure accounts for the distribution of a significant portion of material–financial reserves among consumers, specified as to type and location. This process makes the planning specific, and it partially eliminates another defect of medium-range planning models, the absence of explicit geographical factors.

5. Finally, choice and control elements are introduced by the procedure of calculating multiple variants of the plan. The process is essentially similar to the informal iterative coordination that occurs when calculating a single variant of the medium-range plan.

Because of the many elements of control, the medium-range planning model is not only a system for coordinated forecasting, it is a system for prediction–planning – combining normative, directive elements along with partial control.

Next, let us summarize the structure of this system and its functional principles. Successive elements in the five levels of the system are represented in the form of vertically and horizontally linked systems of passive and active accounts (representing income as value added or payment to factors, as the cost of final output or as resource capacity, respectively).

On level 1, for given assumptions about growth of population, military factors, and technical progress, a one-sector disequilibrium growth model generates seventy-five basic economic parameters – rates of growth of the economy, fixed and working capital, employment, productivity, the shares of personal and governmental consumption, accumulation and capital investment, the aggregate structure of governmental consumption, rates of return to capital, interest rates, and the dynamics of prices. On this level, the economic reformulation of the model was carried through in great detail applying the principle of structural disequilibrium, but the actual empirical calculations were carried out using a much simpler one-sector equilibrium model. The information generated on the first level is used as an input to level 2 for construction of more

109

detailed calculations of the basic material and financial balances of the medium-range plan, but, at this level, the plan is not yet broken down into separate industries. This level provides forecasts for the three main ownership sectors, provides disaggregation into detailed financial sectors of all output variables from level 1, supplementary calculations for the aggregate financial plan (such as forecasts of income and expenditure of the government budget and of the collective farm sector), and disaggregated characteristics of technological progress.

Calculations are coordinated in current and in constant prices, first vertically and then horizontally for seven basic accounts: (1) accumulation of fixed capital, (2) amortization, (3) accumulation of working capital less accounts payable, (4) personal consumption of the population, (5) collective consumption of the population, (6) governmental consumption for governmental and non-governmental purposes, (7) passive and active monetary balances.

The specific economic mechanism of level 2 is still insufficiently understood, so statistical equations are used as the main formal instrument. Structural disequilibrium at this level follows from the disequilibrium model of level 1 and from application of non-stationary statistical equations on this level.

The planning information of level 2 serves, in turn, as an input to level 3, and the whole cycle of calculations and estimates of the extent of imbalance is repeated for a breakdown of approximately twenty branches and twenty-four financial sectors. At this level, the following basic economic parameters are estimated: (1) disaggregated forecasts of personal and collective consumption for twenty sectors, including source and destination, formation of consumption funds, and the corresponding system of retail prices; (2) investment in fixed and working capital, allocated by producer and user, by investment types, and by physical structure, along with the aggregate financial structure; (3) a price system for investment goods; (4) physical volume and prices for the structure of exports, imports, and government consumption for the twenty branches; (5) valuation of gross output and productive capacity, broken down by type, by financing, and by source and origin for twenty branches; (6) the price system for gross output; (7) the projected structure of fixed and working capital and employment; (8) disaggregated estimates of type and rate of technical progress for the above sectors; (9) projected structure of income distribution and financing corresponding to the physical aspects of the medium-range plan.

On level 3, structural disequilibrium is introduced by four factors: (a) forecasting of elements of final demand based on results from levels 1 and 2, (b) shifting technological coefficients that take into account errors of forecasting and measurement, (c) a system of disequilibrium prices for elements of final demand and gross output, (d) a multi-dimensional system of disequilibrium relations among gross output, fixed and working capital, levels of employment and consumption analogous to the relationships on level 1.

On level 4, which utilizes the results of level 3 as inputs, the number of industries is extended to 80–100. This allows balancing in physical terms and also a more detailed specification of products and of the chief directions of technical progress that are reflected by the introduction of new products.

Finally, on level 5, the aggregate medium-range plan is so disaggregated that it becomes 'directed' (*adresnost'*) planning on the basis of an optimal list of investment projects, taking into consideration risk and uncertainty. These projects are allocated within the limits imposed by level 4. On level 5, the principal problems are determination of substitution possibilities among technologies, valuation of alternative techniques, and choice of projects within the feasible range where such choice is possible.

The level 5 model does not offer a single perfect method for investment choice, since there is not such a method. However, the model attempts to diminish or eliminate the main shortcomings of traditional methods of choice. (For discussion, see Mikhalevsky, 1968.)

The functional principles of the five-level system may be summarized as follows: on level 1, an integrated set of economic variables is expressed in a single, simultaneous system. Levels 2–4 are organized on the decomposition principle and disaggregate into successive balances – first, balances of each section of the physical plan, then of the internal structure of prices, then between plans in physical and value terms, and finally, in financial terms.

Consistency between levels and between blocs within each level is achieved by representing the model as a separable system with vertical (recursive) and horizontal links. As in the case of any vertical–horizontal structure with successive and parallel connections among blocs, vertical coordination is achieved by the introduction of control totals at higher and parallel levels as well as by special procedures for disaggregation and coordination of multi-component forecasts. Such procedures include regressions with constrained coefficients and, in some cases, matrix models. Horizontal coordination between parallel subsystems makes it possible to take into account simultaneous errors in dependent variables. Horizontal coordination is achieved by imposing autonomy on the subsystems by breaking the horizontal links and substituting binding constraint equations equal to zero or to a constant in place of the variables of the previous system. Thus, a system with two types of links can be reduced to a fully separable system of three-part and binary relationships. Corresponding to this procedure, there is a man–machine iterative mechanism for simultaneous vertical and horizontal coordination.

However, the nature of this iterative cycle depends crucially on the number of horizontally connected subsystems or on the number of groups of variables within the single system. If the number of groups is two, the iterative cycle will be comparatively simple, allowing consecutive co-ordination of parallel, pair-wise groups of variables which already have been coordinated at each previous step. If the number is three, then imposition of subsystem autonomy and the corresponding iterative cycle both become more complicated, but calculation is still practicable. But in this case, the role of informal elements (expert estimates) increases substantially.[11]

From this description, it follows that it is advantageous to carry out vertical disaggregation as far as possible, in spite of the accumulation of errors, while simultaneously specifying a recursive chain of pair-wise relationships of parallel groups of input and output variables on the horizontal, these variables being balanced by equating to zero or to a constant. Thus, an explicit mechanism is introduced at each step that compensates for the accumulation of error of aggregation and of estimation.

In practice, the coordination process, including both computer calculation and informal correction, takes place in the following manner:

1. Disaggregation of any aggregate endogenous variable occurs on the next two lower levels.

2. Taking into account the derived structural estimates, a small correction is made in the control total of the higher level. This yields a final structure and total, allowing a transition for the model to actual planning and accounting data.

3. An input–output table is used to estimate future gross output and prices. The table takes into account the effects of substitution, and of measurement and forecasting errors and provides for vertical and horizontal coordination. Transitional classifications and coefficients transform the model indices into actual planning and accounting information.

4. Then operations 1 and 2 are repeated for price aggregates.

5. Then horizontal coordination finds that set of prices that balances the physical and value forecasts.

6. If there are any inconsistencies in the various elements of the price structure, a partial recalculation is made – on the previous level as well, if necessary. This completes the coordination of production, resource, and price accounts. Then the transitional classifications and coefficients are used to express endogenous variables in current prices as real accounting and planning information.

7. The corresponding value elements are used as control totals for forecasting the distribution of income to factors in real and nominal terms and for coordinating forecasts of value added and payment to resources. Coordination of resource and income accounts occurs in a similar way,

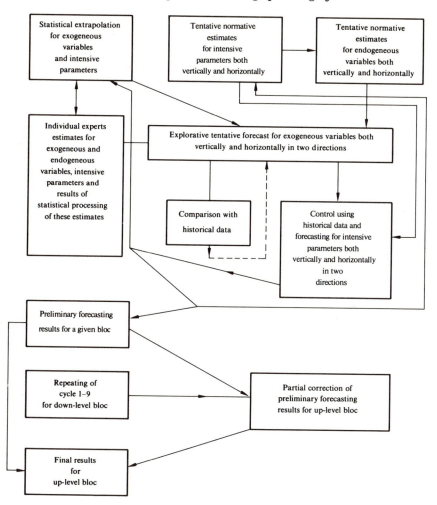

Fig. 4. Iterative forecasting cycle for a single bloc.

completing the transformation of model indices to real planning and accounting data.

8. Income and expenditure estimates in real and nominal terms, based on the results of the seven preceding steps, form a subordinate system of financial sectors, and a balance is derived for each financial sector by using transfer norms as control variables.

Thus, the whole process consists of a series of small iterations coordinating individual values of the vertical, one or two large iterations on each level that provide horizontal agreement to the vertically coordinated variables, and one or two global iterations providing coordination among levels. The iterative forecasting cycle for a single bloc is given in fig. 4.

FORMAL APPARATUS, INFORMATIONAL–COMPUTATIONAL
CHARACTERISTICS OF THE SYSTEM, EXPERIMENTAL RESULTS

'In this very log we sit upon, Mrs Sampson,' says I, 'is statistics more wonderful than any poem. The rings show it was sixty years old. At the depth of two thousand feet it would become coal in three thousand years...A box four feet long, three feet wide, and two feet eight inches deep will hold one ton of coal...A man's leg contains thirty bones. The Tower of London was burned in 1841.'

'Go on, Mr Pratt,' says Mrs Sampson.

'Them ideas is so original and soothing. I think statistics are just as lovely as they can be.'

O. Henry, *The Handbook of Hymen*

The formal model includes the dynamic model of level 1 and the following main types of statistical equations:

We use the following basic notation:

$\mathbf{R}$ correlation coefficient

r_1 first non-cyclical coefficient of autocorrelation of residual variance

$\mathbf{S}^2$ variance

$\vee$ has the meaning 'or'

$\wedge$ the diagonal matrix

M mathematical expectation

$'$ indicates transposition

Case 1. The basic, four equation system.

$$\mathbf{X}^q_{T+\theta} = a_{gq,\,T+\theta} + \sum_{r=1}^{k} \mathbf{b}^g_{rgq,\,T+\theta} \mathbf{Z}^q_{r,\,T+\theta} + \mathbf{U}_{gq,\,T+\theta} \qquad (1)$$

$$\mathbf{U}_{gq,\,T+\theta} = \mathbf{R}_{1gq} \mathbf{U}_{gq,\,T+\theta-1} + \xi_{gq,\,T+\theta}, \quad \mathbf{S}^2 \neq \text{const} \qquad (2)$$

$$\sum_{g\vee q} \mathbf{W}_{gq,\,T+\theta} \cdot a_{gq,\,T+\theta} = \sum_{g\vee q} \mathbf{W}_{gq,\,T+\theta} \cdot \mathbf{U}_{gq,\,T+\theta} = 0 \qquad (3)$$

$$\sum_{g\vee q} b_{gqr,\,T+\theta} \cdot \mathbf{W}_{gqr,\,T+\theta} = b_{r,\,T+\theta} \vee 1, \quad \Sigma \mathbf{W}_{T+\theta} = 1. \qquad (4)$$

Case 2. The second variant is case 1 subject to $r = 1$ or $r \geqslant 1$, $a = $ constant, $b = $ constant.

Case 3. The third variant expresses cases 1 and 2 in logs.

Case 4. The fourth variant:

$$\mathbf{X}_{T+\theta} = a_{T+\theta} + b_{T+\theta} + \lambda_{T+\theta} \mathbf{X}_{T+\theta-1} + \mathbf{U}_{T+\theta} \qquad (5)$$

$$\mathbf{U}_{T+\theta} = \mathbf{R}_1 \mathbf{U}_{T+\theta-1} + \xi_{T+\theta}. \qquad (6)$$

Case 5. The fifth variant:

$$\mathbf{X}_{T+\theta} = f(\mathbf{Z}_{T+\theta}, b) + \mathbf{U}_{T+\theta} \qquad (7)$$

estimated in the form:

$$\mathbf{X}_{T+\theta} = f(\mathbf{Z}_{T+\theta}, \mathbf{B}) + \frac{\partial f}{\partial \mathbf{B}}\bigg|_{\mathbf{Z}_{T+\theta,\,B}} \cdot (b - B) + \xi \qquad (8)$$

$$\mathbf{X}^*_{T+\theta} = \overline{\mathbf{X}}_{T+\theta} \pm t \sqrt{\left[\sum_{j=1}^{k} \sum_{l=1} \left(\frac{\partial f}{\partial b_j}\right)\left(\frac{\partial f}{\partial b_l}\right) \mathbf{R}_{jl} \cdot \mathbf{S}_{b_j b_l} \right]}. \qquad (9)$$

Case 6. The sixth variant is a non-strictly identified stochastic linear equations system in which the number of variables is reduced by the principle components method.

Case 7. Variant 7 is a strictly identified system:

$$[\mathbf{X}_{T+\theta}] = (\pi)' \, (\mathbf{F}_{T+\theta}) + \mathbf{P}[\xi_{T+\theta}], \tag{10}$$

$$\mathbf{M}[\xi_i][\xi_i]' = (\hat{\mathbf{S}}_{ii}) \, (\hat{\mathbf{E}}),$$

$$[\mathbf{V}_{i, T+\theta}] = \mathbf{R}_{1i}(\hat{\mathbf{P}}_i) \, [\xi_{i, T+\theta}] + [\xi_{i, T+\theta}], \tag{11}$$

$$|\mathbf{R}_{1i}| < 1, \quad \mathbf{M}[\xi_{i, T+\theta}] = 0, \quad (\mathbf{L}) = (\mathbf{P}) \, \{\underset{c}{\textstyle\sum} \oplus (\hat{\mathbf{E}})\} \, (\mathbf{P})' \tag{12}$$

$$(\mathbf{P}_i) = \left\{ \begin{matrix} (1-\mathbf{R}_{1i}^2)^{-2} & 0 & 0\dots0 \\ \mathbf{R}_1^{T-1}(1-\mathbf{R}_{1i}^2)^{-2} & \mathbf{R}_{1i}^{T-2} & \mathbf{R}_{1i}^{T-3}\dots1 \end{matrix} \right\}, \tag{13}$$

$$\mathbf{V}_{i1t} = (1-\mathbf{R}_{1i}^2)^{-\frac{1}{2}}\xi_{1t} \quad \text{for} \quad t = 1. \tag{14}$$

We have made preliminary estimates of the informational and computational demands for the first three levels. The results for levels 2 and 3 are given in appendix 1. In calculating the computer requirements of the model, we used the standard of a computer capable of a million operations a second and took into account the time requirements of each type operation. Separate calculations are made for detailed, comprehensive forecasts and for simpler, more aggregate forecasts at the first three levels.

A summary of the aggregate forecasting system is presented in table 1. a decompositional system of the form shown in fig. 3 has a distinct advantage in the flexibility of its mathematical form; whenever necessary, any subsystem may be treated as non-linear, and, for levels 2–4, the subsystems may be assumed to include cumulative uncertainty and compensation of aggregation and forecasting errors.

Empirical verification of the medium-range planning system will require a number of stages. At present, only the first stage is partially complete. This stage includes the following: on level 1, the computation cycle was completed for a one-sector equilibrium model based on a ten-year planning period and separated into five-year periods employing different planning hypotheses.

On level 2, the computation cycle was completed on the basis of a simplified procedure. The procedure involved, first, linear and log-linear forecasting that includes transformation procedures to reduce first-order autocorrelation of residuals and rough adjustment for heteroscedasticity [nonhomogeneity of variance]. Critical values were established for autocorrelation coefficients and Durbin–Watson statistics. And the power of the combined criteria was estimated for small sample cases. Vertical coordination was almost all informal, since the sum of the

Table 1. *Summary of machine time for one computational cycle for the top three levels of an aggregated medium-range planning system*

	Number of equations	Computer time for 1 equation (minutes)	Total computer time (minutes)
Level 1			
Linear regressions	55	0.024	1.32
System of 75 equations	—	55.88	52.88
Total for 2 global iterations			108.4
Level 2			
Linear regressions	2000	0.024	48
Total for 1 global iteration for $\frac{1}{3}$ endogenous variables			64
Level 3			
Linear regressions for current values of variables	12,000	0.024	360
Linear regressions with a general type of distributed lag	283	1.000	283
Non-linear regressions	73	1.000	73
Transcendental equations	130	0.024	3.1
Total for 1 global iteration for $\frac{1}{5}$ endogenous variables			743
Total for levels 1–3			915.4 = 15.27 hours

individual forecasts diverged from the control totals by less than 5 % on level 2, as on other levels. So parameter estimates for individual equations were treated as restricted least squares estimates, and the divergence was distributed proportionally to those components of the independent variables for which the physical or statistical values were in doubt.

On level 3, one whole computing cycle was carried out, covering a ten-year forecast of final demand and gross output at constant prices broken down for sixteen producing sectors of the input–output table together with the corresponding distributions of fixed capital, employment of labor, gross and net capital investment, and the internal structure of investment for the sixteen consuming industries. The output of these forecasts was then transformed to correspond to actual accounting information, and forecasts were made of types and rates of technical progress and the role of technical progress in economic growth. Partial results for one variant of the plan are given in table 2 (see Mikhalevsky, 1970, for further details).

So far, all that has been completed on level 4 is a set of detailed forecasts for some basic products in physical units.

Table 2. *Rates of technological progress and shares of intensive and extensive types of economic growth for industries (with value added as endogenous variable, in %)*

	Rates of technological progress	
	Years 0–5	Years 5–10
Economy as a whole	2.278(1.908–2.350)	2.465(2.150–3.639)
Productive sphere	2.512(2.506–2.171)	2.345(2.286–3.254)
Services	0.228 (−0.162,+0.577)	0.707(−0.402, +2.238)
Industry	2.711(2.729–2.618)	2.638(2.417–4.254)
Building	2.045(2.696–1.165)	3.175(9.600–2.980)
Transportation and communication	2.487(0.419–4.857)	1.915(1.283–1.915)
Agriculture	3.516(3.516–4.828)	3.100(2.150–3.439)
Circulation sphere	3.188(3.389–2.625)	3.984
Metallurgy	2.258	1.364
Fuel industry	2.681	2.828
Power industry	3.057	3.724
Metal-working and engineering industries	1.530	1.485
Chemical industry	1.445	1.468
Timber, paper, timber-manufacturing industries	3.092	2.067
Production of building materials	3.974	3.077
Light industry	2.261	5.076
Food and beverages industry	1.112	3.120

	Shares of intensive type	
	Years 0–5	Years 5–10
Economy as a whole	32.49(32.62–26.55)	36.30(43.80–36.30)
Productive sphere	33.81(37.50–27.11)	35.69(47.30–33.69)
Services	6.04(0.00–7.03)	13.44(0.00–36.49)
Industry	31.17(33.68–29.92)	38.82(38.21–46.85)
Building	29.41(40.95–15.60)	43.65(76.41–34.71)
Transportation and communication	33.89(9.93–41.50)	26.10(40.49–15.11)
Agriculture	93.45(100.00–91.80)	89.35(100.00–73.30)
Circulation sphere	34.35(29.00–72.25)	42.35
Metallurgy	28.94	22.11
Fuel industry	38.50	47.19
Power industry	30.00	36.43
Metal-working and engineering industries	18.91	21.79
Chemical industry	19.94	17.00
Timber, paper, timber-manufacturing industries	39.35	36.74
Production of building materials	42.31	39.85
Light industry	34.39	54.30
Food and beverages industry	19.00	37.35

Table 2 (*cont.*)

	Shares of extensive type	
	Years 0–5	Years 5–10
Economy as a whole	67.51(67.38–73.45)	63.70(56.20–63.70)
Productive sphere	66.19(62.50–72.89)	64.31(52.70–66.31)
Services	95.96(100.00–92.97)	86.56(100.00–63.51)
Industry	62.83(66.32–70.08)	61.18(61.79–53.15)
Building	70.59(59.05–84.40)	56.35(23.59–65.29)
Transportation and communication	66.11(90.07–58.50)	73.90(59.51–84.89)
Agriculture	6.55(0.00–8.20)	10.65(0.00–26.70)
Circulation sphere	65.65(71.00–27.75)	57.65
Metallurgy	71.06	77.89
Fuel industry	61.50	52.81
Power industry	70.00	63.57
Metal-working and engineering industries	81.09	78.21
Chemical industry	80.06	83.00
Timber, paper, timber-manufacturing industries	60.65	63.26
Production of building materials	57.69	60.15
Light industry	65.61	45.70
Food and beverages industry	81.00	62.65

Some illustrative estimates of forecasting errors are given in table 3 and in appendix 2.

We intend to continue to extend all elements of the system in the future in a number of ways: (1) by improving the formal description, (2) by improving the computer program, (3) by extension of the data base, (4) through better coordination of the various blocs, (5) by explicit inclusion of changing prices, (6) by extension of empirical estimation to a wider range of elements, (7) by working out the technique of multi-variant planning.

Table 3. *Forecasting errors for gross output with one-and three-year planning horizon (in %)*

	Errors for one-year planning horizon	Errors for three-year planning horizon
Industry	+ 1.7	− 2.88[a]
Agriculture	− 3.4	+ 3.55
Building	+ 2.2	—
Transportation and communication	− 3.6	—
Distribution and other industries	+ 7.1	—
Iron and steel	− 0.33	—
Fuel industry	− 0.25	1.46
Power industry	+ 0.34	+ 3.15
Metal-working and engineering industries	+ 1.27	− 5.80
Chemical industry	− 2.44	− 11.84
Timber, paper, timber-manufacturing industries	+ 0.92	+ 0.51
Production of building materials	− 2.29	− 7.43
Light industry	− 3.09	− 0.64
Food and beverages industry	+ 0.82	+ 8.30
Other industries	+ 0.63	—

[a] Accounting form 'CO'.

Increase in information under the transition from level 2 to level 3

	Total output	Of which		Total input	Of which		
		Out of equations	Derived variables		Out of historical data	Planned data	Statistical parameters
			Number of variables and parameters				
Personal consumption	3.216:1	2.212:1	—	2.142:1	2.250:1	0.430:1	20.20:1
Government consumption	7.940:1	6.790:1	—	7.170:1	7.940:1	—	—
Balance of payments	18.43:1	18.43:1	—	32.54:1	18.43:1	37.00:1	498:1
Fixed capital and corresponding investments	445:1	11.70:1	68.8:1	11.20:1	11.39:1	—	—
Working capital and corresponding investments (accounts receivable excluded)	8.73:1	7.95:1	—	-0.07:1	8.40:1	—	2.56:1
Gross output and capacities	—	—	—	—	—	—	—
Labor force and employment	46.78:1	34.93:1	74.18:1	27.45:1	30.18:1	0.662:1	12.31:1
Natural resources	1.20:1	1.245:1	1.105:1	1.275:1	1.855:1	—	—
Total basic physical and price variables	38:1	22.91:1	69.85:1	20.29:1	21.10:1	6.70:1	139.5:1
Derived general variables	28.35:1	—	28.35:1	—	—	—	—
Total physical and price variables	23.10:1	22.92:1	26.60:1	20.29:1	21.10:1	6.70:1	139.5:1
Sector 'households'	83.50:1	36.90:1	32950:1	48.57:1	42.79:1	3562:1	—
Sector 'state enterprises and organizations'	6.62:1	56.90:1	3.285:1	612.5:1	568.5:1	—	—
Other sectors	9.61:1	16.02:1	6.600:1	25.2:1	24.9:1	34.5:1	—
Total financial sectors	45.10:1	38.79:1	51.9:1	51.0:1	45.00:1	2809:1	—
Basic financial variables at level 3: basic physical and price variables at level 2	0.370:1	0.402:1	0.0724:1	0.506:1	0.470:1	2.010:1	38.7:1
Derived output variables at level 3: basic output variables at level 2	49.63:1	—	—	—	—	—	—
Informational content output/input at level 3 output/input at level 2	—	—	—	—	—	—	—

	Output 3 / Output 2	Equations 3 / Equations 2	Derived variables 3 / Derived variables 2	Input 3 / Input 2	Historical data 3 / Historical data 2	Planned data 3 / Planned data 2	Statistical parameters 3 / Statistical parameters 2
				Informational content (in bits)			
Personal consumption	1.738	1.325	—	1.315	1.360	0.314	4.428
Government consumption	2.650	2.650	—	2.750	2.890	—	—
Balance of payments	4.175	4.175	—	4.925	4.175	5.110	8.950
Fixed capital and corresponding investments	8.942	3.690	6.149	3.360	3.654	—	—
Working capital and corresponding investments (accounts receivable excluded)	3.300	2.885	—	2.890	2.952	—	1.605
Gross output and capacities	—	—	—	—	—	—	—
Labor force and employment	5.502	5.042	6.162	4.595	4.785	0.0997	3.500
Natural resources	0.901	0.915	0.769	0.939	0.927	—	—
Total basic physical and price variables	4.635	4.420	6.060	4.428	4.435	3.007	6.910
Derived general variables	4.650	—	4.650	—	—	—	—
Total physical and price variables	4.603	4.600	4.798	4.230	4.459	2.660	7.102
Sector 'households'	6.219	5.279	43.70	5.624	5.362	11.80	—
Sector 'state enterprises and organizations'	2.984	5.760	1.744	8.940	8.782	—	—
Other sectors	3.148	3.955	2.550	4.540	4.520	5.128	—
Total financial sectors	5.439	5.170	5.693	5.690	5.437	11.450	—
Basic financial variables at level 3 : basic physical and price variables at level 2	0.298	0.304	0.115	0.376	0.353	1.250	5.297
Derived output variables at level 3 : basic output variables at level 2	5.590	—	—	—	—	—	—
Information content output/input at level 3 output/input at level 2	1.94:1	—	—	—	—	—	—

APPENDIX 2

Forecasting errors for basic products in physical units for one-, two-, three-year planning horizon (in %)

	Forecasting errors for planning horizon		
	1 year	2 years	3 years
Steel	− 0.60	+ 0.17	—
Iron	− 1.50	+ 1.16	—
Rolled metal (including finished	− 0.10	0.00	—
rolled metal)	0.00	+ 1.30	—
Steel tubes	− 1.10	+ 0.81	—
Iron ore	− 1.00	—	+ 0.30
Coke (6 % humidity)	− 1.70	—	—
Coal	+ 0.90	− 1.60	—
Oil	− 1.00	− 0.40	—
Gas	+ 1.10	+ 5.58	—
Schists	− 1.00	—	—
Power production	+ 0.63	+ 1.35	—
Power capacities	+ 0.20	—	+ 4.29
Meat (total weight)	—	—	+ 2.49
Meat (industrial processing, subproducts excluded)	—	—	+ 1.61
Sausage	—	—	+ 2.63
Milk (total)	—	—	+ 1.80
Oil	—	—	− 6.28
Granulated sugar	—	—	+ 2.94
Tea	—	—	− 4.20
Potatoes	—	—	+ 2.51
Vegetables	—	—	+ 2.49
Eggs	—	—	− 3.00
Wool	—	—	+ 8.55
Goods turnover at transportation			
Railroads	− 0.06	—	− 0.87
River	+ 1.50	—	− 4.80
Motor-cars	+ 1.70	—	—
Air	+ 1.10	—	—

NOTES

1 For critical analyses of the assumptions of these models, refer to Mikhalevsky (1971), Van Doren (1967), Worland (1967), Rader (1950), Bohnen (1964) and Luhmann (1968).
2 See Mikhalevsky (1971, 1972) and the bibliography included there.
3 Informational metaorganization is defined in Maruyama (1966).
4 Technology is discussed in Young (1969).
5 See Kulikovskii (1968).
6 Echelon is defined in Pliskin (1969) as a union of a higher-level subsystem with at least one lower-level subsystem.

7 See Simon (1965) for discussion. A formal definition of a decomposable system is provided in Wymore (1967).

8 Morphostatic and morphogenetic processes are defined in Buckley (1967) pp. 62–3.

9 By 'activity' we mean a multi-level, incompletely deterministic process for realization of potential by means of combined functions. See Parsons (1951) and Parsons and Shils (1951).

10 This problem was widely discussed in the literature on balanced and unbalanced growth of developing countries, but the problem obviously exists for all countries in a less acute form.

11 We can demonstrate the process of coordination using an example at level 2. The procedure is the following: first, carry out a series of semi-formalized, small iterations within each bloc of level 2.1 and 2.2. Then carry out that part of the first global iteration related to 2.1 together with a partial revision of the level 1 totals. Then carry out the part related to 2.2. By rechecking the totals for level 1, we can get final values for the output variables of level 1. Then, the first global iteration is completed by running a large-scale iteration between the second approximations to 2.1 and 2.2 that makes use of exogenously determined forecasts and revises variables in 2.2 only. This provides final totals for the second approximation on level 2. Intensive control parameters and normative–expert estimates for level 2 are brought into preliminary agreement (non-formally) with the corresponding aggregate totals of level 1, and then they are used as inputs on level 2, first for the execution of a cycle of small iterations and then for a large-scale iteration between 2.1 and 2.2.

REFERENCES

Bohnen, A. (1964). *Die utilitaristische Ethik als Grundlage der modernen Wohlfahrtsökonomik.* Göttingen.

Buckley, Walter (1967). *Sociology and Modern System Theory.* Englewood Cliffs, NJ: Prentice-Hall.

Krasnosel′skii, M., G. Vainikko, P. Zabreiko, Ia. Rutitskii, V. Stetsenko (1970). *Priblizhennoe reshenie operatornykh uravnenii (Operator Equations Approximate Solution).* Moscow: Uzdat Fiziko-Matematicheskoi Lit.

Kulikovskii, R. (1968). Agregatsiia, optimizatsiia i upravlenie organizatsionnoi strukturoi bol′shikh sistem. *Ekonomika i matematicheskie metody* (Aggregation, optimization and control for an organizational structure of a large system. *Econ. and Math. Methods*), **4** (1).

Luhmann, N. (1968). *Zweckbegriff und Systemrationalitat.* Tübingen

Maruyama, Magoroh (1966). A metaorganization of information. *General Systems,* **11,** 55–60.

Mikhalevsky, B. N. (1968). Otbor proektov kapitalovlozhenii po kriteriiu maksimal′noi normy effektivnosti. *Ekonomika i matematicheskie metody* (Investments list choice using maximal rate of return criterion. *Econ. and Math. Methods*), **4** (4), 526–62.

Mikhalevsky, B. N. (1970). Makroekonomicheskii prognoz tekhnologicheskogo progressa i struktury ekonomicheskogo rosta. *Ekonomika i matematicheskie metody* (Macroeconomic forecast of the technological progress and economic growth structure. *Econ. and Math. Methods*), **6** (4), 510–20.

Mikhalevsky, B. N. (1971). Ekonomicheskie modeli mekhaniko–organicheskogo tipa i modeli otkrytoi mnogourovenevoi dinamicheskoi sistemy (kriticheskii analiz predposylok). *Ekonomika i matematicheskie metody* (Mechanical–organic economic models and the models of an open multi-level dynamic system (a critical assumptions analysis). *Econ. and Math. Methods*), **7** (1), 13–30.

Mikhalevsky, B. N. (1972). Kachestvennoe opredelenie razvivaiushcheisia sistemy. *Ekonomika i matematicheskie metody* (A qualitative definition of the developing system. *Econ. and Math. Methods*), **8** (1), 7–27.

Parsons, Talcott (1951). *The Social System*. Glencoe, Ill.: Free Press.

Parsons, Talcott, and E. Shils (eds.) (1951). *Toward a General Theory of Action*. Cambridge, Mass.: Harvard University Press.

Pliskin, L. (1969). Dekompozitsionnaia dinamicheskaia optimizatsiia proizvodstva s ierarkhicheskoi strukturoi upravleniia. *Avtomatika i telemekhanika*. (Decomposable dynamic production optimization with the hierarchical control structure. *Ant. and Telecom.*), no. 4.

Rader, Melvin (1950). *Ethics and Society: an Appraisal of Social Ideals*. New York: Holt.

Simon, Herbert A. (1965). The architecture of complexity. *General Systems*, **10**, 63–76.

Van Doren, Charles L. (1967). *The Idea of Progress*. New York: Praeger.

Worland, Steven (1967). *Scholasticism and Welfare Economics*. Notre Dame, Ind.: University of Notre Dame Press.

Wymore, A. Wayne (1967). *A Mathematical Theory of System Engineering: the Elements*. New York: Wiley.

Young, T. R. (1969). Social stratification and modern system theory. *General Systems*, **14**, 113–17.

An Experimental Polycentric Model of the Soviet Economy

EDWIN G. DOLAN[1]

In the comparative study of economic systems, a useful distinction is made between centralization and polycentricity. In centralized systems, all economic actors (or at least all producers) are subordinated, via a hierarchical structure, to a single center of command, while in polycentric economies, individual members are free to act autonomously, with organization and coordination of efforts secured by means of certain 'signals' which communicate information about each individual's actions to others. Traditionally, most of the analytical work concerning the Soviet economy has proceeded within the framework of the centralized model, leaving the impression that the applicability of the polycentricity principle was confined to market systems, or at most to those few sectors of planned economies where conventional market mechanisms were used as a supplement to centralized resource allocation. However, descriptive accounts of the Soviet economy, especially those focusing attention on the behavior of industrial management, have always made it clear that the informal structure of the system departs rather substantially from the centralized model.

The present paper is in the spirit of a number of recent studies which have in one way or another placed increased emphasis on the role which informal polycentric features of the Soviet economy play in determining resource allocation either directly, in the course of plan execution, or indirectly, through the influence of anticipated execution difficulties on the behavior of central planners.[2] The model and experiments described below, it is hoped, will contribute to the further clarification of the interaction between the formal and informal elements of the Soviet economy in shaping over-all system behavior.

A SKETCH OF THE EXPERIMENTAL MODEL

The differences between the centralized (command economy) and polycentric models show up most clearly in their treatment of managerial behaviour. The former, which views the entire production establishment, from the top political leadership down to the worker at his bench as an integrated hierarchical organization, postulates an enterprise manager

125

whose principal behavioral rule is to execute commands passed down to him from higher levels. In such a system, all of the information and all of the criteria necessary for managerial decision-making are passed to the enterprise along vertical lines of communication; the scope of that decision-making is strictly limited to the translation of plan targets into detailed technical instructions for the control of intra-enterprise production processes; and rewards received by management are based on the fact of obedience to commands rather than on the specific content of those commands.

In contrast, the manager in a polycentric system acts as independent agent. The information which he receives comes to him along 'horizontal' channels of communication, i.e., directly from other low-level decision makers. He must undertake not only intra-enterprise activities affecting the behavior of his own subordinates, but also extra-enterprise activities which will directly influence the behaviour of other participants in the system (other firms, supply agencies, etc.). The rewards which he receives depend directly on the degree of his success in making and implementing some more or less explicit maximizing decisions.

With reference to the Soviet economy, it is the command model which has the sanction of authority. Lenin appears to have thought that after the revolution, 'the whole of society [would] become one office and one factory' (Roberts, 1971, p. 84) and today, in the official party manual *Fundamentals of Marxism–Leninism*, we are told that 'in socialist society, the national economy is an integral organism, directed by a single will' (Manove, 1971, p. 570). Yet brief reflection on the requirements for the successful operation of a command system indicates some grave difficulties in accepting the official Soviet self-image as descriptive of reality. We need only note that in order for a hierarchic organization to function effectively, each order given anywhere within the system must lie within the 'zone of compliance' of its recipient, i.e., it must respect certain limits beyond which the subordinate will be unwilling or unable to execute it. When the command system in question is an economy, this means that the plans received by enterprise management must be at a minimum (1) of feasible magnitude, (2) internally consistent, and (3) free of extraneous payoff implications which might tempt willful disobedience. Clearly, the administrative resources, communications network, and computational capacity of the Soviet planning system are not equal to the task of formulating such a set of plans.

Confronted with impossibly ambitious or internally inconsistent plans, and surrounded with temptations to better his position by violating them in certain respects, the Soviet manager engages in certain characteristic activities which would be quite unthinkable for a well behaved subordinate member of a centralized system. He bargains with planners and hoards raw materials in order to develop a 'safety factor'. He selects some aspects of the plan to fulfill at the expense of others. He uses his *blat* ('pull'), hires a *tolkach* ('pusher'), and engages in blackmarketeering in attempts to procure deficit inputs. He expands his production backward into earlier stages of production to compensate for the unreliability of his suppliers. And if all else fails, he resorts to *shturmovshchina* (storming), *ochovtiratel'stvo* (misleading reporting) or outright falsification of statistics to create at least the illusion of doing the impossible.

Each of these activities – by increasing the importance of horizontal communications channels, by broadening the extra-enterprise effects of managerial decision-making, and by increasing the importance of unofficial rewards relative to official bonuses – increases the degree of polycentricity of the system.

By introducing many simplifying assumptions, and eliminating from consideration many aspects of the prototype system, a mathematical model emphasizing these polycentric features of the Soviet economy was constructed to permit exploration of certain properties of the system by techniques of computer simulation. Limitations of space preclude the possibility of presenting a fully detailed description of the model, but at least an impression of its main features are given here and in the appendix.[3]

Fig. 1 shows, in schematic form, the main flows of information and materials which serve as signals coordinating the activities of the various semi-autonomous economic agents participating in the resource alloca-tion process. A central element of the model is the supply system, through which all material flows pass on their way from producer to user. Output of each product (1) is by convention assumed to flow from its sector of origin into a centrally held inventory. From there, it is distributed both to those sectors using the product in question as a productive input (2) and to final users, who employ it in investment and consumption (3).

The pattern of distribution of materials is influenced by the central planning agency, which issues plans at certain fixed intervals. These include output targets for the enterprises (4) and a distribution plan for the supply system (5), which specifies the quantity of each product to be shipped to each point of intermediate and final use.

In the intervals between the periodic promulgation of plans, the central authorities may intervene to affect the pattern of resource allocation in a second way, by the exertion of *priority pressure* (6) on the supply system. The *ad hoc* setting of priorities during the course of plan execution is of particular importance in cases where the plan currently in force is characterized by such a degree of tautness that 100 % fulfillment of it is impossible. In such circumstances, priorities are necessary to insure that when shortfalls occur, they occur in the right places. For example, if it becomes clear that the output target of the coal industry will not be fulfilled, the planners might wish to specify that the steel industry has

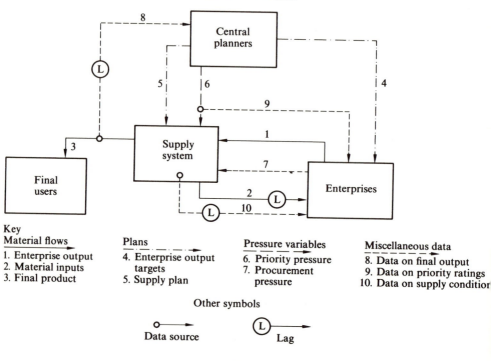

Fig. 1

priority in rationing, so that its needs for fuel may be met while some other activity, say home heating, bears the brunt of the shortage.

By means of the several types of informal behavior mentioned earlier, enterprise managers are also able to influence the pattern of supply distribution during the course of plan execution. In the model, all activities of this type – the dispatch of procurement agents, black-marketeering, cajollery, and so forth – are lumped together and referred to as the exertion of *procurement pressure* (7). The possibility of influencing the pattern of material supply is of particular importance in enabling enterprise management to obtain a balanced mix of productive inputs in the face of widespread disruption of the supply plan. For example, if production in a certain enterprise is being held up by a shortage of one single input, say copper tubing, the manager may concentrate his own procurement efforts on this one bottleneck, rather than hoping or waiting for his general priority rating to be upgraded by the central authorities.

In order for the various economic agents to make decisions governing their priority, production, or procurement policies, they must have access to certain types of information about what is going on elsewhere in the system. Three channels for the transmission of such information were explicitly incorporated in the model, and are shown in the figure. The central planners continuously monitor the rate of fulfillment of consumption and investment targets (8). This enables them to exert priority pressure on behalf of sectors lagging disproportionately far behind in their output of goods for final use. At the same time, in order to make decisions concerning their output and procurement strategies, enterprise managers make it their business to keep well informed about the system of priorities currently in effect (9), and also gather information concerning the tightness of supply conditions prevailing within the supply system for each commodity (10). (The data flowing along this last channel can be thought of as some sort of compilation of all reports on the procurement activities of rival firms gathered from the press, conversations with suppliers, reports of *tolkachi*, general gossip, or other 'horizontal' information sources.)

Given this outline of the communication system, description of the model can be completed by specifying how the behavior of each type of economic agent is determined on the basis of the material and informational inputs received. Beginning with the supply system, we note that four factors act to influence the rate at which any given commodity is shipped to any given user. First, the model was so constructed that this rate would be proportional to the level of the inventory, determined over time by the difference between the inflows (1) and outflows (2) of the item in question. Second, the rate of shipment is influenced by the supply plan (5), in such a way that, *ceteris paribus*, the rate of shipment of a given good to a given user would be proportional to the backlog of unfilled planned shipments accumulated at any given moment. Next, the equations governing supply system behavior were specified in such a way that, *ceteris paribus*, an increase in the priority rating (6) of a given sector would result in a proportional increase in the volume of shipments going to it. Finally, a similar proportional effect was incorporated for the procurement pressure exerted on the supply system by enterprise management (7).

Since all simulation experiments conducted with the model focussed on the behavior of the system within the period of execution of a single plan, it was not necessary to specify a method of plan compilation based on internally generated data. Plans could simply be introduced exogenously by the experimenter at the beginning of each simulated plan interval. The priority pressure variables, on the other hand, are determined endogenously. The central authorities are assumed to adjust priorities from moment to moment during the execution of a plan with the object of maintaining certain desired proportions among the final output of the various commodities (3).[4] On the basis of information received concerning final outputs (8), they adjust priority pressure (6) upward for lagging sectors, and downward for leading ones.

The most important and complex part of the model has been left until last. This is the specification of the behaviour of enterprise management. The manager is assumed to realize certain benefits and incur certain costs both dependent on the quantity of output produced. Like his counterpart in a market economy, he must take into account the technological conditions of production within his own enterprise, together with the expected reactions of his customers and suppliers, in order to determine the level of output which will maximize for him the excess of benefits over costs. Let us see how these considerations interact in our polycentric Soviet-type model to determine enterprise output policy.

We may begin with the factors determining the function which relates managerial benefits to output. Because of the sellers' market and the fixed prices which commonly prevail in the Soviet-type system, it is not unreasonable to assume that marginal revenue is constant with respect to output. But monetary sales revenue does not occupy a very important place in the payoff function of the enterprise manager. Two other factors, the bonus schedule and the 'ratchet effect' are more important, and neither of these is constant at the margin. The typical Soviet-style bonus schedule provides very large rewards for plan fulfillment, and relatively modest ones for over-fulfillment: hence, it may be thought of as contributing to declining marginal benefits beyond the target output level. Equally important, managers are said to operate under the assumption that the level at which their planned output for the next period will be set is dependent on their actual performance in the current period. An overfulfillment in this year may mean that one's carefully nurtured safety factor will be wiped out by a 'hard' plan in the next – the ratchet effect. Thus if the managerial maximum is thought of as the present value of current *and* future bonuses, a second reason for diminishing marginal benefit of output expansion beyond the planned level is introduced.

Let us turn now to the manager's cost function. This is determined by the material requirements for sustaining a given level of output, and the cost of procuring these inputs. In order to focus more clearly on the latter, a very simple form, with fixed coefficients, a single process, and a single output, was chosen for the production function. In the polycentric Soviet type system as we have depicted it, the real test of a manager's competence is his ability to influence the supply rationing process in his favor, and the dominant costs of production become for him those costs which must be incurred in order to obtain the scarce inputs allocated to him by the plan, but not in practice freely forthcoming. In addition to expenditures made through official channels, these costs include both unofficial monetary costs such as payments for black market purchases and salaries of procurement personnel, and also less tangible costs such as the expenditure of a limited budget of credibility and good will, the psychic strain of battling red tape, and the risk of criminal prosecution for doing many of these things.

Given information on the current priority of his sector and the state of competitive demand for the needed inputs, the manager is able to calculate the procurement cost of obtaining the materials required for a given level of output. Together with his knowledge of the benefit function, this allows him to determine a level of output which will equate marginal cost with marginal benefit, much as a capitalist firm would equate marginal cost to marginal revenue in order to maximize profits. Note, however, that in contrast to his capitalist counterpart, costs and benefits must be measured in rather ill-defined units of managerial welfare rather than precisely calculated in terms of monetary units. Depending on conjunctural circumstances, the output chosen by the manager may be above, below, or just equal to the planned output.

SOME EXPERIMENTALLY DETERMINED PROPERTIES OF
THE MODEL

With a completed mathematical model incorporating the main features sketched in the previous section, it was possible to generate simulated time series showing the behaviour of the polycentric Soviet-type system under various conditions. Fig. 2 represents a typical set of experimental results. The figure shows the time paths of net output deliveries from the producers of a four-sector version of our model. The horizontal axis measures time, in arbitrary short intervals, and the vertical axis measures output on an arbitrary scale, with the targeted value of each sector equal to 100.

Time $t = 0$ marks the moment of introduction of a new central plan. The plan, drawn up by the experimenter, was a taut one, purposely constructed to exceed the productive capacities of the economy by 10 %. Since the system could not sustain production at the targeted levels in all sectors at once, deliveries to final use fell off rapidly as mounting pressure from enterprises for intermediate products brought about declines in supply system inventories. As the relative rates of decline of net output from the four sectors were determined simply by the relative simulated procurement skill of the enterprises, the net output proportions desired by the central authorities were violated, and as early as the seventh and eighth intervals it can be seen that changes in priority pressure reversed the decline in the net outputs of sectors two and three. Cyclical fluctuations ensued as first one, then another sector gained a temporary advantage, but by the end of fifty intervals, the final rank ordering of the sectors was established. After about the seventy-fifth interval, fluctuations became imperceptible, as the countervailing pressures of the center and the enterprises reached values just balancing off one another.

Table 1 shows an interesting property of the equilibrium attained, not clear from the figure alone. This is that as measured after ninety periods,

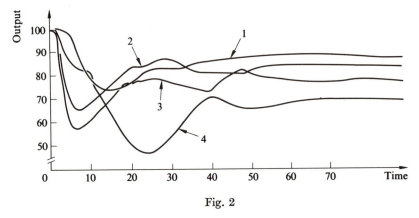

Fig. 2

Table 1. *Comparison of planned, optimal, and actual output rates for the experiment shown in fig. 2*

Sector	Actual imperfect plan	Perfect optimal plan plan	Actual rates after 90 periods
1	158.8	140.2	137.2
2	163.2	135.3	132.4
3	113.2	85.3	84.4
4	119.8	77.9	79.9

the actual net output rates achieved by the system closely approached the targets of a perfect, optimal plan[5] compiled as a control by the omniscient experimenter. This occurred despite the fact that the original plan gave net output targets of neither the right level nor the right proportions.

This experimental run and many others like it demonstrated that the communications system and behavioral specifications of the model were adequate to bring about mutual polycentric adjustment to equilibrium production levels even under conditions where those levels were not adequately defined by the central plan.

It is natural to wonder just which of the many assumptions and structures built into the model are the really crucial ones in giving the system its self-steering capabilities. In answer to this, the results of other simulation runs draw attention clearly to the interplay of the priority and procurement pressure mechanisms. The vital role played by each of these is revealed rather dramatically by a simple experiment.

In the first part of this experiment, all parameters and inputs to the program were set exactly as for the experiment of fig. 2, with the single exception that the priority ratings were artificially fixed at the neutral

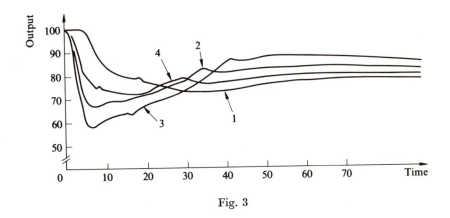

Fig. 3

Table 2. *Comparison of desired and actual net outputs*
for the experiment shown in fig. 3

Sector	Desired net outputs	Actual net outputs after 90 periods
1	140.2	120.3
2	135.3	129.7
3	85.3	92.6
4	77.9	91.8

value, thus entirely depriving the center of any mechanism for influencing the behavior of the system during the course of plan execution. Fig. 3 and table 2 give the results of a run under such conditions. The competing procurement pressures of the enterprises still steer the system to an equilibrium set of net output rates. (Indeed, fig. 3 indicates the approach to equilibrium to be even more rapid than before.) However, the net output proportions of the new equilibrium no longer correspond so closely as before to the desires of the political authorities.

This is visible directly from table 2, but it can be seen even more clearly by calculating for both experiments the relative deviation of the actual output proportions from those desired by the planners.[6] The experiment of fig. 1 showed only a 12 % deviation from planned proportions, but when the priority pressure mechanism was disabled, although the overall volume of output showed no decline the deviation from planned proportions increased to 32 %, indicating a much less satisfactory performance from the point of view of the central authorities.

The second half of our diagnostic experiment was performed by

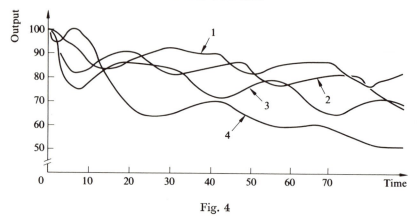

Fig. 4

restoring the priority pressure mechanism to normal operation, and disabling the procurement pressure mechanism instead.

The results of a run under these conditions are shown in fig. 4, which contrasts sharply with figs. 2 and 3. As is clear from the figure, the ability to converge to equilibrium has been lost. When the run is extended a few more intervals, complete collapse to zero output is the eventual result. During the process of decline, the center makes every effort to maintain desired output proportions. It aids lagging sectors and penalizes leading ones by adjusting their priority ratings. This keeps the net output rates on paths which fluctuate only narrowly about their desired proportions, as evidenced by the fact that after ninety periods of this run, output proportions showed only a 10 % deviation from preferences. However, since the center has no information on the relative scarcities of inputs from the point of view of the enterprise, its help to a lagging sector can take the form only of an across-the-board proportional increase of all inputs. In fact, the lagging sector is usually held up only by a single bottleneck, so that the additional supplies of non-bottleneck goods sent by the supply system are wasted at the receiving enterprise and diverted from another where they may be needed. This wastage causes inventories to decline and sets off the downward spiral observed in the figure.

Before leaving the subject of disabled pressure mechanisms, one curious extreme case deserves mention, since, with a little stretch of the imagination, it can be given a theoretically meaningful interpretation. This is a case in which neither pressure mechanism is needed to achieve equilibrium. Suppose that the procurement pressure mechanism is entirely disabled, but that the central plan is precisely optimal and balanced. Normally, with the procurement mechanism active, introduction of even a perfect plan at $t = 0$ still results in some small output fluctuations about a horizontal trend before equilibrium is reached, since the initial reaction of each firm is to employ just a little pressure to slightly overfulfill its share of the plan. Without the priority mechanism, however, a perfect plan gets executed without the slightest deviation – the graphs of all outputs are straight and horizontal, and the priority pressure mechanism, even if not deactivated, is never brought into use.

If our model with both pressure mechanisms absent is interpreted as representing a strict command economy model, this experiment would seem to indicate that such an economy can function if, but only if, it is able to generate flawless plans. In the more complicated conditions of the real world, however, it is likely that the ability to generate perfect plans comes closer to being a necessary than a sufficient condition for the functioning of a command system.

A SUMMARY AND SOME COMPARISONS

Alfred Marshall once wrote that

in spite of a great variety in detail, nearly all the chief problems of economies agree in that they have a kernel of the same kind. This kernel is an inquiry as to the balancing of two opposed classes of motives, the one consisting of desires to acquire new goods and thus satisfy wants, while the other consists of desires to avoid certain effects or retain certain immediate enjoyments... in other words, it is an inquiry into the balancing of demand and supply.

The validity of this generalization is supported by the interpretation of the Soviet economic system presented here. The basic homeostatic properties of our model, like those of a market economy, arise from the impact of forces of supply and demand on productive decisions, with crucial differences between the two systems lying in the institutional forms in which these forces are expressed. In the Soviet-type system, 'demand' is expressed via the mechanisms of plan and priority, rather than via the market, while 'supply' functions, reflecting the willingness of managers to produce given their expectations concerning the benefits of production, are more strongly influenced by psychological and political factors, and less closely related to technological and monetary considerations than in the market system.

Despite their unorthodox institutional nature, the equilibrating forces of supply and demand enable our model to achieve a rather high degree of efficiency, relative to an internally defined standard, when all of its features are permitted to operate. However, it would be very misleading to interpret the experimental results reported in this paper as suggesting that the efficiency of such a system might compare favorably to that of a market economy when measured by standards applicable in the real world. True, the forces of pseudo-demand and pseudo-supply have a general tendency in the Soviet-type polycentric system to push scarce resources in the direction of those users who cry out the loudest for them, much as one might expect the hungriest pig to fight most vigorously and thus obtain an ear of corn thrown into a pigpen. This does prevent certain gross and flagrant forms of waste. But the homeostatic mechanisms of this system completely lack the precision of those which operate in a market system. In particular, although the Soviet manager is led to operate at a point where 'marginal cost' equals 'marginal benefit', it is not possible to discern in this any invisible hand aligning the manager's interest with those of other participants in the system. The marginal cost with which the manager is concerned has nothing to do with the marginal opportunity cost to the economy of the inputs used up in production – it simply represents the risk and inconvenience which the manager must incur in order to procure them. Likewise, the marginal benefit of production to the manager is in no way equated to the marginal benefit of the product to its ultimate consumers, but rather reflects the manager's subjective tradeoff between the value of current bonuses and the value of maintaining a safety factor.

If the structure of the real world were as simple as that of our model – with fixed-proportions production functions, fixed technology and factor supplies, and a simple, explicitly expressed social welfare function – then the inability of the Soviet-type system to find tune resource allocation might be relatively unimportant. But as things are, its efficiency relative to a market system would seem to be rather low. This is why many economists intimately acquainted with the operation of such economies are searching for a 'New Economic Model' which would move the system away from the crude type of polycentricity described in this paper toward the more rational polycentricity of some sort of market socialism.

APPENDIX

This appendix gives a brief summary of the key behavioral equations of the model, as a supplement to the verbal description given above in the first section of the paper. Throughout the appendix, numbers in parentheses refer to the schema of fig. 1.

The supply system

The supply system decision-maker with whom we are concerned is one whose function it is to control the rate of shipment of a given commodity from the central stock, and to divide this quantity among the various users who want it. His activities are broken down into two separate steps: first a decision is made regulating the over-all rate at which goods are released for use from the hypothetical central stock. This can be represented as

$$S_i = (\Sigma_j B_{ij} P_j p_{ij}) \, I_i / D_i, \qquad\qquad [1]$$

where S_i is the total rate of shipment of the ith good (sum of the flows in (2));

$\quad\;\; B_{ij}$ is the backlog of unfilled orders for the ith good for shipment to user j;

$\quad\;\; P_j$ is an index of the priority attached to the jth sector by the central planners (6);

136

P_{ij} is the amount of pressure exerted by the jth user for procurement of the ith good (7);

I_i is the current central inventory of the ith good; and

D_i is a stock/flow conversion constant.

The priority and procurement pressure variables take on values from slightly less to slightly greater than 1.0. The multiplicative form indicates full substitutibility between these two factors, although a case could be made that this is not always realistic, especially in extreme instances.

The total supply of the product released for distribution is divided among users in proportions corresponding to the volume of unfilled orders weighted by the sectoral priority and the urgency with which the good is demanded, as measured by procurement efforts expended:

$$G_{ij} - S_i(B_{ij}P_j p_{ij}) \Big/ \sum_{k=1}^{n} B_{ik}P_k p_{ik}, \qquad [2]$$

where G_{ij} is the shipment rate of the ith good to the jth user (the flows in (2) broken down by sector of destination; and S_i, B_{ij}, P_j, and p_{ij} are as in equation [1]).

Central planners

Central plans are formulated exogenously, and injected into the system in the form of an output target X_i^* and a sector of input quotas $(x_{i1}^*, ..., x_{in}^*)$ for each sector i, both expressed in flow dimensions.

The priority pressure variables P_j are determined endogenously, in accordance with current economic performance and the planners' objective function. The latter was given the simple form

$$U = \min[y_1/f_1(W), ..., yn/fn(W)], \qquad [3]$$

where U is an index of 'planners' welfare', i.e., a reflection of the preferences of the individuals wielding state power;

y_i is net output of the ith good;

f_i is a function giving the desired proportion of output for the ith good;

W is a weighted sum of the y_is (e.g. GNP at constant prices).

This functional form implies that state authorities want to maximize a fixed-proportions bundle of net outputs, although the desired proportions may vary with the size of the whole. Use of this simple objective function makes it possible to set the priority ratings according to the following procedure:
(1) At the end of each of the short intervals by which time moves during a simulated planning 'year', the central planners compute the net output of each commodity to date. Let us denote these accumulated deliveries, expressed as annual rates, as $\bar{Y} = (\bar{y}_1, ..., \bar{y}_n)$, and their sum as $\overline{W}$. (2) The planners next calculate the desired levels of outputs corresponding to the total level of economic activity as measured by $\overline{W}$. Denote these as $Y^* = (y_1^*, ..., y_n^*) = [\overline{W}f_1(\overline{W}, ..., Wf_n(\overline{W})]$. (3) Priority ratings for the next short interval are then assigned according to the formula

$$P_i^{t+1} = P_i^t(y_i^*/\bar{y}_i)^k, \qquad [4]$$

where P_i^t is the priority ratings in the previous interval for the ith sector, and k is a constant.

(As might be expected, experiments showed the stability of the system to be sensitive to the value chosen for the parameter k. If it was set too high, the system tended to succumb to explosive cycling, while if it was set too low, the ability of the planners to control the process of plan execution was impaired. There was, however, a rather broad

137

middle range of values where both of these problems were avoided, and the parameter was set within this range for the experiments reported later in this paper. Setting k to lie within this safe range, in fact, amounts simply to giving the benefit of the doubt to the intuitive ability of the planners to avoid over- or under-reaction in priority setting.)

Enterprise management

Enterprise managers adjust their behavior to that of the supply system and the central planners. To determine output and procurement policy, the managers must be able to calculate the amount of pressure necessary for the given firm to obtain a given quantity of a needed input.

Solving equation [2] for p_{ij}, we get

$$P_{ij} = g_{ij}(G_{ij}) = G_{ij}Q_{ij}/B_{ij}P_j(S_i - G_{ij}) \qquad [5]$$

in which

$$Q_{ij} = \sum_{k=1} B_{ik}P_k p_{ik};$$

and $g_{ij}(G_{ij})$ is a shorthand notation giving the amount of pressure necessary to obtain G_{ij} units of the ith good for the jth user, other things equal.

Little can be said with confidence about the shape of the benefit function except that it increases up to at least the level of the output target, and, because of the ratchet effect, then increases less rapidly and eventually declines. The simplest function having these characteristics is a quadratic. In the model itself, the corresponding marginal function appears:

$$r'(X) = a - b\frac{X}{X^*}, \qquad [6]$$

where a and b are constants, $a \geqslant b$; X is gross output; and X^* is the gross output target.

The assumptions leading to the choice of a form for the cost function are, if anything, even more arbitrary than those for the benefit function. Neglecting monetary costs, we may concentrate on the cost factors involved in the exertion of procurement pressure by the enterprise. We begin by assuming that the cost of maintaining the pressure index p_{ij} at the neutral level of 1.0 is zero. This means that if everything goes according to the plan, the manager may sit back and relax while supplies roll in at just the right rate without his taking any special action. In addition, we assume that the procurement pressure process is irreversible, that is, values of p_{ij} less than 1.0 are not permitted. This is not only realistic, but necessary to avoid the absurd results obtained in some early simulation experiments where managers tended to maximize their payoffs by shutting down production and selling all inputs back to suppliers. It follows from these assumptions that there is an unassisted rate of input receipt, call it $\overline{G}_{ij}$, which represents the amount of the ith product received by the jth firm when it engages in no procurement activities on its own behalf. This unassisted input rate, determined by solving equation [2] with $p_{ij} = 1.0$, provides a reference point for further analysis of the cost function. Notice, incidentally, that this unassisted rate is not necessarily the planned rate, although it would be in the case of a perfectly balanced plan being smoothly executed.

Now the total cost function for the enterprise can be written as

$$c(X_j) = \sum_i h[g_{ij}(a_{ij}X_j - \overline{G}_{ij})], \qquad [7]$$

where X_{ij} is the gross output of the jth firm;
       a_{ij} is the input norm of the ith input to the jth firm;
       $\overline{G}_{ij}$ is the unassisted level of input receipt;

$g_{ij}(x)$ is from equation [5] and gives the amount of pressure needed by the jth firm to obtain x units of the ith good; and

$h(z)$ is a function giving the cost of exerting z units of procurement pressure.

The only element of this equation remaining to be specified is the cost-of-pressure function $h(z)$. This function is a proxy for all of the sacrifices which the manager must make to obtain scarce inputs. As mentioned earlier, these include such factors as the expenditures of money and *nariady* (purchase authorizations) through official channels, the real cost of black market purchases and of hiring a procurement staff, the judicious use of a limited budget of credibility and good will, the psychic costs of battling red tape and stubborn suppliers, the risk of criminal prosecution, and many more. It would be possible to come up with a story to justify virtually any shape for the function $h(z)$ (or of $h'(z)$, since that is the form in which the function enters the simulation program). Several possibilities were the subject of experiments including (1) step functions with constant, non-zero marginal cost per pressure unit above $p_{ij} = 1.0$, (2) a linear function with marginal cost increasing in proportion to pressure, and (3) marginal cost functions approaching a vertical asymptote somewhere above $p_{ij} = 1.0$. The formula most frequently used in experimentation was

$$h'(p_{ij}) = a(p_{ij} - 1)^2. \qquad [8]$$

This function is smooth and flexible, since by means of the parameter a it can be varied from almost flat to almost vertical without producing an actual kink at $p_{ij} = 1.0$. It represents a hypothesis somewhere between the proportional and asymptotic possibilities mentioned above.

In addition to the cost and benefit functions given above, the manager must keep one more factor in mind when choosing welfare maximizing levels for his intra- and extra-enterprise activities – the capacity of his capital equipment. This was treated as an absolute ceiling on output, and when it was encountered, the capacity output became the basis for determining input requirements. However, in order to observe the effects of other limitations on output, many experiments were run with the capacity constraint at such a high level that it never became binding.

NOTES

1 This paper is based on the author's PhD dissertation (Dolan, 1969). A related paper concerned with certain aspects of the historical development of the Soviet economy has appeared in *Yale Economic Essays* (Dolan, 1970). The author wishes to thank J. M. Montias, Raymond Powell, and Martin Weitzman for their constructive criticisms of the original dissertation, and to thank P. J. D. Wiles and P. C. Roberts for helpful comments on an earlier draft of this paper.

2 The work of Roberts (1969, 1971) and Powell (n.d.) most closely parallels the line of thought pursued in this paper. Ames, in Ames (1970) and in his paper 'The Marshallian Planned Econonomy' in this volume, has developed models incorporating a similar view of the interaction of planners' and managers' behavior. Weitzman (1971) and Manove (1971) have focused on the problem of how central planners should formulate their control strategy in the light of polycentric aspects of the system.

3 Those readers interested in such a detailed description are referred to Dolan (1969, 1970).

4 It should be mentioned that the final users themselves play no active role in determining resource allocation in our model. They are mere passive residual claimants to whatever part of gross material output is not used up as inputs to production. The

size of this residual is determined by the plans and priorities issued by the central authorities.

5 In the context of the model, an optimal plan means one which specifies outputs which maximize planners' preferences subject to the existing technology and resource constraints. Since all of these things have simple, well defined forms in the model, an optimal program can easily be calculated and used as a standard of comparison.

6 This calculation was not difficult since the model used a fixed-proportions type function to express the planners' preferences.

REFERENCES

Ames, Edward (1970). The structure of general equilibrium in a planned economy. *Jahrbuch der Wirtschaft Osteuropas*, Band 1.

Dolan, Edwin G. (1969). The role of non-price information in decentralization and control of resource-allocation decisions: the Soviet industrial supply system during the first Five Year Plan. Unpublished PhD dissertation. Yale University.

Dolan, Edwin G. (1970). The teleological period in Soviet Economic Planning. *Yale Economic Essays*, **10**, 3–41

Manove, Michael (1971). A model of Soviet-type economic planning. *American Economic Review*, **61**, 390–406.

Powell, Raymond (n.d.). Plan execution and the workability of Soviet Planning. Mimeographed.

Roberts, Paul Craig (1969). The polycentric Soviet economy. *Journal of Law and Economics*, **12** (1).

Roberts, Paul Craig (1971). *Alienation and the Soviet Economy*. Albuquerque: University of New Mexico Press.

Weitzman, Martin (1971). Material balances under uncertainty. *Quarterly Journal of Economics*, **85**, 262–82.

Financial Planning in the Soviet Economy

JOYCE E. PICKERSGILL

INTRODUCTION

It may seem incongruous to discuss monetary policy in a planned economic system where the emphasis of the planning process is placed on physical targets. Most studies on financial planning in the USSR have treated it as merely an adjunct of the physical plan designed to facilitate the achievement of output targets (Garvy, 1964; Hodgeman, 1960). It is nevertheless true that an economy in which goods and services are exchanged for money, and in which workers are paid in units of generalized purchasing power will have an implicit monetary policy, where monetary policy is defined as changes in the money supply. It is the thesis of this paper that the amount of money which an enterprise or individual holds will affect its behavior and thus the economic variables in any economy but one with totally centralized physical allocation of resources.

It is the purpose of this study to examine the process of financial planning and the achievement of financial balance in the Soviet economy, and to analyze the effects of changes in monetary variables on economic activity. This paper will examine the effects of these changes using a simplified model of a Soviet-type economy.

At least three conditions are required if changes in the quantity of money are to be regarded as important for the explanation of changes in other variables in the economy. (1) There must exist an operational definition of money over which the monetary authority has direct control; (2) the demand function for money must be stable; and (3) the demand and supply functions must be independent. If these conditions are satisfied, money holders will not be content to hold any arbitrary quantity of money which the monetary authorities make available, but will attempt to achieve an optimum quantity of cash balances through portfolio adjustments. These portfolio adjustments will, in turn, affect prices and real variables in the economy. In order to evaluate the applicability of these conditions to the Soviet economy, we must define the money stock and analyze the determinants of the supply of money and the demand for money.

Joyce Pickersgill

THE DETERMINANTS OF THE SUPPLY AND DEMAND FOR MONEY

Traditionally, money is said to fulfill certain functions. It is a generally accepted medium of exchange; it is a store of value; and it is a standard of value. Although only a few assets perform the first of the above functions, there are many that perform the second and can be converted into a medium of exchange at relatively low cost. Thus, one is faced not with a two-way classification of assets, but rather with a continuum of assets which meet these requirements in varying degrees. Therefore, in the absence of evidence on rates of substitution, arbitrary decisions must be made.

For the purpose of analyzing the effects of monetary policy, we will consider those assets which represent a store of generalized purchasing power and which are, or can be, quickly converted into a means of payment. This includes those assets which represent a claim on the goods and services produced in the Soviet economy, and which come under direct control of the authorities.

Studies of the money supply in the United States have traditionally included currency in circulation, demand deposits and occasionally time deposits and short term government securities. In the Soviet economy, it is more difficult to distinguish the set of assets which meets the criteria set forth above because of the strict limitations often in force on the use of the financial assets held in the firm and household sectors. Except for currency in circulation, the Soviet collection of assets has no exact counter-part in the United States. An acceptable definition might include currency in circulation, deposits of firms and collective farms and various smaller non-budgetary organizations in the State Bank and the savings deposits of private individuals. (For a discussion on the definition of the money stock see Powell, 1951; Pickersgill, 1966.)

In Western economies monetary authorities determine the level of high-powered money-currency outside banks plus bank reserves. Given the level of high-powered money, the total money supply depends on the desired currency deposit ratio, time deposit to deposit ratio and the desired reserve deposit ratio. In the Soviet Union, the primary source of the money supply, as defined above, is the State Bank which has control over the issue of currency and is the predominant supplier of credit. Garvy (1966, pp. 12–27, 122–36), in one of his works on banking, describes the banks' loan policy as following a real bills doctrine, thus tying the quantity of money supplied to the planned level of output and the share of working capital to be bank financed.

Once the bank makes a loan, it is entered into a firm's account. Transfers are made between the accounts of different firms as intermediary and final products are purchased and sold. Withdrawals in cash from a firm's deposit are used primarily for making wage and salary

142

payments. Thus the money economy can be divided up into two sectors. Firms and collective and state farms hold money in the form of deposits, and inter-enterprise transfers consist almost exclusively of transfers between deposit accounts. Private individuals hold their money either in accuracy or savings deposits, and transactions between individuals and between the firm and the individual take place in cash.

One might question the inclusion of savings deposits in the definition of the money stock on the grounds that savings deposits are less liquid than currency and are not a medium of exchange. Savings deposits are, however, the only alternative liquid financial assets available to the private citizen in the Soviet Union, and they do bear some resemblance to demand deposits in that rent and certain utilities may be paid directly from the savings account.

Let us assume that people desire to hold cash balances in order to distribute their purchases over time. There will be costs and benefits derived from holding cash, and the individual's demand for money may be analyzed as a problem in the theory of rational choice. Thus, the demand function will contain arguments that are similar to those of conventional demand analysis. Specifically, the variables to be considered as defining the desired nominal quantity of money are the cost of holding cash balances, wealth, and the price level. The cost of holding cash balances is represented by a real rate of interest which measures the opportunity cost of holding non-cash assets. If the expected rate of change of prices is not zero, there is a second cost of holding cash balances – their expected appreciation or depreciation due to the rate of decrease or increase in the price level. This cost must be added to the real earnings foregone, represented by 'the real interest rate'. The desired level of cash balances varies directly with the level of wealth since cash is a superior good, and thus has a positive income elasticity. Further if individuals expect the quality or variety of goods available to be improved in the future, this would have the same effect on the demand for money as the expectation of deflation.

All of these variables affect the demand function for money in a planned economy, but their relative importance may be significantly different. To consider the institutional framework of the Soviet Union in particular, it is useful to separate the demand functions of private individuals from those of firms and collective farms.

The consumer

The range of assets which the individual can hold is quite narrow. He is primarily limited to currency, savings deposits, and physical assets, since there is no private securities market, and the history of the sale of government securities suggests that in most cases they should be regarded as a form of taxation rather than as a possible non-cash asset. Since physical assets can be purchased solely for the individual's own consumption, the relevant interest rate is the implicit rate that measures the return in kind. Due to this institutional arrangement, measurable interest rates would be of relatively little importance in determining the portions of one's assets held in the form of cash balances, including both currency and savings deposits.

The cost of holding cash balances due to the rate of change of prices, however, has been significant. Phillip Cagan (1956) has shown in his work on hyperinflation in Russia during the 1920s that the rate of change of prices was certainly an important variable in determining the demand for cash balances. Additional work on the period of the first two five-year plans also indicates that price expectations are a determinant of the demand for money (Pickersgill, 1970).

An additional factor that affects the demand function for money in the Soviet Union is rationing. There are several effects of rationing on the demand for money. First, there is a welfare effect which results in a decrease in real income. Much work has been done on the welfare loss resulting from the introduction of rationing, and little need be said about it here (see Samuelson, 1947, pp. 163–71). Because rationing reduces real income, it will have a partial negative effect on the demand for cash balances.

Second, there is a substitution effect between rationed and unrationed commodities. Let us assume the existence of rationing by coupons or bare shelves rationing. The individual's demand for rationed goods will depend upon his income, the price of rationed goods and the price of non-rationed goods. The individual will also have a demand for un-rationed goods which is dependent upon the same arguments. If we consider money as an unrationed good, it is argued that the demand for money will increase in proportion with the number of goods that are rationed and the size of the rations (Tobin, 1952). Rationing will, in this instance, have a partial positive effect on the demand for real cash balances. One can also argue, however, that the existence of rationing reduces the services that money provides and thus results in a decrease in the demand for money (Turbio, 1968). An effective system of rationing will cause a discrepancy between desired and actual cash balances. This discrepancy grows as rationing continues or is extended, and inflationary pressures may build up to the point that controls break down. If, on the other hand, individuals believe that the rationing apparatus will be dismantled shortly, the services of money are restored and the demand for money will increase.

Rationing also effects the measurement of price changes and the construction of the price index used in measuring the demand for money. Ideally, one would like to choose a price index which reflected both the quantities and prices of rationed and unrationed goods. If, however, only one price index is available, it will show a bias. The amount of this bias will depend upon the quantities of goods in each category and the disparity between official prices and black market prices.

The final effect of rationing is the uncertainty of the time pattern of the availability of goods. This will result in uncertainty in the time pattern of desired expenditures, inducing an increase in the desired level of cash balances.

The enterprise

One would expect these same factors to affect the enterprise's demand for money, but the influences are more difficult to analyze than those affecting private individuals because of the presence of additional institutional constraints. The enterprise cannot freely determine its mix of cash, materials, capital, and labor since this is determined to a large extent by the plan. The enterprise does not have free access to its bank deposits, and the amount of currency which it may hold is limited. This does not imply, however, that the manager of the enterprise has no decision-making power. Due to the nature of the institutional arrangement of control over the enterprise, it has been possible for it to convert a portion of its demand deposits into currency for the purchase of labor. Because of the less stringent controls over the use of currency relative to demand deposits, it has attempted to make this conversion. It has also attempted to increase its stock of raw materials and inventory at the expense of its deposits in the State Bank. Thus, given the constraints on the enterprise, it has tended to adjust its portfolio of holdings in those areas where physical and monetary controls have been most slack.

If this is the case one would expect to observe the enterprise using extra-legal means to adjust its holding of money balances and real stocks. The rate of return on this action, however, can be expected to vary considerably over time depending upon the degree of planner control and the penalty for discovery.

THE DETERMINANTS OF FINANCIAL EQUILIBRIUM

Having briefly described the determinants of the supply and demand for money in the Soviet Union, we will now turn to the problem of achieving financial equilibrium. In order to examine the process of achieving financial equilibrium and the consequences of financial disequilibrium it is necessary to set up a simplified model of the workings of the Soviet economy. Certainly many aspects of Soviet financial institutions have undergone substantial change over time, although it can be argued that the broad outlines of the system have remained fairly constant. The remarks which follow are an attempt to outline the essential conditions of financial balance and the consequences of imbalance in a centrally planned economy rather than an attempt to completely describe the financial institutions of the USSR at any particular moment of time.

Let us begin our examination of the role of financial assets in Soviet economic activity by first assuming that all of the interactions of the various sectors of the economy are planned as illustrated in the accompanying input–output table (table 1).

The following assumptions will be made concerning the institutional framework within which the plan is carried out.

(1) The production and distribution by sector of all intermediate and final products are determined by the planners.

(2) The prices of all intermediate and final products are set by the planners.

(3) Firms exchange cash balances for primary inputs and intermediate products and they receive revenue for all products sold. All receipts and expenditures take the form of changes in enterprise deposits at the State Bank.

(4) Households are free to determine their employment and receive income in the form of wages, which they may use to purchase the consumer goods made available to them by the planners.

In equilibrium all markets must clear. Enterprises must have an adequate supply of cash balances to purchase all planned inputs at planned prices. Households must have an adequate income to purchase the available supply of consumer goods at planned prices. Desired and actual holdings of cash balances must be the same. Let us examine the meaning of financial equilibrium in the enterprise and household sectors.

The enterprise sector

The equilibrium condition for the enterprise can be stated as follows:

$$TR = \epsilon P_I Q_I + \epsilon P_p Q_p + wL + \bar{\pi} + T + \Delta M_D,$$

where

$P_I Q_I$ = planned payment for intermediate goods

$P_p Q_p$ = planned payment for primary goods

w = wage rate

L = quantity of labor

$\bar{\pi}$ = planned level of profits to be distributed in the form of bonuses

T = planned tax payments

M_D = desired holdings of cash balances.

146

Table 1. *Soviet inputs and outputs (billions of rubles)*

Inputs	Outputs							
	Agriculture	Textiles	Machine tools	Investment	Military	Collective consumption	Individual consumption	Total
Agriculture	5	10	0	15	10	10	50	100
Textiles	5	0	0	0	10	5	30	50
Machine tools	25	15	50	20	30	0	10	150
Wages of labor	50	20	70	10	5	5	15	175
Profits on capital	15	5	30	—	—	—	—	50
Taxes	—	—	—	—	—	—	70	70
Total	100	50	150	45	55	20	175	595

Leaving aside the problem of financing long term investments, to achieve financial equilibrium, the enterprise requires sufficient cash balances to meet its obligations, which include payments for raw materials, intermediate products, wages, planned profits, and to add to or subtract from its cash holdings, at the desired rate. Over the plan period total revenue from the sale of its product will be set to just cover the enterprise's planned expenditures. Since revenues and expenditures will not be perfectly synchronized, it will be necessary for the State Bank to make short term loans to the enterprise to finance work in progress. A crucial question for the determination of the average cash holdings of the enterprise and thus for financial balance is the amount and duration of the credit extended by the State Bank.

Consider the case of the machine tool industry, which, over the plan period, will receive R150 in revenue. Let us suppose for convenience, that this revenue will be received on the last day of the planning period but that it must make payments equal to R150 over the course of the plan period. One possible credit plan would be for the Bank to loan the industry R150 at the beginning of the planning period, which it would then pay back at the end of the period.

This procedure would result in the enterprise holding an average cash balance of R75 over the course of the plan period (see fig. 1). More frequent extensions of loans for shorter periods would reduce the average cash balances of the enterprise. What is the optimum credit plan? Surely, the larger the loan, the higher the average level of cash balances and the smaller the transaction costs of the lending process. What are the disadvantages of this type of credit plan?

If the enterprise had an infinitely elastic demand for money, with respect to the planned level of output, the optimum credit plan would be to grant all necessary credit at the beginning of the plan period. If this is not the case the enterprise may attempt to reduce its holdings of cash in order to achieve its desired holdings of cash and non-cash assets. This behavior may result in unplanned activity. The enterprise may attempt to increase its use of labor by converting deposits into currency. If all enterprises attempt to do this, it will result in an increase in the wage bill, as the wages are bid up through extra-legal means such as job reclassification. The enterprise may then find it necessary to apply for additional credit to enable it to purchase planned inputs other than labor.

Financial equilibrium in the enterprise sector requires that the enterprise's desired holdings of cash balances be equal to its actual holdings of cash balances. The consequences of financial disequilibrium may result in unplanned activity if the enterprise's expenditures are not closely monitored.

Another possible source of financial disequilibrium in the enterprise sector is the application for credit based on expected over fulfillment of

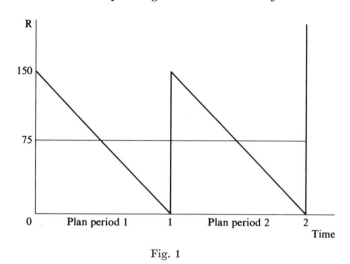

Fig. 1

the targeted level of output. Suppose the enterprise applies for credit in order to hire additional workers to produce a total output in excess of R150. Additional cash will be created which will flow into the consumer sector in the form of wages. Adequate revenues will be generated to repay the loan if

$$dLw \leqslant MPP_L \cdot P_m,$$

where

L = quantity of labor

w = wage rate

P_m = price of machine tools.

If the value of the marginal product of labor is less than the additional wage bill the enterprise will not be able to repay completely its loan. Regardless of the repayment ability of the enterprise, this process has resulted in the creation of new money, now in the hands of the household sector. This occurrence may result in excess cash balances in the consumer sector. Let us now turn to the question of achieving financial equilibrium in the consumer sector.

The consumer sector

We have outlined the rationale for the household's demand for cash balances in the second section. We can examine the conditions for equilibrium in the consumer sector using the Patinkin analysis of an exchange economy in which the size and composition of real output is determined outside of the household sector (Patinkin, 1965, pp. 403–39). It is assumed in our model that individuals start out each period with a zero stock of consumer goods, so no distinction is made between the

149

individual's total demand for the jth commodity and his excess demand for the jth commodity.

The consumer in the Soviet economy holds two types of goods – money and commodities. Additions to or subtractions from savings are identical with increases or decreases in cash balances. Financial equilibrium in the consumer sector implies that households are just willing to purchase the existing supply of consumer goods at the existing set of prices, where prices include a turnover tax.

$$P_c C = W - T_p - S,$$

where

P_c = price of consumer goods including the turnover tax

C = quantity of real consumer goods

W = the wage bill

T_p = personal taxes

S = savings.

Equilibrium implies that households are adding to or subtracting from their holdings of cash at the desired rate. What determines the individual's demand for cash balances or conversely, his demand for commodities? Each individual starts with a given income, in the form of wages, and holdings of cash. Given prices he will allocate his income among the available goods in such a way as to maximize his satisfaction. We can specify the ath individual's demand function for the jth commodity for a given time period as follows, where $n-1$ goods represent commodities, and the nth good is money.

$$Z_j^a = F_j^a \left(\frac{P_1}{P}, \ldots, \frac{P_{n-1}}{P}; \frac{P_n \Sigma_n^a}{P} + \frac{\overline{w}^a}{P}; \dot{p}^e \right),$$

where

$P_1, \ldots, P_{n-1}$ are the prices of commodities

P_n is the price of money

P is the general price level $= \sum_{j=1}^{n-1} W_j P_j$, where the Ws are a set of price weights

$\overline{Z}_n^a$ is the initial quantity of cash held by individual a

$\overline{W}^a$ is individual a's income

$\dot{p}^e$ is the expected rate of change of prices.

The demand for any commodity for a given time period depends upon relative prices, cash balances, the expected rate of change of prices and real income, which may best be represented by some concept of permanent or expected income rather than current income.

Individual a's demand for money balances may be expressed as follows:

$$Z_n^a = F_n^a\left(P_1, ..., P_{n-1}, P; \frac{P_n \bar{Z}_n^a}{P} + \frac{\bar{W}^a}{P}; \dot{p}^e\right),$$

where the individual's demand for money depends upon the prices of commodities, the general price level, cash balances, and his real income and the expected rate of change of prices.

Assuming that the marginal propensity to save out of wealth on any good is always the same for all individuals, we can sum the individual demand functions to obtain the market demand functions, which depend upon the same variables as the individual demand functions.

In equilibrium the demand for all commodities must be equal to the supply made available by the planners, and individuals must be adding to their cash balances at the desired rate. By setting the demand function for each good equal to the available supply we can solve for an equilibrium set of prices, given the wage bill. (For an analysis of the solution for equilibrium prices see Patinkin, 1965, pp. 427–8.)

This analysis assumes that at the equilibrium set of prices the real wage is sufficient for adequate supplies of labor to produce the planned supplies of consumer goods. In the event that this is not true financial equilibrium in the enterprise sector may not be compatible with financial equilibrium in the consumer sector.

THE CONSEQUENCES OF FINANCIAL DISEQUILIBRIUM

Let us assume that we are starting from a position of financial equilibrium in the enterprise and the household sectors. What will be the effect of a movement away from equilibrium, and what mechanisms if any, exist in the Soviet context to restore equilibrium? Suppose that there is an increase in the money stock as a result of the extension of bank credit for wage payments. The quantity of money supplied will now be greater than the quantity demanded, implying that there is an excess demand for commodities. Inflationary pressures will develop. The consequences of these inflationary pressures will depend upon the degree of control over output and prices maintained by the planners. If all real variables and the price level are completely determined, there exists no mechanism to restore equilibrium. The consumer and the enterprise, facing infinite prices for goods and services above the planned allocation, can only add to their cash balances when their money receipts are greater than desired. The implication of this model is that cash balances will increase indefinitely with no effect on the economic variables in the system.

If the quantity of money supplied is less than the quantity demanded, some goods will remain unpurchased, given constant quoted prices, and the planned level of consumption or investment, or both, will not be achieved.

Recalling the demand function for money described above, where the demand is a function of wealth, the price level, and the expected rate of change of prices, one would observe the level of real balances (M/P) held by the individual to vary significantly over time. Measuring velocity as Y/M, the ratio of money income or output to the nominal quantity of money, one would observe it to fluctuate over time. As the supply of money increased or decreased, average balances would increase or decrease. Since price levels and output are determined by the planners and can be considered constant for a planning period, velocity would fall in the first instance and rise in the second.

Since the measurable factors which determine the demand function for money are constant, one might infer from the movement in velocity either an unstable demand function, a demand function not independent of the supply function, some combination of both of the above, or a continuing state of disequilibrium in which the individual is constantly trying to restore his equilibrium level of cash balances. If the latter is the case, and the individual is unwilling to hold any arbitrary amount of cash, one would look for extra-legal methods of adjustment, such as the black market, or for informal methods by the government to alter prices.

Now let us change our previous set of assumptions about the institutional framework by introducing individual decision-making and analyze the results of doing so on our analyses of the consequences of financial disequilibrium. Let us alter our previous assumptions by assuming that prices in at least one sector of the economy are flexible.

Starting from a position of financial equilibrium what will be the effect of a movement away from equilibrium, and what mechanisms exist to restore equilibrium under the assumptions of limited price flexibility? If the quantity of money supplied is greater than the quantity demanded, inflationary pressures may now take the form of increased prices or wages or some combination of the two. An increase in money wages which is accompanied by an equiproportional increase in the weighted average of prices will have no effect on the real wage rate, and thus no effect on the quantity of labor supplied. This is unlikely, however, to be the case.

Assuming the inflationary pressures develop only in the sector with flexible prices, what devices can the planners use to restore financial equilibrium without an upward adjustment of the level of fixed prices?

According to Professor Franklyn Holzman (1955, pp. 29–44), inflationary pressure can be divided into two categories, anticipated and unanticipated. If all inflationary pressure was anticipated, the problem of controlling it would be relatively simple. The goal would be to mop up the excess purchasing power of the consumers and firms through taxation. The tax problem becomes more difficult when there are unanticipated inflationary pressures which could result from a shift in the demand function for money or unplanned loan extensions to enterprises. If one could not estimate correctly the desired level of cash balances, it would be impossible for the planners to determine the equilibrium quantity of taxes, and they would have to remedy the situation ex-post.

Another possible remedy for a disequilibrium quantity of money and rate of taxation would be to impose rationing. Instead of letting prices rise to allocate scarce goods among consumers and firms it would be possible to introduce a formal rationing device. If the effect of rationing is to reduce the monetary properties of cash balances, one would expect to find a growing disparity between desired and actual cash balances.

Examining the effect of rationing more closely, as a larger share of total output is rationed, the second model is transformed into the first where all real variables are determined by the planners and all prices are fixed so that an increase in the quantity of money can result only in an increase in the level of cash balances. One would again expect black market methods to appear if rationing were the only adjustment mechanism employed. In fact, in the Soviet Union there is a legalized free market in the form of the collective farm market, where agricultural commodities are sold at free market prices. During the first and second five-year plans, the collective farm market was supplemented by state-owned commercial shops which sold goods at prices substantially higher than those in state and cooperative stores where both cash and ration tickets were necessary to purchase any item. These markets served as an equilibrating mechanism, enabling individuals to alter their portfolio of holdings.

An alternative possibility for controlling inflationary pressures is a currency conversion, which is designed to restore financial equilibrium by reducing the supply of real cash balances. (For a discussion of the 1948 Soviet currency conversion see Ames, 1954; for a more general discussion of the effects of monetary reform see Pesek, 1958.) This solution may be desirable if the existence of large holdings of currency and savings deposits are resulting in a decreased work incentive. To be successful, however, the conversion must appear to be a once and for all measure that will not be repeated. If individuals come to expect currency conversions this will decrease the demand for money and further aggravate inflationary pressures.

We can use the framework we have developed for the analysis of monetary disequilibrium to examine the phenomenon of rising inventories of unsold consumer goods accompanied by the accumulation of savings deposits observed in the late 1950s and 1960s. (For a discussion of Soviet consumer behaviour in this period see Goldman, 1965.)

Since World War II we have observed rising real incomes in the Soviet Union accompanied by a slower rate of inflation. From our model we would expect that the demand for real cash balances would rise due to increasing real incomes and the lower cost of holding cash balances due to the lower rate of inflation.

Under the assumption of flexible wages and prices in a standard Western macroeconomic model, an increase in the demand for cash balances relative to the supply in the system as a whole will result in a decline in the price level, which satisfies the initial desire for increased money balances. When prices are rigid in a downward direction, however, the effect of an increase in the demand for cash balances may be increased inventories and unemployment.

There is no doubt that in the Soviet economy prices are not perfectly flexible. The accumulation of unsold goods may represent a case of the demand for money increasing faster than the supply. Furthermore, during this period there was much discussion of reforms of the Soviet economy which would increase efficiency and improve product quality. If consumers expect quality to increase in the future this is tantamount to the expectation of deflation and can be expected to increase the demand for cash balances.

CONCLUSION

An analysis of the determinants of monetary equilibrium can result in significant insights into the type and degree of inflationary controls effective in the Soviet economy. If one can assume that consumers and enterprises, within the institutional constraints of the system, are maximizing individuals and units, they will attempt to optimize their portfolio of holdings of cash and non-cash assets. This will result in observed changes of real cash balances which can be explained by changes in measurable variables. The observed demand function for money will be unstable the more inoperative are the adjustment mechanisms and the more completely physical controls are applied.

The existence of one market with flexible prices provides the mechanism by which the consumer and the firm can adjust its portfolio and obtain its equilibrium position. In this case, increases in the quantity of money will result in increased prices, all other factors constant, which may directly affect real variables in the economy. Due to the existence of at least one sector with flexible prices, changes in the level of real balances can be explained by changes in observed variables.

These conclusions are supported in empirical studies of the stability of the demand function for money in the Soviet Union over the period 1919 to 1937 (for 1921–6 see Cagan, 1956; for 1924–38 see Pickersgill, 1970). The results indicate a demand for money which is a stable function of certain measurable variables, namely, the expected level of real per capita income and the expected rate of change of prices. Rationing is also shown to be an important variable affecting the demand for real cash balances.

The empirical results demonstrate that individual households and enterprises will not passively hold any quantity of cash balances. Their attempts to obtain an equilibrium portfolio of cash and non-cash assets may have serious repercussions on the size and composition of output and on the level and structure of prices. The history of open and repressed inflation in the Soviet Union suggests that planners have not adequately considered the relationships between financial and real variables.

REFERENCES

Ames, Edward (1954). Soviet Bloc currency conversions. *American Economic Review*, **64**, 339–53.

Cagan, Phillip (1956). The monetary dynamics of hyperinflation. In *Studies in the Quantity Theory of Money*, ed. Milton Friedman, pp. 25–120. Chicago: University of Chicago Press.

Garvy, George (1964). The role of the State Bank in Soviet planning. In *Soviet Planning: Essays in Honor of N. Jasny*, ed. Jane Degras and Alec Nove, pp. 46–76. Oxford: Basil Blackwell.

Garvy, George (1966). *Money, Banking and Credit in Eastern Europe.* New York: Federal Reserve Bank of New York.

Goldman, Marshall (1965). The reluctant consumer and economic fluctuations in the Soviet Union. *Journal of Political Economy*, **73**, 366–80.

Hodgeman, Donald (1960). Soviet monetary controls through the banking system. In *Value and Plan*, ed. Gregory Grossman, pp. 105–24. Berkeley: University of California Press.

Holzman, Franklyn (1955). *Soviet Taxation.* Cambridge, Mass.: Harvard University Press.

Patinkin, Don (1965). *Money, Interest and Prices*, 2nd edition. NewYork: Harper & Row.

Pesek, Boris (1958). Monetary reforms and monetary equilibrium. *Journal of Political Economy*, **66**, 375–88.

Pickersgill, Joyce (1966). Soviet monetary policy and the demand for money, 1914–1938. Unpublished PhD dissertation. Seattle.

Pickersgill, Joyce (1970). A long run demand function for money in the Soviet economy. *Journal of Money, Banking and Credit*, **1**, February.

Powell, Raymond (1951). Soviet monetary policy. Unpublished PhD dissertation. Berkeley.

Samuelson, Paul (1947). *Foundations of Economic Analysis.* Cambridge, Mass.: Harvard University Press.

Tobin, James (1952). A survey of the theory of rationing. *Econometrica*, **20**, 521–53.

Turbio, Juan (1968). On the effects of repressed inflation. Paper presented at the Money and Banking Workshop, University of Chicago, April 1968.

2. Foreign Trade

A Model of Foreign Trade Planning in an East European-Type Economy

EDWARD A. HEWETT[1]

INTRODUCTION

In this paper I discuss a theoretical model of short-term planning in what I will call an East European-Type Economy (EETE). This is a centrally planned economy (CPE) highly dependent on foreign trade, and planned non-optimally using material balances.[2] The eventual goal, of which this paper is an intermediate product, is to produce a quantitative model which can be used to simulate foreign trade planning in an EETE.

Those familiar with East European planning may well find aspects of the model somewhat quixotic. The data needed to implement it are relatively incomplete, especially for an outsider. The 'behavior' underlying those data is attributable to a mysterious and amorphous group of men called central planners, about whom we know very little, and whose behavior often seems sprinkled with a capriciousness defying quantified functions. The East European economies have gone through reforms, revolutions and growth cycles of such magnitude that 'the' system is a moving target, a discouraging development given the difficulty of coping with similar problems for immobile targets.

Admitting to all of these difficulties, it still seems useful to persevere and attempt to build a model, since many questions about the EETE seem unanswerable without at least some simple, quantified, general equilibrium model of the EETE. It is important to know, for example, the nature of the East European economies' dependence on foreign trade, about which export/national income ratios are uninformative. It would be more useful to know the importance of foreign trade in supplementing the gross output of specific sectors, and the importance of such sectors to the economy. A model of the economy which would allow us to estimate the elasticity of national income with respect to imports in each sector, could bring us closer to understanding the contribution of the foreign sector to plan fulfillment.

Similarly, we know that national income moves cyclically in the Soviet and East European economies, and that these countries are tightly interlocked in the CEMA trade network.[3] Hence natural questions which arise are to what extent do EETE national income cycles and trends

156

affect foreign trade? While the possibility of an international transmission of growth-rate fluctuations is fairly obvious conceptually, a quantified model for specific EETEs might make it possible to derive more precise notions of the nature of such interdependencies.

Again, a third question concerns the determinants of the level and composition of trade among centrally planned economies. Here too an essential starting point is a foreign trade planning model. Though the question would then have to be considered by means of a bargaining model, this is an extension of the single-country models discussed below.

These are all reasonable inquiries of a sort which frequently appear in the literature on CPEs. If one were trying to answer these questions for a market-type economy, he would often proceed with a model. I see no justification for using a different approach for the EETE.

Most work on the Soviet and East European economies does indeed contain models. There are, for example, many *descriptive models* concerning regularities and irregularities observed in real Soviet and East European decision processes. Although these are invaluable sources of information on actual decision processes, they emphasize the complexity of details, hence are not well suited either to prediction or to studying basic quantitative properties of the systems.

A second approach involves the use of *optimization models*. These, whether or not quantified, yield single-valued solutions which the model-builder implicitly recommends to the planner (assuming they share the same objective function). Optimization models may prove useful as evaluators of planning behavior and even as guides to improved pricing and incentive systems in actual planning situations.[4] However, they carry little descriptive power, at least in the Soviet–East European situation, and can be safely ignored in a discussion concerning models of actual planning processes.

Between the poles of literary description and single-point optimization are *behavioral models* which seek to portray the essentials of planners' behavior through descriptions of the planning process posed in quantifiable form. This group includes the theoretical work on material balances planning by Montias (1959) and Manove (1971), and a simulation model of Soviet economic planning in the 1930s by Dolan (1970).[5]

The model discussed in this paper is proximate to the behavioral models. It seeks to capture the essence of EETE planning in a small set of equations, which, nevertheless, can be claimed to be an adequately accurate reflection of basic forces in real EETEs. Although much of the complexity of real planning decisions is not to be found in the model, this is an unavoidable cost one must pay for uncovering basic relationships. Obviously, this is also a high cost which cannot be ignored in evaluating usefulness and relevance.

Edward A. Hewett

A THEORETICAL MODEL OF FOREIGN TRADE PLANNING IN AN EETE

The EETE

When specialists on the CEMA countries have studied actual planning processes there, they have relied on the Soviet economy as their main source of institutional information. For the most part Eastern Europe has been neglected, the rationale being that East European economic systems faithfully copy the more important Soviet institutions. The result has been the terminological convention of interchangeability between the terms 'CEMA economies' and 'Soviet-type economies', a truly remarkable identity since there is no foreign sector in the STE model, yet there are large foreign sectors in every CEMA economy *except* for the Soviet economy! East European reality has never conformed with the STE model since planning problems in Eastern Europe are foreign trade planning problems by definition. Changes in East European economic institutions, the level and pattern of their foreign trade, their economic literature, and their most recent economic policies all leave no doubt that foreign trade is, and always was, *de facto* a critical factor in the outcome of all East European planning. Very few major decisions on production, consumption, or investment in this region can be separated from their foreign trade implications.

In brief, there are no Soviet-type economies in Eastern Europe, only Soviet-type institutions whose problems are unique to small countries with a large foreign sector. It is this combination of central planning, material balances (non-optimal) planning, and a high dependence on foreign trade which is the EETE prototype here.

What we require for an EETE is a model which describes planners' interactions with structural, stock, and flow constraints as they seek a feasible way to achieve their goals. It will be a foreign-trade planning model, thus emphasizing the importance of that process to the attainment of goals. The descriptions which are available of East European planning (Kornai, 1959, *passim*; Montias, 1962, ch. III; Pryor, 1963, chs. II–IV; Keren, 1971, pp. 220–331) indicate that the actual process by which planners integrate foreign trade into a plan is complex, probably inconsistent and partially unconscious. In turn, the problem of analytically portraying export and import decisions involves constructing a framework that would convert more or less simultaneous decisions, made either during a plan period or inherited from past plan periods, into identifiable sets of consecutive decisions. The goal of the following model will be to highlight such identification rather than to portray the actual course of the decision-making process faithfully. For simplicity, the model below will only concern the process of deriving annual plans for a single period.

Structure of the model

Among the basic features of EETE planning is that the government is assumed to present the planner with a set of annual goals for which he is to find a feasible plan. Next, the planner is assumed to be so constrained by the structure of his economy and the capacity to produce in each sector that the set of choices he can make in an attempt to achieve government goals is severely limited. Nethertheless, the planner does make choices within constraints, and behavioral equations need to be constructed to reflect the 'non-optimality' (to be defined later) of his decision procedure.

The goals. Assume that the government's quantitative goals are in the form of a desired vector of net output ($f*$).[6] This vector contains targets for consumption, investment and inventory changes. Exports are not included and are determined endogenously. In actual situations many more targets come to planners than just those on net output while, conversely, some net output targets may not be made explicit. Here it is assumed, however, that actual plan targets either specify or imply a complete set of net outputs (an $f*$ with all positions filled).

It is likely that compromises will be necessary in the course of the planning process between the government and planners on certain elements in $f*$. This will be allowed for in the model by having the government specify floors for certain components of $f*$ and trade-offs (relative prices) among all elements. How the planner goes about changing $f*$ within these constraints will be discussed below when we specify planners' behavior.

The constraints. The EETE planner is constrained in a number of ways. He has inherited a structure of the economy, to be designated here by a technology matrix A. No one in the planning hierarchy knows all of A; that is the motivation for using material balancing. We may presume that planners will, at times, try to decrease coefficients in A, but that they will encounter little success.

Another important set of constraints concerns capacity by sector, expressed as a ceiling on gross output (denoted here by the vector $\bar{x}$). Maximum gross output is a function of labor and capital constraints (or possibly 'land' constraints in the cases of some raw materials); only one of the two (three) constraints will, in the usual case, be binding. The elements of $\bar{x}$ are variable to a certain extent for a number of reasons.

1. In any sector where labor is constraining, it is probably easy to move labor into that sector from another sector, thus changing the distribution of elements within $\bar{x}$. Since the plans are being made in year t for year $t + 1$, the only constraints on this type of movement are the requirements

in the different trades and the retraining capacity available in the economy.

2. Capital stock is probably not all sector-specific; that is, some capital is malleable. This applies, for example, to transportation equipment, computing equipment, buildings, and some machinery. Also, there are probably multi-product firms that 'span' the rows of the input–output table. Those can be assumed to possess a concave set of production possibilities among which they can maneuver. Different sets of outputs will show up as different $\bar{\mathbf{x}}$s.

3. Additions to the stock of capital and labor are malleable. For additions to the stock of labor the point seems obvious; however, it needs justification for changes in the stock of capital. Most capital for $t+1$ will be in the pipeline in t and the question is how variable is the destination of the capital already in process?

(a) In the case of construction projects there probably is a good deal of variability. There are usually more construction projects going on in Eastern Europe at each point in time than can be justified by the capacity to produce structures. Therefore, it is a matter of choice which projects will be accorded relatively higher priorities and be finished relatively sooner. Each possible configuration of priorities implies a set of possible additions to $\bar{\mathbf{x}}$ reflecting different priorities.

(b) Additions to capital mentioned in point 2 contribute to variability in $\bar{\mathbf{x}}$.

4. Finally, there is the possibility of fast-recuperating investments in some sectors which creates another set of possibilities for varying potential capacities.

These considerations suggest that $\bar{\mathbf{x}}$ is a planners' variable and we can speak of the constraints on gross output in $t+1$ as a set $\bar{\mathbf{x}}$. Each vector in $\bar{\mathbf{x}}$ is a different possible configuration of capacity gross outputs using up available stocks of capital, land, and labor. The number of vectors in $\bar{\mathbf{x}}$ and the magnitudes of differences between the vectors are both empirical questions which can only be answered for specific economies.

Finally, there are constraints in the foreign sector. One very important constraint is in the form of the balance of trade, a target $(\bar{\pi})$ which is given to planners by the government. The initial $\bar{\pi}$ reflects foreign currency reserves, forecasted net loans, and government goals for reserves at the end of the period. At certain points in the planning process, it may be that either $\mathbf{f}^*$ or $\bar{\pi}$ must be changed in order to locate a feasible plan. Although it is true that in some cases the EETE can increase net short term loans and therefore maintain $\mathbf{f}^*$ by decreasing $\bar{\pi}$, it seems realistic to presume that the general case is the opposite. We will assume therefore that $\bar{\pi}$ is fixed.

Constraints on exports and imports of individual products, which arise from demand and supply circumstances in partner countries can be important, as they are for example, in intra-CEMA trade for 'hard-good' imports and 'soft-good' exports.[7] Specific constraints on commodity trade are necessary in any empirical version of the EETE model if it is to provide a realistic view of reality. However, they add little to the theoretical model (after $\bar{\pi}$ has restricted the feasible space, the export and import constraints are simply a further restriction) and will be left out of it in order to simplify the exposition.

The mechanics of iterations

Structural equations can be combined with constraints and targets to show how the planner iterates towards a solution, that is, to show the mechanics of his search for the feasible space.

The planners' problem is to solve the equation:

$$Ax + f^* + e = x + i \tag{1}$$

subject to:
$$x \leqslant \bar{x}, \quad x \in \overline{X}, \quad p_f(e-i) \geqslant \bar{\pi},$$

where
p_f = the vector of foreign trade prices

e = exports

i = imports

x = gross output

A = the technology matrix.

It is assumed he does not know all of the components of A, and that he will try to solve equation (1) by the technique called balancing. This is an algorithm for identifying and eliminating the surpluses and deficits implied by a certain set of net outputs. The planner who uses balancing first guesses at the solution to (1), then sends out gross output targets based on the guesses to all firms. Firms then send back their estimates of inputs necessary to fulfill those targets (which is equivalent to Ax) and the planner checks for disequilibria by drawing up balances of the following form:

$$\begin{array}{cccc} \text{supplies} & \text{demands} & \text{balances} \\ x+i & -Ax - f^* - e = & m, \end{array} \tag{2}$$

where m = material balances.

If there are negative elements in m then further iterations are necessary, i.e., the planning process is successfully completed when all elements in m are positive or zero.[8] How the planner behaves in choosing the first guess at x and all subsequent xs is the subject of the following section.

Although balancing is the core of the solution algorithm to the model, it is cumbersome to work with a model in the form of equations (1) and (2). It is easier to work with a reduced form which can be derived by making a few assumptions.

1. Planners tend to fix taut plans (given the **f***s they receive from the government) and we may assume that gross output targets in each iteration are equal to a capacity vector from $\overline{\mathbf{X}}$.

2. Net exports (or net imports) are the important variable in the model, so we can speak of the vector $\mathbf{e} - \mathbf{i}$ (or $\mathbf{i} - \mathbf{e}$).

3. Planners wish that each iteration were their last. Although an EETE planner may encounter negative elements in **m** at some iteration, that still could be the last iteration if, after negative elements are added to the import plan and positive elements added to the export plan, the balance of trade is satisfactory. Therefore, in depicting the planners' search for a balanced plan, **m** and $\mathbf{e} + \mathbf{i}$ need not be treated separately. Instead, we can add them together, making $\mathbf{e} - \mathbf{i}$ the foreign trade vector which *must* obtain for any given solution to the **f*** problem to be feasible.[9]

As a result of these assumptions, the planning equation becomes:

$$(\mathbf{I} - \mathbf{A})\,\overline{\mathbf{x}} - \mathbf{f}^* + (\mathbf{i} - \mathbf{e}) = 0 \tag{3}$$

subject to:
$$\mathbf{p}_f(\mathbf{e} - \mathbf{i}) \geqslant \overline{\pi}.$$

The test for feasibility reduces to a balance of trade test, emphasizing the importance of foreign trade to the planning problem. Non-feasible solutions, i.e., unattainable balances of trade, indicate that for a given $(\mathbf{f}^*, \overline{\mathbf{x}}, \mathbf{p}_f)$ combination, the planner would be forced to supplement domestic gross output capacity to a much greater extent than is possible, given the domestic export capacity, available stocks of foreign exchange and net loans.

As equation (3) shows, there are only three planners' variables in an EETE: $\overline{\mathbf{x}}$, $\mathbf{f}^*$, and $\mathbf{i} - \mathbf{e}$. Choosing elements of any two of those vectors automatically chooses the corresponding element of the third.[10] Thus, if the planner is given $\mathbf{f}^*$, he searches for feasible solutions by trying different $\overline{\mathbf{x}}$s and $(\mathbf{i} + \mathbf{e})$s. It doesn't matter whether we depict the choices he is making by stating that he chooses different vectors of gross outputs or different foreign trade vectors; $\overline{\mathbf{x}}$ and $\mathbf{i} - \mathbf{e}$ are two sides of the same function and, given $\mathbf{f}^*$, choosing $\overline{\mathbf{x}}$ implies $\mathbf{i} - \mathbf{e}$ and vice versa.

Behavior of the EETE planner

We now turn to the most difficult portion of the model: the specification of how the EETE planner behaves in this world we have constructed for him. The main assumption is, it will be remembered, that the planner uses balancing to search for a feasible solution to his $\mathbf{f}^*$ problem. The questions we must answer specifically are what criteria will he use for choosing his $\overline{\mathbf{x}}$s from **X** and will his balancing algorithm converge towards a feasible solution? It is useful in understanding the behavior of the EETE planner to review the behavior of his predecessor, the STE planner. Therefore, I discuss Montias' assumptions about planners behavior; modify his model to fit the more realistic assumptions of sector-specific gross output limitations; then compare that version of the model with EETE behavior.

There is no foreign sector in Montias' STE model; planners must use domestic gross output to achieve all goals. In the first iteration, planners guess a feasible solution and draw up material balances:

$$\mathbf{x}(1) - \mathbf{A}\mathbf{x}(1) - \mathbf{f}^* = \mathbf{m}(1). \qquad (4)$$

where the numbers in parentheses refer to the number of the iteration. Should a second iteration prove necessary (some elements in $\mathbf{m}$ are negative), the planners attempt a second guess on $\mathbf{x}$, sector by sector, taking the first guess in each sector and adding or subtracting the shortfall or over-run indicated by the material balance in that sector. They then construct balances on the basis of the new gross output vector:

$$\mathbf{x}(1) - \mathbf{m}(1) - \mathbf{A}[\mathbf{x}(1) - \mathbf{m}(1)] - \mathbf{f}^* = \mathbf{m}(2). \qquad (5)$$

The planners will continue the process until they locate a balanced plan. Montias has shown that the algorithm will converge towards the balanced plan (Montias, 1959, p. 968):

$$(I - A)^{-1}\mathbf{f}^* = x^*. \qquad (6)$$

The main features of the STE model are:

(a) There is only one possible solution to any $\mathbf{f}^*$ problem.

(b) Planners can find the solution using a very simple criterion: they derive targets at each iteration by taking the previous target and changing it by the surplus or deficit indicated by the last balance vector.

(c) Although the total supplies of labor do limit total gross outputs, there are no limits on gross output in specific sectors. Therefore, the feasibility of the $\mathbf{f}^*$ referred to in (a) turns only on total labor demands generated by the balanced plan associated with $\mathbf{f}^*$.[11]

The discussion below will show that points (a) and (b) do not apply in an EETE economy. However, before we can consider EETE behavior, we must discuss (c) which contradicts the EETE assumptions and, I believe, contradicts reality in both STEs and EETEs.

Because, in the STE model, there are no capacity limitations on any sector other than those internal to the input–output system, the implication is that iterations always fall either within, or on the border of $\overline{\mathbf{X}}$. One of two assumptions are possible to justify this interpretation. It could be that planners' initial gross output targets are all below firms' capacities to produce and that planners iterate towards full capacity while staying below it. Or, it may be that planners always send out full capacity targets, but in each industry any gross output is possible from zero to the amount which would just use up the total amount of labor available to the economy.

Neither assumption seems realistic. If planners send out **x**s dominated by some $\bar{\mathbf{x}}$, then they are consciously planning for unemployed capital and labor in one or more sectors. While this is certainly possible, it hardly is so widespread in real CPEs that it should be a systematic feature in a model of their behavior.[12] Presumably planners are moving around the boundaries of $\overline{\mathbf{X}}$ during Montias' iterations. However, they need give no thought to that since $\bar{\mathbf{x}}$ is always large enough to accommodate their gross output targets; the only constraint on $\overline{\mathbf{X}}$ is total labor force. This assumption can hardly bear scrutiny. The history of sectoral distributions of investments in the economy loses all relevance in the model; no *composition* of **f*** is unattainable (although certain levels may be, due to the labor constraint). If **f*** in period t is just the opposite in composition of **f*** in period $t-1$ planners simply 'unbolt' all the capital and special labor used in high demand sectors in $t-1$ and nimbly shift them to the sectors important to plans in t. No doubt central planners wish their economies were so agile; yet they certainly are not.

Although it is not realistic to pretend that iterations will never take the economy into non-feasible compositions of gross output, it may be that **f***s change very little from year to year, hence iterations can usually be expected to go on within the small amount of flexibility given by $\overline{\mathbf{X}}$. However, this is not specifically stated in Montias' version of the STE model and should be explicity clarified. I do not think a workable specification of the nature of the set $\overline{\mathbf{X}}$ can be avoided.

How does Montias' model change if we introduce the assumption used in the EETE model that there are constraints in every sector on the amount of gross output, and that the planners can change those capacities by some amount specified by the set $\overline{\mathbf{X}}$? Since there is no foreign trade in Montias' model, $\overline{\mathbf{X}}$ uniquely defines a set of feasible final demands:

$$\overline{\mathbf{F}} = (\mathbf{I} - \mathbf{A})\,\overline{\mathbf{X}}, \tag{7}$$

where $\overline{\mathbf{F}}$ is the set of maximum possible net output vectors.

When planners receive an **f*** in Monias' model, they have also 'received' a specific vector, call it **x***, which is the unique solution to the **f*** problem. Planners will use the equivalent of Montias' solution algorithm and they will begin to approach **x***. However, they may discover long before they arrive that further interations would require more gross output capacity than they can muster in at least one sector. In that case, their only means of achieving **f***, domestic gross output, is unavailable, and they will be forced to negotiate with the government for a new **f***. Since it is possible that **f*** will not be in $\overline{\mathbf{F}}$, it is possible that the need to change **f*** will arise. A full specification of Montias' model will require a sub-model explaining when and how planners sacrifice **f***. We will be considering that problem below for the EETE model and therefore will leave it aside for the moment.

Were the STE planner to consider foreign trade as a possible aid in finding a feasible plan, i.e., were he to take the EETE planners' approach, he would discover that (a) there is the possibility of a larger feasible set; and (b) it is much harder to 'iterate' into the feasible set from the non-feasible region when balancing is the solution algorithm.

The feasible set is now defined as:

$$\mathbf{F}' = g(\overline{\mathbf{X}}),\qquad(8)$$

where $\mathbf{F}'$ = all feasible final demand vectors attainable with foreign trade; defined as all non-zero final demand vectors such that

$$\mathbf{p}_f(\mathbf{e} - \mathbf{i}) \geqslant \overline{\pi}.^{13}$$

The size of $\mathbf{F}'$ is not directly related to the size of $\overline{\mathbf{X}}$ (as it is in the STE model). For each $\mathbf{x}$ there may be a large number of non-zero $\mathbf{f}$s which leave a satisfactory balance of trade; there may be only one such $\mathbf{f}$; and there may be none. It all depends on π and $\mathbf{p}_f$:

In the STE model, each $\mathbf{f}^*$ has one solution $\mathbf{x}^*$ (from equation (6)), which may or may not be feasible, depending on whether or not $\mathbf{x}^*$ is in $\overline{\mathbf{X}}$. Either of these cases could also hold for the EETE model. However, in addition, $\mathbf{f}^*$ could well be feasible for an entire set of $\overline{\mathbf{x}}$s (and assorted $\mathbf{i} - \mathbf{e}$ values). Thus foreign trade introduces the real possibility of a much larger feasible set. The question is whether the balancing algorithm common to the STE and EETE models is likely to lead the EETE planner into a feasible set.

Assume the EETE planner begins with a guess at $\overline{\mathbf{x}}$ and $\mathbf{e} - \mathbf{i}$. The guess for $\overline{\mathbf{x}}$ may, for example, be some mark-up on the previous period's capacities, with exceptions for sectors where unusually high or low changes in capacities are anticipated to meet net output targets for $t + 1$. Before the $\mathbf{e} - \mathbf{i}$ choice can be discussed it is necessary to introduce several concepts.

Data on East European trade indicate that for a typical EETE there are certain sectors which, year after year, do not produce sufficient gross output to meet the needs of the economy. Sectors such as these probably represent consciously designated, long-term import sectors. Investments and resources have not been provided in adequate amounts for import substitution purposes, probably because such decisions would be obviously irrational if not impossible.[14] Imports into these sectors are a predictable, annual phenomenon, and important enough as inputs that no reasonably high set of net outputs for all sectors is possible in their absence. In each import sector they will be large relative to gross output; they will be closely correlated (though not necessarily linearly) with national income. Thus it should be possible, emulating the planner, to estimate a functional relationship with national income, designating the trend value so derived as *hard-core imports* (which they are in a very real sense). Any serious planner, regardless of his predisposition towards foreign trade, will be forced from the very beginning of each planning cycle to accept an approximation of hard-core levels, and the exports necessary to pay for them, if he wishes to achieve full capacity output. In this model, hard-core imports are assumed to account for the major part of all imports in all iterations.

At each stage in the iterative process (including probably the final stage) there will also be a set of *residual imports* which represent (a) variations from the trend in hard-core import sectors, and (b) imports which occur for only one or two periods in a sector which is usually self sufficient. Residual imports arise in the normal course of affairs when there is an unforeseen change in capacity gross output in some sector (agriculture is the most important case), or when there is a dramatic change in the composition of **f***compared to the previous period. In certain sectors they may well become hard-core if they continue to arise year after year as a result of the confluence of the net outputs and gross outputs planners choose.

There are also *hard-core exports*. Although the EETE tends to export whatever it has, or can create, in surplus sufficient to pay for imports, certain industries do become annual producers of much of the export proceeds. The definition of hard-core exports is analogous to that for hard-core imports: (a) the exports are large relative to domestic gross output; (b) they occur annually; and (c) they tend to be closely correlated with national income. There are also *residual exports* which are: (a) fluctuations around the trend rate of hard-core exports and (b) exports for only a few years from a sector which usually does not participate in foreign trade. It is quite possible for residual exports to occur in the final solution year after year if hard-core trade is in deficit. The *sum* of residual exports may be as predictable a phenomenon as individual hard-core exports. However, if the specific products which arise each year to fill the need for a certain sum of residual exports differ from year to year, then to the model, as presumably to the planner, those individual exports should not be treated as predictable annual phenomena.

The concept of hard-core trade is obviously an empirical one. Its only real justification is if planners tend to be fairly sure that an identifiable set of traded commodities will, in the main, show up in the final solution.

Thus, for the first iteration the EETE planner chooses the $\bar{x}$ as described above and his initial estimate of $e - i$ as the balance, sector by sector, in hard-core trade. It makes common sense that he begins the iterative process already planning for a substantial amount of trade. Reading Western accounts of material balances planning, one receives the impression that imports and exports are practically random variables, a non-systematic, annual record of planners' failure to achieve autarky. The latter may be true, but the former is certainly false. No EETE planner is likely to begin year t with, for example, plans to wipe out all imports of iron ore, steel, petroleum, cotton, etc.[15]

Thus the first iteration, and the resulting material balances are:

$$\bar{\mathbf{x}}(1) + \mathbf{i}_h - \mathbf{A}\bar{\mathbf{x}}(1) - \mathbf{e}_h - \mathbf{f}^* = \mathbf{m}(1), \tag{9}$$

where $\mathbf{i}_h$ = hard-core imports, $\mathbf{e}_h$ = hard-core exports. The balance of trade implied by the first iteration is:

$$\mathbf{p}_f[\mathbf{e}_h - \mathbf{i}_h + \mathbf{m}(1)] = \pi(1), \tag{10}$$

where $\mathbf{m}(1)$ is residual trade implied by the first iteration.

If $\pi(1) < \bar{\pi}$, the planner is assumed to go through further iterations seeking to locate a feasible solution (find a satisfactory $\pi(\mathbf{i})$). If we assume that $\mathbf{i}_h - \mathbf{e}_h$ are firmly set positions in the material balances tables, equivalent to $\mathbf{f}^*$, we can assume that the EETE planner uses material balances as the STE planner does: to change production continually in search for a balanced plan. Thus, the second iteration is:

$$(\mathbf{I} - \mathbf{A})[\bar{\mathbf{x}}(1) - \mathbf{m}(1)] + (\mathbf{i}_h - \mathbf{e}_h) - \mathbf{f}^* = \mathbf{m}(2)$$

$$\mathbf{p}_f[\mathbf{e}_h - \mathbf{i}_h + \mathbf{m}(2)] = \pi(2), \tag{11}$$

where $\bar{\mathbf{x}}(1) - \mathbf{m}(1) = \bar{\mathbf{x}}(2)$.

Would such a process converge towards a feasible solution and, if so, at what rate? We will examine these questions first by introducing three rather unrealistic assumptions, then analyzing the effects of relaxing them one at a time.

Case 1. *Hard-core trade balanced at $\bar{\pi}$; composition of $\overline{\mathbf{X}}$ unconstrained; number of iterations unconstrained.* In this case the balancing algorithm will produce a set of $\bar{\mathbf{x}}$s which converge on feasible space, and the number of iterations required to arrive is probably less than, and certainly no more than, those required in the STE model.

To understand this, note that in assuming $\mathbf{i}_h - \mathbf{e}_h(\pi_h)$ fixed, we can add it to f^* to produce a new vector $\mathbf{f}^{**}$ $(= \mathbf{f}^* + \mathbf{i}_h - \mathbf{e}_h)$. Then the planners' iterations amount to seeking solutions to the equivalent of our equation (4) from Montias' model, namely:

$$\mathbf{x} - \mathbf{A}\mathbf{x} - \mathbf{f}^{**} = \mathbf{m} \tag{4'}$$

where $\mathbf{m}$ is now residual trade. Since we have assumed all $\mathbf{x}(i)$s are in $\overline{\mathbf{X}}$, Montias' theorem that the balancing algorithm converges to a balanced plan applies here with equal force.

At this point similarity with the STE model ends. Since for the EETE planners $\mathbf{m}$ is residual trade, whenever $\mathbf{p}_f\mathbf{m} \geq \bar{\pi}$, the iterative process can cease long before it has played itself out as it must in the STE model. Whether or not the EETE planners will enter feasible space during the iterative process depends mainly on the path of $\mathbf{m}$ during the process and the vector $\mathbf{p}_f$. Although these are primarily empirical properties, something can still be said at the theoretical level. While the vector of material balances will eventually converge towards zero, individual elements of $\mathbf{m}$ will change at different rates, particularly during the first few iterations. In fact, if the initial guess at $\bar{\mathbf{x}}$ exceeds the equilibrium

$$\bar{\mathbf{x}}^* \; [= (\mathbf{I} - \mathbf{A})^{-1}\mathbf{f}^{**}]$$

in at least one sector, some elements of $\mathbf{m}$ may oscillate about zero during the first few iterations before they settle down to steady convergence.[16] Thus, elements in $\mathbf{m}$ behave erratically, and so will the balance of residual trade. Depending on $\mathbf{p}_f$, the balance $\mathbf{p}_f\mathbf{m}$, could well exceed $\bar{\pi}$ at some iteration and stop the process. There is no way of telling where that will happen unless we know $\mathbf{p}_f$, $\mathbf{A}$, $\mathbf{f}^{**}$ and the initial guess at $\bar{\mathbf{x}}$. The last three determine the time path of $\mathbf{m}$ through the iterative process as $\mathbf{p}_f$ combines with $\mathbf{m}$. Different relative values in $\mathbf{p}_f$ could produce opposite movements in the balance of trade from one iteration to the next, depending on the relationship between elements in $\mathbf{p}_f$ and those in $\mathbf{m}$.

Case 2. Hard-core trade balanced below $\bar{\pi}$; composition of $\bar{\mathbf{X}}$ unconstrained; number of iterations unconstrained. We can now release the first of three restrictive assumptions, that being $\pi_h = \bar{\pi}$. We could assume that $\pi_h > \bar{\pi}$; however, that is the easy way out and our analysis of $\pi_h < \bar{\pi}$ will provide all the essentials for dealing with this problem.

If $\pi_h < \bar{\pi}$, it is probably a reflection of the fact that $\mathbf{p}_f\Delta\mathbf{i}_h > \mathbf{p}_f\Delta\mathbf{e}_h$, which, from what is known of EETE experience, seems realistic. East European planning systems seem prone to chronic balance of payment crises; trend values of import demand exceed the trend values reflected in developing export industries (see, e.g. Brown, 1968). We cannot be completely sure of this argument until we specify what has happened to the net barter terms of trade (NBTT) over time in hard-core trade. For East European trade with the Soviet Union (which accounts for about 0.35 of total trade)[17] the NBTT have significantly improved during this period (Hewett, 1974, ch. III). If applicable to hard-core trade, this would alleviate somewhat the negative effects of increasing dependence on imports. Nevertheless, let us assume for now that the net effect is to leave the EETE with a growing deficit (falling surplus) in hard-core trade ($\pi_h < \bar{\pi}$), and analyse the effect on the planning process.

The balancing process will always converge towards π_h, which under these assumptions is a non-feasible solution. (From equation (4'), $\mathbf{f}^*$ cannot be retained simultaneously with $\bar{\pi}$.) The only hope of a feasible solution in this case is that at some iteration, $\mathbf{p}_f \cdot \mathbf{m}$ will be large enough to produce a satisfactory total balance of trade. Nothing specific can be stated about the chance that the planner will locate a feasible solution on his way, in this case, to an unfeasible one.

168

Probably, given $\mathbf{f}^*$ and some total factor limits on $\overline{\mathbf{X}}$ (whose composition can remain flexible), the lower $\mathbf{p}_f \cdot (\mathbf{e}_h - \mathbf{i}_h)$ the lower is the probability of finding a feasible solution.

If a feasible solution is not located, some elements of $\mathbf{f}^*$ will have to be decreased, which increases the size of the feasible space and thus the probability of reaching a feasible solution. We can approximate the negotiations that go on between planners and politicians about $\mathbf{f}^*$ by positing a politicians' preference function for net output. The function will contain lower bounds on some goods and trade-offs among all goods. The planner then uses the function as a guide when he chooses a new lower $\mathbf{f}^*$. (We discuss below specifically how the planner uses preferences.) If at the iteration where the planner stops, π is only slightly below $\overline{\pi}$, decreasing $\mathbf{f}^*$ may push $\mathbf{p}_f \mathbf{m}$ up high enough to achieve feasibility. For larger differences, the planner recommences the iterative process with a higher probability of success.

Case 3. *Hard-core trade balanced below* $\overline{\pi}$; *composition of* $\overline{\mathbf{X}}$ *constrained; number of iterations unconstrained.* It may occur during the iterative process that gross output in at least one sector should be increased and cannot be, since the required $\mathbf{x}$ is outside $\overline{\mathbf{X}}$. In this case the planner is assumed to get as close to the $\mathbf{x}$ he seeks as possible and continue the process in that fashion. Therefore, constraints on $\overline{\mathbf{X}}$ decrease the size of the feasible space further still and, for a given $\mathbf{f}^*$, decrease the probability of finding a feasible solution. Again, a decrease in $\mathbf{f}^*$ may be the only solution.

Case 4. *Hard-core trade balanced below* $\overline{\pi}$; *composition of* $\overline{\mathbf{X}}$ *constrained; number of iterations constrained.* Iterations are a costly affair for any central planner and the EETE model must reflect this if it is to be realistic. The iterative process poses a dilemma for the planner. Higher $\mathbf{f}^*$s, which keep politicians happy, decrease the probability of finding a feasible solution in a few iterations; many iterations may overtax the entire system and produce an *a priori* inconsistent plan. Lower $\mathbf{f}^*$s increase the probability of finding a feasible solution quickly but make for unhappier politicians, as do *a priori* inconsistent plans. It is an optimization problem, although one doubts that the planner takes the requisite steps to solve it as such.

We can represent the actual situation in the model by assuming the following:

1. Politicians send planners $\mathbf{f}^*$, lower bounds on the set of all acceptable **f**s and relative values for moving from $\mathbf{f}^*$ to a lower, acceptable, **f**. Giving up any significant portion of $\mathbf{f}^*$ is regarded as a serious affair; whenever it is decreased, the value (in politicians' prices) of the decrease is to be minimized.

2. The costs to planners of keeping an $\mathbf{f}^*$ increase at an increasing rate as the number of iterations increases. Iterations eat up time and overload

facilities for generating and processing information. Thus the more iterations which are accumulated, the closer becomes the date by which the plan must be sent down, and the more desperate the planner.

3. There are also subjective and objective benefits to achieving f^*. In the first iterations these presumably exceed the costs of retaining an initial f^*, thus explaining the planners' predisposition to hold on to the same f^* for several iterations.

4. There is finally some point where f^* becomes too 'costly' for the planner to hold on to and he moves down to a lower but still acceptable f^*.

5. He then resumes iterations and presumably retains the new f^* for at least a few iterations (although quite possibly a smaller number than for the previous f^*).

6. When the planner is forced to sacrifice f^*, we assume he does it by decreasing the 'cheapest' elements in f^* (in politicians' prices), first until it hits its lower bound, and so on until he has sacrificed the value he intends to sacrifice before resuming the iterative process.

7. Theoretically we can specify the value of f^* he will sacrifice as a function of (a) his perception of the costs he will incur by presenting politicians with a lower f^* and (b) the benefits that he will obtain by presenting politicians with a consistent f^*. The higher the number of iterations, the higher is the amount of f^* (in politicians' prices) the planner will give up.

8. Eventually a solution must be located, although politicians may be forced to sacrifice some lower bounds in their preference functions.

SUMMARY AND CONCLUSIONS

Fig. 1 contains a simplified flow chart which summarizes the main characteristics of the EETE model.

The first f^* comes from the political process. Planners then choose an $\bar{x}$ which, for most elements, is some uniform mark up and the previous years' capacity. This is the first iteration. The vector $e - i$, which contains both hard-core and residual trade, determines (with p_f) whether the plan is feasible. If it is, then the process is finished; any potential balance of payments surplus can be distributed among final demanders or used to augment foreign exchange reserves.

If the plan is not feasible, further iterations are necessary. Based on planners' expected payoffs from achieving f^* and the costs of iterations, it is estimated that σ iterations will be attempted before f^* is changed.

Before planners change f^*, they may explore the possibility of buying present f^* with future f^*s (a foreign loan from the Soviet Union, for example). If this ploy fails, then f^* will be changed and iterations resumed.

The amount of f^* (in politicians' prices) which the planner will give up

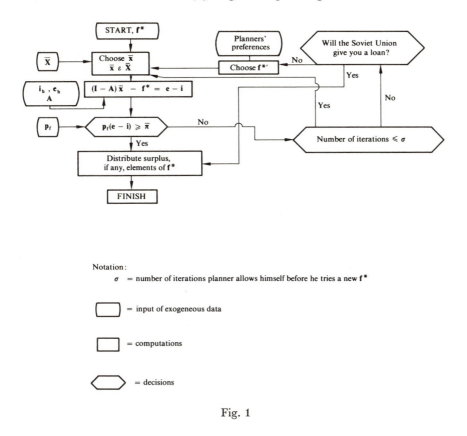

Notation:

σ = number of iterations planner allows himself before he tries a new f^*

= input of exogeneous data

= computations

= decisions

Fig. 1

is a non-linear (increasing) function of the number of iterations he has accumulated in the search for a feasible solution. The composition of the f^* sacrificed is a function of politicians' preferences.

The iterative process under a more restricted f^* resumes with an enlarged probability of finding the feasible space. The only feature we need to note about subsequent rounds with new f^*s is that we assume each time that the planner searches σ times for a feasible solution to whatever f^* he has.[18] A continuingly decreasing value of f^*, hence increasing probability of a feasible solution, guarantee the planners' eventual success.

The flow chart is consistent with all four cases we have discussed. These simply outline the increasingly severe restrictions on feasible space one encounters as more realistic assumptions are imposed on the model about the constraints on planners' behavior.

The final version of the model (Case 4) with all of the unrealistic assumptions removed, is what I regard as the nearest to a viable model of actual EETE behaviour. It captures what is, in my mind, the essence of

171

EETE planning: the use of a non-optimal balancing algorithm to seek solutions to $\mathbf{f^*}$, feasible within constraints on the possible range of sectoral gross outputs and on the balance of trade. The planner has only a relatively few iterations to 'spend' in his quest for feasibility, so that it becomes a matter of chance whether or not he finds his feasible solution to $\mathbf{f^*}$ quickly or must sacrifice some of it to get at least some kind of feasible solution in time to send a balanced plan to lower levels. Conversely, the set of feasible solutions to $\mathbf{f^*}$ may be large, yet the planner may not find it simply because he has little time to look. Obviously he almost certainly will have no chance of coming up with the optimal solution. To adopt a linear programming approach as follows:

$$\text{Max: } \mathbf{p}_f \mathbf{m} \tag{12}$$

subject to: $\qquad (\mathbf{I} - \mathbf{A})\,\bar{\mathbf{x}} - \mathbf{f^*} = (\mathbf{e}_h - \mathbf{i}_h + \mathbf{m}), \quad \bar{\mathbf{x}} \in \bar{\mathbf{X}},$

where the following variables are exogenous: $\mathbf{p}_f$, $\mathbf{f^*}$, $\mathbf{e}_h$, $\mathbf{i}_h$, $\mathbf{A}$, would require a leisurely stroll around a feasible space the planner has a hard time even entering.

There is, of course, much left out of the present model, or at least only implicitly included. The iterative process in the model is a proxy for all of the total and partial iterations which planners go through as they seek a feasible plan. Those are no doubt much less clearly defined than the model's iterations.

In practice, a feasible solution may be the result of an infeasible plan sent down from the top (after a few iterations) along with a priority list, with which lower levels interact to produce the final solution. In this model such behaviour is proxied by steps along the planner's preference function. Thus, although it is not explicit, and that may be a shortcoming of the model, it is implicit.

In practice, too, planners may negotiate with politicians on $\mathbf{f^*}$ before the iterative process begins, since they (the planners) know their economy well and can guess with a fair amount of accuracy if a given $\mathbf{f^*}$ is likely to be attainable. Again this is implicit in the model in the artificial convention that planners must each time learn what the capabilities of their economy are (through iterations) and then begin sacrificing $\mathbf{f^*}$.

It is probably unrealistic to assume that politicians have explicit preferences for all elements of $\mathbf{f^*}$. They may not, or, conversely, they may have very explicit preferences for some elements of *gross* output (e.g. steel). This just cannot happen in the model (unless the politician simultaneously specifies $\mathbf{e} - \mathbf{i}$) but certainly can occur in actual situations. It seems safe to assume, however, the politicians have fairly definite preferences for most net outputs.

These objections need not vitiate the model. The interaction of foreign trade with the planning process in small CPEs has been neglected and this model is one way of thinking about it. Also, as I indicated in the introduction, scholars studying the CEMA economies are concerned with other questions for which this model may provide a basis of analysis. It could be quantified and used to study the role of foreign trade in planning EETEs. It could be extended, theoretically and empirically, to consideration of the determinants of intra-EETE and EETE–STE trade. Although these extensions are important, they will not be discussed here since the problems associated with them are formidable enough to merit separate treatment.

NOTES

1 I am grateful to Edwin Dolan, Paul Marer and George Stolnitz for their very perceptive comments on an earlier draft. The remaining errors and ambiguities are mine.

2 Balancing is an algorithm designed to identify and eliminate surpluses and deficits associated with specific net output plans. A detailed discussion is presented in the section 'The mechanics of iterations'.

3 CEMA is the abbreviation for Council for Mutual Economic Assistance, also referred to as CMEA or COMECON. It is the economic coalition of the Soviet and East European countries; its membership is Bulgaria, Czechoslovakia, East Germany, Hungary, Mongolia, Poland, Rumania and the Soviet Union.

4 See, for example, my discussion of the application of a decomposition algorithm to Polish planning practices in Hewett (1974, pp. 156–66).

5 Recently econometric models of the Soviet and East European economies have begun to appear in the literature. These include Montias' model of foreign trade and industrialization in Rumania (Montias, 1968) and models of the economies of the Soviet Union (Niwa, 1971), Hungary (Halabuk, 1972), and Poland (Barczak *et al.*, 1968). These models are conceptually similar to models of market-type economies: government (here, planners') behavior is exogenous; instead the 'behavior' appears in demand and production functions. Econometric models and models of planners' behavior complement each other; they each focus on behavioral elements set aside by the other. Although the former are undoubtedly an important tool for studying the EETE, I have chosen to ignore them in this paper in order to highlight planners' behavior.

6 Throughout this paper, the following notational rules will be used: bold capital letters are matrices and bold lower-case letters are vectors. Small Greek letters are scalars. All matrices and vectors have the correct dimensions. A bar over any variable indicates that it is a constraint.

7 'Soft' commodities are those for which there is a relative excess supply in CEMA; they tend to be those with no market in hard currency areas. 'Hard' commodities are those which are in excess demand in CEMA; they are generally raw materials and agricultural products, many of which do have a potential market in hard currency areas.

8 Based on the information about **A** gained from the first iteration, planners may be able to do subsequent iterations without consulting industrial organizations or firms (Manove, 1971, pp. 396–71). Whether or not that is the case, the model remains the same.

9 Material balances **m** could also go into changes in stocks (if the stocks are available for negative **m**s). However, that is a change in f^* and, as I discuss below, I assume that planners only change f^* as a last resort after the iterative process fails to produce a feasible solution to the initial f^*.

10 Equation (3) can be used to define 'complete' plans which were implicitly assumed when we stated that government targets would contain or imply a complete $\mathbf{f}^*$ vector. The assumption is, therefore, that government specifies for each sector two of the three variables listed above, and it doesn't matter which two.

11 Montias' basic model is written with one scarce factor only, labor. Other scarce factors are not considered in the aggregate, but only when he discusses the possibility of sectoral limitations on gross outputs. Thus he notes that some industries may be limited by primary factors in the amount of gross output they can produce. The solution in this case is to treat net output in those sectors as variables and then go through the iteration process in all other sectors to solve for their gross outputs plus intermediate demands for the capacity-limited sectors (which determines net outputs in those sectors). (Montias, 1959, p. 973.) The solution could yield negative final demands in the capacity-limited sectors, in which case net outputs in other sectors will be scaled down. (Montias, 1962, p. 343.)

While this solution to the problem of capacities is technically correct, the fact remains that sector-specific capacity constraints are treated as the exceptional case in the STE model. In most sectors, iterations can go on with absolutely no attention given to capacity limitations in those sectors.

12 Of course plans may imply excess capacity in the utilization of capital stock because the amount of labor applied to the sector is insufficient to utilize all capital. However, that sector is still working at full capacity by the definition of $\overline{\mathbf{x}}$ used in this paper as long as its targeted gross output will cause it to use up all of its scarcest factor (e.g., in this case, labor).

13 The function g is of the following form:
   (1) $(\mathbf{I} - \mathbf{A})\,\overline{\mathbf{x}} = \mathbf{f} + \mathbf{e} - \mathbf{i}$ for each $\overline{\mathbf{x}}$ in $\overline{\mathbf{X}}$.
   (2) Now for each $\overline{\mathbf{x}}$, the vectors $\overline{\mathbf{F}}$ are formed by finding the set of all $\mathbf{f}$s such that:
      (*a*) the equation in point (1) is satisfied.
      (*b*) $\mathbf{p}_f(\mathbf{e} - \mathbf{i}) \geqslant \overline{\pi}$.
   (3) A similar operation on the entire set $\overline{\mathbf{X}}$ will produce the set of all $\mathbf{f}$s possible given, $\mathbf{X}$, $\mathbf{p}_f$, and $\overline{\pi}$.

14 For example, most EETE have low capacity in their raw materials sector. Investments to increase capacities in these industries are usually far less efficient than elsewhere, in particular because of the absolute physical limits imposed by meagre natural endowments in Eastern Europe of some major types of raw materials.

15 It also makes statistical sense to use hard-core trade as the first guess at $\mathbf{e} - \mathbf{i}$ since $\mathbf{e}_h$ and $\mathbf{i}_h$ are the only vectors with non-zero expected values.

16 Evans (1954) already showed direct convergence when all $\overline{\mathbf{x}}$s $< \overline{\mathbf{x}}^*$. A modification of the numerical example in Evans (1954, p. 70) to $\hat{\mathbf{x}} = (7, 4, 6)$ shows the possibility of oscillatory movements in $\mathbf{m}$.

17 If an adjustment were made for the over-valuation of $\mathbf{x}$ the official exchange rates between CEMA foreign trade prices and world market prices then this number would be lower. For a discussion of the problem, see Marer (1971).

18 As a simplifying assumption for the flow chart, σ is the same for each new $\mathbf{f}^*$.

REFERENCES

Barczak, A., B. Ciepielewska, T. Jakubczyk, Z. Pawlowski (1968). *Model ekonometryczny Gospodarki Polski Ludowej (Econometric Model of the Polish Peoples' Economy)*. Warsaw: Państwowe Wydawnictwo Naukowe.

Brown, Alan A. (1968). Towards a theory of centrally planned foreign trade. In *International Trade and Central Planning*, ed. Alan A. Brown and Egon Neuberger, pp. 57–93. Berkeley: University of California Press.

A model of foreign trade planning

Dolan, Edwin G. (1970). The teleological period in Soviet economic planning. *Yale Economic Essays*, **10**, 3–41.

Evans, W. D. (1954). Input–output computations. In *The Structural Interdependence of the Economy*, ed. T. Barna, pp. 53–102. New York: Wiley.

Halabuk, L. (1972). Otsenka i struktura vtoroi ekonometriccheskoi modeli Vengrii (Estimation and structure of the second econometric model of Hungary). *Ekonomika i Matematicheskie Metody (Economics and Mathematical Methods)*, **8**, 28–43.

Hewett, Edward A. (1974). *Foreign Trade Prices in the Council for Mutual Economic Assistance*. Cambridge: Cambridge University Press.

Keren, Michael (1971). Planning and uncertainty in a Soviet-type economy. *Yale Economic Essays*, **11**, 219–61.

Kornai, Janos (1959). *Overcentralization in Economic Administration*. Oxford: Oxford University Press.

Manove, Michael (1971). A model of Soviet-type economic planning. *American Economic Review*, **61**, 390–406.

Marer, Paul (1971). An empirical estimate of foreign trade price levels and ratios. Indiana University, International Development Research Center, January 1971 (mimeographed).

Montias, J. M. (1959). Planning with material balances in Soviet-type economies. *American Economic Review*, **49**, 963–85.

Montias, J. M. (1962). *Central Planning in Poland*. New Haven: Yale University Press.

Montias, J. M. (1968). Socialist industrialization and trade in machinery products: an analysis based on the experience of Bulgaria, Poland and Rumania. In *International Trade and Central Planning*, ed. Alan A. Brown and Egon Neuberger, pp. 130–59. Berkeley: University of California Press.

Niwa, Haruki (1971). An econometric forecast of Soviet economic growth. In *The Prediction of Communist Economic Performance*, ed. Peter Wiles, pp. 339–72. Cambridge: Cambridge University Press.

Pryor, Frederic L. (1963). *The Communist Foreign Trade System*. Cambridge. Mass.: MIT Press.

3. Rationing

The theory of consumer rationing, Pareto optimality, and the USSR: a non-linear programming approach

JOHN A. SHAW[1]

DEFINITION OF THE PROBLEM

When the theory of consumer rationing is discussed in relation to Pareto optimality, it is usually in terms of a single market structure for a particular commodity. Samuelson (1961, p. 171) arrives at this single market structure by allowing for exchange of ration coupons for ration coupons (where several commodities are rationed) and of ration coupons for money.[2] If a ration card may only be used by the person to which it was issued, the exchange of coupons may be impossible, and instead what develops is a two-market system. The primary market involves ration cards, money, and goods. The secondary market no longer involves ration coupons, but simply money and commodities. Rather than indirectly exchanging goods to achieve Pareto optimality in a single market system, the exchange process is dichotomized.

In other words, suppose there exists a single price under consumer rationing, then the result may not be Pareto optimal. It can be made Pareto optimal by the creation of a dichotomized system.

Ames (1965, part I) considers the conditions for equilibrium in a market with more than one price. The relationship of this market to Pareto optimality is not discussed. A multi-price market may or may not be Pareto optimal even if all individuals attempt to maximize their respective utilities. It is shown in this paper that a dichotomization of the market can lead to a Pareto optimal solution in this case also. Thus economic theory should lead to a prediction that under rationing there should be a dichotomized market. It is therefore unnecessary to postulate separately the existence of the second set of prices.

UTILITY MAXIMIZATION UNDER CONSUMER RATIONING:
n INDIVIDUALS, m COMMODITIES

The problem here is to discover the conditions by which individuals may maximize their utility when they are subjected to consumer rationing. If human behavior is to be significantly altered by consumer rationing, then

176

many consumers must buy their entire allotment. In such a case the constraints imposed on behavior do not take the form of equalities, but inequalities. By observation it is not difficult to find examples where consumers do not consume their entire ration.

Let us define the following:

$y_{ij} \equiv$ the quantity of the jth commodity belonging to the ith individual;

$y_{ij}^0 \equiv$ the initial endowment of the ith individual of the jth commodity.

The excess demand of the jth commodity by the ith individual will be denoted by,

$$E_{ij} = y_{ij} - y_{ij}^0, \qquad \begin{matrix} i = 1, \dots, n \\ j = 1, \dots, m \end{matrix} \qquad (1.1)$$

$$y_{ij} = E_{ij} + y_{ij}^0. \qquad (1.1a)$$

The price of the jth commodity will be p_j, and is the same for all $i = 1, \dots, n$. The value of the i's initial endowment is,

$$Y_i = \sum_{j=1}^{m} p_j y_{ij}^0, \quad i = 1, \dots, n. \qquad (1.2)$$

Expenditure of i on all goods is the sum of the prices he pays times the quantity of goods he buys and is equal to his income, i.e.,

$$Y_i = \sum_{j=1}^{m} p_j y_{ij}, \quad i = 1, \dots, n. \qquad (1.3)$$

When all goods are considered, including money, the value of the initial endowment must be equal to the value of the expenditures by individual i.

$$\sum_{j=1}^{m} p_j y_{ij}^0 = \sum_{j=1}^{m} p_j y_{ij}, \quad i = 1, \dots, n,$$

$$\sum_{j=1}^{m} p_j y_{ij} - \sum_{j=1}^{m} p_j y_{ij}^0 = 0, \quad i = 1, \dots, n,$$

and, $$\sum_{j=1}^{m} p_j(y_{ij} - y_{ij}^0) = \sum_{j=1}^{m} p_j E_{ij} = 0, \quad i = 1, \dots, n. \qquad (1.4)$$

Each of the i individuals is assumed to possess a continuous and differentiable utility function everywhere under range of discussion. This utility function is given by

$$U_i = U_i(y_{i1}, \dots, y_{im}), \quad i = 1, \dots, n. \qquad (1.5)$$

From (1.1) it follows that,

$$U_i = U_i(E_{i1} + y_{i1}^0, \dots, E_{im} + y_{im}^0), \quad i = 1, \dots, n. \qquad (1.5a)$$

The quantity of the jth commodity for the ith individual set by the rationing authority will be denoted by $\bar{y}_{ij}$, $i = 1, \dots, n$, and $j = 1, \dots, r$, where $r < m$.[3] The rationing constraint will then take the form,

$$y_{ij} - \bar{y}_{ij} \leqslant 0, \qquad \begin{aligned} i &= 1, ..., n, \\ j &= 1, ..., r, \text{ where } r < m. \end{aligned} \qquad (1.6)$$

We wish to find the conditions so that each individual maximizes his utility, (1.5a), subject to his budget constraints, (1.4), and the rationing constraints, (1.6), imposed on him. The principles of classical marginalism are not applicable if any of our constraints fail to be satisfied, i.e., if inequalities rather than equalities hold. It was argued that under consumer rationing inequality constraints were not at all rare. Fortunately, we have at our disposal the Kuhn–Tucker conditions of nonlinear programming to handle such situations.[4]

Our maximization problem is equivalent to the problem of maximizing the following Lagrangean expressions,

$$\Phi_i = U_i(E_{i1} + y_{i1}^0, ..., E_{im} + y_{im}^0) - \lambda_{i0} \left(\sum_{j=1}^{m} p_j E_{ij} \right)$$

$$- \sum_{j=1}^{r} \lambda_{ij}(y_{ij} - \bar{y}_{ij}), \quad i = 1, ..., n, \quad (1.7)$$

where the nonnegative $\lambda_{i0}, \lambda_{i1}, ..., \lambda_{ir}$ (one for each constraint) are the undetermined Lagrangean multipliers or imputed values. To obtain an expression for the values that maximize (1.7) it is necessary to differentiate (1.7) with respect to the $m + r + 1$ variables, i.e. the E_{ij}s and the λ_{ij}s, for each of the i individuals.[5]

The necessary conditions for an optimal solution are:

(1) $\quad \dfrac{\partial U_i}{\partial y_{ij}} - \lambda_{i0}(p_i) - \lambda_{ij} \leqslant 0,$ $\qquad \begin{aligned} i &= 1, ..., n, \\ j &= 1, ..., m, \\ \lambda_{i, r+1} &= ... = \lambda_{i, m} = 0. \end{aligned}$ $\qquad (1.8)$

(2) $\quad$ If $\dfrac{\partial U_i}{\partial y_{ij}} - \lambda_{i0}(p_i) - \lambda_{ij} < 0$, then $y_{ij} = 0.$ $\qquad (1.8a)$

(3) $\quad \displaystyle\sum_{j=1}^{m} p_i E_{ij} \leqslant 0,$ $\qquad i = 1, ..., n.$ $\qquad (1.9)$

(4) $\quad$ If $\displaystyle\sum_{j=1}^{m} p_i E_{ij} < 0$, then $\lambda_{i0} = 0.$ $\qquad (1.9a)$

(5) $\quad (y_{ij} - \bar{y}_{ij}) \leqslant 0,$ $\qquad \begin{aligned} i &= 1, ..., n, \\ j &= 1, ..., r. \end{aligned}$ $\qquad (1.10)$

(6) $\quad$ If $(y_{ij} - \bar{y}_{ij}) < 0$, then $\lambda_{ij} = 0.$ $\qquad (1.10a)$

It will be assumed throughout the paper that the sufficient conditions for a *maximum maximorum* are satisfied.[6]

UTILITY MAXIMIZATION UNDER CONSUMER RATIONING:
$n = 2, m = 2$, AND $m = 3$

A special case of the foregoing section is when there exist only two consumers and two commodities. Let us assume that the rationed commodity is $j = 1$ for $n = 1, 2$. If for individual one '=' holds in equations (1.8) and (1.9), i.e., some of both commodities is used and the budget constraint is fulfilled, and '<' holds in equation (1.10), then it can easily be shown that

$$\frac{\partial U_1}{\partial y_{11}} \bigg/ \frac{\partial U_1}{\partial y_{12}} = p_1/p_2. \tag{2.1}$$

This is the usual result in the unconstrained case, which in fact is the case here since it was assumed that equality did not hold in equation (1.10).

If for individual two '=' holds in equations (1.8), (1.9), and (1.10), then the following result is deducible:

$$\left(\frac{\partial U_2}{\partial y_{21}} - \lambda_{21} \right) \bigg/ \frac{\partial U_2}{\partial y_{22}} = p_1/p_2. \tag{2.2}$$

Since λ_{21} must be nonnegative, the marginal utility of y_{21} per dollar must be greater than or equal to the marginal utility of y_{22} per dollar. λ_{21} is the imputed value of an additional unit of y_{21}, i.e., the price individual two would pay per unit of $y_{.1}$ to have the rationing constraint lifted.

Graphically the solutions (2.1) and (2.2) might be represented as in figs. 1(a) and (b) respectively. Fig. 1(a) is the usual tangency solution between the indifference curve and the budget–price line. Fig. 1(b), on the other hand, is a corner solution. The inadequacy of the classical calculus techniques becomes obvious from the results of equation (2.2) and fig. 1(b).

We may combine equations (2.1) and (2.2)

$$\frac{\partial U_1}{\partial y_{11}} \bigg/ \frac{\partial U_1}{\partial y_{12}} = \left(\frac{\partial U_2}{\partial y_{21}} - \lambda_{21} \right) \bigg/ \frac{\partial U_2}{\partial y_{22}}. \tag{2.3}$$

From (2.3) it is clear that as long as λ_{21} is positive the rates of commodity substitution for $y_{.1}$ and $y_{.2}$ between individuals one and two are not the same.

In the case where there are three commodities the results are basically unchanged. Let us assume the conditions regarding the equalities and inequalities of equations (1.8), (1.9), and (1.10) are the same as those at the beginning of this section. If there are one or two rationed commodities it can be easily shown that for individual one the following results hold:

$$\frac{\partial U_1}{\partial y_{11}} \bigg/ \frac{\partial U_1}{\partial y_{12}} = \frac{p_1}{p_2}, \tag{2.4}$$

$$\frac{\partial U_1}{\partial y_{11}} \bigg/ \frac{\partial U_1}{\partial y_{13}} = \frac{p_1}{p_3}, \tag{2.5}$$

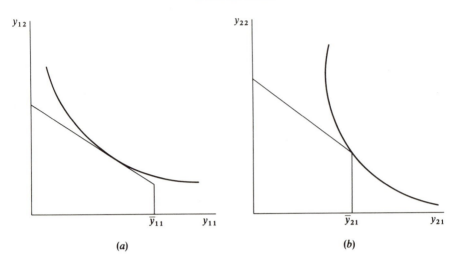

(a) (b)

Fig. 1

and
$$\frac{\partial U_1}{\partial y_{12}} \bigg/ \frac{\partial U_1}{\partial y_{13}} = \frac{p_2}{p_3}. \tag{2.6}$$

If there is one rationed commodity, say $j = 1$, then for individual two the following hold:

$$\left(\frac{\partial U_2}{\partial y_{21}} - \lambda_{21}\right) \bigg/ \frac{\partial U_2}{\partial y_{22}} = \frac{p_1}{p_2}, \tag{2.7}$$

$$\left(\frac{\partial U_2}{\partial y_{21}} - \lambda_{21}\right) \bigg/ \frac{\partial U_2}{\partial y_{23}} = \frac{p_1}{p_3}. \tag{2.8}$$

and
$$\frac{\partial U_2}{\partial y_{22}} \bigg/ \frac{\partial U_2}{\partial y_{23}} = \frac{p_2}{p_3}. \tag{2.9}$$

If there are two rationed commodities, say $j = 1, 2$, then for individual two we have

$$\frac{\dfrac{\partial U_2}{\partial y_{21}} - \lambda_{21}}{\dfrac{\partial U_2}{\partial y_{22}} - \lambda_{22}} = \frac{p_1}{p_2}, \tag{2.10}$$

$$\left(\frac{\partial U_2}{\partial y_{21}} - \lambda_{21}\right) \bigg/ \frac{\partial U_2}{\partial y_{23}} = \frac{p_1}{p_3}, \tag{2.11}$$

and
$$\left(\frac{\partial U_2}{\partial y_{22}} - \lambda_{22}\right) \bigg/ \frac{\partial U_2}{\partial y_{23}} = \frac{p_2}{p_3}. \tag{2.12}$$

Of these last nine equations, (2.4) to (2.12), the first three and the sixth are completely analogous to those in ordinary demand theory. The others, instead of being simply ratios of partial derivatives of the utility function, contain terms of the form $(\partial U_2/\partial y_{2j} - \lambda_{2j})$. The equation (2.10) contains such terms in both numerator and denominator, while the other four contain such a term only in the numerator. Thus the difference between the case where one commodity is rationed and the case where two commodities are rationed is basically the replacement (for individual two) of the usual equilibrium conditions, by terms involving

$$(\partial U_2/\partial y_{2j} - \lambda_{2j}).$$

Where the economy involves $m > 3$ commodities, the analysis generalizes readily, and the analyst need only be careful about specifying which commodities are rationed, for the equilibrium conditions affecting such commodities involve terms such as those in (2.10) or (2.11).

PURE EXCHANGE AND PARETO OPTIMALITY: $n = 2$, $m = 2$, $m = 3$

Assume that individual two has a constant utility, U_2^0. If individual one is to maximize his utility subject to the constraint, $U_2 = U_2^0$, then he must maximize the following Lagrangean, π_1.

$$\pi_1 = U_1(k_{11}, k_{12}) + \mu[U_2(k_{21}, k_{22}) - U_2^0],$$

where k_{ij}, $i = 1, 2$, and $j = 1, 2$ are the quantities of the two commodities held by each individual. The total quantity of each commodity is fixed and is given by k_1^0 and k_2^0. Therefore,

$$k_1^0 = k_{11} + k_{21} \quad \text{and} \quad k_2^0 + k_{12} + k_{22}.$$

Equation (3.1) can be rewritten as

$$\pi_1 = U_1(k_{11}, k_{12}) + \mu[U_2(k_1^0 - k_{11}, k_2^0 - k_{12}) - U_2^0]. \tag{3.1a}$$

By setting the appropriate partial derivatives of (3.1a) equal to zero a necessary condition for Pareto optimality can be obtained. It is given by

$$\frac{\partial U_1}{\partial k_{11}} \Big/ \frac{\partial U_1}{\partial k_{12}} = \frac{\partial U_2}{\partial k_{11}} \Big/ \frac{\partial U_2}{\partial k_{12}}. \tag{3.2}$$

The necessary condition for Pareto optimality is that the rate of commodity substitution for each of the two individuals after the exchange be made equal.

If each of the individuals maximizes his utility and the necessary condition is equation (2.3), then unless $\lambda_{21} = 0$ (2.3) does not yield a Pareto optimal solution. It would therefore be possible to redistribute the commodities without reducing the utility of one of the individuals, while at the same time increasing the utility of the other.

For the case where there are three commodities the results extend to require that the rates of commodity substitution between the various commodities and individuals be equal. Again, if the λs do not equal to zero a redistribution of the commodities would improve the utility of at least one individual.

CONSUMER RATIONING AND THE MEANING OF PRICE

The necessary equilibrium condition in the secondary exchange is the same as that derived in the ordinary non-rationing pure-exchange case between two individuals. The condition is that the rate of commodity substitution for the two commodities between the two individuals be equal, or just the condition (3.2) for the existence of Pareto optimality. It is therefore possible for the existence of rationing not to hamper the achievement of Pareto optimality, if a secondary market is permitted (or if illegal, at least entered into by the individuals of the economy).[7] Since theorems concerning the path to an equilibrium are not available, we cannot state what the price in the secondary market that yielded Pareto optimality will be. What has been shown, though, is that at least one such price exists.

My formulation differs from, say, Tobin (1952, pp. 541–2) in that he assumes there exist no unused ration coupons, i.e., all rations are effective. He must make this assumption since prices in his system (a single market system) are determined by the interaction of supply and demand. If excess coupons existed and were subsequently used on a fixed quantity of goods the price of the commodity would be forced up. This would impel individuals to pay higher prices. Some individuals would not be able to buy the same bill of goods as before. In an economy where the prices of the rationed commodities are fixed, such as the USSR, and the economy functions as my dichotimized system does, the determination of price is not a relevant problem.

Under pure competition it is assumed that there exists a single set of prices with only one price per commodity, and that all individuals are faced with the same set of prices. The first-order condition for utility maximization is that the rate of commodity substitution of goods be equal to the ratio of their prices. Since the prices faced by all individuals are the same it follows that the rates of commodity substitution for all individuals must be equal. In the two-person two-commodity case each individual's indifference curve must be tangent to the given budget–price line.

If two individuals have a non-Pareto optimal distribution of goods, such as point N in figs. 2(a) and (b), and wish to move to a Pareto optimal state where each is maximizing his utility for one price vector, then the entire amount of goods available must be completely distributed, and the indifference curve of each individual must be tangent to the price line (point M, fig. 2(a)). It is clear that no boundary point meets these conditions.

Point R, fig. 2(b), is feasible since individual two is indifferent between R and N by definition. Such a boundary point R is a Pareto optimal solution, but violates the condition that both individuals maximize their utility for a given price vector. For the price vector in fig. 2(b), $\bar{P}''$,

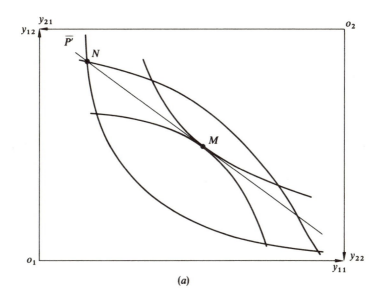

(a)

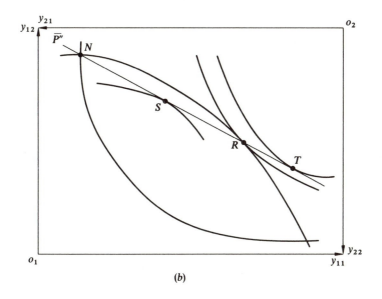

(b)

Fig. 2

individual two would maximize his utility at point S and individual one would maximize his utility at point T. Of course, the pure competition assumption of the inability to influence price is no longer met.

When individual one has a superior bargaining position, i.e. he is able to force individual two to remain on the same indifference curve after the exchange, neither individual one nor two maximizes his utility given the price vector $\bar{\mathbf{P}}''$ even though an exchange occurs and a pareto optimal solution is achieved for the price vector $\bar{\mathbf{P}}''$.

If in the secondary exchange individual one is to maximize his utility under the constraint that individual two's utility may not change, then it is not surprising that the result obtained is not identical with the result that would have been obtained had the constraint not been in force. This fact, i.e. individual one must maximize his utility subject to the constraint that individual two's utility be constant, explains why it would be reasonable to expect that for the Pareto optimal solution neither individual would have commodity bundles that would maximize their utility function for the given price vector.

If it is true that there is a point which leaves individual one indifferent and individual two better off, then there is also a point (perhaps a lot of them) which leaves both individual one and individual two better off.

SOVIET CONSUMER RATIONING DURING THE 1930s

Food and non-food products were sold to consumers in a number of different markets and at a number of different prices in the USSR in the 1930s. First of all, there was rationing in effect from the latter part of 1928 to 1935–6 (Bergson, 1964, p. 52). Prices of rationed goods were generally the lowest of any of the various markets. The Soviet government legalized the free market trade of the peasant on 20 May 1932. This had become known as '*kolkhoz* markets'. The government began selling part of their procurements of food from the agricultural sector in so-called commercial stores at prices usually a little below the *kolkhoz* market prices, which were considerably above the ration prices. Thus at least three markets and three prices existed at which consumers could purchase food products. There were sales in state commercial stores of non-food goods without ration, as well as rationed non-food goods. The prices peasants faced were higher in the cooperative stores than the prices faced by wage and salary workers in the state commercial trade (Jasny, 1961, p. 151).

The size of one's ration was dependent on one's need, e.g. manual laborers', and on one's relative position (undoubtedly Stalin had a larger 'ration' than did those at the bottom of the heirarchy). However, the ration was not intended to provide the entire amount of goods consumed by any individual, as it was in the United States or the United Kingdom during World War II (Dobb, 1948, p. 368).

Let us consider now such a tri-chotomized market system. It is assumed that the different levels of prices are the same for all individuals and are denoted in the following manner:

$_1p_j \equiv$ rationed price for the jth commodity, $j = 1, ..., r, r < m$;

$_2p_j \equiv$ commercial store price for the jth commodity, $j = 1, ..., m$;

$_3p_j \equiv$ free market price[8] for the jth commodity, $j = 1, ..., m$.

In accord with the Soviet Government's policy it is assumed that all individuals' rations are not necessarily equal. These are given by,

$y'_{ij} \equiv$ the maximum amount the ith individual may purchase of the jth good at its rationed price, $_1p_j, j = 1, ..., r$,

$y''_{ij} \equiv$ the maximum amount the ith individual may purchase of the jth good at the commercial store price, $_2p_j, j = 1, ..., m$,

where $0 < {_1p_j} < {_2p_j} < {_3p_j}$. The initial endowment of money of each individual may differ and is denoted by $Y_i, i = 1, ..., n$.

The total expenditure of the ith individual on the jth commodity, $i = 1, ..., n$, and $j = 1, ..., r$, may be expressed as the improper Riemann integral[9]

$$\int_{z_{ij} \leqslant y_{ij}} e_{ij}(z_{ij})\, dz_{ij}$$

$$= \begin{cases} 0, & \text{if } y_{ij} = 0 \\ {_1p_j} y_{ij}, & \text{if } y_{ij} \leqslant y'_{ij} \\ {_1p_j} y'_{ij} + {_2p_j}(y_{ij} - y'_{ij}), & \text{if } y'_{ij} < y_{ij} \leqslant y''_{ij} \\ {_1p_j} y'_{ij} + {_2p_j}(y''_{ij} - y'_{ij}) + {_3p_j}(y_{ij} - y''_{ij}), & \text{if } y''_{ij} < y_{ij} \end{cases} \quad (5.1)$$

The integrand, $j = 1, ..., r$,

$$e_{ij}(y_{ij}) = \begin{cases} 0, & \text{if } y_{ij} = 0 \\ {_1p_j}, & \text{if } y_{ij} \leqslant y'_{ij} \\ {_2p_j}, & \text{if } y'_{ij} < y_{ij} \leqslant y''_{ij} \\ {_3p_j}, & \text{if } y''_{ij} < y_{ij} \end{cases} \quad (5.2)$$

For $j = r + 1, ..., m$, the total expenditure of the ith individual is

$$\int_{z_{ij} \leqslant y_{ij}} e_{ij}(z_{ij})\, dz_{ij} = \begin{cases} 0, & \text{if } y_{ij} = 0 \\ {_2p_j} y_{ij}, & \text{if } y_{ij} \leqslant y''_{ij} \\ {_2p_j} y''_{ij} + {_3p_j}(y_{ij} - y''_{ij}), & \text{if } y''_{ij} < y_{ij} \end{cases} \quad (5.3)$$

185

The integrand, $j = r+1, ..., m$,

$$e_{ij}(y_{ij}) = \begin{cases} 0, & \text{if } y_{ij} = 0 \\ {}_2p_j, & \text{if } y_{ij} \leqslant y''_{ij} \\ {}_3p_j, & \text{if } y''_{ij} < y_{ij} \end{cases}. \qquad (5.4)$$

Again we assume that each individual attempts to maximize his utility function subject to the constraint that his income be equal to his total expenditures.[10] This is equivalent to maximizing the Langrangean

$$\Gamma_i = U_i(y_{i1}, ..., y_{im})$$

$$-\gamma_i\left[Y_i - \sum_{j=1}^{r} \int_{z_{ij} \leqslant y_{ij}} e_{ij}(z_{ij})\, dz_{ij} - \sum_{j=r+1}^{m} \int_{z_{ij} \leqslant y_{ij}} e_{ij}(z_{ij})\, dz_{ij}\right], \quad n = 1, ..., n. \qquad (5.5)$$

Differentiating (5.5) and setting the derivatives equal to zero we get the necessary conditions for (5.5) to take on its maximum value (as before, the second order conditions are assumed to hold), that is,

$$\frac{\partial \Gamma_i}{\partial y_{ij}} = \frac{\partial U_i}{\partial y_{ij}} - \gamma_i \frac{\partial}{\partial y_{ij}} \int_{z_{ij} \leqslant y_{ij}} e_{ij}(z_{ij})\, dz_{ij} = 0, \quad \begin{matrix} i = 1, ..., n, \\ j = 1, ..., m, \end{matrix} \qquad (5.6)$$

$$\frac{\partial \Gamma_i}{\partial \gamma_i} = Y_i - \sum_{j=1}^{m} \int_{z_{ij} \leqslant y_{ij}} e_{ij}(z_{ij})\, dz_{ij} = 0, \quad i = 1, ..., n. \qquad (5.7)$$

In the case where $n = 2$, and $m = 2$ the necessary conditions for a maximum can be written easily. For individual one,

$$\frac{\partial U_1}{\partial y_{11}} - \gamma_1 \frac{\partial}{\partial y_{11}} \int_{z_{11} \leqslant y_{11}} e_{11}(z_{11})\, dz_{11} = 0, \qquad (5.8)$$

$$\frac{\partial U_1}{\partial y_{12}} - \gamma_1 \frac{\partial}{\partial y_{12}} \int_{z_{12} \leqslant y_{12}} e_{12}(z_{12})\, dz_{12} = 0, \qquad (5.9)$$

$$Y_1 - \sum_{j=1}^{2} \int_{z_{1j} \leqslant y_{1j}} e_{1j}(z_{1j})\, dz_{1j} = 0. \qquad (5.10)$$

For individual two,

$$\frac{\partial U_2}{\partial y_{21}} - \gamma_2 \frac{\partial}{\partial y_{21}} \int_{z_{21} \leqslant y_{21}} e_{21}(z_{21})\, dz_{21} = 0, \qquad (5.11)$$

$$\frac{\partial U_2}{\partial y_{22}} - \gamma_2 \frac{\partial}{\partial y_{22}} \int_{z_{22} \leqslant y_{22}} e_{22}(z_{22})\, dz_{22} = 0, \qquad (5.12)$$

$$Y_2 - \sum_{j=1}^{2} \int_{z_{2j} \geqslant y_{2j}} e_{2j}(z_{2j})\, dz_{2j} = 0. \qquad (5.13)$$

If we take commodity two as *numéraire*, then for individual one equation
(5.9) becomes

$$\frac{\partial U_1}{\partial y_{12}} - \gamma_1 = 0, \tag{5.9a}$$

since $e_{i2} = 1$ for all values of y_{i2}, $i = 1, 2$.

By transposing and dividing (5.8) by (5.9a) we obtain

$$\frac{\partial U_1}{\partial y_{11}} \Big/ \frac{\partial U_1}{\partial y_{12}} = \left(\frac{\partial}{\partial y_{11}} \int_{z_{11} \leqslant y_{11}} e_{11}(z_{11})\, dz_{11} \right) \Big/ 1. \tag{5.14}$$

Therefore, $\qquad\qquad \partial y_{12}/\partial y_{11} = {}_h p_1, \tag{5.15}$

where,

$${}_h p_1 = \begin{cases} 0, & \text{if } y_{11} = 0 \\ {}_1 p_1, & \text{if } y_{11} \leqslant y'_{11} \\ {}_2 p_1, & \text{if } y'_{11} < y_{11} \leqslant y''_{11} \\ {}_3 p_1, & \text{if } y''_{11} < y_{11} \end{cases}. \tag{5.16}$$

By a similar argument for individual two involving equations (5.6)
and (5.7) the following result may be deduced:

$$\partial y_{22}/\partial y_{21} = {}_k p_1, \tag{5.17}$$

where,

$${}_k p_1 = \begin{cases} 0, & \text{if } y_{21} = 0 \\ {}_1 p_1, & \text{if } y_{21} \leqslant y'_{21} \\ {}_2 p_1, & \text{if } y'_{21} < y_{21} \leqslant y''_{21} \\ {}_3 p_1, & \text{if } y''_{21} < y_{21} \end{cases}. \tag{5.18}$$

Consequently, if ${}_h p_1 = {}_k p_1$, then from (5.15) and (5.17)

$$\frac{\partial y_{12}}{\partial y_{11}} = \frac{\partial y_{22}}{\partial y_{21}}, \tag{5.19}$$

and from equation (3.2) it can be seen the solution is Pareto optimal. If,
on the other hand, ${}_h p_1 \neq {}_k p_1$ the solution does not meet the necessary
condition for Pareto optimality. By the same reasoning as in the previous
section an additional exchange would be advantageous for at least one
individual while the other would be at worst indifferent.

In fact, if there exists a system where the marginal cost function has
w steps and is not Pareto optimal, then there also exists a system with $w + 1$
prices that is Pareto optimal. This is easily shown by defining the total
expenditure of the ith individual on the jth commodity, for $j = 1, \ldots, r$,
as in equation (5.1) and its integrand as in equation (5.2), but extending
the definition to w prices. The total expenditure for the $j = r + 1, \ldots, m$,
commodities is analogous to equation (5.3) and the integrand to equation
(5.4).

If $n = 2$ and $m = 2$, then equations analogous to (5.6) through (5.18)
can be derived. If ${}_h p_1 = {}_k p_1$, then the w price system is Pareto optimal. If

$_h p_1 \neq {}_k p_1$, then the system is not Pareto optimal, but as before can be made Pareto optimal by adding an additional exchange and price, thus making the system have $w + 1$ prices. Consequently, for every w price non-Pareto optimal system, there exists a $w + 1$ price Pareto optimal system.

To write out explicitly the equilibrium conditions for more than two commodities becomes exceedingly cumbersome, although it is conceptionally straightforward, i.e. simply solving equations (5.6) and (5.7).

CONCLUSION

The theoretical model presented above is consistent with the observed fact of secondary and 'black' markets that are known to exist in economies where rationing is prevalent. The existence of a dichotomized market allows individuals to achieve a Pareto optimal distribution of commodities, both in the case where rationing provided the only means of acquiring commodities and where rationed and non-rationed markets existed simultaneously. Rationing introduces the possibility of non-Pareto optimal solutions, but the existence of a secondary exchange can lead to Pareto optimality.

Nonlinear programming gave an easy method of handling the rationing situation where some rations were ineffective. In the 1930s in the USSR rations were of the minimum type and consequently the need for inequality constraints is absent.

If individual one would buy less than his full ration under the condition that he maximize his utility in the primary exchange it may still be to his advantage to purchase a large, non-utility maximizing, quantity when the following relationships exist.

Individual one knows the *minimum* amount that he will take for his extra ration, i.e. how much money he had to give up to acquire the extra ration. The *maximum* amount individual two will pay for the extra ration will be that amount of money given up that will leave his utility constant after the gain of the extra ration. If the *maximum* individual two will pay is greater than the *minimum* individual one will take, then trade will take place. If we assume individual one's bargaining position is such that he can also exact this *maximum* amount from individual two, then individual one's utility still increases with individual two's utility remaining constant. It is therefore clear that the original position was not Pareto optimal.

Individual one, in this case, would find that to maximize his ultimate utility, i.e. after the secondary exchange, he should not maximize his immediate utility, i.e. after the primary exchange. Thus, the nature of utility maximization takes on a decidedly different appearance in a dichotomized market system.

NOTES

1 I wish to express my deepest thanks to Edward Ames for his counsel at the various stages of this paper. I am also indebted to an unknown referee on several points. Of course, I retain the rights to all remaining errors.

2 This approach is also followed by other writers. In particular, see Tobin (1952) and McManus (1956).

3 If the budget constraint (1.4) is to hold, then the rationing authority does not have the prerogative to ration all m commodities. For a fuller discussion of this point see Samuelson (1961, p. 164).

4 For a succinct statement of the Kunn–Tucker conditions and their implications see Smith (1961, pp. 321–7). Of course, for the original formulation see Kuhn and Tucker (1951, pp. 481–92).

5 Thus,

$$\frac{\partial \Phi_i}{\partial E_{ij}} = \frac{\partial U_i}{\partial E_{ij}} - \lambda_{i0}(p_i) - \frac{\partial \left[\sum\limits_{j=1}^{r} \lambda_{ij}(y_{ij} - \bar{y}_{ij}) \right]}{\partial E_{ij}}, \tag{a}$$

$$i = 1, \dots, n,$$

$$j = 1, \dots, m,$$

$$\frac{\partial \Phi_i}{\partial \lambda_{i,0}} = \sum_{j=1}^{m} p_i E_{ij}, \quad i = 1, \dots, n,$$

and,

$$\frac{\partial \Phi_i}{\partial \lambda_{ij}} = (y_{ij} - \bar{y}_{ij}), \quad \begin{array}{l} i = 1, \dots, n, \\ j = 1, \dots, r. \end{array} \tag{b}$$

Since, $\dfrac{\partial E_{ij}}{\partial y_{ij}} = 1$, (a) can be rewritten as

$$\frac{\partial \Phi_i}{\partial E_{ij}} \cdot \frac{\partial E_{ij}}{\partial y_{ij}} = \frac{\partial U_i}{\partial E_{ij}} \cdot \frac{\partial E_{ij}}{\partial y_{ij}} - \lambda_{i0}(p_i) - \frac{\partial \left[\sum\limits_{j=1}^{r} \lambda_{ij}(y_{ij} - \bar{y}_{ij}) \right]}{\partial E_{ij}} \cdot \frac{\partial E_{ij}}{\partial y_{ij}}, \tag{c}$$

$$i = 1, \dots, n,$$

$$j = 1, \dots, m,$$

or equivalently as

$$i = 1, \dots, n,$$

$$\frac{\partial \Phi_i}{\partial y_{ij}} = \frac{\partial U_i}{\partial y_{ij}} - \lambda_{i0}(p_i) - \lambda_{ij}, \quad j = 1, \dots, m, \tag{d}$$

$$\lambda_{i,r+1} = \dots = \lambda_{i,m} = 0.$$

6 For a lucid discussion of Kuhn and Tucker's results on this point see Dorfman *et al.* (1952).

7 Perhaps expected utility is to be maximized if the secondary exchange is illegal. If one considers the probabilities of being caught, then the penalties for violations might be used as weights in the expected utility function.

8 At this level of abstraction it is assumed that the free market price is constant over the entire quantity for sale on the free market. In reality, of course, the free market was free to fluctuate with variations in supply and demand.

9 For a further elaboration of this see Shaw (1966).

10 A difficulty is introduced at this point if the solution turns out to be at a 'corner' on the budget constraint. At the point $y_{11} = y'_{11}$, for example,

$$\frac{\partial}{\partial y_{11}} \int_{z_{11} \leqslant y_{11}} e_{11}(z_{11})\, dz_{11}$$

189

in (5.14) does not exist. Therefore there is no guarantee that the solution is Pareto optimal since equation (5.19) is invalid. If a non-Pareto optimal solution is achieved in the tri-chotomized market, trade would be advantageous for a least one individual while the remaining individuals would be at worst indifferent. An additional round of exchange would be needed to achieve a Pareto optimal solution. Since this possibility can be handled straight-forwardly as shown in the section above on 'Consumer rationing and the meaning of prices', the necessary complications will not be introduced in this discussion.

REFERENCES

Ames, Edward (1965). *Soviet Economic Processes*. Homewood, Ill. Irwin.

Bergson, Abram (1964). *The Economics of Soviet Planning*. New Haven: Yale University Press.

Dobb, Maurice (1948). *Soviet Economic Development Since 1917*. London: Routledge & Kegan Paul.

Dorfman, Robert, Paul A. Samuelson, and Robert M. Solow (1958). *Linear Programming and Economic Analysis*. New York: McGraw-Hill.

Jasny, Naum (1961). *Soviet Industrialization 1928–52*. Chicago: University of Chicago Press.

Kuhn, H. W. and A. W. Tucker (1951). Nonlinear programming. In *Proceedings of the Second Berkeley Symposium on Mathematical Statistics and Probability*, ed. U. Neyman. Berkeley: University of California Press.

McManus, M. (1956). Points rationing and the consumer. *Metroeconomica*, **8**, 118–34.

Samuelson, Paul Anthony (1961). *Foundations of Economic Analysis*. Cambridge, Mass.: Harvard University Press.

Shaw, John A. (1966). The integration of discontinuous marginal functions. *Indian Economic Journal*, **14**, 114–15.

Smith, Vernon L. (1961). *Investment and Production*. Cambridge, Mass.: Harvard University Press.

Tobin, James (1952). A survey of the theory of rationing. *Econometrica*, **20**, 521–53.

Pressure and Suction on the Market

JANOS KORNAI[1]

INTRODUCTION

The subject of this paper is disequilibrium on the market, a phenomenon which has existed for close to thirty years in the Hungarian national economy. It is evidenced by a regular shortage of many products and services. The Hungarian consumer has grown accustomed to hearing 'shortage of goods' as explanation for a product's unavailability. Many products are completely out of stock for long periods of time, while others are available only in limited selection. Thus, while clothing, shoes and chinaware are available, there is little choice in size, color or style. Although there may be a regular supply of some products and services, the quantity is insufficient, meaning that the consumer may wait for months or even years for a flat, telephone, car or foreign exchange allocation for a trip abroad.

We find a similar phenomenon in the market for producers and investment goods. There is continuous scarcity of construction capacity and basic building materials. In many fields there are repeated shortages of material and component parts. There is a lack of foreign exchange to import essential inputs. And last but not least, there is a shortage of manpower.

We do not intend to call attention to sporadic and temporary disturbances in equilibrium, but to the fact that in a *number* of markets, shortages are *continuous*. Some have become used to this phenomenon. Young people born during or following the war who have not travelled abroad consider it natural that in Hungary, despite its outstanding cattle breeding, veal is never available in the shops. (In order to obtain veal one must either be hospitalized, or dine in an expensive restaurant.)

Many of those giving any thought to the shortage phenomenon draw one-sided or even distorted conclusions. Some may explain the shortage phenomenon as due to the economic backwardness of the country, some may give a political 'explanation'. Opponents of the system gloat while its supporters admit with anxiety that a shortage of goods must, by necessity, exist in a socialist economy. The spread of these views is unfortunately aided by those economic policymakers and economists who 'rationalize' shortage conditions by stating: 'This is a good thing, for demand will force production to advance.'[2]

191

There are phenomena which the uninitiated do not even note, and must be discovered by the scientist, but this is not the case with a shortage of commodities. The layman, the housewife or the staff of the purchasing department in the factory experience it day by day whereas economists pay very little attention to what they call market disequilibrium. At most, only a few studies touch on it and none presents a comprehensive theory of disequilibrium.[3]

CONCEPTUAL CLARIFICATION

Several new concepts must be introduced to facilitate analysis. In formulating the basic terminology used to describe the market (effective demand, equilibrium price, excess demand and supply, etc.) economists have had in mind a *special* economic system: the decentralized market in which prices serve as the sole or major source of information. However, this special system of concepts cannot conveniently be used in describing other economic systems, for instance allocation controlled by central directives. This is why we would like to introduce a *conceptual framework of more general validity*, with which we can describe the most diverse types of markets and control mechanisms.

By way of illustration, let us first look at a household. Expenses for large items (e.g., furniture, car, trip abroad) are planned well in advance, while other purchases (e.g., buying daily food supplies) are done by everyday routine, although the housewife may have advance ideas about the later type of purchases. In our analysis we differentiate between original idea at the beginning of a decision process and the final decision. We will call the former *aspiration level*[4] or *intention* and the latter *decision*.

A household's aspiration level can be determined by a questionnaire interview.[5] 'Let us assume', we might say to the consumer, 'that (1) you have a given expected income for the coming period and accumulated savings until now, (2) current market prices are known, and (3) everything which you might want is available, there being no supply limit to your purchases. How would you spend your money in the forthcoming period?' Their reply would give us the aspiration level for procurement. By carrying out similar interviews with a sufficient number of families, we would draw general conclusions on aspirations for consumer procurement.[6]

Let us assume that there are n number of households and m types of *alternative expenses*. (Alternative expenses include different forms of consumer savings: keeping money at home, bank accounts at 3 % interest, etc.) The procurement aspiration level of the ith household can be described by a vector of m components denoted $\mathbf{q}_i$. To summarize the entire economy, we can derive as the total consumption aspiration level:

$$\mathbf{q} = \sum_{i=1}^{n} \mathbf{q}_i. \tag{1}$$

On the basis of *ex post* observation, we can determine the quantity of *actual procurement* for the period under question for each of the m-type expense alternatives. In the case of the ith household, we denote this vector by $\mathbf{r}_i$, and in total by $\mathbf{r}$.

The difference between the two vectors gives us the deviation between intentions and fulfillment. For example the housewife, if all types of meat were available, might have spent a portion of the money on steak, veal and sweetbreads. Since she did not find these available, she purchased pork chops and salami instead. In the former, the $(q_{ij} - r_{ij})$ difference is positive, in the latter it is negative. The event which, in our example, was made unavoidable by a shortage of commodities, is called *forced substitution*.[7] Dissatisfaction of the consumer is expressed by a positive deviation, indicating an aspiration which she could not satisfy because of a shortage of commodities.

Let us introduce the following notation:

$$p_{ij} = \begin{cases} q_{ij} - r_{ij}, & \text{if } q_{ij} - r_{ij} > 0 \\ 0, & \text{if } q_{ij} - r_{ij} \leqslant 0 \end{cases}. \tag{2}$$

The $\mathbf{p}_i$ vector gives the *tension* of the procurement aspirations of the ith household.

We can develop symmetrical concepts for the sphere of production. For the sake of simplicity, let us leave out the intermediary of commerce and view producing enterprises. Just as we did before with members of a family, we must now interview enterprise managers. 'Assuming that (1) the production capacity and inventory of final goods of the enterprise is given (we are concerned with short-term decisions and thus will not consider the affect of capacity increase through investment), (2) current market prices are given, and together with this, the relative proportions of demand for the different products of the enterprise, (3) sales are not limited by demand considerations, how much would you produce and sell in the forthcoming period?' The reply would give us the aspiration level of production and sale for the enterprise concerned. After completing similar interviews in a suitable number of enterprises, we could draw general conclusions about the aspiration level of producers.

Let us assume there are N enterprises and m products. The aspiration level of the nth enterprise is described by a vector of m components, denoted by $\mathbf{x}_h$. In summarizing for the entire economy, we receive the total producer aspiration level:

$$\mathbf{x} = \sum_{h=1}^{N} \mathbf{x}_h. \tag{3}$$

193

Ex post observation can give us actual production during the period under question, which in the case of the *h*th enterprise is denoted by $\mathbf{y}_h$, and in summarizing for all enterprises by $\mathbf{y}$.

We measure dissatisfaction in producer aspirations in a similar way of that for consumers:

$$z_{hk} = \begin{cases} x_{hk} - y_{hk}, & \text{if} \quad x_{hk} - y_{hk} > 0 \\ 0, & \text{if} \quad x_{hk} - y_{hk} \leqslant 0 \end{cases}. \tag{4}$$

The vector $\mathbf{z}_h$ expresses the *tension of the production-sale aspiration level* of the *h*th enterprise.

There is *pressure* on the market for a product if the tension of production-sale aspirations is substantial and, compared with it, the tension of procurement aspirations is negligible. (The pressure is felt by the producer and it is caused *not* by production bottlenecks but by insufficient demand.) There is *suction* on the market if the tension of procurement aspirations is substantial, and in comparison, the tension of production–sale aspirations is minimal. There is *general pressure* over the entire economy if pressure exists on a large number of important products on the market, and suction appears only sporadically. The state of *general suction* can be defined analogously.

Conceptually, one may envision an index for measuring pressure and suction as follows:

$$S = \frac{p'\boldsymbol{\pi}}{r'\boldsymbol{\pi}}, \quad P = \frac{z'\boldsymbol{\pi}}{y'\boldsymbol{\pi}}, \tag{5}$$

where S is the degree of suction, P is the degree of pressure, and $\boldsymbol{\pi}$ is the vector of current market prices. According to this, the strength of suction is measured by the ratio of dissatisfied procurement aspirations to actual procurement, both summed at valid prices. We can interpret the degree of pressure in a similar way.

We have borrowed the concept of 'pressure–suction' from the vocabulary of metallurgical engineers. If the output capacity of an iron foundry is smaller than that of a steel works and that of the latter is smaller than the demands of the rolling mill, then the steel works voraciously consumes crude iron and the rolling mill likewise consumes steel. If, on the other hand, the situation is reversed so that the output capacity of the iron works is larger than the demands of the steel works, and the steel works' capacity is larger than the demands of the rolling mill, then the iron works puts pressure on the crude iron, and the steel works on the steel, all in the direction of the user.

The 'pressure–suction' pair of concepts is related to (though not identical with) the concepts of 'buyers' market–sellers' market'.

In speaking of pressure and suction, we are not thinking of momentary, temporary fluctuation from equilibrium. Here we are concerned with two types of *permanent one-way* deviations from the state of equilibrium, as illustrated in fig. 1.

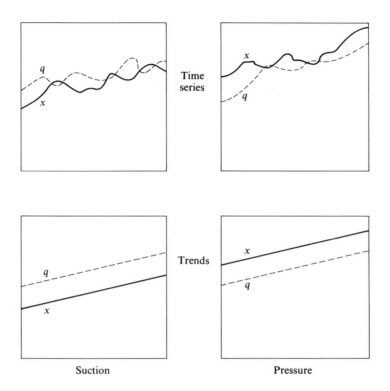

Fig. 1. Dotted line: procurement intentions. Continuous line:
production–sales intentions.

The graphs clearly show, in both the case of pressure and suction, that not only do the actual values in the time series of q and x deviate from one another, but so do the trends. We could speak of dynamic equilibrium if the actual values of intentions of procurement and of sale deviated but the two trends coincided.

In the case of pressure, procurement intentions and actual procurement more or less coincide. For this reason, by observing actual procurement data (from trade statistics or household statistics) we can draw conclusions on aspirations or intentions. This is what happens in estimating demand functions. The situation is different in the case of suction. Actual purchases do not reflect original intentions but rather realizations distorted by forced substitution. If, in a suction economy, we use customary methods for estimating a demand function (on the basis of trade statistics or household statistics), we cannot receive a true picture of the buyer's aspirations.

These comments indicate not only problems of measurement, but also the reason it was necessary to introduce new concepts in describing market disequilibrium. According to the traditional concept of 'demand' q and r, original intention and realization are used interchangeably. We must, however, be able to sharply separate these categories in order to characterize dissatisfaction and tension. We find ourselves facing a similar problem with the traditional concept of 'supply'.

While it is true that determining intentions and aspirations is not easy, it can be done.[8] In any event, and no matter how difficult this may be, the difficulties cannot be avoided by simply confusing intentions and realization or by dealing with actual purchases and sales only.

To be sure, we cannot consider the system of concepts introduced above as final. No doubt, following a large number of empirical observations, it will become possible to define concepts more accurately and to introduce new and better indices. However, we hope that the proposed concepts provide a useful initial framework for measuring disequilibrium and a point of departure for analysis.

THE EFFECTS OF PRESSURE AND SUCTION

We turn now to describing the effects of a lasting general pressure or suction on different economic processes of the economy. Although these effects are many-sided and mutually interrelated, in order to simplify analysis we divide them into four major groups.

Use of resources

First let us take as a simple example the housing situation. If there is pressure on the housing market, there are always flats awaiting rental. In suction this is inconceivable. Buyers must stand in line and dozens of people apply for a flat before it has been built.

In practical terms this means:
(a) In suction, the fixed assets of the producers are much more fully utilized than in pressure; generally the number of weekly shifts is higher, and reserve capacity is lower.
(b) The condition of pressure is generally accompanied by unemployment, while in suction there is a shortage of labor.
(c) When production and commerce are carried out under conditions of pressure, inventories are larger and better assorted, while under suction, inventories tend to be small and the buyer's choice is limited.

Therefore, in the state of suction, there is a fuller utilization of resources in general than in pressure. But here we should add that there are also adverse effects because in suction different types of friction appear, as discussed below.

196

Quality

The development of better-quality products is a complex process. It often begins with the introduction of revolutionary new products which differ considerably from older products of similar purpose (see Jewkes *et al.*, 1958). Examples of new products that were revolutionary at the time they appeared are the television, nylon, the transistor and Xerox duplicating. After the revolutionary new product became available, often first in simple form, its gradual improvement began, which is an evolutionary process. Here we distinguish between the pioneering enterprise which first introduces a product, from those which simply take over the innovation once it has been introduced. Finally, an important concept of quality is product reliability. Whether achieved through revolutionary or gradual change, every product has a quality parameter at any given time and stage of technical development. An important question is: how many products of a given enterprise achieve quality standards fully, and how many products show larger or smaller deficiencies or deviations from the quality standard? From here on, in speaking of 'quality', we generally mean a combination of all these aspects.

Many factors influence the development of better-quality products: general economic and cultural level of a country, financial support for research, technical development, effects of defense, etc. Without taking a stand on the order of importance of such factors, one thing we can say with certainty is that the absence or presence of pressure or suction on the market is one of the most important variables. For instance, the history of the most important inventions of nonmilitary revolutionary new products shows that with few exceptions, these products first appeared in 'pressure' economies. Yet in suction economies (particularly the more highly developed ones), we can find outstanding scientists, inventors, trained engineers and skilled workers capable of introducing new products to industry. The explanation for the anomaly lies not in technology but in the economic environment. In suction economies there tends to be lack of incentive for the extra effort, expense, and risk-bearing involved in introducing a new product. In a pressure economy the producers struggle with sales problems. The total production–sale aspirations of all producers are generally higher than their total sales opportunities. Under such circumstances, price reductions may be used to increase sales temporarily but this cuts down on profits. Or an advertising campaign might help to some extent. However, the major method through which a producer can draw buyers away from competitors and, at least in his own case, narrow the gap between his sales aspirations and actual results is to improve quality or introduce a new product, thereby creating new demands and developing a new market. *Tension in production–sale aspirations is the fundamental driving force behind improvement of quality and revolutionary product innovation.*

While emphasizing this, we must state that a suction economy may also be subject to factors which contribute to improving quality, innovation and technical development. In the sphere of consumption, rising living standards may cause strong demands to appear for more modern, better-quality products, particularly for products known to be available abroad. Also, the professional motivations of engineers and workers may contribute to improving quality, as may their interest in new technologies. They may also be spurred on by administrative regulations which protect industrial quality standards, as well as by financial awards for innovations and inventions. And finally, the shortages themselves may initiate innovations, although this possibility should not be overrated.

In describing technical development it is customary to differentiate product innovation from innovation in the production process. Many recognize that suction is unfavorable for product innovation but add that it provides incentives for production innovation, for careful economizing of scarce resources. However, in the majority of cases this statement does not hold true. In reality an improvement in the production process is nearly always closely associated with product innovation: the introduction of new machines, new instruments, new materials. Such new means of production are for the most part neither designed nor introduced by the consumer, but rather by the producer. Synthetic fibers were not invented by the textile industry but by the chemical industry; Xerox duplication was not brought about by offices or libraries which make use of it, but by the factory producing Xerox machines. The process of instant developing of film within cameras (Polaroid) was not discovered by the photography servicing industry but by the photography equipment industry. The key incentive for technical development derives from the *producing* enterprise, desiring to innovate by widening its product selection, rather than from the *user* enterprise seeking more efficient utilization of resources. The latter is important but plays a secondary role.

Looking again at a pressure economy, to be objective we must further point out that quality deterioration tends to appear along with quality improvement. For example, producers with lagging sales may try to increase their markets by decreasing the durability of their products, thereby forcing buyers to purchase replacements more frequently.

Yet, even after weighing such counterforces to the basic trend, we must still state that *suction slows down and pressure speeds up quality improvements and product development.*

Adaptation

The process of mutual adaptation of production and consumption is closely connected to the question of quality. First we look at short-run adaptation. *Suction* places the consumer at the mercy of the seller, whether the former is the housewife in the consumer goods market or a producing enterprise in the producer goods market. This affects consumer–seller relationships: the seller may behave carelessly and unconcernedly with the buyer or may continually ignore his demands. Suction forces the consumer or use of a product to accept the given supply and make substitutions. Thus, so long as a housing shortage exists, it is impossible to compel the construction industry to build high quality flats; again, so long as one must stand in line for repair and maintenance services, it is impossible to demand high quality.

Let us compare two consumers with identical consumption, that is with identical $\mathbf{r}_i$ vectors. In one case suppose $\mathbf{t}_i = 0$, that is the consumer has purchased what he wants. In the second case assume $\mathbf{t}_i > 0$, so that the consumer was unable to satisfy his original aspirations. Despite identical actual consumption, the former consumer would be satisfied and the latter dissatisfied. *Rising living standards in a suction economy give less satisfaction to the consumer since there is continuous tension due to unfulfilled aspirations.*

Under pressure conditions, the consumer–seller relationship is reversed, with the seller forced to court the buyer and meet his demands. Nevertheless, it would be incorrect to say that complete 'consumer sovereignty' is realized. This is only true in the short run; *long-run adaptation* takes place differently. The truth is that the consumer's preferences, tastes and demands change continually, being affected by technical development and innovations. 'Consumer preference' is not an inborn human quality but a social product; it is shaped by the available choice of products. Man has always wanted to see things happening in distant places, but this has become an effective demand only since industry produced the television set and made it available at acceptable prices. In a pressure economy as we have explained previously, there are strong incentives for product innovations. In the final analysis, therefore, *it is production which plays the primary role in the long run in the mutual adaptation of production and consumption in a pressure as well as a suction economy. From the point of view of technical development, more progress takes place in a pressure than in a suction economy.* The producer does not force the buyer to purchase his product due to forced substitution but attempts to produce new products attractive to the buyer.

Both from moral and economic points of view, it is debatable whether an unceasing flood of new products and the creation of newer and newer needs truly serve the welfare of humanity. It is not the role of this study, however, to take a stand on this but to state the facts. It is clear that new demands arise even in a suction economy, if for no other reason than to imitate consumption customs in pressure economies. If new products are creating new demands somewhere in the world and reports about them spread, these same new demands will sooner or later appear in other countries too.

It is also clear that product innovation and quality improvement are more likely and production–consumption relationships more pleasant for the consumer and freer of friction in a pressure than in a suction economy.

Informational activity

Producers and consumers, sellers and buyers, are connected by a flow of information. To a certain extent it is unavoidable that most informational activity be initiated by the producer. This division of labor can, however, be influenced by suction or pressure conditions. In the case of pressure, the seller increases his informational activities: he sends salesmen to the buyer and floods him with advertisements. To be sure, distinguishing objective from misleading information may become difficult. A shower of advertisements can overflow into a giant flood, which, from the social point of view, means waste of resources, going well beyond the level at which information is truly needed.

In a suction economy, the buyer is burdened with a disproportionately large share of the cost of obtaining information. He is forced to go from ship to shop, to return again and again to inquire until he finally finds the desired commodity. An enterprise must repeatedly urge and beg suppliers to send materials or component parts that are badly needed.

Rationing, a frequency occurrence in suction economies, must also be listed as an informational activity. Items in excess demand are not allocated by the market but are rationed by licensing agencies and administrators of material supply offices. While under pressure it is exaggerated advertisement which causes social waste, under suction it is the administrative cost of rationing that has similar consequences.

Having examined the effects of pressure and suction, we can proceed to some normative conclusions. We cannot state that either pressure or suction is more favorable in all respects. Both types of disequilibria have advantages and disadvantages which, unfortunately, are usually closely interconnected. In a pressure situation one must reckon with unutilized resources and excessive advertising activity, but there are also strong incentives for technological development and quality improvement, as well as attention to purchasers' interests. In a suction situation there are fewer idle resources and no flood of advertising, but strong incentives for improving quality and introducing new products are lacking and the purchaser is at the mercy of the producer.

Which situation is more favorable for a country depends upon numerous factors. Such may be more favorable in a very poor country where it may be important to give something to everyone as soon as possible through maximum utilization of resources, while in the meantime, satisfaction of more discriminating demands can be neglected. A country like this must accept the fact that owing to its level of development it cannot play a pioneering role in the introduction of innovations and new products; it must be content to adopt them in ready-made form from the 'pressure' countries.

Suction is a necessary condition in a war economy (or an economy preparing for war). Here maximum use of resources is required; 'civilian' demands can be neglected and the demands of defense technology are well served by noneconomic incentives.

It is the opinion of the author that (assuming comparatively peaceful international conditions) an economy in the middle range of economic development – when satisfaction of more discriminating consumer demands comes to the fore – is likely to find that the advantages of pressure conditions and the disadvantages of suction are becoming increasingly pronounced. As long as pressure is not too strong, it is more favorable than either equilibrium or suction.[9] The benefits to be gained outweigh the disadvantages, especially since the latter can be limited with careful planning and appropriate state intervention.

Is it possible to establish pressure conditions in a socialist economy? The author is convinced that *it is*. To understand the basis of this positive answer, factors which create suction and pressure conditions must be analyzed. So far, we have discussed the *consequences* of two types of disequilibria. Let us now examine the underlying causes, realizing of course that 'cause' and 'effect' cannot always be clearly separated, since there are many phenomena which are simultaneously cause and effect due to complex interactions.

CAUSAL FACTORS AFFECTING SUCTION

Suction conditions can exist in both socialist and nonsocialist countries. Suction often accompanies war in capitalist economies. It has also appeared in several nonsocialist developing Asian and African countries. This indicates that suction is not exclusive to socialist ownership relations, but rather arises due to certain economic situations or policies.

Here, however, we would like to deal solely with suction as it appears in one socialist economy, Hungary. We would like to emphasize that the study of this phenomenon is rather new for this country; we can only postulate hypotheses which will subsequently require careful examination and correction if necessary.

Four interrelated causal factors will be examined: (1) an excess of purchasing power over commodity supply; (2) structural disproportions; (3) emphasis on quantity production; and (4) high investment tension.

Excess purchasing power

Suction on the consumer goods market can be explained to a great extent by the fact that with given prices (mostly fixed by the state) 'superfluous' purchasing power appears, i.e. purchasing power is greater than the available commodity supply.

This phenomenon can only be understood by studying the dynamic processes of development over time. Consumption in physical terms may increase, quite independently of financial developments; it may rise while prices are constant or during inflation – under suction or pressure. In suction, the state fixes most prices while at the same time attempts to hold in check the increase of nominal incomes by trying to link salary increases to rising productivity. However, the latter two endeavors will not be wholly successful. On the one hand, purchasing power in excess of the value of commodity supplies will push prices upwards in the form of government measures, administrative price changes or indirect hidden price increases (e.g., price remains unchanged but quality deteriorates or an improved quality product is sold at a disproportionately higher price). On the other hand, total wages and incomes – both employment and per worker incomes – will uncontrolledly increase again and again, much faster than planned.

It would seem that of these two endeavors – regulating both prices and purchasing power – the former has been carried out comparatively more consistently. This is why *the total process can be regarded as repressed inflation, repressed both in prices and wages, the former being more successful than the latter.* Since in the Hungarian economy it is easier to hold back prices than employment and income, 'superfluous' purchasing power appears repeatedly, and together with this, excess demand; hence suction.

Price rigidity may also contribute to suction. Flexible prices might aid short-run *adaptation* by lowering demand for commodities in short supply and making more attractive products which the purchaser is forced to buy because of shortages. Flexibility could thereby serve as incentive to the producer to increase production of items in short supply and lower the production of goods bought only as a result of forced substitution. At the same time, however, no matter how significant are *relative* prices, the ratio of the general price level to the wage level – that is, the ratio of total commodity supplies to total purchasing power – plays a much more important role as a cause of inflation.

Structural disproportions

When introducing the concepts of pressure and suction, we used as examples of disproportions vertically connected enterprises in the metallurgy industry. To a certain extent, the entire economy can be conceived of as a single, gigantic vertical enterprise.[10] The structure of the economy as it was developed in Hungary in the recent past has created many examples in which the production capacity of 'earlier steps' was smaller than the requirements of the 'later steps', even when the latter's production capacity was fully utilized. Raw material production may lag behind processing, expansion of the highway network behind the increase in the number of cars, export production behind import demands, etc. Such structural disproportions lead to suction within the production sphere.

Obsession with quantity

For a long time Hungarian enterprises have been stimulated to achieve maximum quantity production. This has been the aim of taut production plans, production propaganda, state-sponsored 'competition' among workers, and the system of managerial bonuses. Yet, internal reserves of raw materials, component parts and production capacity have not been sufficient. In the national economic plan, input projections were based on the optimistic assumption that all plants would fulfill their output plans. If, in this sort of *over-optimistic taut plan with no reserves*, mistakes occurred, e.g., enterprises lagged in output, there was an immediate disturbance in the input of the next user. This could take the form of a lack of materials, lack of component parts, lack of electric current or lack of commodities.

The pursuit of quantity is a characteristic example of how a cause at the same time is also an effect of suction.[11]

Over-taut investment intentions

Generally, lengthy decision-making processes precede reconstruction of an old factory, establishment of a new factory, hospital or university, construction of a highway or railway station, or the general mechanization of a technically backward branch of industry, in other words, all investments of major importance. The process begins with proposals; later bodies of higher authority (the Planning Office, the ministries), the Investment Bank, and perhaps local district or city councils join in and at last a final decision is made. Yet a 'final' decision is never so final after all: plans frequently change during execution. And since the decision-making process is lengthy, sometimes lasting for years, we are particularly justified in differentiating among original intentions, or aspiration levels as they were formed in the beginning of the process, the final decision itself, and both of these from realized investments.

Let us take a given point of time, denoted by t_0. Investment intentions and decisions at different levels of maturity exist side by side – from the first carefully formulated proposals to government decisions accepted and modified to investment plans that are in the process of being executed. The total of these is what we call *investment intentions* at t_0. If investment intentions were completely realized and in accordance with the original time-schedule of individual decisions, then they would imply determined physical input demands in the coming $t_1, t_2, t_3, \ldots$ periods. Let the number of types of different capital goods – machines, installations, instruments, buildings – be M. Let foreign exchange needed for imported machines and installations be listed under special 'capital goods'. Denote the M component vectors of *capital good requirements* for the investment intentions valid at time t_0 by $\mathbf{g}(t_1), \mathbf{g}(t_2), \mathbf{g}(t_3), \ldots$. These requirements must be met by the branches producing capital goods (including foreign trade, which must product the foreign exchange). Denote the M component vectors, describing the maximum available quantities of capital goods by $\mathbf{h}(t_1), \mathbf{h}(t_2), \mathbf{h}(t_3), \ldots$, and call them *investment potential*.

Investment intentions are overtense if the following inequality holds:

$$\mathbf{g}(t) \geqslant \mathbf{h}(t), \quad t = t_1, t_2, \ldots, \tag{6}$$

and at least for some important capital goods:

$$\mathbf{g}_i(t) > \mathbf{h}_i(t), \quad 1 \leqslant i \leqslant M, \tag{7}$$

that is, *if some important capital good requirements for which investment intentions are higher than the output capacity of the branches producing these capital goods, i.e. the investment potential.*

The actual use of capital goods can, of course, be no greater than the quantity available. *Ex post*, instead of the inequality in (7), we must have equality or inequality in the opposite direction:

$$\bar{\mathbf{g}}(t) \leqslant \mathbf{h}(t), \tag{8}$$

where $\bar{\mathbf{g}}(t)$ is actual (not intended) use of capital goods in time t. However, disproportions can exist *ex ante*; intentions can be oversized, leading to too many or too large a volume of investment actions beginning at the same time, forcing shortages of materials, queues of requests for building capacity and inadequate funds to import. The result is that the execution of investment plans is continually interrupted and dragged out over time. Tension appears on the capital goods market.

Of the factors causing suction, oversized investment intentions, i.e. tension on the investment market, is the most important. The relationship between $\mathbf{g}(t)$ and $\mathbf{h}(t)$ is the major regulator of suction as well as pressure.

Investment tension has an effect on the above other three sets of factors too, particularly on the first, i.e., on tensions on the consumer market. On the one hand, investments and consumption compete with one another for various products and resources. The consumer awaiting a new flat and the producing enterprise awaiting a new industrial hall both expect their demands to be met by the construction industry and the building materials industry. Hard currency could be used to purchase either foreign consumer goods or foreign industrial machines. Aside from this, dragging out investment actions can directly contribute to disproportions between purchasing power and commodity supply. While wages are received by those working on an investment project, the additional production which results enters the economic bloodstream later.

Let us make a slight digression here. In the introductory section it was emphasized that we are striving to develop a system of concepts more *generally* valid than is usually the case. The need for this endeavor is illustrated by this description of investments. When a Hungarian institution – the government, the planning office, or even an enterprise – makes an investment decision, the national economic plan contains indices expressed in physical units, indicating the required production of so many tons of various materials or the use of this or that important machine for the investment project. Investment activities are to begin according to a documented schedule: procurement and installation of machines, construction of facilities, etc., as designated. Once the project has begun, one can be practically certain that it will not be stopped owing to insufficient *funds* (Hungarian forints). It may have been delayed because blueprints, machines or cement arrived late or because the construction enterprise did not begin work on time, or perhaps because of a shortage in hard currency to buy imported components, but a slow-down or stoppage of an investment project has never been caused by a lack of domestic 'financing'. This means that tension on the investment market of a socialist economy cannot be described in depth using customary theoretical concepts, i.e. by contrasting supply and demand expressed in value terms. We need categories which help to contrast 'real' demand caused by investment intentions and physically available 'real' potential.

In the final analysis, suction as it appears in a socialist economy cannot be fully explained by phenomena in the *financial* sphere, by disproportions between effective supply and demand or between purchasing power and the quantity of commodities offered for sale at given prices. The latter descriptions would appear to hold by and large only on consumer markets. The main problem on the producer goods market is not that the purchaser has 'too much money', to use a simplified expression, but that the producing enterprise, in order to meet its current production requirements, to use its capacity optimally or tautly, needs more materials, component parts, machines and labor than are available. In order to realize investment decisions, more machines, building capacity, and hard currency are needed than are available, given the investment potential of the country. This means that we are not facing disproportions in the financial sphere but between *real* requirements implied by plan decisions on the one hand, and *real* possibilities on the other.

Let us now go on to an analysis of pressure. Temporary pressure on individual markets can exist in socialist countries too. For a time, general pressure existed in Yugoslavia, taking the economy as a whole. However, in this paper we will turn our attention exclusively to general pressure in the markets of developed capitalist countries.

In debating the question with Western economists, the author has frequently encountered the following view: it is incorrect to describe the markets of capitalist economies as typically in pressure, i.e., exhibiting disequilibrium. In their opinion, the capitalist market, looking at long-run trends, is in equilibrium, there being only partial and temporary fluctuations around equilibrium. There is no need here for a debate on semantics; what is important is not how to define the typical state of the capitalist market but how to describe its characteristics correctly. There are reasons for holding to the view that present capitalist markets are characterized by permanent and one-way deviations from equilibrium, i.e., in a pressure-type of disequilibrium.

All sciences – be they mechanics, thermodynamics, or biology – view equilibrium as a symmetric state, as the equalization of two opposing forces. The capitalist market in this sense is asymmetric. The key question is: who is faced with the greater problem in the market – the buyer or the seller? Who has to 'court' whom – is it the buyer courting the seller, or the seller the buyer? There would be equilibrium if market pressures were divided '50–50'. However, the typical state of affairs in a capitalist economy is that problems of buying–selling are divided unequally, with a greater burden being placed on the seller. He sends his salesmen to the buyer, he tries to win him over with quality improvements, with new products (sometimes pseudo 'novelties') and with objective information and untrue advertisements alike. It is not the buyer who is worried about whether he will be able to buy the desired goods with the money he has, but the seller who is worried about whether he will win the favor of the buyer.

There are many unutilized resources in a capitalist economy. Many authors point to the gap between the potential and actual output of the economy.[12] Perhaps we could better understand the dynamics of a capitalist economy if we would accept permanent disequilibrium to be a fact and try to analyze the factors which continually produce a state of pressure. We would like to call attention to four closely interrelated factors.

Price inflation

Just as in discussing suction, a first factor is the ratio between prices and wages. It is well known that the majority of capitalist countries have experienced inflationary processes for decades. We do not want to deal with the historical starting points of these processes nor with the way the state of pressure had been initially created. Let us assume that creeping inflation is a fact and that pressure is the typical state. Beginning here, both prices and incomes could continue to increase and the value of money to decrease while a state of pressure is maintained. The only thing needed is growth in income not to exceed increases in prices. Although rising prices and wages are mutually interdependent, in a capitalist pressure economy price inflation plays the leading role. This, and the lack of full employment, ensures that, despite continuous wage and price rises, *total purchasing power intended by the population for consumption is incapable of consuming the mass of commodities offered for consumption at any single moment.* Such disproportions affect further production through financial and credit relations among enterprises. In the final analysis, *effective purchasing intentions lag behind commodity supplies as well as behind sales intentions based on potential production.*

This phenomenon is also related to the influence of large business concerns on price determination. Prices are quite rigid on many markets in today's capitalist economy. Even if sales are difficult, the enterprise would rather produce new products than reduce its prices to adjust to the momentary market situation.

Uncertainty and excess capacity

In a state of pressure, as was pointed out earlier, the buyer can choose among many sellers. Knowing this, every seller tries to prepare for the fact that he might be the one whose product will be chosen. This is why he creates extra capacity which, at the same time, increases pressure, in the form of added selection opportunities for the buyer. In the end this decreases from the point of view of the individual seller, the changes for his product to be chosen by the buyer.

This same idea can be described in another way. The market is ruled by uncertainty and all producers plan excess capacity in order to lower the uncertainty of sales. The size of this slack is as large as *individual* certainty requires; they do not want to miss potential buyers. However, on the *scale of the entire economy* the sum of individual slack capacities is substantially larger than would be needed to supply all buyers. (This is why a planned economy feels the urge to decrease radically such 'exaggerated' slack.) The fact that extra capacity, exaggerated from the point of view of 'safety of operation', also serves as an incentive for important and continuous technical progress and improvement of quality, etc., is another matter.

Succession of new products

Product innovation is not only a consequence but also a cause of pressure. Let us assume that at a given technological level there is equilibrium and that a new product appears, creating new demands. The buyer turns to the new, but the old is still produced simultaneously or at least capacity exists for producing it (perhaps unsuited for the new product). This contributes to unutilized capacity in the entire economy.

Unutilized investment potential

As with suction, the most important factor here is investment proportions. The Keynesian school deals in depth with equilibrium and disequilibrium of saving and investment but always keeps the financial side of the problem in mind as fundamental. We would like here to put emphasis on the real sphere: the ratio of real capital goods (machines, buildings, etc.) required by investment intentions to actual investment potential, i.e., to the output capacity of all branches producing the machines, buildings, etc.

A state of pressure results if *ex ante* (that is, during the time of proposals, decisions, plans) *the need for capital goods induced by investment intentions is smaller than the available supply of investment goods, that is, investment potential.* Using the notation introduced earlier:

$$\mathbf{\hat{g}}(t) \leqslant \mathbf{h}(t), \quad t = t_1, t_2, \dots \tag{9}$$

and for at least some important capital goods:

$$\mathbf{\hat{g}}_i(t) < \mathbf{h}_i(t), \quad 1 \leqslant i \leqslant M. \tag{10}$$

As we can see, the direction of inequality is exactly the opposite of that observed under suction in (7), where the need for investment goods was higher than investment potential.

Levels of investment intentions which are too low can be explained by many factors. Financial savings which could serve as resources for decentralized investments may be insufficient; investors may be too cautious and too pessimistic; the government and the banking system follows an investment credit policy which is too restrictive; there are too few government investments. These factors (and perhaps others too) can appear alone, though joint effects are more frequent. In the final analysis, in a pressure economy there is always some unused real capital for new investment.

We would like to call attention to the fact that we have not asked the Keynesian question here on the relationship between savings and investments but a more general question which is related to it: the ratio between investment intentions and investment potential.

The four economic factors contributing to pressure just reviewed, do not of course, always prevail to the same extent. In capitalist economies as elsewhere, increases in wages and employment may be the dominant force, sometimes supplemented by extension of credit for investment purposes. In order to avoid a recession, following Keynesian lines, many countries are increasingly applying economic policies which stimulate investment intentions. Inflation may then speed up and the economy become 'overheated', but a recession may be avoided and pressure abated, while one or more suction symptoms may appear.

TRANSITION FROM SUCTION TO PRESSURE

In reviewing the causes of suction and pressure, we hope we have convinced the reader that neither one nor the other is a direct and automatic result of the political nature of the system. There can be suction in a capitalist economy and pressure in a socialist economy.

The author is convinced that Hungary will sooner or later have to prepare for a transition from the state of suction to that of pressure. The economic reform successfully introduced in Hungary in 1968 can only bring halfway results if market suction continues (see Friss, 1969). It is true that enterprises have been freed from an entire series of bureaucratic ties and become interested in profits. So long as suction rules there will be friction in that producers will continue to dominate consumers and will not be truly forced to improve quality or to innovate. However, it is already noticeable that the New Economic Mechanism has brought about most favorable results in those branches (e.g., the food industry, light industry, and certain parts of the engineering industry related to consumption branches) where the market has become increasingly saturated with products, and a more or less pressure-like state has developed. The situation is similar with enterprises working solely or mainly for export; we find 'pressure' here too, where producers face selling difficulties and are forced to produce new, better quality products to gain markets. In contrast, the building industry, where strong suction continues, has not improved quality to any noticeable extent.

Many believe that the key means to develop the reform is to make the price system more flexible. Although it would be useful, its importance should not be overrated. Sensitivity and speed of adjustment in production does not depend very strongly on whether prices and profit rates react like seismographs to all fluctuations in supply and demand. *Global proportions are more important: selling should become more difficult in general.* The producer then would be forced to adjust to demand even if this would not be reflected directly in differential profit margins.

We frequently encounter the view that the main problem following the recent Hungarian reform stems from a monopolistic position of enterprises, i.e., lack of competition. But this too is secondary to the problem of 'pressure–suction'. So-called monopoly enterprises only rule individual groups of products or services, that is, are monopolies *within one branch.* However, in the case of pressure, there is competition among branches too. Even if railway transportation and air transportation were monopolized by individual large-scale enterprises, they would compete for passengers with each other and with highway transportation. In a general pressure situation the consumer can decide whether to spend more on travel, entertainment, furniture, or for other purposes. Although transportation is not a direct 'substitute' for the cinema or furniture, at least for that portion of consumer spending which is 'discretionary', transportation, services of the entertainment industry, furniture, together with a good many other products, are in competition with one another. In situations of pressure, with few or rare exceptions, all enterprises are in competition with all others, even if they can maintain monopolies in their own specialty or territories. In contrast, under suction, even the most strongly atomistic branches (e.g., private craftsman offering repair services) can dominate the consumer like monopolists.

There is a certain asymmetry in transforming the economy from suction to pressure as compared to a pressure to suction transformation. Transitions from pressure to suction tend to be very easy. Enterprises can quickly utilize internal reserves as the economy switches tight production plans. As nominal wages surge, many new investments may be eagerly undertaken. During the period of transition this can produce spectacular results and the growth rate may speed up due to the transition alone.

The reverse road is much more difficult to traverse. If we ignore the possibility of resources from abroad (either gradual indebtedness through foreign trade, long-term credit or aid) and take into account domestic resources only, four types of measures would have to be executed in Hungary to achieve this type of transition. (1) Investment plans would have to be compiled in such a way as not to reach the upper bound of investment potential, but should allow slack in the building and engineering industries. (2) Some investment should be designed to create excess capacity which would not contribute instantly to social production. (3) Real wages and employment should be increased in a way such that surplus purchasing power would be gradually eliminated and a more extensive and better assortment of commodity stocks allowed to accumulate. (4) Reform in economic management must be consolidated and then further developed so that production could become more efficient, and expansion of enterprises more dependent on profitability. This would cause enterprises to become more interested in market adaptation and in lowering costs. In general, we can say that the *economic policy* problem of pressure–suction, together with other economic policy issues, is most closely connected with further development of reforms in economic management.

One or the other of the conditions just listed would temporarily 'damage' the indices which are frequently handled as fetishes, such as the capital–output ratio or the growth rate of national income and real wages. Despite this, modification of economic policy in these directions will sooner or later be unavoidable.

We cannot say when these changes should begin or how fast they should proceed. That is not a problem for economics alone since it would have deep-reaching political effects.

It would be a mistake to take practical measures too hastily, but now is the time to propose a fundamental theoretical debate on the above issues. This leads us to a final topic: the tasks of scientific research.

CONFRONTATION WITH TRADITIONAL ECONOMIC THEORIES AND THE TASKS OF SCIENTIFIC RESEARCH

Discussion of disequilibrium in this article deviates from general equilibrium theory and neo-classical price theory in a number of respects. For the sake of summary, let us return to several questions touched on previously.

System of concepts

We have endeavored to develop a system of concepts more general than those in traditional theory. For instance, the customary concept of 'demand' is a narrow, special case of the new, broader concept 'procurement aspirations'. This embraces purchase intentions appearing at the beginning of the decision process of procurement and subsequently modifiable by many different factors (e.g., a shortage) prior to actual purchase. The customary interpretation of 'demand' does not distinguish between original and final or 'validated' intention. Under conditions of pressure the fact that these coincide is self evident. However, this distinction can become very important in describing suction.

The term 'procurement aspiration' appears a suitable one for a number of reasons. For instance, in a centralized socialist economy the input requirements of state enterprise are influenced by central directives. 'Demand', considered primarily or solely as a function of price and income, would be a special case of 'procurement aspiration' in this situation.

'Procurement aspiration' does not deal with hopes, but rather with *serious* intentions. For example, in a socialist economy 'seriousness' of investment intentions could be judged by asking: Is there a valid state resolution authorizing the investment? In contrast, in the traditional interpretation of 'demand', the sole criterion of 'seriousness' is the willingness of the buyer to spend money.

Mechanism of adaptation

Although they are obviously related, the two concept pairs 'pressure–suction' and 'excess supply–excess demand' are not synonymous. The latter is associated by traditional theory with the following adaptation mechanism (see Arrow and Hurwicz, 1960). On one side are producers with given production possibilities, on the other consumers with given preferences. Mutual adjustment of production and consumption takes place under unchanged technical conditions. If there happens to be excess supply under a given price, then the price drops; with excess demand, it increases. Thus price is the sole information feed-back, adjusting production and consumption to approximate a state of equilibrium.

This paper has described a more complex adaptation mechanism. In situations of pressure, adaptation takes place in the midst of technological development over time.[13] If there is excess supply of a product, its price may drop but a more important adjustment response may be that the enterprise tries to correct the situation by marketing new, better quality products. Also, consumer preferences are not objectively given but are part of an economic process developing preferences, adjusted to continuous product innovation.

In the case of suction there are again two sides to adaptation: response of the buyer to procurement possibilities through forced substitution and of the seller to demand information received primarily through non-price channels (e.g., state directives, rationing, length of waiting lines, and complaints by purchasers).

Normative standpoint

Perhaps the most essential difference between the traditional theory of equilibrium and that presented in this article is normative standpoint. Most economists consider it self-evident that equilibrium is the most desirable economic state. In contrast, the author is of the opinion that while equilibrium is more favorable than suction, slight pressure is more advantageous than equilibrium. The theoretical definition of equilibrium is a state of rest – a position of the economy which no participant in the system wants to disturb. It would be unfortunate if an economy were ever to find itself in that state. It would lead to inertia, which is much less preferable than some sort of healthy disturbance.

The author would like to emphasize that he considers the present paper and his book *Anti-Equilibrium* (Kornai, 1971), which discusses the topic in more detail, to be only the beginning of needed research in this area. Many research problems remain. To mention but a few examples:

(1) Observation is needed of shortage phenomena, market tension and aspirations. Systematic description of pressure and suction should be supported by data for Hungary and other countries.

(2) Questions of quality improvement, product innovation, techno-logical development, and the interrelations of these processes with market disequilibrium, need explanation.

(3) Adaptations of production and consumption under both suction and pressure should be distinguished.

(4) Examination of factors regularly producing suction and pressure (a related issue is differentiating 'suction' and 'pressure' types of in-flation); the relationship between investment intentions and investment potential; the creation of enterprise excess capacities; disproportions in branch structure; the interdependence of disequilibrium and prices (price structure and flexibility).

(5) Study of the relationship between disequilibria and economic adjustment mechanism.

We are sure that many statements in this paper will provoke debate. If this paper has been able to show that the study of disequilibrium can be important and fruitful it has then achieved its purpose.

NOTES

1 This paper summarizes some of the author's ideas as they appeared in Kornai (1971). The author expresses his gratitude to the institutes through which he completed the preparatory research for the book: the Institute of Economics of the Hungarian Academy of Sciences in Budapest, the Institute of Mathematical Studies in the Social Sciences at Stanford University, and the Cowles Foundation for Research in Econmics at Yale University. My special thanks go to those who provided valuable advice in helping me clear up my concepts. They include K. J. Arrow, W. Fellner, T. C. Koopmans, T. Liptak, B. Martos, and many other colleagues from Hungary and abroad.

This paper is an expanded version of a lecture the author gave at Indiana University in April 1970 and which has since appeared in the January 1971 issue of *Közgazdasági Szemle* (Budapest). The author would like to thank the International Development Research Center for its facilities, the Center's Director, George J. Stolnitz, for helpful comments and Paul Marer and Mrs Kathleen Sparkes for editorial assistance. The help of Alan A. Brown in providing liaison between the author and the Center is gratefully acknowledged. An earlier version of this paper appeared in the Working Paper Series of the International Development Research Center at Indiana University.

2 Stalin stated: 'here in the Soviet Union consumption [purchasing power] of the masses grows continually, advancing ahead of the rise in production, serving as a stimulant to production ... the growth of the domestic market will advance beyond the growth of industry, serving as a spur to industry to continually expand production' (see Stalin, 1949). This view has frequently appeared in economic literature.

3 Articles and studies from 1954–8, initiating the reform in Hungary's economic mechanism, refer meaningfully to problems of disequilibrium. We often come across contrasts between 'buyers' market' and 'sellers' market' in the literature comparing economic systems. Keynes (1936) and Keynesian literature deal with certain types of disequilibrium in the sphere of investment and employment. Others, including J. K. Galbraith (1947) and P. Streeten (1959), also discuss problems of disequilibrium, in a manner which deviates from the train of thought of the present paper.

4 The concept of *aspiration level* has been introduced by the psychologist Kurt Lewin (1936), and has since been used by many sociologists and economists.

5 We are speaking of the aspiration level for 'procurement' and not for 'purchasing'. The former is a more general concept; the latter is a special form of procurement. We consider the concept 'aspiration level for procurement' applicable also to the procurement of materials by enterprises in a highly centralized planned economy. Here the financial side of procurement (its 'purchase' nature) is completely secondary, since administrative consignment of materials plays the major role.

6 We are describing the aspiration level and related concepts in deterministic form for the sake of simplicity. In truth, however, there is much uncertainty of intentions and aspirations, and for this reason it would be more accurate to use stochastic formalism.

7 Deviation between intention and realization can be caused by other factors as well: the purchaser housewife simply changes her mind, she gains knowledge of new information, etc. This paper does not deal with these deviations.

8 For instance, regular interviews with consumers, completed by the Michigan Survey Center, USA, are held expressly to inquire into consumers' purchase intentions (see Katona, 1969). In compiling the McGraw-Hill Index, measuring the production dynamics of the United States, questions are put to the managers of many enterprises; a number of such questions yield replies from which we can draw conclusions on production aspirations.

9 A similar conclusion appears in Marx. He raises the question of how to organize the economy 'after having eliminated the capitalist form of reproduction'. He refers to the fact that 'in one year, more fixed capital and in the next year less fixed capital may be used up in the form of *de facto* depreciation. To replace fixed capital, its total output should be increased one year and decreased the next. This can only be accomplished if there is general comparative overproduction. On the one hand somewhat more capital must be produced than is really needed, while, on the other hand and primarily, levels of raw material and other inventories must be established which go beyond direct annual requirements (particularly valid prospects for essential consumer commodities). This type of overproduction means that society has taken under its own control the reproduction of fixed capital.' (See Marx, 1967, vol. II, p. 473.) As we see, Marx is not speaking simply of reserves, but of *permanent comparative over-production*.

10 The concept of 'the national economy as a vertical enterprise', can be interpreted in the following way: Consider the triangularization of an economy-wide Leontief

214

matrix, at least with respect to the larger coefficients. Although full triangularization cannot be executed, the problem can be solved with respect to the large
coefficients so that we arrive at a block–triangular structure. This means that blocks
consisting of sectors with lower row numbers channel products to sectors with
higher serial numbers, but do not receive inputs from them. (Mutual input–output
connections appear only within the blocks.) The blocks with lower serial numbers
represent sectors in the 'earlier steps' in the production process, as discussed above,
while those with higher numbers are the 'subsequent steps'.

11 We list the pursuit of quantity among causal factors of suction although since the
reform in economic management, in Hungary at least, this factor is no longer valid.

12 See, for example, a paper by Okun (1962). Noteworthy from the point of view of
indicating 'slack' are the McGraw-Hill Indexes of capacity utilization based on
questionnaire surveys of business enterprises. According to these, actual capacity
utilization of American industry is regularly 10–15 % below the capacity utilization
rate preferred by management.

13 Here we are reminded of Schumpeter's important ideas on 'creative destruction'
(*Schöpferische Zerstörung*); see Schumpeter (1942).

REFERENCES

Arrow, K. J. and L. Hurwicz (1960). Decentralization and computation in resource
allocation. In *Essays in Economics and Econometrics*. Chapel Hill: University of North
Carolina Press.

Friss, I. (ed.) (1969). *Reform of the Economic Mechanism in Hungary*. Budapest: Akademiai
Kiado.

Galbraith, J. K. (1947). The disequilibrium system. *American Economic Review*, **37**,
287–302.

Jewkes, J., D. Sawers, and R. Stillerman (1958). *The Sources of Inventions*. London:
Macmillan, 1958.

Katona, G. *The Powerful Consumer*. New York: McGraw Hill, 1969.

Keynes, J. M. *The General Theory of Employment, Interest and Money*. London:
Macmillan.

Kornai, J. (1971). *Anti-Equilibrium: On Economic Systems Theory and the Tasks of Research*.
Amsterdam: North-Holland.

Lewin, K. (1936). *Principles of Topological Psychology*. New York: McGraw Hill.

Marx, K. (1967). *Capital*. Moscow: Progress Publishers.

Okun, A. (1962). Potential GNP: its measurement and significance. *American Statistical
Association Proceedings*, **57**, 98–104.

Schumpeter, J. A. (1942). *Capitalism, Socialism and Democracy*. New York: Harper.

Stalin, J. V. (1949). Politicheskiy otchnot Centralnovo Comitata XVI Syezdu VCP/b
(Political account of the Central Committee to the XVIth Congress of the Soviet
Communist Party). *Sochineniya*, vol. 12. Moscow: Gosuderstvennoe Izdatelstvo
Politicheskoi Literature.

Streeten, P. (1959). Unbalanced growth. *Oxford Economic Papers*, **11**, 176–81.

4. The Socialist Enterprise

Economic Reform and the Maximizing Behavior of the Soviet Firm

J. MICHAEL MARTIN

INTRODUCTION

Despite the economic reform of 1965, the Soviet Union has not been able to recapture the once rapid pace of economic development. Preliminary figures suggest the slowdown of growth has continued. Admittedly, the reform failed in part because of the way it was administered. The provisions of the reform had to be enacted by the petty bureaucracy that was most opposed to the reform in the first place.[1] Yet, given the specific nature of the reform there was no way efficiency (as compared to perfect competition) could be obtained. This paper will concentrate on one provision of the reform, the change in managerial incentives, by constructing a model of the reformed enterprise.[2] This new firm will fail to achieve the conditions of perfect efficiency but in a way that differs significantly from the pre-reform enterprise.

Before the reform was enacted firms were given up to thirty targets. The size of their bonus funds depended on the fulfillment of these targets. However, so many targets left the managers with few degrees of freedom. While the gross output target and a few others were met, the rest were undoubtedly violated. All of these goals were replaced with just two main targets by the reform: the growth of profits (or in some cases the growth of sales) and the profit rate (profit divided by the sum of fixed and working capital). The size of the incentive funds is now tied to these targets in a manner described below. There are other targets but they can be thought of as inequalities that must be satisfied before any bonuses are paid at all.[3]

The reforms enhance the role of the three so-called enterprise funds: the material incentive fund, the social–cultural fund, and the fund for production development. The first is to be used for ruble bonuses to managers and workers, the second for housing and other communal activities, and the third for reinvestment in the firm. These three funds are deducted from profits after fixed percentage capital charges, rent, and certain other payments are made to the government. The size of each one of these funds depends on how well the growth of profits and profit rate indicators are fulfilled. Additional planned bonuses are included in the material incentive fund, but since these bonuses are out of the firm's control we will not consider them in our analysis.

216

There is a fixed norm for deduction for each 1 % growth of profits and one for each 1 % of profit rate – different norms for different funds. These norms are to be held stable for long periods of time. The wages fund is used as a base for the calculation of the deductions for the material incentive and social–cultural funds; fixed capital is used as a base for the development fund. The enterprise manager is presumed to maximize a weighted average (his subjective weights) of the material incentive and social–cultural funds. That is, these two funds appear as arguments in his utility function. The development fund is best treated as affecting the charge against capital and will be omitted from this first model.

Thus, the objective function the firm maximizes can be written:

$$Z = \alpha_1 MIF + \alpha_2 SCF$$
$$Z = \alpha_1(awL\sigma + bwL\phi) + \alpha_2(cwL\sigma + dwL\phi)$$
$$= (\alpha_1 a + \alpha_2 c)\, wL\sigma + (\alpha_1 b + \alpha_2 d)\, wL\phi,$$

where:

MIF	Material incentive fund
SCF	Social-cultural fund
α_1, α_2	Subjective weights given to each of these funds
a, b, c, d	Norms for deduction
wL	Wages fund
π_t	Accounting profit. It is net of all capital and labor costs and fixed rental payments
K	The sum of fixed and working capital
σ	Growth of profits; i.e. $\dfrac{\pi_t - \pi_{t-1}}{\pi_{t-1}}$
ϕ	Profit rate, i.e. $\dfrac{\pi_t}{K}$.

We let:

$$\alpha_1 a + \alpha_2 c = \gamma_1$$
$$\alpha_1 b + \alpha_2 d = \gamma_2,$$

and assume the subjective weights are known and constant so that γ_1 and γ_2 are also known and constant.[4] It should be noted that γ_1 and γ_2 will not add up to one. The objective function in its final form is:[5]

$$Z = \gamma_1 wL\sigma + \gamma_2 wL\phi.$$

This is a simplified version of the actual accounting formula used by Soviet planners for calculating incentive funds. We will analyze the behavior of the Soviet firm as it seeks to maximize this function assuming first one variable factor and then two variable factors. In a second model we will replace growth of profits in the objective function with growth of sales and compare the results.

J. Michael Martin

ONE VARIABLE FACTOR

The single variable factor case constitutes the basic model. Unlike usual microeconomic analysis, we shall make that variable factor capital. This, in the Soviet planning context, is a plausible assumption. The wages fund (wL) is one of the targets still specified in the plan and wage levels are determined by the central planners. Therefore, labor is fixed. This model will enable us to discover what combination of the profit rate and the growth of profits the firm chooses and how it goes about choosing it. We will also see how much capital the firm employs and how much output it produces.

The relevant equations for this model are:

$$Z = \gamma_1 \overline{wL}\sigma + \gamma_2 \overline{wL}\phi \qquad \text{Objective function} \qquad (1)$$

$$X = f(K, L); \; L = L_0; \quad f_K > 0; f_{KK} < 0 \quad \text{Production function} \quad (2)$$

$$\pi = TR - TC = P_X X - rK - \overline{wL} - R. \qquad \text{Profit.} \qquad (3)$$

Output is a function of capital and labor, but the quantity of labor is fixed at L_0. Both the wages fund, wL, and rent, R, are considered fixed costs. Capital is assumed to be in perfectly elastic supply at price r. The demand for the single output is perfectly elastic at price P_X.

For the present we shall analyze a one period case. This means that last year's profit, π_{t-1}, is fixed and out of control of the manager. No action of his can change it. Thus, the way for him to maximize the growth of profits is to maximize profit this year. Actually, this may not be a bad assumption. Soviet managers are transferred from firm to firm quite often and so are likely to have short time horizons with respect to the operation of any one enterprise. Doubt about the permanence of the reforms would enhance that attitude. Entrepreneurs are unlikely to develop a long term strategy of how to maximize profits over time (which might mean earning lower profit this year so the growth of profits would be much larger next year). Such behaviour would probably be noticed and punished by the planners.

Our objective function contains two elements: the growth of profits and the profit rate. The growth of profits is a monotonic transformation of profit. This term alone would cause the firm to behave in the same way as a profit maximizing firm. A firm that maximized only the profit rate would behave in a way very similar to a firm that maximized the dividend rate (profit per worker) where the conclusions with regard to employment of labor would apply to capital instead (see Ward, 1958; Domar, 1966; Oi and Clayton, 1968). The new Soviet firm will be an intermediate case between a firm that maximized profit and one that maximized the profit rate.

The first step in our analysis is to draw a production function for output

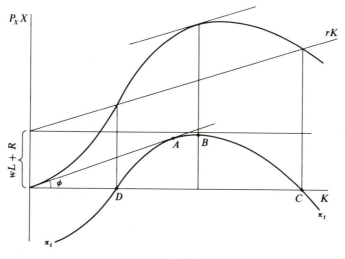

Fig. 1

with respect to capital (fig. 1).[6] The vertical axis is multiplied by the price of the product so everything is in value terms. Labor cost is fixed at wL, rent at R. Capital has a constant price of r per unit of capital. Thus, variable cost is a straight line with a slope of r. Total costs are the vertical sum of the wages bill, rent, and capital cost. We can find the amount of profit for any output simply be subtracting total costs from total revenue. This procedure generates another curve which represents the amount of profit earned by the firm for the given production function and given output price ($DABC$ in fig. 1). The profit rate (profit divided by capital) can be represented as the slope of a line drawn from the origin to the curve. It is at its maximum when the line is tangent to the curve.

We can find the numerator of the growth of profits expression, $\pi_t - \pi_{t-1}$ simply be a vertical displacement up or down of the profits curve – up if π_{t-1} is negative, down if π_{t-1} is positive. Comparison of the resulting curve with a vertical line segment representing will give the growth of profits. Two possibilities are shown in fig. 2. Negative profits are losses. The firm would require and presumably receive a subsidy to stay in operation. When both current and past profits are negative, the term σ needs to be multiplied by minus one to give the correct sign (or alternatively, we could take the absolute value of that expression).[7]

What combination of growth of profits and profit rate does the firm choose? To answer this question, we plot σ against ϕ (fig. 3). We can generate a 'feasibility surface' from fig. 1. That is, how much does profit grow at each level of profit rate? At point D the profit rate is zero; growth of profits is negative (assuming π_{t-1} to be positive). The profit rate and growth of profits increase up to point A where the profit rate is at a maxi-

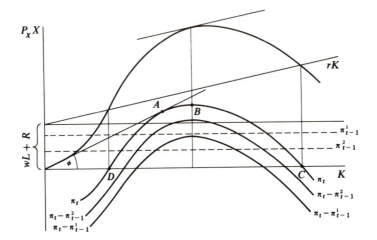

Fig. 2

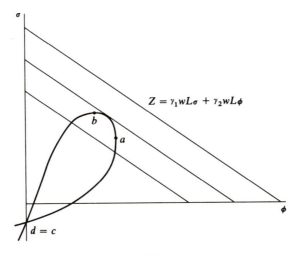

Fig. 3

mum. From A to B the growth of profits continues to increase, but the profit rate falls. Both fall after point B. The profit rate equals zero again at C, and the growth of profits is negative and equal to what it was at D. In such a manner we generate the feasibility surface. Small letters on the feasibility surface show points corresponding to those shown by capital letters on the profit curve.

A few comments about the nature of this surface are in order before we proceed further. The curve bears some resemblance to a production function if we think of the growth of profits and the profit rate as the outputs. Both capital and output vary as we move along the curve; only labor is fixed. We can say the feasibility surface is a function of capital and output, $S = S(K, X)$; or since output is a function of capital (labor fixed), $X = f(K)$, we have $S = S'(K)$. The vertical intercept of the surface will always take place at -100% whether last year's profits were positive or negative since $\sigma = \pi_t/\pi_{t-1} - 1 = -1$ if $\pi_t = 0$.

The objective function plots as a straight line in fig. 3, since $\gamma_1 wL$ and $\gamma_2 wL$ are constant. The slope is $-\gamma_2/\gamma_1$; the vertical intercept $Z/\gamma_1 wL$. There are a family of these lines, each representing a constant incentive fund. Lines to the northeast represent larger funds. They are exactly analogous to budget lines. The enterprise selects that combination of the growth of profits and profit rate that earns it the largest incentive fund – i.e. where the slope of the feasibility surface equals the slope of the incentive line. We have:

$$\frac{d\sigma}{d\phi} = -\frac{\gamma_2}{\gamma_1}. \tag{4}$$

The firm will pick a point where neither the growth of profits nor the profit rate is maximized. Actually, if the firm operates on the frontier of the feasibility surface only that portion of the curve between the two maximums is relevant.

Different π_{t-1}s would generate different feasibility surfaces. Curves resulting from the π_{t-1}s of fig. 2 are shown in fig. 4. All curves have the same maximum profit rate since it is unaffected by last year's profit. Maximum growth of profits also occurs at the same profit rate. As π_{t-1} approaches zero, the growth of profits approaches infinity. This will elongate curves representing a low last year's profit (π_{t-1}^2 in fig. 4). Obviously a firm earning low profit last year will be in a better position to earn a large incentive fund this year.[8]

Fig. 1 reveals the new firm will employ less capital than a firm that maximizes profit. Differentiating Z (the objective function) with respect to K yields the same result and gives us a better idea of what the factor market looks like. The result of this operation is:[9]

$$r = P_X f_K + \frac{\gamma_2 \pi_{t-1}}{\gamma_1 K}\left(P_X f_K - \frac{P_X X - wL - R}{K}\right). \tag{5}$$

The firm will hire capital to a point where its price equals the value of the marginal product (VMP) plus some fraction of the difference between the VMP and the value of the net average product (net of rent and fixed labor costs). The fraction is the ratio of the weights given to profit rate and growth of profits weighted itself by the ratio of past profit to capital. If past profits are positive, this ratio will be positive. Accordingly, we draw a demand curve for capital (fig. 5). The demand curve DD is above the VMP when $(P_X X - wL - R)/K$ is less than $P_X f_K$, below it when the reverse is true. Where the two terms are equal and the curves cross, the profit rate is zero.[10] It is positive to the right of that point, negative to

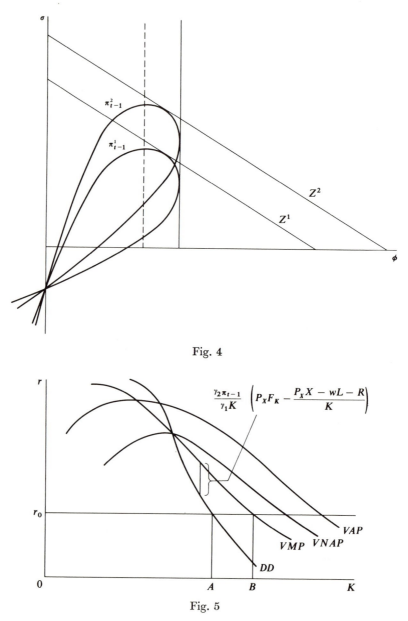

Fig. 4

Fig. 5

the left. OA is the amount demanded by the firm after economic reform; OB is the amount demanded by the profit maximizer. Note that demand curve DD is less elastic than the demand curve of the profit maximizing firm (VMP).

Differentiation of the objective function with respect to output establishes what output will be produced at the given price. For our purposes here cost is defined as a function of output, $C = C(X)$. The equation for the supply curve is :[11]

$$P_X = MC + \left(\frac{\gamma_2 \pi_{t-1}}{\gamma_1 K + \gamma_2 \pi_{t-1}}\right) \phi \left(\frac{\partial K}{\partial X}\right). \tag{6}$$

There are two components to this supply curve. The first results from the σ term; the second from ϕ. If this year's profit is positive, the supply curve is about the profit maximizer's marginal cost (MC) curve. The difference is determined by the product of three terms. One is composed of the coefficients weighted by past profit and capital; one is the profit rate; the third is the change in the employment of capital that results from an incremental change in output. All terms are positive if last year's profit is positive; the first is less than one. When this year's profit is zero, the supply curve crosses the MC curve. When π_t is negative, it lies below the MC curve. Hence, it is less elastic than the MC curve. The resulting supply curve is shown in fig. 6. For positive profit, the new Soviet firm produces less output than its profit maximizing counterpart – a not too surprising result since it uses less capital.

Throughout this analysis we have assumed last year's profit to be positive. If it were negative, we would have a perverse case where our conclusions were reversed – i.e. at positive π_t the firm would use more capital and produce more output than a profit maximizer. If either this year's profit or last year's equals zero, then the equilibrium condition for capital (equation 5) and the supply condition (equation 6) collapse to the corresponding conditions for the profit maximizing firm. However, a zero last year's profit still means an infinite incentive fund. In a steady state equilibrium at zero profit the new Soviet firm would behave exactly as a profit maximizer. It would hire capital until its price equals the value of the marginal product and produce output at the point where the product's price equalled profit maximizing marginal cost.

Five major conclusions emerge from our one variable factor model. When the firm is earning positive profits, it employs less capital, produces less output, has a less elastic demand curve for capital, and has a less elastic supply curve of the output. The firm also produces each output at a higher cost than the profit maximizing firm since it uses a different combination of factors than the cost minimizing combination. Now we are ready to consider labor a variable factor. How will our conclusions about the Soviet firm's performance change and what additional conclusions can we derive when we add this second variable factor?

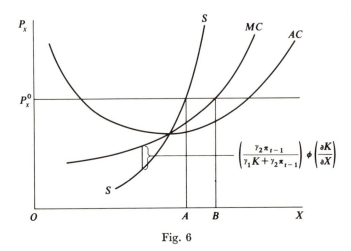

Fig. 6

TWO VARIABLE FACTORS

Adding labor as a second variable factor complicates the maximizing behaviour of the firm. Since the wages fund, wL, is the base on which the incentive funds are calculated, a larger wL means larger total incentive payments. However, a larger wL also means less profit assuming diminishing returns. Thus, the firm must choose the optimal combination of the profit rate, the growth of profits, and the wages fund. This section will discuss how the firm makes that choice and also will examine how much of each factor the firm employs and what the resulting capital labor ratio is.

The equations for this model are much the same as for the single variable factor case:

$$Z = = \gamma_1 wL\sigma + \gamma_2 wL\phi \qquad \text{Objective function} \qquad (7)$$

$$X = f(K, L, E); \; E = E_0; \quad f_K > 0; f_{KK} < 0; \quad \text{Production function} \quad (8)$$

$$f_L > 0; \; f_{LL} < 0$$

$$\pi = TR - TC = P_X X - rK - wL - R. \qquad \text{Profit.} \qquad (9)$$

Unlike the single variable factor case, wL is free to vary in the objective function. We assume labor is in perfectly elastic supply at wage rate w. Capital is supplied perfectly elastically at r. Assume there is some fixed factor such as a given supply of socialist managers, E, in order to make the supply curve slope upward and insure a determinant firm size. The demand for the product is perfectly elastic at P_X. Again we assume the one time period case so that past profit is fixed.

The graphical procedures of the last section could be repeated for this two variable factor case (Martin, 1969). Some changes would need to be made. Rather than start with a production function (output versus capital) an output isoquant (capital versus labor) would be more appropriate. Again we would obtain a feasibility surface and constant incentive fund lines. These incentive fund lines would have to be reinterpreted in light of the fact that the wages fund is now variable. The mechanics of such a procedure yields little new knowledge however. If we interpret the previous section as a partial model (what is the demand for capital given a fixed supply of labor?), we have almost the same result. Therefore, we will go directly to the equilibrium conditions.

To obtain the equilibrium conditions (the demand for each factor) we proceed as before differentiating the objective function with respect to capital and labor.[12]

$$r = P_X f_K + \frac{\gamma_2 \pi_{t-1}}{\gamma_1 K} \left(P_X f_K - \frac{P_X X - wL - R}{K} \right), \tag{10}$$

$$w = P_X f_L + \frac{1}{L} \left(\frac{\pi_{t-1} K}{\gamma_1 K + \gamma_2 \pi_{t-1}} \right) (\gamma_1 \sigma + \gamma_2 \phi). \tag{11}$$

The partial equilibrium condition for capital is the same as before. The conclusion that the new Soviet firm uses less capital remains.

If wL did not appear in the objective function as a base for calculating the inventive payments, then the objective function would be a monotonic transformation of profit as far as labor was concerned, and the equilibrium condition for labor would duplicate that of a profit maximizing firm.[13]. The inclusion of the wages fund results in the more complicated expression above. If the growth of profits is positive and the profit rate is also positive, then the amount of labor hired by this firm exceeds that hired by the profit maximizer. The firm will hire labor to the point where the wage rate equals the value of the marginal product plus some positive sum. The change in the magnitude of the sum as we move down the demand curve is determined by two forces. As more labor is employed the sum steadily decreases. But the growth of profits and the profit rate increase this term until they reach their maximums and then they reinforce the effect of increasing labor. The resulting demand curve is shown in fig. 7. The firm hires OB of labor compared to the profit maximizer's OC.

It is very useful to examine the capital–labor ratio implied by these equilibrium conditions. The ratio of the marginal products of the factors will not equal the ratio of their prices. Solving each of the equilibrium conditions for their marginal products and dividing the marginal product of labor by the marginal product of capital we obtain:[14]

$$\frac{f_L}{f_K} = \frac{w - \frac{1}{L} \left(\pi_t - \frac{\gamma_1 \pi_{t-1} K}{\gamma_1 K + \gamma_2 \pi_{t-1}} \right)}{r + \left(\frac{\gamma_2 \pi_{t-1}}{\gamma_1 K + \gamma_2 \pi_{t-1}} \right) \phi}. \tag{12}$$

225

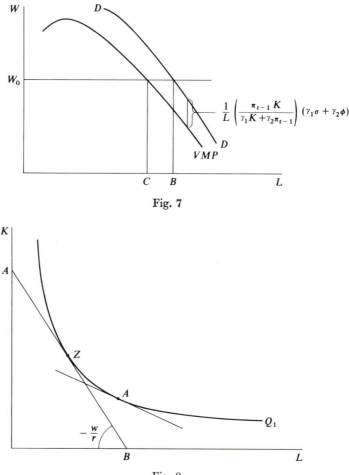

Fig. 7

Fig. 8

For a firm earning positive profit, the ratio of the marginal products for this firm will be less than the ratio for the profit maximizing firm. Thus we have equilibrium at a point such as A rather than the profit maximizing Z (fig. 8).

If $1/L(\pi_t - \gamma_1 \pi_{t-1} K / \gamma_1 K + \gamma_2 \pi_{t-1}) > w$, then the marginal product of labor will be negative.[15] This clearly is impossible since the socialist manager could always throw away labor rather than suffer decreasing output due to the negative marginal product of labor. He might pay these marginal workers in order to have a larger wages fund as a base on which to calculate incentive funds, but he certainly will not use them.

Before economic reform capital was essentially a free good for high priority industries. Firms in these industries would use capital until its marginal product was zero. Thus, the firm would choose a capital labor ratio on the upper ridge line (where the isoquant changes its slope). This model of the Soviet firm suggests the firm will move a great distance towards the lower ridge line – a very drastic shift!

This is not the end of the story. Equations (10) and (11) are partial equilibrium conditions. The firm uses less capital than a profit maximizer if it uses the same amount of labor. It uses more labor if it uses the same amount of capital. Obviously, this is not full equilibrium. In full equilibrium we cannot tell how the employments will compare unless we know how the outputs will compare. Let us examine the supply condition.

Differentiation of the objective function with respect to output yields:[16]

$$P_X = MC + \left(\frac{\gamma_2 \pi_{t-1}}{\gamma_1 K + \gamma_2 \pi_{t-1}}\right) \phi \left(\frac{\partial K}{\partial X}\right)$$

$$- \left(\frac{\pi_{t-1} K}{\gamma_1 K + \gamma_2 \pi_{t-1}}\right) \left(\frac{1}{L}\right) \left(\frac{\partial L}{\partial X}\right) (\gamma_1 \sigma + \gamma_2 \phi). \qquad (13)$$

Each of the three variables in the objective function contributes a term. Maximizing σ tells the entrepreneur to produce at the point where marginal cost will equal price. The inclusion of ϕ adds a second term which shifts the supply curve up (use less capital; produce less output). The wages fund adds a third term which shifts the supply curve down (use more labor; produce more output). Without information on numerical magnitudes, we do not know if this supply curve will be above or below the profit maximizing marginal cost curve.[17] The output is indeterminate in comparison with a profit maximizer, and hence so are the employments of capital and labor.

In conclusion, all we know for sure in this model is that even if the firm produces the same output as the profit maximizer (which is possible) it will not do so with the same factor proportions. But this is an important result. These differing capital labor ratios suggest a possible empirical test to verify this theoretical model.

GROWTH OF SALES

As stated in the introduction, some firms are given growth of sales rather than growth of profits as one of their targets. In fact, this may be the more important case. Out of the first forty-three firms to switch to the new reforms, thirty-three were given growth of sales as a target. Growth of sales is adopted 'for those enterprises for which an especially important task is an increased output to fully satisfy the needs of the economy' (Krylov, Rothshtein and Tsarev, 1966, p. 7) – a rather loose criterion and one that implies cost is of no concern. Sales as a target does differ from the previous gross value of output target. The plan is not satisfied until the goods are sold thus solving the problem of large inventories of goods no one wanted to buy.

Our primary objective in this section will be to compare this model with the basic model in the one and two variable factor cases – i.e. how much labor and capital does the firm employ; how much output does it produce? We will set the problem up in a way that best enables us to make these comparisons.

The relevant equations for his model are:

$$Z = \gamma_1 wL\left(\frac{P_X X_t - V_{t-1}}{V_{t-1}}\right) + \gamma_2 wL\phi \qquad \text{Objective function} \quad (14)$$

$$X = f(K, L, E); \; E = E_0; \; f_K > 0; f_{KK} < 0; \quad \text{Production function} \quad (15)$$

$$f_L > 0; f_{LL} < 0$$

$$\pi = TR - TC = P_X X - rK - wL - R. \qquad \text{Profit.} \qquad (16)$$

Past sales, $V_{t-1}(= P_X X_{t-1})$, is considered to be fixed and out of the firm's control. The demand for the product is assumed to be perfectly elastic at P_X in both periods.[18] We make the same assumptions about the supplies of the factors as we did in the two variable factor case: capital is supplied elastically at r; labor at w. As before, fixed entrepreneurship, E, generates an upward sloping supply curve.

Growth of sales in the above objective function is a monotonic transformation of the value of output. If there were no cost constraint, a firm maximizing only growth of sales would hire an infinite amount of factors and produce an infinite amount as long as the marginal products of the factors were positive. Edward Ames (1965) develops a model of a firm that maximizes output subject to the constraint that it covers costs – i.e. maximize $Z = P_X X + \lambda(P_X X - TC)$. It is not necessary to add any such Lagrangian type constraint to our objective function; the profit rate term already fulfills that purpose. If the firm is making losses, the profit rate will be negative and the incentive payments will be less. This is a valid constraint as long as γ_1 is not many times larger than γ_2. In practice, the planners have set the norms for deduction so that the norm applied to the profit rate is approximately twice as large as the norm applied to growth of sales. The subjective weights should not substantially change the relationship.

Suppose we begin by reverting to the one factor case (or partial equilibrium model). We draw a production function and derive a feasibility surface from it in a manner similar to the previous example. In fig. 9 the value of sales is maximized at C with employment of capital of OD. Notice that this is more than employed by the profit maximizing firm (OE). A firm that maximized a combination of growth of sales and profit rate will employ an amount of capital somewhere between OD and

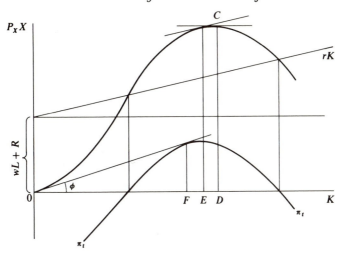

Fig. 9

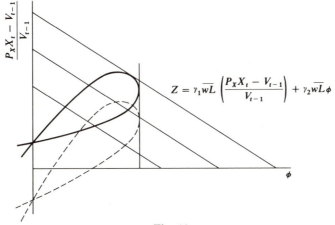

$$Z = \gamma_1 \overline{wL} \left(\frac{P_X X_t - V_{t-1}}{V_{t-1}} \right) + \gamma_2 \overline{wL} \phi$$

Fig. 10

OF; it could employ an amount of capital exactly equal to that employed by the profit maximizing firm.

The feasibility surface appears in fig. 10 (the solid curve). The dashed curve represents the feasibility surface that would result from the growth of profits and profit rate case and is drawn in for comparison. Growth of sales would be maximized at a lower profit rate than growth of profits.

By differentiating the objective function, we get the equilibrium condition for capital in the one factor case.[19]

$$0 = P_X f_K + \frac{\gamma_2 V_{t-1}}{\gamma_1 K} \left(P_X f_K - \frac{P_X X - wL - R}{K} \right). \tag{17}$$

The amount of capital employed is completely independent of the price at which it is sold. Thus, the demand curve is really not a curve but a point. We do not know if this is more or less than the amount employed by the growth of profits and profit rate maximizing firm for equal amounts of labor. (Call it Firm A; call the growth of sales and profit rate maximizer Firm B.) Assume γ_1, γ_2, P_X, w, and r are the same for both firms. Comparing Firm A's demand for capital with Firm B's, we see there are two offsetting factors. Suppose, for the moment, that the left-hand term of equation (17) is not zero but r. This will facilitate the comparison. V_{t-1} exceeds π_{t-1} and thus $\gamma_2 V_{t-1}/\gamma_1 K$ exceeds $\gamma_2 \pi_{t-1}/\gamma_1 K$.[20] For any given amount of capital the difference between the VMP and the value of the net average product is the same in both cases so

$$\frac{\gamma_2 V_{t-1}}{\gamma_1 K}\left(P_X f_K - \frac{P_X X - wL - R}{K}\right) > \frac{\gamma_2 \pi_{t-1}}{\gamma_1 K}\left(P_X f_X - \frac{P_X X - wL - R}{K}\right).$$

This means the demand curve for Firm B will be displaced a greater distance up from the VMP curve when $P_X f_K > (P_X X - wL - R)/K$ and a greater distance down when $P_X f_K < (P_X X - wL - R)/K$. That is, it is more inelastic than Firm A's demand. This alone means that Firm B would employ less capital (if we are to the right of the crossover point as we must be if the profit rate is to be positive). In effect, Firm B has given a greater weight to the ϕ term. However, Firm B is only in equilibrium when the left-hand term equals zero not r in equation (17). If r is really positive, then this will work in the opposite direction. Firm A will hire less capital than Firm B. We do not know which tendency will dominate and which firm will employ more capital. Nor do we know how the employment of capital by Firm B will compare with the profit maximizing firm. The demand curves are shown in fig. 11. Remember, however, only point B is relevant for Firm B.

The direction of output is also ambiguous. Differentiating the objective function with respect to X and defining profit as $\pi_t = P_X X - C(X)$ we obtain:[21]

$$P_X = \frac{\gamma_2 V_{t-1}}{\gamma_1 K + \gamma_2 V_{t-1}}\left[MC + \phi\left(\frac{\partial K}{\partial X}\right)\right] \tag{18}$$

or in terms easier for comparison:

$$P_X = \frac{\gamma_2 V_{t-1}}{\gamma_1 K + \gamma_2 V_{t-1}}\,MC + \frac{\gamma_2 V_{t-1}}{\gamma_1 K + \gamma_2 V_{t-1}}\,\phi\left(\frac{\partial K}{\partial X}\right). \tag{18'}$$

Firm B's supply curve is some fraction of the marginal cost curve $\gamma_2 V_{t-1}/(\gamma_1 K + \gamma_2 V_{t-1}) < 1$ plus some positive term assuming profit to be positive. We do not know which side of the marginal cost curve the supply curve will lie on and thus we do not know how its output will compare with either Firm A or a profit maximizing firm.[22]

Let us now examine the two variable factor case. Differentiation of the

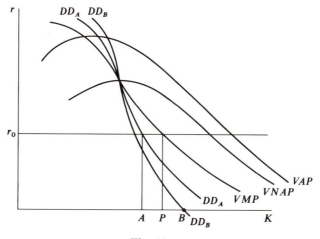

Fig. 11

objective function gives the partial equilibrium conditions for capital and labor.[23]

$$0 = P_X f_K + \frac{\gamma_2 V_{t-1}}{\gamma_1 K}\left(P_X f_K - \frac{P_X X - wL - R}{K}\right) \tag{19}$$

$$w = P_X f_L \left(\frac{\gamma_1 K + \gamma_2 V_{t-1}}{\gamma_2 V_{t-1}}\right) + \frac{K}{L}\left[\frac{\gamma_1}{\gamma_2}\left(\frac{P_X X_t - V_{t-1}}{V_{t-1}}\right) + \phi\right]. \tag{20}$$

The equilibrium condition for capital is, of course, the same as before and our conclusions remain the same. With regard to labor, however, the situation is not so ambiguous. Comparing the two demand curves for labor (equations 11 and 20) for Firms A and B, we see Firm A hires labor until the wage equals something greater, $(\gamma_1 K + \gamma_2 V_{t-1})/\gamma_2 V_{t-1} > 1$, than the VMP plus a second term. This alone would imply that Firm B uses more labor. The second term reinforces the direction of the first. Since:

$$\frac{1}{\gamma_2 \pi_{t-1}} > \frac{1}{\gamma_1 K + \gamma_2 \pi_{t-1}},$$

$$K > \frac{\gamma_2 \pi_{t-1} K}{\gamma_1 K + \gamma_2 \pi_{t-1}}.$$

Assuming[24]
$$\frac{P_X X_t - V_{t-1}}{V_{t-1}} = \sigma,$$

$$K\left[\gamma_1\left(\frac{P_X X_t - V_{t-1}}{V_{t-1}}\right) + \gamma_2 \phi\right] > \frac{\gamma_2 \pi_{t-1} K}{\gamma_1 K + \gamma_2 \pi_{t-1}}(\gamma_1 \sigma + \gamma_2 \phi);$$

$$\frac{K}{L}\left[\frac{\gamma_1}{\gamma_2}\left(\frac{P_X X_t - V_{t-1}}{V_{t-1}}\right) + \phi\right] > \frac{1}{L}\left(\frac{\pi_{t-1} K}{\gamma_1 K + \gamma_2 \pi_{t-1}}\right)(\gamma_1 \sigma + \gamma_2 \phi).$$

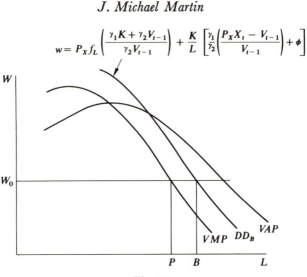

$$w = P_X f_L \left(\frac{\gamma_1 K + \gamma_2 V_{t-1}}{\gamma_2 V_{t-1}} \right) + \frac{K}{L} \left[\frac{\gamma_1}{\gamma_2} \left(\frac{P_X X_t - V_{t-1}}{V_{t-1}} \right) + \phi \right]$$

Fig. 12

Thus, Firm B unambiguously uses more labor. Both firms employ more labor than a profit maximizing firm. The demand curve for labor is shown in fig. 12.

Solving the partial equilibrium conditions for the marginal products and dividing f_L by f_K as we did before, we obtain:[25]

$$\frac{f_L}{f_K} = \frac{w - \frac{K}{L} \left[\frac{\gamma_1}{\gamma_2} \left(\frac{P_X X_t - V_{t-1}}{V_{t-1}} \right) + \phi \right]}{r + \phi}. \tag{21}$$

Again we discover that the reformed firm is likely to make a drastic change in factor proportions. Comparing this expression with equation (12) (the ratio of the marginal products for the growth of profits and profit rate case), we see that the numerator is smaller and the denominator larger.[26] The ratio of the marginal products is unambiguously smaller for Firm B. Hence, for the same output Firm B will have a lower capital–labor ratio than either Firm A or a profit maximizing firm (fig. 13).

Allowing the socialist manager to vary his supply of labor adds another term to the output condition.[27]

$$P_X = \frac{\gamma_2 V_{t-1}}{\gamma_1 K + \gamma_2 V_{t-1}} \left[MC + \phi \left(\frac{\partial K}{\partial X} \right) \right]$$
$$- \left(\frac{V_{t-1} K}{\gamma_1 K + \gamma_2 V_{t-1}} \right) \left(\frac{1}{L} \right) \left(\frac{\partial L}{\partial X} \right) \left[\gamma_1 \left(\frac{P_X X_t - V_{t-1}}{V_{t-1}} \right) + \gamma_2 \phi \right]. \tag{22}$$

Since the entrepreneur is induced to hire more labor to increase the size of his incentive fund, the amount of labor he employs is larger, and this logically results in the supply curve being shifted down and out. However,

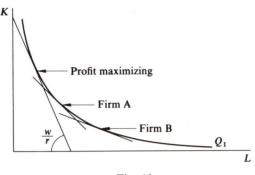

Fig. 13

we still do not know if this supply curve will lie above or below the marginal cost curve. The term that results from the profit rate,

$$\frac{\gamma_2 V_{t-1}}{\gamma_1 K + \gamma_2 V_{t-1}} \phi\left(\frac{\partial K}{\partial X}\right),$$

may shift the curve up more than the other two terms can shift it down.

We do not know if the socialist manager will produce more or less output than the profit maximizing firm, and thus we do not know if he will employ more or less capital and labor in full equilibrium. We do know that for any level of output the capital–labor ratio will be lower in the growth of sales and profit rate case.

The results of our comparisons are summarized in table 1 for the two variable factor cases. We divide the comparisons into factor proportion effects – what capital–labor ratio is chosen for a fixed level of output – and scale effects – what output level is chosen. These comparisons assume that both profits and the growth of profits are positive for all cases.

Finally, it is useful to compare the marginal firms for the three cases (Firm A, Firm B, and the profit maximizer). We consider the marginal firm to earn zero profits and also have zero growth of profits (thus $\pi_{t-1} = 0$) or zero growth of sales. Comparing the equilibrium and output conditions for the three cases we see that a marginal Firm A behaves like a profit maximizer. It hires the same amount of each factor and produces the same amount of output. But the marginal Firm B hires more capital, more labor, and produces more output with a different capital–labor ratio than the profit maximizing firm.[28] Under socialism there is no mechanism for capitalizing rent so that situations of positive excess profits can persist. Soviet firms will not necessarily behave as marginal firms in the long run.

Table 1. *Comparisons of factor proportions and outputs*

Firm	K/L per unit of output	Level of output
Firm A Maximize: ϕ and σ	Lower than profit maximizer	Indeterminate compared to profit maximizer 1. Profit rate effect – less output 2. Wages fund effect – more output 3. Growth of profits effect – no change
Firm B Maximize: ϕ and $\dfrac{P_X X_t - V_{t-1}}{V_{t-1}}$	Lower than profit maximizer	Indeterminate compared to profit maximizer 1. Profit rate effect – less output 2. Wages fund effect – more output 3. Growth of sales effect – more output
	Lower than Firm A	Indeterminate compared to Firm A 1. Profit rate effect – less output 2. Wages fund effect – more output 3. Growth of sales effect – more output

EXTENSIONS AND CONCLUSIONS

The theory of the Soviet firm after economic reform is by no means completed with these pages. If the economic reform as described above becomes a permanent feature of the Soviet economy, then there is every reason to make this model as complete as that of the neoclassical firm. We will briefly note the several obvious topics that need further analysis.

First, it would be very useful to study the reaction of this firm to changes in various parameters – price of the product, prices of both factors, and rent. The supply curves of both Firm A and Firm B should be analyzed further to insure they are indeed upward sloping. The analysis might be done assuming a Cobb–Douglas production function (rather than the general production function we used) in order to give more precise results.

The fund for production development has been omitted from these models. The fund could be included in either of two ways. The socialist manager could be assumed to maximize a weighted sum of all three funds instead of just the material incentive and social–cultural funds. However, this does not seem a satisfactory procedure to use since the manager is then essentially maximizing his supply of capital. We suggest instead

234

that the fund be treated as affecting the charge against capital. Including the fund this way makes it possible to develop a growth model for the firm where the supply of capital depends on the previously existing stock plus that earned by the production development fund in the last period.

Finally, an attempt should be made to provide empirical verification of our theoretical results. The most fruitful area of search would be to examine the capital–labor ratios since the changes here are our main conclusions. The capital–labor ratio has been increasing in the Soviet Union over the past decade. Therefore, if our hypothesis is correct we would expect the rate of increase to fall at the very least.

Unfortunately, statistics on Soviet firms before and after reform are very scarce. In addition, as far as this author knows, there are no capital, labor, and output figures available that will allow us to distinguish between those firms maximizing growth of profits and the profit rate and those maximizing growth of sales and the profit rate. Indeed, it is difficult to tell to what degree the available data represent firms still operating on the old system and to what degree firms operating under the new system.

The matter is certainly worth further research. However, until the nature of the reform changes or more precise information is available, our main conclusions stand. In the one factor case, the growth of profits and profit rate maximizing firm will use less capital and produce less output. When we add labor as a second variable factor, this firm will produce using a lower capital–labor ratio than its profit maximizing counterpart providing they produce the same output. The output condition itself is indeterminate. Finally, the growth of sales and profit rate maximizing firm will use a lower capital–labor ratio than either of the other two.

NOTES

1 We will not consider the problems in implementing the reforms since several good articles have been written on that subject. See Bush (1968, 1967); Frankel (1967).

2 The other provisions of the reform were increased autonomy for the firm, a change from regional to branch direction of industry, and an introduction of a charge for capital (6 % on the undepreciated sum of fixed and working capital).

3 These other targets were such items as the wages fund, the volume of goods to be sold, payments to and from the budget, and the main assortment of goods.

4 It is a simplification to consider the norms for deduction fixed. The norms applied to above and below plan growth of profits and profit rate are lower than the norms applied when the plan is fulfilled. More specifically, taking the case of growth of profits: if the actual growth of profits is less than the planned growth of profits then the *ruble* value of the deduction is reduced by 3 % (minimum) for each 1 % underfulfillment. If the actual growth of profits exceeds the planned growth of profits, the *norms* applied to above plane growth of profits are reduced 30 to 40 %. Above and below plan profit rate is treated similarly. We could replace the norms with some sort of function, but it would have to be discontinuous since above and below plan achievements are treated differently. Our simplification makes the analysis much

easier; and, as long as the firm's performance does not differ greatly from the plan, the results should not be very different.

5 A numerical example may make things clearer. Suppose:

$\gamma_1 = 0.18$ for each % growth of profits,

$\gamma_2 = 0.25$ for each % profit rate,

$wL = 10,000,000$ rubles,

$\sigma = 15\%$,

$\phi = 21\%$.

Then:

$$Z = \gamma_1 wL\sigma + \gamma_2 wL\phi$$
$$= (0.18)\,(15)\,(10,000,000) + (0.25)\,(21)\,(10,000,000) = 795,000 \text{ rubles.}$$

6 After formulating the relationships in this diagram, I discovered a somewhat similar analysis (Horwitz, 1968). I believe I have gone much further with this analysis than he has.

7 Suppose $\pi_t = -20$ and $\pi_{t-1} = -25$. Then $\sigma = \dfrac{-20 - (-25)}{-25} = -20\%$. The firm

has a negative growth of profits although its performance is better this year than last. (Losses are less.) $+20\%$ is a more accurate indicator of its performance.

8 If π_{t-1} is variable, then the optimal strategy is clearly to earn zero profits this year, any positive amount at all next year, and retire to the Black Sea on the infinite incentive funds earned (that will result from the infinite growth of profits) the third year.

9 Differentiate Z with respect to K:

$$Z = \gamma_1 wL\sigma + \gamma_2 wL\phi,$$

$$\frac{\partial Z}{\partial K} = 0 = \frac{\gamma_1 wL}{\pi_{t-1}}\left(P_X \frac{\partial X}{\partial K} - r\right) + \frac{\gamma_2 wL}{K^2}\left(P_X \frac{\partial X}{\partial K} K - rK - P_X X + wL + rK + R\right),$$

$$0 = \frac{\gamma_1 wL}{\pi_{t-1}}(P_X f_K - r) + \frac{\gamma_2 wL}{K^2}(P_X f_K K - P_X X + wL + R),\quad \frac{\partial X}{\partial K} = f_K,$$

$$0 = (P_X f_K - r) + \frac{\gamma_2 \pi_{t-1}}{\gamma_1 K}\left(P_X f_K - \frac{P_X X - wL - R}{K}\right),$$

$$r = P_X f_K + \frac{\gamma_2 \pi_{t-1}}{\gamma_1 K}\left(P_X f_K - \frac{P_X X - wL - R}{K}\right).$$

10 At the point where the two curves cross $P_X f_K = \dfrac{P_X X - wL - R}{K}$. Hence:

$$r_0 = P_X f_K + \frac{\gamma_2 \pi_{t-1}}{\gamma_1 K}\left(P_X f_K - \frac{P_X X - wL - R}{K}\right),$$

$$r_0 = P_X f_K.$$

But:

$$\frac{P_X X - wL - R}{K} = \frac{\pi_t r K}{K},$$

$$= \phi + r.$$

Since $r = P_X f_K$, ϕ must equal zero.

11 Differentiate Z with respect to X:

$$Z = \gamma_1 wL\sigma + \gamma_2 wL\phi, \qquad\qquad \pi = P_X X - C(X),$$

$$\frac{\partial Z}{\partial X} = 0 = \frac{\gamma_1 wL}{\pi_{t-1}}\left(P_X - \frac{\partial C}{\partial X}\right) + \frac{\gamma_2 wL}{K^2}\left[K\left(P_X - \frac{\partial C}{\partial X}\right) - \pi_t\frac{\partial K}{\partial X}\right],$$

$$0 = P_X - MC + \frac{\gamma_2 \pi_{t-1}}{\gamma_1 K}\left[P_X - MC - \phi\left(\frac{\partial K}{\partial X}\right)\right], \qquad\qquad \frac{\partial C}{\partial X} = MC,$$

$$0 = P_x\left(1 + \frac{\gamma_2 \pi_{t-1}}{\gamma_1 K}\right) - MC\left(1 + \frac{\gamma_2 \pi_{t-1}}{\gamma_1 K}\right) - \left(\frac{\gamma_2 \pi_{t-1}}{\gamma_1 K}\right)\phi\left(\frac{\partial K}{\partial X}\right),$$

$$P_X = MC + \left(\frac{\gamma_2 \pi_{t-1}}{\gamma_1 K + \gamma_2 \pi_{t-1}}\right)\phi\left(\frac{\partial K}{\partial X}\right).$$

12 Differentiate Z with respect to L:

$$Z = \gamma_1 wL\sigma + \gamma_2 wL\phi,$$

$$\frac{\partial Z}{\partial L} = 0 = \frac{\gamma_1 wL}{\pi_{t-1}}\left(P_X\frac{\partial X}{\partial L} - w\right) + \frac{\gamma_2 wL}{K}\left(P_X\frac{\partial X}{\partial L} - w\right) + \gamma_1 w\sigma + \gamma_2 w\phi,$$

$$0 = \frac{\gamma_1 L}{\pi_{t-1}} + \frac{\gamma_2 L}{K}(-w) + (P_X f_L)\left(\frac{\gamma_1 L}{\pi_{t-1}} + \frac{\gamma_2 L}{K}\right) + \gamma_1\sigma + \gamma_2\phi, \qquad \frac{\partial X}{\partial L} = f_L,$$

$$w = P_X f_L + \frac{1}{L}\left(\frac{\pi_{t-1}K}{\gamma_1 K + \gamma_2 \pi_{t-1}}\right)(\gamma_1\sigma + \gamma_2\phi).$$

13 This is the way a third factor would be hired – until its price equaled the value of its marginal product.

14 Solve for the marginal products of capital and labor and divide f_L by f_K:

$$w = P_X f_L + \frac{1}{L}\left(\frac{\pi_{t-1}K}{\gamma_1 K + \gamma_2 \pi_{t-1}}\right)(\gamma_1\sigma + \gamma_2\phi),$$

$$P_X f_L = w - \frac{1}{L}\left(\frac{\pi_{t-1}K}{\gamma_1 K + \gamma_2 \pi_{t-1}}\right)\left(\frac{\gamma_1 \pi_t}{\pi_{t-1}} + \frac{\gamma_2 \pi_t}{K_t} - \gamma_1\right),$$

$$P_X f_L = w - \frac{1}{L}\left(\pi_t - \frac{\gamma_1 \pi_{t-1}K}{\gamma_1 K + \gamma_2 \pi_{t-1}}\right),$$

$$r = P_X f_K + \frac{\gamma_2 \pi_{t-1}}{\gamma_1 K}\left(P_X f_K - \frac{P_X X - wL - R}{K}\right),$$

$$r = P_X f_K\left(1 + \frac{\gamma_2 \pi_{t-1}}{\gamma_1 K}\right) - \frac{\gamma_2 \pi_{t-1}}{\gamma_1 K}\left(\frac{P_X X - wL - R}{K}\right),$$

$$P_X f_K\left(1 + \frac{\gamma_2 \pi_{t-1}}{\gamma_1 K}\right) = r + \frac{\gamma_2 \pi_{t-1}}{\gamma_1 K}(r + \phi),$$

$$P_X f_K = r + \frac{\gamma_2 \pi_{t-1}}{\gamma_1 K + \gamma_2 \pi_{t-1}}\phi,$$

$$\frac{P_X f_L}{P_X f_K} = \frac{w - \dfrac{1}{L}\left(\pi_t - \dfrac{\gamma_1 \pi_{t-1}K}{\gamma_1 K + \gamma_2 \pi_{t-1}}\right)}{r + \dfrac{\gamma_2 \pi_{t-1}}{\gamma_1 K + \gamma_2 \pi_{t-1}}\phi}.$$

15 The expression inside the parentheses will always be positive if profit (this year's and last's) and the growth of profits are positive. Rewriting the expression we see:

$$\pi_t - \frac{\gamma_1 K}{\gamma_1 K + \gamma_2 \pi_{t-1}}(\pi_{t-1}) > 0,$$

since $\gamma_1 K / \gamma_1 K + \gamma_2 \pi_{t-1}$ is less than one and π_t exceeds π_{t-1}.

16 Differentiate Z with respect to X:

$$Z = \gamma_1 wL\sigma + \gamma_2 wL\phi, \quad \pi = P_X X - C(X),$$

$$\frac{\partial Z}{\partial X} = 0 = \frac{\gamma_1 wL}{\pi_{t-1}}\left(P_X - \frac{\partial C}{\partial X}\right) + \frac{\gamma_2 wL}{K^2}\left(KP_X - K\frac{\partial C}{\partial X} - \pi_t\frac{\partial K}{\partial X}\right) + \gamma_1 w\frac{\partial L}{\partial X}\sigma + \gamma_2 w\frac{\partial L}{\partial X}\phi,$$

$$0 = \left(\frac{X_1 L}{\pi_{t-1}} + \frac{\gamma_2 L}{K}\right)P_X - \left(\frac{\gamma_1 L}{\pi_{t-1}} + \frac{\gamma_2 L}{K}\right)MC - \left(\frac{\gamma_2 L}{K}\right)\phi\left(\frac{\partial K}{\partial X}\right)$$

$$+ \frac{\partial L}{\partial X}(\gamma_1\sigma + \gamma_2\phi), \qquad \frac{\partial C}{\partial X} = MC,$$

$$P_X = MC + \left(\frac{\gamma_2\pi_{t-1}}{\gamma_1 K + \gamma_2\pi_{t-1}}\right)\phi\left(\frac{\partial K}{\partial X}\right) - \left(\frac{\pi_{t-1}K}{\gamma_1 K + \gamma_2\pi_{t-1}}\right)\left(\frac{1}{L}\right)\left(\frac{\partial L}{\partial X}\right)(\gamma_1\sigma + \gamma_2\phi).$$

17 We can see it depends largely on the relative elasticities. Comparing the second term with the third:

$$\left(\frac{\gamma_2\pi_{t-1}}{\gamma_1 K + \gamma_2\pi_{t-1}}\right)\phi\left(\frac{\partial K}{\partial X}\right) \gtreqless \left(\frac{\pi_{t-1}K}{\gamma_1 K + \gamma_2\pi_{t-1}}\right)\left(\frac{1}{L}\right)\left(\frac{\partial L}{\partial X}\right)(\gamma_1\sigma + \gamma_2\phi),$$

$$\gamma_2\phi\left(\frac{\partial K}{\partial X}\right) \gtreqless \left(\frac{K}{L}\right)\left(\frac{\partial L}{\partial X}\right)\sigma + (\gamma_1\sigma + \gamma_2\phi),$$

$$\gamma_2\phi\left(\frac{\partial K}{\partial X}\right) \gtreqless \gamma_1\left(\frac{K}{L}\right)\left(\frac{\partial L}{\partial X}\right)\sigma + \gamma_2\left(\frac{K}{L}\right)\left(\frac{\partial L}{\partial X}\right)\phi,$$

$$\gamma_2\pi_t\frac{X\partial K}{K\partial X} \gtreqless \gamma_1 K\sigma\frac{X\partial L}{L\partial X} + \gamma_2\pi_t\frac{X\partial L}{L\partial X},$$

$$\frac{X\partial K}{K\partial X} \gtreqless \frac{X\partial L}{L\partial X}\left(1 + \frac{\gamma_1 K}{\gamma_2\pi_{t-1}}\sigma\right).$$

18 If demand is perfectly elastic, then the firm has no trouble selling its output – something that was not true before the reforms. We are thus ignoring the problem that output produced may not equal output sold. Our simplified model answers the questions we pose for it; we will leave the treatment of this problem to others.

19 Differentiate Z with respect to K:

$$Z = \gamma_1 wL\left(\frac{P_X X_t - V_{t-1}}{V_{t-1}}\right) + \gamma_2 wL\phi,$$

$$\frac{\partial Z}{\partial K} = 0 = \frac{\gamma_1 wL}{V_{t-1}}(P_X f_K) + \frac{\gamma_2 wL}{K^2}[K(P_X f_K - r) - (P_X X - wL - rk - R)], \quad \frac{\partial X}{\partial K} = f_K,$$

$$0 = \frac{\gamma_1 wL}{V_{t-1}}(P_X f_K) + \frac{\gamma_2 wL}{K}\left(P_X f_K - \frac{P_X X - wL - R}{K}\right),$$

$$0 = P_X f_K + \frac{\gamma_2 V_{t-1}}{\gamma_1 K}P_X f_K - \left(\frac{P_X X - wL - R}{K}\right).$$

20   $P_X X_{t-1} = V_{t-1} > \pi_{t-1} = P_X X_{t-1} - wL_{t-1} - rK_{t-1} - R.$

21   Differentiate Z with respect to X:

$$Z = \gamma_1 wL \left(\frac{P_X X_t - V_{t-1}}{V_{t-1}} \right) + \gamma_2 wL\phi, \quad \pi = P_X X - C(X),$$

$$\frac{\partial Z}{\partial X} = 0 = \frac{\gamma_1 wL}{V_{t-1}} (P_X) + \frac{\gamma_2 wL}{K^2} \left[K \left(P_X - \frac{\partial C}{\partial X} \right) - \pi_t \frac{\partial K}{\partial X} \right],$$

$$0 = \frac{\gamma_1 wL}{V_{t-1}} (P_X) + \frac{\gamma_2 wL}{K} (P_X) - \frac{\gamma_2 wL}{K} \left[MC + \phi \frac{\partial K}{\partial X} \right], \quad \frac{\partial C}{\partial X} = MC,$$

$$0 = P_X \left(\frac{\gamma_1 wLK + \gamma_2 wLV_{t-1}}{V_{t-1}K} \right) - \frac{\gamma_2 wL}{K} \left[MC + \phi \left(\frac{\partial K}{\partial X} \right) \right],$$

$$P_X = \frac{\gamma_2 V_{t-1}}{\gamma_1 K + \gamma_2 V_{t-1}} \left[MC + \phi \left(\frac{\partial K}{\partial X} \right) \right].$$

22   This is true even though we do know that the upward shift term is greater for Firm B.

$$\frac{\gamma_2 V_{t-1}}{\gamma_1 K + \gamma_2 V_{t-1}} > \frac{\gamma_2 \pi_{t-1}}{\gamma_1 K + \gamma_2 \pi_{t-1}}.$$

23   Differentiate Z with respect to L:

$$Z = \gamma_1 wL \left(\frac{P_X X_t - V_{t-1}}{V_{t-1}} \right) + \gamma_2 wL\phi,$$

$$\frac{\partial Z}{\partial L} = 0 = \frac{\gamma_1 wL}{V_{t-1}} \left(P_X \frac{\partial X}{\partial L} \right) + \frac{\gamma_2 wL}{K} \left(P_X \frac{\partial X}{\partial L} - w \right) + \gamma_1 w \left(\frac{P_X X_t - V_{t-1}}{V_{t-1}} \right) + \gamma_2 w\phi,$$

$$0 = \frac{\gamma_2 wL}{K} (-w) + \left(\frac{\gamma_1 wL}{V_{t-1}} + \frac{\gamma_2 wL}{K} \right) P_X f_L + \gamma_1 w \left(\frac{P_X X_t - V_{t-1}}{V_{t-1}} \right) + \gamma_2 w\phi, \quad \frac{\partial X}{\partial L} = f_L,$$

$$w = \left(\frac{\gamma_1 K + \gamma_2 V_{t-1}}{\gamma_2 V_{t-1}} \right) P_X f_L + \frac{K}{L} \left[\frac{\gamma_1}{\gamma_2} \left(\frac{P_X X_t - V_{t-1}}{V_{t-1}} \right) + \phi \right].$$

24   If we have constant returns, this is true. If there are diminishing returns, then:

$$\frac{P_X X_t - V_{t-1}}{V_{t-1}} > \sigma,$$

and this further reinforces the effect we predict.

25   Solve for the marginal products of capital and labor and divide f_L by f_K:

$$w = P_X f_L \left(\frac{\gamma_1 K + \gamma_2 V_{t-1}}{\gamma_2 V_{t-1}} \right) + \frac{K}{L} \left[\frac{\gamma_1}{\gamma_2} \left(\frac{P_X X_t - V_{t-1}}{V_{t-1}} \right) + \phi \right],$$

$$P_X f_L = \frac{\gamma_2 V_{t-1}}{\gamma_1 K + \gamma_2 V_{t-1}} \left\{ w - \frac{K}{L} \left[\frac{\gamma_1}{\gamma_2} \left(\frac{P_X X_t - V_{t-1}}{V_{t-1}} \right) + \phi \right] \right\},$$

$$0 = P_X f_L + \frac{\gamma_2 V_{t-1}}{\gamma_1 K} \left(P_X f_K - \frac{P_X X - wL - R}{K} \right),$$

$$P_X f_K \left(1 + \frac{\gamma_2 V_{t-1}}{\gamma_1 K} \right) = \left(\frac{\gamma_2 V_{t-1}}{\gamma_1 K} \right) \left(\frac{P_X X - wL - R}{K} \right),$$

$$P_X f_K = \frac{\gamma_2 V_{t-1}}{\gamma_1 K + \gamma_2 V_{t-1}} (r+\phi), \quad \frac{P_X X - wL - R}{K} = r+\phi,$$

$$\frac{P_X f_L}{P_X f_K} = \frac{\dfrac{\gamma_2 V_{t-1}}{\gamma_1 K + \gamma_2 V_{t-1}} \left\{ w - \dfrac{K}{L} \left[\dfrac{\gamma_1}{\gamma_2} \left(\dfrac{P_X X_t - V_{t-1}}{V_{t-1}} \right) + \phi \right] \right\}}{\dfrac{\gamma_2 V_{t-1}}{\gamma_1 K + \gamma_2 V_{t-1}} (r+\phi)},$$

$$\frac{f_K}{f_L} = \frac{w - \dfrac{K}{L} \left[\dfrac{\gamma_1}{\gamma_2} \left(\dfrac{P_X X_t - V_{t-1}}{V_{t-1}} \right) + \phi \right]}{r+\phi}.$$

26 Numerator:

$$w - \frac{K}{L} \left[\frac{\gamma_1}{\gamma_2} \left(\frac{P_X X_t - V_{t-1}}{V_{t-1}} \right) + \phi \right] \gtreqless w - \frac{1}{L} \left(\pi_t - \frac{\gamma_1 \pi_{t-1} K}{\gamma_1 K + \gamma_2 \pi_{t-1}} \right),$$

$$w - \frac{1}{L} \left[\pi_t + \frac{\gamma_1 K}{\gamma_2} \left(\frac{P_X X_t - V_{t-1}}{V_{t-1}} \right) \right] < w - \frac{1}{L} \left(\pi_t - \frac{\gamma_1 \pi_{t-1} K}{\gamma_1 K + \gamma_2 \pi_{t-1}} \right).$$

Denominator:

$$r+\phi > r + \left(\frac{\gamma_2 \pi_{t-1}}{\gamma_1 K + \gamma_2 \pi_{t-1}} \right) \phi, \quad \text{since } \frac{\gamma_2 \pi_{t-1}}{\gamma_1 K + \gamma_2 \pi_{t-1}} < 1.$$

27 Differentiate Z with respect to X:

$$Z = \gamma_1 wL \left(\frac{P_X X_t - V_{t-1}}{V_{t-1}} \right) + \gamma_2 wL\phi, \qquad\qquad \pi = P_X X - C(X),$$

$$\frac{\partial Z}{\partial X} = 0 = \frac{\gamma_1 wL}{V_{t-1}} (P_X) + \frac{\gamma_2 wL}{K^2} \left[K \left(P_X - \frac{\partial C}{\partial X} \right) - \pi_t \frac{\partial K}{\partial X} \right]$$

$$+ \gamma_1 w \frac{\partial L}{\partial X} \left(\frac{P_X X_t - V_{t-1}}{V_{t-1}} \right) + \gamma_2 w \frac{\partial L}{\partial X} \phi, \qquad \frac{\partial C}{\partial X} = MC,$$

$$0 = \left(\frac{\gamma_1 wL}{V_{t-1}} + \frac{\gamma_2 wL}{K} \right) P_X - \frac{\gamma_2 wL}{K} \left[MC + \phi \left(\frac{\partial K}{\partial X} \right) \right]$$

$$+ w \left(\frac{\partial L}{\partial X} \right) \left[\gamma_1 \left(\frac{P_X X_t - V_{t-1}}{V_{t-1}} \right) + \gamma_2 \phi \right],$$

$$P_X = \frac{\gamma_2 V_{t-1}}{\gamma_1 K + \gamma_2 V_{t-1}} \left[MC + \phi \left(\frac{\partial K}{\partial X} \right) \right]$$

$$- \left(\frac{V_{t-1} K}{\gamma_1 K + \gamma_2 V_{t-1}} \right) \left(\frac{1}{L} \right) \left(\frac{\partial L}{\partial X} \right) \left[\gamma_1 \left(\frac{P_X X_t - V_{t-1}}{V_{t-1}} \right) + \gamma_2 \phi \right].$$

28 These results are obtained by substituting zero for the relevant variables in the equilibrium equations (10, 11, 19, and 20) and the output conditions (13 and 22).

A SELECTED BIBLIOGRAPHY

Ames, Edward J. (1965). *Soviet Economic Processes*. Homewood, Ill.: Irwin.
Balinsky, A. *et al.* (1967). *Planning and the Market in the USSR: the 1960's*. New Brunswick: Rutgers University Press.
Bush, Keith (1967). The reforms: a balance sheet. *Problems of Communism*, **16**, 30–41.

Bush, Keith (1968). An appraisal of the Soviet economic reforms. In *Soviet Economic Performance 1966–7*, pp. 129–41. 90th Congress, 2nd Session, Joint Economic Committee. Washington: Government Printing Office.

Cambell, Robert (1968). Economic reform in the USSR. *American Economic Review*, 58, 547–58.

Domar, E. D. (1966). The Soviet collective farm. *American Economic Review*, 56, 547–58.

Ekonomicheskaya Gazeta (1966). Systematic instructions on the transfer of various industrial enterprises to the new system of planning and economic stimulation in 1966. *Ekonomicheskaya Gazeta*, February.

Feiwel, George R. (1967). *The Soviet Quest for Economic Efficiency*. New York: Praeger.

Felker, Jere L. (1966). *Soviet Economic Controversies*. Cambridge, Mass.: MIT Press.

Frankel, Theodore (1967). Economic reform: a tentative appraisal. *Problems of Communism*, 16, 29–41.

Goldman, Marshall I. (1963). Economic controversy in the Soviet Union. *Foreign Affairs*, 41, 498–512.

Horwitz, Bertrand N. (1968). Profit responsibility in Soviet enterprise. *Journal of Business of the University of Chicago*, 40, 47–55.

Kosygin, A. N. (1965). On improving industrial management, perfecting planning and enhancing incentives in industrial production. *Current Digest of the Soviet Press*, 17, 13 October 1965, 3–15. Translated from *Pravda*, 28 September 1965.

Krylov, P., L. Rothshtein, and D. Tsarev (1966). On the procedure and conditions for changing to the new system. *Problems of Economics*, 9 (September), 3–14. Translated from *Plannovoe Khoziaistvo*, 43, 55–66.

Martin, J. Michael (1969). Economic reform and the maximizing behavior of the Soviet firm. Unpublished Doctor's dissertation, University of Washington.

Oi, Walter Y. and E. M. Clayton (1968). A peasant's view of a Soviet collective farm. *American Economic Review*, 58, 37–59.

Schroder, Gertrude E. (1968). Soviet economic reforms: a study in contradictions. *Soviet Studies*, 20, 1–21.

Sharpe, Myron E. (ed.) (1966). *Planning, Profit, and Incentives in the USSR:* vol. i, *The Liberman Discussion: A New Phase of Soviet Thought;* vol. ii, *Reforms of Soviet Economic Management*. White Plains, New York: International Arts and Sciences Press.

Ward, Benjamin (1958). The firm in Illyria: market syndicalism. *American Economic Review*, 48, 566–89.

Ward, Benjamin (1967). *The Socialist Economy – A Study of Organizational Alternatives*. New York: Random House.

Zaleski, Eugene (1967). *Planning Reforms in the Soviet Union*, trans. Marie-Christine MacAndrew and G. Warren Nutter. Chapel Hill: University of North Carolina Press.

The Labor-Managed Firm and Bank Credit

SVETOZAR PEJOVICH[1]

The purpose of this paper is to contribute to our understanding of the relationship between the availability of bank credit and the investment behavior of the firm in a socialist state of the general type that is frequently referred to as the labor-managed economy. Since Yugoslavia is a variant, and the only one in the world today, of the labor-managed economy, it stands to reason that a theory of the investment behavior of the labor-managed firm must not ignore that country's experience. Indeed, the institutional framework in the paper reflects the legal and other institutional arrangements in Yugoslavia. Yet, the paper is intended to be a contribution to the microeconomic theory of socialism. For that reason my discussion of the relationship between bank credit and the investment behavior of the labor-managed firm will occasionally deviate from the economic situation in Yugoslavia.

I shall define the labor-managed economy quite broadly as a socio-economic arrangement featuring (i) the state's right of ownership in capital goods, (ii) the workers' right of ownership in the earnings of their respective firms, (iii) the workers' right to approve, police and enforce the decisions made by the managers, and (iv) the substitution of bank credit for the system of budgetary and other administrative (planned) allocation of funds. It follows that the labor-managed firm has two major sources of funds: retained earnings and bank credit.[2] Thus, the banking system is a crucial and, if one is to judge from the Yugoslav experience, quite powerful institution in the labor-managed economy.[3]

The analysis of the investment behavior of the labor-managed firm in this paper rests on the following major premises: First, our hypothetical firm has a given net earnings π^0. The employees are free to determine the allocation of that sum between the wage fund and retained earnings.[4] To simplify the analysis I will assume that the firm's undistributed profits are set aside to finance net additions to its stock of capital. That is, the analysis will ignore the effects of past debts as well as other uses for retained earnings on the collective's allocative decisions. Second, the firm must maintain the book value of its assets *via* depreciation or other means (e.g. the enterprise must reinvest the proceeds from sale of capital goods). This proposition reasserts the state ownership in capital goods

242

held by the labor-managed firm. The employees' decision to leave a part of the earnings with the firm for investment in additional assets is irreversible. If and when a worker leaves the firm he loses all his claims to the future returns despite the fact that his earlier sacrifice of current income helped the enterprise to purchase additional assets. Yet the proposition also implies a substantial attenuation in the state ownership rights. The employees have the right to control both the composition as well as the rate of growth of the firm's stock of capital. Moreover, they have adequate incentives to seek the highest-valued uses for the firm's resources.

Third, the banks' earnings are distributed in the manner of other firms. It follows that commercial banks in the labor-managed economy have adequate incentives to compete for deposits and seek profitable and low risk outlays for their funds. Fourth, the acquisition of additional capital goods is likely to increase the firm's demand for liquid assets on account of information and operating costs, lack of coincidence between expenditures and receipts, and the accompanying increase in the demand for the goods in process. To simplify the analysis I will assume a constant relationship between the firm's demand for liquid assets and its stock of capital, i.e. $L = aF$, and $dL/dF = a$. Liquid assets are taken to consist of cash balances, near money and physical inventories.[5] Fifth, following the Yugoslav case the bank lending rate as well as interest paid on time deposits are taken to be controlled by the state.

The paper begins with a brief discussion of the behavioral relationship between the content of property rights in capital goods, the collective's allocation of the labor-managed firm's earnings, and the availability of bank credit. This section summarizes the analysis developed elsewhere (Furubotn and Pejovich, 1970; Pejovich, 1973) and provides a useful and possibly necessary background for my discussion in the rest of the paper. The analysis in the second section of the paper offers some important insights into the investment behavior of the labor-managed firm. It also suggests a number of refutable consequences concerning the relationship between the firm's schedule of investment opportunities, its demand for short- and long-term funds, the collective's allocation of profit between the wage fund and retained earnings, and the availability of bank credit. The purpose of the final section of the paper is to indicate that the economic situation in Yugoslavia does not refute the line of reasoning developed in the first two sections.

Given the institutional structure described above, the employees of the labor-managed firm face two fundamentally different wealth-increasing alternatives: (i) the option to leave a part of the residual with the firm to purchase additional capital goods, or (ii) the option to take the residual out as wages and, then, to invest individually in savings accounts, jewelry, or in anything else the law allows. In Yugoslavia, those individual investment alternatives are restricted to monetary assets, human capital, and some limited types of physical assets such as small houses, taxis, small artisan shops, restaurants and motels employing no more than five hired workers, etc., where the right of ownership does not necessarily and obviously violate the principle of self-management.[6] It is important to recognize, however, that there is a significant difference in the bundle of rights under (i) and (ii). And that difference in the bundle of rights must affect the comparison of returns in the respective areas. I shall take the rate of interest on savings accounts to represent the highest return available to the employees from taking the residual out as wages and investing it individually. To consider explicitly other alternatives would only complicate the analysis without adding anything to the basic analytical argument which rests on the existence of two fundamentally different types of wealth-increasing alternatives in the economy. I will also assume that savings accounts and joint investment *via* retained residual are alike with respect to risk level and liquidity, that the employees of our firm have identical time preference, and that they have the same expectation about the length of employment by *that* firm. Those assumptions will help us to capture the essential factors governing the behavior of the collective of the labor-managed firm.

The workers are free to choose to exchange their current consumption for higher future income by leaving a part of the residual with the firm for investment in additional capital goods. Yet, they can neither sell their claims to future earnings from fixed assets acquired by the firm during the period of their employment nor continue to receive their share of those earnings once they leave the employ of *that* firm. The comparison between the rate of return required on internal investment in fixed assets and the rate of interest paid on individual savings must then recognize the important fact that the former alternative does not provide for the withdrawal of invested capital. From the standpoint of the Yugoslav workers those are *owned* and *nonowned* assets.

The contrast in the conditions of returns makes this distinction between owned and nonowned assets clear. In the former case savings of S dinars in period one permit additional consumption of $S + i_0 S$ dinars in period two. But the same number of dinars left with the firm for purchase of additional capital goods makes possible additional consumption of only rS in the second period. It follows that the worker who saves one dinar out of his current wages purchases a stream of income equal to

$$a = \frac{i_0(1+i_0)^n}{(1+i_0)^n - 1},$$
(1)

where i_0 is the prevailing rate of interest on savings deposits (i.e. owned assets) and n is the common time horizon of the working collective.

The employee will then have incentive to vote for and accept a reduction in his take home pay if he can expect to receive in the form of higher wages a stream of income at least equal to (1). Given the firm's legal obligation to maintain the value of its fixed assets, the rate of return from investment in nonowned assets which would generate the stream of income equal to (1) is

$$r = \frac{i_0(1+i_0)^n}{(1+i_0)^n - 1}. \tag{2}$$

For example, the rates of return that would make investment in nonowned capital goods as attractive to the employees as savings deposits at 5 % are 23 %, 19 %, 13 % and 9 % for time horizons of 5, 6, 10 and 15 years. It follows that for each given i and n there exists the rate of return r from investment in nonowned capital goods which would make the employees of the labor-managed firm indifferent between investment in nonowned assets and the highest-valued investment alternative in owned assets. The rate of interest i_0 is taken to represent the latter.

Equations (1) and (2) permit the comparison of the two basic wealth-increasing alternatives available to the employees of the firm in an environment in which they have the right of ownership in the income from capital goods but not in capital goods themselves.[7] This is a very important proposition that could be explained with the aid of a diagram. The $S_1 S_1$ schedule in fig. 1 represents the savings that will be forthcoming at various interest rates. Given the length of employment expected by the employees of the firm, the $S_2 S_2$ schedule can easily be calculated.[8] It shows the amount of income π the collective is willing to set aside for investment in nonowned assets at each given r. 'More specifically, the $S_2 S_2$ curve is the $S_1 S_1$ curve *adjusted* for the behavioral effects of a change in property rights from owned to nonowned assets. The rate of return r on nonowned assets has to be greater than the corresponding rate of return i on owned assets to elicit any given volume of saving from the employees' (Pejovich, 1969).

Given the employees' time preference and time horizon n, the firm's income π^0, and the required equalizing differential between incremental wages resulting from the workers' joint investment in nonowned assets and the highest-valued investment alternative available to them individually (i.e. r_0 and i_0 in fig. 1), the allocation of π^0 between the wage fund and retained earnings must depend on the properties of the schedule of investment opportunities in additional capital goods. If the expected rate of return from investment in a fixed asset is above r_0 the employees will find it in their interest to increase the share of retained earnings and capture the returns *via* higher wages in the future. If the expected rate of return is below r_0 the employees will prefer to save individually at i_0. However, the portion of the $S_1 S_1$ curve lying above i_0 does not come into effective play. It follows that failing the special condition that $r \geqslant r^0$ and the possibility of bank credit, each collective is effectively cut off from

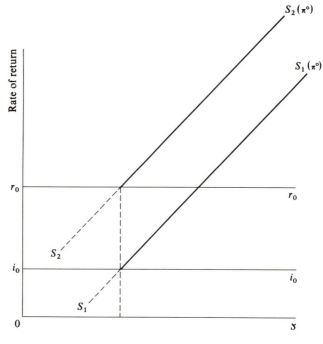

Fig. 1

investment alternatives promising higher rewards than i_0. In other words, consumption is likely to become the most attractive alternative open to workers.

Examples relating our analytical reasoning to the observed behavior of workers in Yugoslavia are many, to wit:

(i) As early as in 1966 it was said in a Yugoslav weekly newspaper that 'workers of a very successful enterprise in Slovenija wish to renounce a good part of what they have earned in order to help build a new workshop. But they say they would like, in turn, a paper which would indicate what they have given and what rights they would have to the future income of the enterprise.'[9]

(ii) A leading Yugoslav economist wrote:

If one wants to expand and improve entrepreneurial activity, one cannot avoid the flow of entrepreneurial product to entrepreneurs, whoever they may be . . . one cannot negate the economic necessity that entrepreneurs be proprietors of their products . . . entrepreneurial activity . . . is merely a special kind of work which it is necessary to supply in adequate quantities and quality to production . . . entrepreneurial incomes can never be regarded as state or society incomes . . . I would not be surprised, therefore, if somewhere in the future this will find its expression in giving enterprises property rights in their means of production. (Bajt, 1968, p. 3.)

(iii) In the summer of 1973 the Yugoslav press reported that the ruling elite was seriously debating the possibility of allowing business firms to distribute annually a share of profits to former employees in recognition of their past contributions

Let us assume that in the absence of bank credit the employees of our firm would decide to leave X dinars with the enterprise for self-financed investment activity. According to our earlier assumption that the firm's demand for liquid assets is a constant percentage of its fixed assets the allocation of X dinars would be as follows:

$$F = \frac{X}{1+a},\qquad(3)$$

$$L = X\left(1 - \frac{1}{1+a}\right).\qquad(4)$$

The important question must now be raised: what are the likely effects of bank credit on the firm's allocation of profit π^0 between the wage fund and retained earnings or, what is the same thing, the employees' distribution of their non-consumed income $\pi^0 - C$ between *joint* investment in nonowned assets and *individual* savings? For the purpose of this paper the following two effects are important:

(i) The law of diminishing returns and the penality–reward system in the labor-managed economy combine to suggest that the firm's investment decision can be – in the absence of outside administrative interferences – analyzed in the context of a conventional downward sloping schedule of investment opportunities. Assuming that investments are perfectly divisible rather than discrete[10] and that the employees can save individually any amount at i_0, it could be easily shown that the expected rate of return r from investment in capital goods will fall when a bank loan is added to the firm's retained earnings. As the rate of return falls, the employees will find it in their interest to change the allocation of profit π^0 in favor of the wage fund, i.e. to reduce their purchase of nonowned assets. At the rate of return r_0 and below it the employees will prefer to allocate the entire profit π^0 to the wage fund, save individually at i_0 and finance the entire investment by bank credit. It follows that as we start from the *extreme* case (the absence of bank credit) and then allow for debt financing *each additional dollar the firm can and wants to borrow from banks will increase its total investment by less than a dollar.* Moreover, as long as the bank lending rate is below r_0 the labor-managed firm will prefer debt financing to internally financed investment.

If our reasoning is correct it could be argued that the labor-managed firm would prefer to utilize bank credit *before* allocating a part of its profits for self-financed investment projects.[11] Yet, I believe that a sequence of financial operations followed in this paper is – and once again we have to fall back on the Yugoslav experience – more realistic. First, the firm cannot quickly and readily adjust its distribution guidelines to each and every change in either the price or availability of bank credit. It is much simpler for the firm to shift undistributed profits earmarked for investment projects into the money balances subject to holding preference. Moreover, the firm could also use retained earnings to enlarge the wage fund indirectly by placing these into the so-called collective consumption fund. Second, in 1972 the Yugoslav government ruled that the firm must secure at least 20 % of the total cost of investment in order to qualify for bank credit.

(ii) It is equally important to observe the effects of bank credit on the distribution of retained earnings between fixed and liquid assets. Given the assumed proportional relationship, or for that matter any other positive relationship, between the firm's need for additional liquid assets and its investment in fixed assets, *a long-term loan will induce the enterprise to increase the percentage of retained earnings earmarked for investment in liquid assets while a short-term loan will do just the opposite.* And if retained earnings happened not to be sufficient to finance the firm's need for additional liquid assets its demand for long-term loans will be accompanied by an increase in the demand for short-term credit. To simplify the analysis I will assume that the firm will seek short-term credit only when retained earnings are not sufficient to satisfy its demand for liquid assets. This assumption in no way affects the basic thrust of our analysis.

Our discussion thus far provides enough information to relate the firm's net investment in capital goods to its need for long- (F_b) and short- (L_b) term borrowings. The AF_b and BL_b curves in fig. 2 show the volumes of long- and short-term credits the firm would require in order to finance various levels of investment in new capital goods ΔF, given the employees time preference, time horizon and income π^0, the firm's schedule of investment opportunities, the rate of interest i_0 on individual savings, and the behavioral relationships discussed above. The OA investment in capital goods represents the extreme case which is associated with zero bank credit. As bank loans are made available to the firm, the level of investment in fixed assets will increase beyond A in fig. 2. At B the firm will be financing its entire investment in capital goods *via* bank credit while retained earnings will be just sufficient to satisfy its need for additional liquid assets.

It follows that investment in fixed assets between OB and OC levels in fig. 2 will be possible only if short-term credits are made available to the firm. To put it differently, *if and when* the economic situation permits the volume of investment in capital goods in excess of OB, retained earnings of our hypothetical firm will become inadequate to finance its rising demand for liquid assets. Also, the rate of investment in fixed assets OC

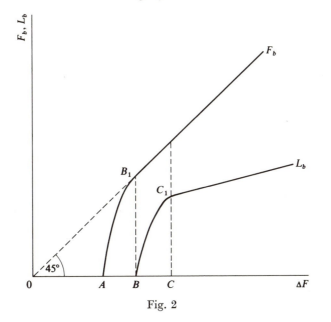

Fig. 2

will be undertaken if the entire cost of investment could be financed by bank credit. In that case, the workers will want to take the entire profit π^0 out as wages and save individually at i_0. The slope of AF_b curve between A and B_1 as well as the slope of BL_b curve between B and C_1 conform to the proposition discussed earlier that each dollar borrowed from the bank increases the firm's total investment by less than one dollar.

The set of diagrams in fig. 3 combines the firm's marginal efficiency of investment schedule with its accompanying need for long- and short-term credit. The MM curve is the marginal efficiency of investment schedule. This schedule is traditionally taken to reflect the opportunities the *given* firm possesses for the use of additional fixed assets and is based on the firm's initial position, current prices and the labor input, and the characteristics of the existing production function. The $F_b M$ and $L_b L_b$ curves represent the volumes of long- and short-term borrowings which are required for each given level of investment in fixed assets, given the background data.[12] The $F_b B_1$ curve then represents the labor-managed firm's combined need for bank credit.

In the absence of bank credit the firm's investment in fixed assets will be OA in fig. 3(d). The availability of bank credit will then induce the collective to increase its investment in additional capital goods beyond the OA level. However, it is important to note that the firm's need for bank credit (short plus long) will exceed the monetary value of its investment in additional fixed assets as the level of investment in capital goods exceeds OB.

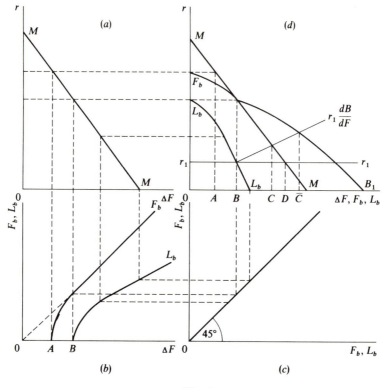

Fig. 3

The fact that the aggregate demand schedule for investable funds and the marginal efficiency schedule of the firm do not coincide raises the problem of assigning a separate rate of return to liquid assets. Lutz and Lutz (1951, esp. p. 161) argued that in a private property free-market community we can treat those assets as just earning what they cost; that is, the short-term market rate of interest. In that case, conventional proposition that the firm's rate of investment depends on its schedule of investment opportunities and the market rate of interest remains valid. An important question is: does economic logic support the extension of this proposition to the investment decision of the labor-managed firm in a decentralized *socialist* state?

The common feature of those items that are included into my definition of liquid assets (cash balances, near money, inventories) is that they are productive because they help business firms (i) to economize on the high cost of information and (ii) to maximize the extent of exchange. And I know of no obvious reason why a difference would exist between the demand for liquid assets (as defined in this paper) by the capitalist and socialist firms. On the other hand, the set of alternative forms in which business firms can hold liquid assets differs between those two systems. In a private property capitalist economy the firm can use some of its liquid assets to purchase interest-bearing securities (i.e. to hold financial inventories). While the distribution of liquid holdings of the capitalist firm between interest-bearing assets (near money) and non-interest-bearing assets such as money balances and physical inventories depends on a multitude of factors including transaction costs and the market rate of interest, the essential point is that the enterprise can *choose* to hold some of its liquid assets in interest bearing securities (see Baumol, 1952). The fact that capitalist firms have been consistent in using some of their liquid holdings to purchase interest-bearing securities suggests that they view the alternative of holding all liquid assets in non-interest-bearing forms (i.e. physical inventories and cash) as an inferior (costlier) one (see Bloch, 1963).

Financial markets do not exist in socialist states. Thus, the socialist firm has no choice but to hold its liquid assets in non-interest-bearing forms. In other words, the socialist firm is compelled to choose the alternative which the capitalist firm considers costlier. Assuming that the demand for liquid assets does not differ between the capitalist and the socialist firm, it is then possible to assert that the cost of each given investment in fixed assets is higher in socialism, other things being the same. This difference in costs is then a price the socialist state has to pay for its refusal to allow the future consequences of current allocative decisions to be capitalized *via* the right of private ownership in earning assets.

Following the line of reasoning suggested above and letting r_1 be the lending rate on bank loans,[13] the labor-managed firm would add to its stock of capital less than OD in fig. 3(d), that is less than the capitalist firm, all other things being the same. But how much less? To answer this question let us make an extreme assumption that liquid assets yield no return at all. Then, the marginal cost of borrowing becomes $r_1(dB/dF)$, where $r_1 < r_1(dB/dF)$ beyond OB investment in fixed assets because $dB > dF$. In this extreme case the labor-managed firm will increase its stock of capital by OC and borrow the $O\bar{C}$ amount from the bank to finance that investment.

However, liquid holdings *do* yield positive returns. Thus the labor-managed firm's demand for investment in fixed assets will fall between OC and OD levels in fig. 3d. The fact that the cost of holding liquid assets is higher in socialism than in capitalism will stop the socialist firm from increasing its investment in fixed assets up to D where the lending rate and the internal rate of return are equal. In other words, the differences in the costs of liquid assets between the capitalist and labor-managed firm suggest that the demand for new capital goods by the latter is likely to be below that of the former, other things being the same.

The analysis of the relationship between the firm's demand for outside funds, the collective's decision concerning the allocation of profits, the schedule of investment opportunities facing the enterprise, and the price and availability of bank credit yields some important insights into the investment behavior of the socialist firm, suggests a number of verifiable consequences, and implies that the management of firms by labor might not represent an optimal structure for decentralization. Some of those expected consequences are: (i) The growing dependence of business firms in the labor-managed economy on the banking system as a major if not the only outside source of long- and short-term funds. (ii) As long as the bank lending rate is set below the crucial rate of return from nonowned assets r_0 in fig. 1, bank credit will tend to enlarge the share of profits allocated to the wage fund relative to that which would otherwise prevail. (iii) The crucial role played by the banking system in freeing the volume of investment from the limitations imposed by the rate of voluntary savings. (iv) High costs of liquidity of the labor-managed firm relative to that of the capitalist firm. (v) Relative changes in the sources of assets of the labor-managed firm in favor of debt financing.

The logic of economics suggests that the consequences derived from our analysis will then translate themselves into the liquidity crisis, inflation, seemingly insatiable demand for bank credit, and possibly unemployment. Significantly, the Yugoslav economy – the only country in which a sort of the management of firms by labor has been introduced on a large scale – has been plagued with precisely those problems since the 1965 reform (see Pejovich, 1973). In the early 1970s the rate of inflation exceeded 20 %, the share of bank credit in financing net investment approached 70 %, the share of profit allocated to retained earnings fell from 40 % in 1965 to about 24 % in 1972, while short- and long-term credits rose from 18.2 and 53.6 billion dinars in 1965 to 54.5 and 134.4 billions in 1972. Table 1 reveals estimated changes in the sources of assets held by business firms between 1966–71.

Table 1. *Sources of assets of business firms in Croatia* (%)

	1966	1971
Retained earnings (i.e. firms' 'own' assets)	54.50	35.00
Bank credit	33.10	35.00
Other sources	12.40	30.00

Source: B. Cota, 'Likvidnost Privrede', *Ekonomski Pregled*, **21**, June–July 1970, p. 426; and *Ekonomska Politika*, **21**, 28 August 1972, p. 18.

In addition to revealing some interesting and certainly significant changes in the structure of 'ownership' of earning assets held by business firms, table 1 indicates the seriousness of the liquidity crisis in Yugoslavia as well. The 'other sources' entry primarily reflects debt financing *via* accounts payable and other types of firms's unsettled obligations.

While better experts might, it is hoped, test the expected consequences of the analysis for finer and more extended applications, the crude statistical data such as those mentioned above generate some important information, postulate measurable relationships and, most significantly, do not seem to contradict the suggested line of reasoning. If the basis thrust of the analysis is acceptable, there would be no presumption that Yugoslavia has arrived at an optimal structure of decentralization. More significantly, the analysis suggests that the question of precisely which set of institutions is capable of promoting efficient allocation of resources within a socialist framework is still open.

NOTES

1 The writing of this paper was facilitated by a grant from the National Science Foundation.

2 Retained earnings and bank credit amounted to about 80 % of the total investment in Yugoslavia in 1972. See *Statisticki Godisnjak*, Belgrade, 1973, p. 263.

3 For a detailed analysis of the banking system in Yugoslavia see Furubotn and Pejovich (1971).

4 This represents a deviation from the Yugoslav situation. See Furubotn and Pejovich (1973).

5 Physical inventories are not customarily regarded as liquid assets. However, inventories help the firm to economize on the high costs of information and to facilitate exchange. And with respect to this function inventories are similar to other liquid assets. For example, the manager of, say, a pizza place could try to spend money to obtain complete information as to who is going to buy pizza each day. He could also stock just enough material to make one pizza, and each time he sold one he could order material for another one, getting special delivery service. The manager is likely to decide that to hold inventories in excess of the average daily sales is a less costly alternative to either trying to purchase *complete* (*perfect*) *information* or making *instantaneous adjustments* in the number of pizzas. See Alchian and Allen (1968, pp. 153–7).

6 People who hold full-time jobs in Yugoslavia cannot readily use their savings to purchase some of these physical assets (e.g. small restaurants). The right to operate those assets is frequently contingent on the owner's continued presence.

7 To quote Professor Vanek 'The confusion and the inefficiency that this [differential between the market rate of interest and the rate of return on internal investment] will generate ... will be easily recognized by anyone with even a rudimentary training in economics' ('Some Fundamental Considerations of Financing and the Right of Property Under Labor Management', p. 8, unpublished paper). An objection that no evidence exists that the employees of Yugoslav firms think in terms of relative rates of returns when they allocate the firm's profit is a naive one. First, there is also no evidence that the employees in Yugoslavia do not think in terms of relative rates of interest. Secondly, it is the workers' *observed behavior* rather than what they say that they *think* which is relevant to an analyst. Becker's 'Irrational Behavior and Economic Theory' is recommended reading on this point. Finally, if our model is to be used to explain the real economic situation in

Yugoslavia it should be necessary to adjust it for (i) political influence of the state on the allocation of profits, (ii) the expected effects of the utility maximizing of the firm's manager on the allocation of profits, and (iii) the fact that some savings deposits are similar to, i.e. used *in lieu* of, short-term securities.

8 We assume the average length of employment expected by the employees to be the same. Information on the age distribution of the workers is important, of course, but it would not affect the essential features of the model.

9 *Vijesnik u Srijedu*, 23 November 1966.

10 This is a simplifying assumption which does not change the general results of our analysis. For detailed diagrammatic analysis see Pejovich (1969).

11 For detailed analysis see *Sluzbeni List SFRJ*, 30 December 1972, pp. 1443–4.

12 The availablility of funds is not implied here. If the funds are not available the rate of investment will slide up the *MM* schedule.

13 A difference between rates of interest on short- and long-term loans could easily be introduced into the model. Also, provisions for repayment of bank credit at a rate shorter than the workers' time horizon are likely to have some effect on borrowing. The result would be a change in the specific investment decision of the labor-managed firm but not in the general pattern of its investment behavior.

REFERENCES

Alchian, A. and W. Allen (1969). *Exchange and Production: Theory in Use*. Belmont, Calif.: Wadsworth.

Bajt, A. (1968). Property in capital and the means of production in socialist economies. *Journal of Law and Economics*, **11**.

Baumol, S. (1952). The transactions demand for cash: an inventory theoretical approach. *Quarterly Journal of Economics*, **66**, 545–56.

Bloch, E. (1963). Short cycles in corporate demand for government securities and cash. *American Economic Review*, **53**, 1058–77.

Furubotn, E. and S. Pejovich (1970). Property rights and the behavior of the firm in a socialist state: the example of Yugoslavia. *Zeitschrift für Nationalökonomie*, **3**.

Furubotn, E. and S. Pejovich (1971). The role of the banking system in Yugoslav economic planning. *Revue Internationale D'histoire de la Banque*, **4**, Summer.

Furubotn, E., and S. Pejovich (1973). The evolution of the Yugoslav firm, 1965–72. *Journal of Law and Economics*, **16**, October.

Lutz, F. and V. Lutz (1951). *The Theory of Investment of the Firm*. Princeton: Princeton University Press.

Pejovich, S. (1969). The firm, monetary policy and property rights in a planned economy. *Western Economic Journal*, **7**.

Pejovich, S. (1973). The banking system and the investment behavior of the Yugoslav firm. In *Plan and Market*, ed. M. Bornstein. Yale University Press.

Price, Appropriability and the Soviet Agricultural Incentives

ELIZABETH CLAYTON

Western economists have commonly supposed that price increases in Soviet agricultural products must have incentive effects and thus increase output, labor productivity, or both. The purpose of this paper is to examine this common assertion using mathematical tools of explication and analysis. There is clearly a nexus between Soviet agricultural prices and the distribution of income to rural areas; this area will not be examined. However, to assume that changes in income distribution will change productivity is a complex leap requiring generous economic assumptions and flexible economic institutions and structure. This paper will examine these, emphasizing the role of appropriability.

In the first section of the paper, the economic meaning of incentive is examined and the concept of appropriability developed. In the second section, an economic model of Soviet agricultural incentives is proposed. The third section extends the analysis of the proposed theory, and the fourth draws some conclusions.

The concept of incentive has been used variously by both Soviet and Western economists when referring to Soviet agriculture. Encompassed in an incentive are several attributes: an actor, a stimulus and a resultant action. Uses of the word may vary in any of these attributes. Action resulting from an incentive stimulus may increase total output, labor productivity (output per unit of labor), or output of a specific crop. The actor upon whom the incentive operates usually is labor, but this may be either managerial or production labor. Further, other inputs (capital, material supplies) also may respond to price incentives though one must acknowledge that there would be labor incentives intervening through managerial decision-making. An exogenous stimulus may be the price of either an input or an output. In general, Soviet theorists have emphasized the price incentive in reference to direct (input) responses, while western theorists have used price incentives to refer to both direct and indirect (output) responses.

Many examples of differences in 'incentive' may be cited. Bronson and Krueger (1971) imply that operative price incentives would result in an increase in labor productivity. Diamond (1966) discusses commodity prices as 'incentives' but notes that the connection between stimulus (reward) and action (effort) is 'tenuous' for the individual member of a collective. Spulber (1969) and Nove (1969) clearly regard prices as 'incentives' but do not specify the action that might result from an operative incentive effect. Bornstein (1966) refers to prices as incentives to perform the action of allocating resources between various crops. Bergson (1964) speaks of 'material incentives' but says their complexity has reduced effectiveness. Nimitz (1965) defines incentives as a stimulus of 'cash-plus-kind earnings', and details their trend in relation to 'intensity of labor'.

Soviet views of price incentives are narrower than western views. Kaluzhskii (1971) discusses increases in labor productivity attributed to work incentive premiums though in industry. Stoliarov (1969) mentions the 'principles of material incentives' as a basis of price-formation but in further discussion, considerations of equity, growth and balance dominate; output prices as labor incentives are not discussed. In summary, the Soviets acknowledge material inventives but dissociate labor supply from output prices; this dissociation is based on the implicit assumption that work payment levels set by the state are independent of output price levels set by the state. Note that Bergson (1964) and Diamond (1966) have reached the same conclusion of dissociation of stimulus and activity for somewhat different reasons.

Incentive effects are defined in this paper by resultant action; 'output response to price'. This meaning may be expressed in quantitative terms: if an incentive effect exists, then an increase (decrease) in price must result in an increase (decrease) in quantity produced. As a first approximation, only production effects will be studied in the socialized sectors. Marketing incentive effects will be limited to private sector activities. This boundary was chosen for two reasons: first, production in the socialized sectors clearly determines marketing to a large degree and should receive prior attention; second, socialist sector market response to price incentives is sufficiently complex to warrant extended separate analysis, due to the diversity among Soviet prices: quota, over-quota, *rynok*, cooperatives.

The nexus between output, a real variable, and price, a money variable, is a production function, a statement of the relation between outputs and inputs in real terms. Two output responses may be distinguished: response due to changes in input supplies and response due to shifts of fixed input supplies from one output to another.[1] The first response may be illustrated by a production function of the form:

$$X = f_1(N, K, T) \tag{1}$$

where X is aggregate output and N, K, T are inputs of labor, capital and land respectively. An input-response definition of incentive effects states that at least one input (say, N) may respond to the aggregate price level:

$$N = g(P). \tag{2}$$

Substituting (2) into (1) yields:

$$X = f_1[g(P), K, T]. \tag{3}$$

Thus, both input supply response (2) and output supply response (1) must be related to the effects of price incentives.[2]

Alternatively, one may view incentives in terms of outputs. If inputs (N, K, T) are fixed and there are two crops X and Y, production functions become:

$$X = f_2(N_x, K_x, T_x),$$

and

$$Y = f_3(N - N_x, K - K_x, T - T_x). \tag{1'}$$

An output-response definition of incentive effects states that the producer will choose outputs to maximize the sum of:

$$P_x f_2(N_x, K_x, T_x) + P_y f_3(N - N_x, K - K_x, T - T_x). \tag{2'}$$

If the price of one crop were to increase, resources would be shifted from the other crop, diminishing its production. Thus, one must consider the mobility of resources when investigating the effects of price changes under these definitions.[3]

This discussion of incentive effects and the traditional supply curve of economic literature are related closely. As shown, output response to price may result from either an increase in the total input supply or shifts in inputs from one output to another. Prices may be incentives for input suppliers, particularly labor; or for managerial decision-makers, who determine input uses, particularly land. Economists commonly refer to prices as 'market' indicators or 'market' incentives; the market communicates information through the price mechanism to producers. To return to the previous behavioral analogy, the market transmits a stimulus to the actor to induce a response. If prices are to change output in a planned economy, there must be channels for communicating an incentive effect to a producer, whether he be decision-maker or input supplier.[4] In the next section, the channels between producer and price will be examined.

The ability of inputs and outputs to respond to price depends on institutional constraints and economic organization. In this section, the institution of economic planning and its relation to price incentives will be examined. The channels for communicating price information to labor and land inputs are examined explicitly. The role of appropriability of rewards is drawn from these observations. Finally, a formal model of response based on the discussion will be presented.

If inputs and outputs are planned wholly and the production function is given, there can be no response to price at the level of production.[5] Planning directives, if binding, may determine either the aggregate supply of inputs (quantitative planning) or the inputs to a single output (use planning). The effect of wholly deterministic planning is a perfectly inelastic supply of input and output and there can be no response to price incentives.[6] In such a circumstance prices distribute income but do not allocate resources. Channels for communicating price incentives have been totally abrogated.

Soviet agricultural land has been planned with respect to both quantity and use. While empirical correlation of price increases 1953–62 with total land use is significant and positive, there is no statistically significant correlation between price increases for any specific crop in the socialized sector and the land input to that crop.[7] Surprisingly, this same observation may be made in the subsidiary household sector. Thus, there is no empirical verification of land response to price incentives with respect to use, but some verification with respect to quantity.

In general, it is believed that the Soviets have relied on 'material incentives', for the aggregate supply of labor, but there is no significant empirical correlation between the aggregate quantity of labor employed in the socialized sectors and the level of agricultural prices. There are both empirical and theoretical reasons. First, there are problems of gathering and interpreting such statistics: several independent observers cannot agree on the direction, let alone the magnitude, of changes in the supply of labor.[8] There is a theoretical reason for this unexpected response as well; economic theory demonstrates that an increase in income increases demand for leisure as well as supply of labor. These effects are offsetting. Minimum workday requirements testify to the strength of the demand for leisure. While material incentives may be used to plan aggregate labor supply, institutional choices, i.e., leisure, may mitigate their effectiveness.

Price may determine producer revenue, producer income, or both. Income need not be related to revenue. Organizational methods of paying income to producers need not use output prices as incentives. In state farms (*sovkhozy*), production workers are paid according to fixed wage scales. While there are bonuses for over-quota production, these are a small proportion of income. Further, wages are guaranteed by the state budget and state farms are subsidized; this weakens the link between revenues and income and, thus, incentive effects. It is unlikely that the prices paid to state farms are incentives to increase production.[9] On collective farms (*kolkhozy*), production workers until recently were paid by shares of total revenue received by the collective. In theory, these should act as incentives to increase production; in practice, the number of members in the collective is so large as to make changes in income due to individual effort imperceptible. In effect, the collective farm worker has long worked for a fixed wage which reflects skill rather than effort. This practice was formalized in recent reforms which instituted wage payments.[10] Only in the subsidiary household sector does the producer perceive directly the effects of prices on income. Price increases in the collective farm market increase or decrease the income from production in this sector.

The discussion above demonstrates significant institutional differences between price appropriability in socialized and subsidiary household agriculture. While land is 'socialized' in all sectors of Soviet agriculture, the ability to appropriate rewards from the sale of products differs vastly. It is this difference which lies at the heart of a discussion of price incentives under socialism. Increases in prices do not, *per se*, increase income. Institutional constraints in the appropriability of the price increase (output or income planning) may abrogate potential incentive effects entirely. Even if appropriable, rewards may be shared. While the collective farmer may appropriate rewards, they are not his exclusively; he must share them with other members of the cooperative, and this number may be substantial – in 1963, an average collective had 411 households sharing 2900 hectares (7000 acres).[11] In such an environment, returns to the individual from changes in price may be imperceptible.

Socialized farm workers derive their income from both the revenue of the socialized farm and their household sector returns. It remains to be shown formally that individual Soviet agricultural workers would respond to price incentives. Under present circumstances, the Soviet agricultural worker views his socialized sector income (M_s) to be determined exogenously to the parametric wage rate and hours worked (L), i.e.,

$$M_s = wL.$$

Private sector income (M_p) is determined by an exogenously determined price for output (P_x) and the quantity of that output (X). Quantity of private sector output is determined by the production function for that product with land input fixed but labor variable, i.e.,

$$M_p = XP_x$$

where $X = f(N, T)$ is the production function, N is the man-hour input, T is the land input (exogenously determined), and

$$\partial X/\partial N \equiv f_N, \quad \partial X/\partial T = f_T.$$

Alternatively, the worker might choose to spend his time in leisure activities (F). The problem then becomes one of maximizing utility:

$$U = U(M, F) \tag{4}$$

where $\partial U/\partial M \equiv u_M$ and $\partial U/\partial F \equiv u_F$, subject to:

$$M = M_s + M_p = wL + P_x f(N, T), \tag{5}$$

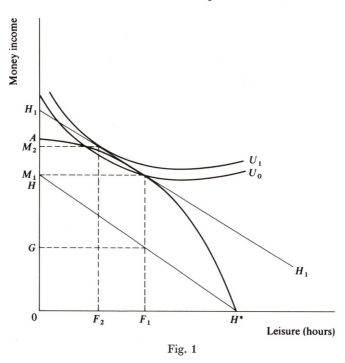

Fig. 1

and a physical and time constraint:

$$L + N + F = H \tag{6}$$

where H is a constant.[12]

As a first approximation, the worker may choose L, i.e. the work-day minimums are not binding. Maximizing the utility function subject to the constraints yields the equilibrium conditions:

$$u_F u_M = w = P_x f_N. \tag{7}$$

These conditions are shown graphically in fig. 1. The horizontal axis shows the number of hours devoted to leisure; if all available hours were devoted to leisure (H^*), no money income would be earned. If all available time were devoted to the production of private sector output (X), money income $= A$ could be earned; the curved line AH^* outlines the opportunities from combinations of N and F; it is curved due to diminishing returns on a fixed quantity of land (T). The straight lines HH^* and $H_1 H_1$ define market wage opportunities, the rate at which leisure may be exchanged for money income. If all available time were devoted to wage earning activities, money income $= H$ could be earned. Indifference curves U_0 and U_1 show the worker's preferences for money income (M) and leisure (F).

260

Moving from H_0, the worker can first maximize his opportunity set by expending $F_1 H^*$ hours on the private plot, i.e., by moving to a position where the market wage rate is tangent to the production opportunity curve, he is on indifference curve U_0, $w = P_x f_N$, and money income $= M_1$. In order to maximize his utility, the worker will expend a further $F_2 F_1 (= L)$ hours of labor in the labor market at the market wage rate (w), moving to the highest attainable indifference curve U_1, where $W = u_F / u_M$. At that point, money income $= M_2$ and leisure $= OF_2$.

While income received from the private plot is derived from land which is socialized, it may be imputed into wage and rent 'shares'. In fig. 1, the income to the worker as 'labor' may be measured by his alternative opportunity, $M_1 G$ in the diagram. His income as a 'landowner' is a residual, OG in the diagram. Taxes on sales price reduce private plot usage and rent, but lump sum taxes do not. Allowing the private subsidiary sector to appropriate money income gains from socialized land ensures a 'capitalistic' distribution of income in this instance.

If a minimum workday requirement ($L = L^*$ is imposed, the conditions for equilibrium become:

$$P_x f_N = u_F / u_M, \tag{8}$$

and the options facing the Soviet agricultural worker can be illustrated by fig. 2. A minimum money income (M_0) has been given to the worker by the workday minimum: his opportunity set is the household plot production, now $A^* H^{**}$ and the income wL, now fixed, $L + F_1 H^*$. The effect on the supply of labor to the household sector depends on the price received in that sector, the worker's preference for leisure, and the marginal productivity of labor in that sector. As the workday minimum is increased, the marginal utility of money decreases, the marginal utility of leisure increases and the impact falls on the household sector. One should expect that, indeed, the private sector will wither away under such circumstances. That this has occurred is evidenced by the predominance of non-wage persons in the household sector, i.e., elderly pensioners.

This extension of the analysis of incentive effects demonstrates the general equilibrium aspects of appropriability: if one source of income *must* be appropriated (i.e., through work-day minimums and a fixed wage) a negative response may occur in the other sector. Even though both average and marginal rewards in the household sector might be very 'high', the high rewards may not be appropriated. In effect, constraint is a tax in kind. In discussion, we have assumed that household sector product would be marketed. However, the Soviet rural household might produce in household production, not for sale but for household consumption. This subject is analyzed in the next section.

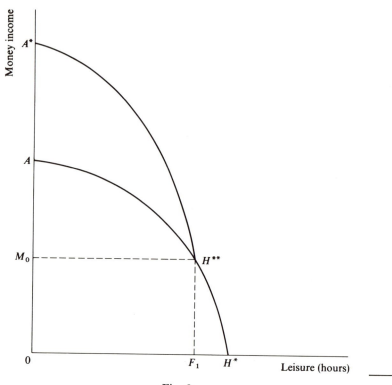

Fig. 2

The previous discussion demonstrated that appropriability of rewards in Soviet agriculture may determine the effectiveness of price incentives. Appropriability of rewards is most obvious in the subsidiary household sector. In that sector, an increase in product price transmits a direct market incentive to the individual producer in the household sector. The presence of planning and the absence of a market in kolkhoz and sovkhoz sectors are observed jointly; the key role in allocation is played by planning, rather than market appropriability. By removing the appropriability of price increases, the incentive effects of prices with respect to quantity of inputs and input use also are removed, and the market ceases to function as an allocator. The purpose of this section is to analyze market-type decisions which remain in the subsidiary household sector and to extend the analysis previously proposed.

In order to extend the analysis, the following model is proposed: the agricultural household derives utility from the consumption of leisure (F), household consumption of agricultural products (Z) and purchased goods (Y).

$$U = U(F, Z, Y). \tag{9}$$

262

Money income of the household is received from two sources: sale of household production (X) at a parametric price (P_x) and sale of labor of the household (L) at a parametric wage (w).[13] The income derived from these activities is spent on the purchase of good (Y) at a parametric price (P_y).

$$wL + XP_x = YP_y. \tag{10}$$

Using one price as a numéraire, this may be stated:

$$\frac{w}{P_y}L + \frac{P_x}{P_y}X = Y. \tag{11}$$

The products produced by the household have production functions:

$$X = f(N_1),$$
$$Z = g(N_2) \tag{12}$$

where $N_1 + N_2 = N$, hours expended in the household sector. The total hours available to the household may be summed:

$$N_1 + N_2 + L + F = H^*. \tag{13}$$

If workday minimums are imposed on the household, (13) becomes:

$$N_1 + N_2 + F = H^* - L, \tag{13'}$$

and equilibrium conditions become:

$$U_y(P_x/P_y)f_N = U_z g_N = U_F. \tag{14}$$

The interdependent effects of policies toward the socialized and household sectors may be analyzed with the aid of the four-quadrant diagram of fig. 3. In quandrant IV, the household faces private sector opportunities H^*Y^*; it may give up leisure to produce product X which is sold on the market. If a minimum workday is established at L^*, the household's preferences and the value of marginal product of labor (VMP_L) determine N, the labor devoted to household production. The value in the decision calculus is the market price of output sold relative to the market price of products purchased.

Given the labor input (N), and the single production function of homogeneous products $(X$ and $Z)$, the household will produce X_0 of product X (quadrant III); this is perfectly substitutable for product Z, as shown by the straight line of quadrant II. The rate of substitution in production between X and Z is -1, due to the assumption that the products are identical in production but not in end use. Quadrant I illustrates the consumer's preferences between consumption of goods produced in the household (Z) and consumption of goods purchased in the market (Y). From the wages of the minimum workday, the consumer may purchase Y_0 goods plus purchases from the sale of X not consumed in the household as Z. The locus of opportunities is the mirror image of

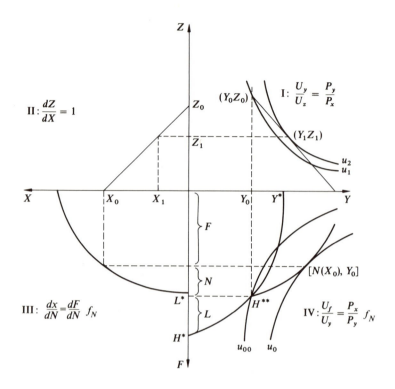

Fig. 3

the line $X_0 Z_0$ in quadrant II, multiplied by the parameteric price ratio P_y/P_x and sloping downward from the initial endowment (Y_0, Z_0).

If the household is satisfied with the goods which can be purchased with wage income, it will remain at $Y_0 Z_0$; alternatively, it may trade Z for further purchased goods, moving to a position of maximum utility $Y_1 Z_1$ where X_1 ($= Z_0 Z_1$) is sold in the market. Availability of consumer goods in rural areas has been assumed with certainty in this decision-making process. If goods past the original endowment $(Y_0 Z_0)$ are unavailable to the rural consumer, then his level of utility is reduced from u_2 to u_1. It does not follow, however, that the household would reduce household labor inputs, for this would reduce household consumption (Z) and thus reduce welfare further.

The model, as described, has more equations than unknowns. If the somewhat unreasonable assumption that workers may choose socialized labor hours (L) is introduced, then the model predicts the effect of a wage increase. Under these assumptions, a wage increase will diminish household sector labor supply. An income effect increases the demand for leisure, and a substitution effect diminishes N for F and L. The net result decreases the supply of labor for household production, if home consumption is an inferior good and purchased consumption is a close substitute. In effect, the wage increase has made purchased goods cheaper, relative to home production, in terms of labor time expended.[14]

NOTES

1 Comparison of these two approaches to incentive effects may be illustrated by familiar graphic means: the first is a shift outward of an agricultural production possibilities curve, the second is a movement along a single production possibilities curve with resources held constant.

2 More specifically, if (1) is of the Cobb–Douglas form $X = N^a K^b T^c$ and (2) is of the form $N = kP_x$, where k is some constant, then the elasticity of producer response to price (dX/dP_x) (P_x/X) is a/k; this implies that a 1 % change in price will yield an a/k % change in output.

3 To give a more specific illustration: if each crop uses identical inputs to produce the same weight of output, producers will produce only that crop with the highest price. An example would be potatoes for starch and potatoes for vodka: inputs are identical but outputs differ by final use. With different outputs, i.e., different production functions, combinations of products will be chosen reflecting the production function relationships and the mobility of resources. See Oi and Clayton (1968) for explication of this point.

4 Estimation of supply curves in market economies has utilized a combined disaggregate and aggregate input approach: Nerlove (1958) and Krishna (1963) have used land response to price to estimate supply elasticity; Falcon has used land, output and yield response to price. These approaches have focused on the producer as decision-maker. The present discussion separates producer functions into decision-maker and input supplier.

5 Planners may respond to price incentives but this possibility is not treated here. The price hierarchy and the agricultural planning hierarchy are separated.

6 This discussion abstracts from considerations of demand by the producing enterprise. While Soviet central planning is termed 'supply' planning, it also 'plans' the *demand* for inputs; it is possible for this demand to be 'de-planned' at a decentralized level. Conklin (1969) illustrates such a situation in his study of fertilizer inputs. While such failures may be attributed to lack of coordination, producers clearly have the choice of not using planned inputs, i.e., a failure of effective demand.

7 In discussion of correlations between input supplies, outputs and prices, the period 1953–63 was studied. See Clayton (1971) for sources of these data.

8 Nimitz (1967), in sectoral data, proposes that there were significant year-to-year differences in labor supply with large fluctuations in this input. Diamond does not concur; he proposes a stable or slightly declining labor supply during the same period.

9 In Clayton (1971), elasticity of supply with respect to price is not significantly different from zero in this sector.

10 The kolkhoz worker receives some income in kind. The share of income received in kind has diminished in recent years but is still significant. Morozov states that there were no *kolkhozniks* receiving all income in money in the RFSFR in 1958.

11 *Narodnoe Khoziaistvo v 1963 g.*, p. 345.

12 Heuristically, H may be viewed as twenty-four hours, with requisite activities such

as eating and sleeping subsumed in F; alternatively H may be all time not spent in requisite activities.

13 Note that goods X and Z are identical in production but not in end use.

14 This assumes that the individual has no preferences for social or household labor and that the disutility of each is the same for him. The equilibrium condition is:

$$\frac{w}{P_y} = \frac{P_x}{P_y} g_N.$$

REFERENCES

Bergson, A. (1964). *The Economics of Soviet Planning*. Yale.

Bornstein, M. (1966). The Soviet price system. In *The Soviet Economy*, ed. M. Bornstein and D. Fusfeld, pp. 66–96. Irwin.

Bronson, D. and C. Krueger (1971). The revolution in Soviet farm household income, 1953–1967. In *The Soviet Rural Community*, ed. James R. Millar, pp. 214–58. University of Illinois.

Clayton, E. (1971). Productivity in Soviet agriculture: a sectoral comparison. In *Jahrbuch der Wirtschaft Osteuropas*, ed. H. Raupach, pp. 315–28. Munich.

Conklin, D. W. (1969). Barriers to technological change in the USSR: a study of chemical fertilizers. *Soviet Studies*, **20**, 353–65.

Diamond, D. B. (1966). Trends in outputs, inputs and factor productivity in Soviet Agriculture. In *New Directions in the Soviet Economy*, Joint Economic Committee, pp. 339–82. Washington.

Kaluzhskii, A. (1971). Tseli stimylirovaniia. *Ekonomicheskaya Gazeta*, **44**, 8.

Krishna, R. (1963). Farm supply response in India–Pakistan. *Economic Journal*, **73**, 477–87.

TsSU, *Narodnoe Khoziaistvo v 1963 g.*

Nerlove, M. (1958). *Dynamics of Supply: Estimation of Farmers Response to Price*. Baltimore: Johns Hopkins.

Nimitz, N. (1965). Agriculture under Khrushchev: the lean years. *Problems of Communism*, **14**, 10–22. Reprinted in M. Bornstein and D. Fusfeld, *The Soviet Economy*, pp. 202–15. Irwin, 1966.

Nimitz, N. (1967). Farm employment in the Soviet Union, 1928–1963. In *Soviet and East European Agriculture*, ed. J. Karcz, pp. 175–205. Berkeley.

Nimitz, N. (1971). Comment. In *Agrarian Policies and Problems in Communist and Non-Communist Countries*, ed. W. A. D. Jackson, pp. 174–7. University of Washington.

Nove, A. (1969). *The Soviet Economy*. Praeger.

Oi, W. and Clayton, E. (1968). A peasant's view of a Soviet collective farm. *American Economic Review*, **58**, 37–59.

Spulber, N. (1969). *The Soviet Economy*. Norton.

Stoliarov, S. G. (1969). *O Tsenax i Tsenoobrazovanii v SSSR*. Moscow.

III. Quantitative Analysis of the Soviet-Type Economy

I. Multi-Sectoral Modelling

A Test of Five-Year Plan Feasibility

HOLLAND HUNTER[1]

INTRODUCTION

This paper reports on an exercise in *ex-post* planning, applying contemporary quantitative methods to data for the first Soviet Five-Year Plan, which covered the years 1929–33. The tools of input–output economics and linear programming were not then available, but the three volumes of the first Soviet plan reflect a massive attempt to lay out a coordinated blueprint for development, and there is considerable interest in using present techniques, forty-five years after the fact, to evaluate this pioneering effort. A test of this sort throws light both on the empirical situation being studied and on the analytic tools themselves. The stress here is methodological. The quantitative estimates, highly simplified and aggregated for expository reasons, yield rather tentative results that mainly suggest directions in which further work appears promising.

The practical application to a national economic plan of a linear programming technique in an intersectoral framework has been demonstrated by Richard S. Eckaus and Kirit S. Parikh (1968) in their study, *Planning for Growth*. They present a theoretic model in four variants that can test the intertemporal and intersectoral feasibility of an aggregate development plan, and review the third and fourth plans of the Government of India in order to identify bottlenecks, compare alternative patterns of resource allocation, and trace the effect of various detailed changes in plan parameters. Differences between the USSR and India, as well as limitations on the resources available for this project, have led me to make a number of changes in the model. The real breakthrough of Eckaus and Parikh lies not so much in the details of their model as in demonstrating the feasibility itself of a comprehensive test of economic plans.

Testing the first Soviet FYP is facilitated by ample documentation which permits greater empirical precision in some respects than is derivable from India's third and fourth plans. Base period stocks of available capital capacity and capital-in-process, for example, can be derived directly from Soviet plan documents. Moreover Soviet data permit detailed reconstruction of the gestation periods for fixed capital formation that were anticipated by Gosplan. In addition, since the focus here is on short-run structural evolution, base period parameters are made to

269

evolve annually toward intended terminal-year values, and the length of the plan period is varied experimentally.

The next section lays out the structure of the model. The third section notes some dimensional decisions and conceptual complications that arise in matching the model with data. Analysis of the capital gestation process appears in the fourth section. Some initial test results are summarized in the final section, which ends with a few reflections on the implications of the exercise. A broader evaluation appeared in the discussion section of the June 1973 issue of the *Slavic Review* (Hunter, 1973).

THE STRUCTURE OF THE MODEL

The core of the Eckaus–Parikh basic model consists of inequalities stating that the uses of each sector's gross output cannot exceed the sources available that year, together with other inequalities stating that each sector's domestic production cannot exceed a ceiling imposed by its current capital capacity. Current flows in an input–output framework link the sectors of the economy together each year as they deliver to five categories of final demand. While the sectors of the economy are linked together each year by an *A* matrix of production coefficients, the years of the plan period (together with several preplan and postplan years) are linked together by the process of building new capital capacity. Fixed capital formation requires deliveries of current output from various sectors over a gestation period of perhaps several years. The claims of capital formation thus reach backward through preceding years and outward through the economy's intersectoral structure.

The Eckaus–Parikh basic model places an objective function within this intersectoral and intertemporal linear framework in order to test the programming feasibility of reaching a set of terminal-year targets, given an initial base-year starting point. If the targets are feasible, an optimal linear programming solution will determine an allocation of resources among the sectors of the economy and the years of the plan period that will maximize the value of the objective function. Imports, exports, and foreign aid can be fitted into the model. As a closed but flexible system, it is a powerful instrument for studying development processes.

For this study, two variants of the Eckaus–Parikh Target model have been constructed. Both make use of a 1928 base-year flow table and 1933 terminal-year flow table involving six sectors, together with the 1928 actual and 1933 intended sectoral capital stocks. The 1928 table displays the dimensions and structure of major intersectoral flows on the eve of the first plan period. Dividing the column entries for each producing sector by that sector's row total, we obtain an *A* matrix for 1928, reflecting the technological structure of the economy as it stood in the

270

base year (see table A 1). Each element of this matrix shows how much of sector *i*s output is required per unit of sector *j*s gross output. The final demand columns show the absolute levels and structural composition of household demand, current inventories, and deliveries to government, exports, and fixed capital formation.

A similar table for 1933 incorporates the terminal-year targets of the official Soviet plan (see table A2). Implicit in its northwest quadrant is another *A* matrix reflecting the technological structure that Gosplan estimated would be brought into being by 1933. Comparison of an element in the 1933 matrix with the corresponding element in the 1928 matrix discloses a small bit of technological change embedded in the plan. Similarly, one can compare the size and structure of a 1933 final demand column with that of its 1928 predecessor to note intended pro-portional changes and also compare expected changes among the final demand columns. In this study the value added rows of the two tables play no part and the totals are only recorded as checks. Though the Soviet Plan dealt with labor supply and training problems in some detail, the present exercise focuses on capital as the binding constraint and therefore makes no use of labor information.

The tables show that deliveries to household consumption were to undergo a noticeable shift in composition, with deliveries from the industry sector showing an increasing share of the column total at the expense of deliveries from agriculture. Intended deliveries to government show an opposite trend. For each year a small fraction of each sector's gross output goes to current inventories: these ratios were slated to be markedly higher in 1933 than in 1928. Together with data on exports and imports, these made up the structural parameters embedded in the plan.

In this study, parameters are not constant over the plan period but instead move smoothly from their base period values to their terminal year values. Input–output coefficients, current inventory coefficients, sectoral shares in household consumption, and required-import ratios are all interpolated arithmetically over the intervening years. Where absolute amounts in each sector are involved, as with deliveries to Government and Exports, the intermediate-year levels are interpolated logarithmically. The effect is to loosen up some of the rigidity that is conventionally attributed to input–output analysis, permitting steady evolution of structural change along lines intended by the plan.

This approach also makes it possible to vary the length of the plan period itself. In order to minimize the rewriting of history, one needs to retain as much as possible of the original plan targets while investigating alternative growth paths. The introduction to the first FYP itself suggests a way to avoid arbitrary departures from plan intentions. Gosplan had prepared two plan variants, basic and 'optimal', and the authors note that the gap between them is roughly 20 %, that is, one year's worth of development. In other words, the same (optimal) program that can be carried out in five years under one set of conditions will extend over six years under other less favourable conditions, as specified in the basic variant. (Gosplan SSSR, 1930; vol. i, pp. 11–12.)

Both of the models employed in this study therefore examine the consequences of stretching the plan period to six, seven, or eight years without altering any of the terminal-year absolute targets. Input–output coefficients, household consumption proportions, inventory–output ratios, required import ratios, autonomously specified final demands, and sectoral capital–output ratios all evolved linearly over a longer period, but plan targets are otherwise left intact. The levels achieved in the fifth year decline, of course, as the plan period lengthens, and by the same token changes in intersectoral structure proceed less rapidly.

In their study of India, Eckaus and Parikh employed a very simple capital gestation period since detailed information was lacking and their interest centered on processes covering several construction periods. Soviet capital data for the first plan period are quite abundant, and it is therefore possible to be more precise. Instead of an arbitrarily assumed three-year gestation period with one third of the outlays being made in each of the three years preceding the introduction of new capital capacity, Gosplan expectations indicate a four-year capital outlay pattern with 8 % coming in the first year, 16 % in the second year, 41 % in the third year, and 35 % in the fourth year, just before a new group of facilities comes into operation. The underlying details are set forth in the next section.

In all their models, Eckaus and Parikh put private consumption into the objective function as the goal to be maximized. My CTAR (Consumption Target) model does the same. A column vector of deliveries from each producing sector to households, in proportions that evolve linearly from base year to terminal year, is summed up for each year and the annual totals are summed over the plan period, subject to a modest rate of social discount (whose size does not significantly affect alternative solutions). Eckaus and Parikh show how bang–bang solutions can be excluded through requiring monotonic growth in consumption at a specified minimum rate, together with a specified minimum for the initial plan year. My tests use the expected rate of population growth as a growth-rate floor, and raise the base-period figure for total household consumption parametrically as provided for in one of the IBM Mathematical Programming System sub-routine options.

Since Soviet purposes centered on capital formation, there is analytic interest in placing terminal-year capital stocks in the objective function and shifting household consumption over to join the constraints that must be met. In this conceptual reconstruction of Stalin's approach, the needs of households are taken care of on some minimum basis, while first priority is given to building the capital base of the economy. Though the first Soviet plan did not state its aims in these terms, Soviet policies in fact developed along these lines during the 1928–40 period. In the KTAR (capital target) model, therefore, a vector of terminal-year capital stocks is maximized, using the sectoral proportions laid down for 1933 in the 'optimal' variant of the first FYP. Household consumption is exogenously specified and moved to the right-hand side of the distribution inequalities. It grows at the same rate as total population, preserving per capita consumption levels.

The sectoral capital stock data in the first FYP require adjustment to separate rural housing from agricultural capital, separate urban housing from capital recorded in the industry sector, and consolidate other entries into our six-sector framework. Beyond this, estimates discussed in detail in the appendix take account of capital in process at the beginning of 1928, and the beginning of 1933. These amounts are deducted in order to obtain capital–output ratios for 1928 and 1933 reflecting only capital capacity available for use.

Turning now to the formal model itself, and following the terminology and symbols of Eckaus and Parikh, but simplifying the treatment of inventories, we have first a set of sources-and-uses inequalities as follows, one for each sector of the economy in each year of the plan period:

$$aX + cC + sX + G + E + N \leqslant X + M, \qquad (1)$$

where

$X =$ the annual gross domestic output of a sector,
$cC =$ the portion of total household consumption that comes from this sector,
$sX =$ the portion of this sector's output that is required for current inventories,
$G =$ deliveries by this sector to Government uses,
$E =$ deliveries by this sector for Exports,
$N =$ deliveries of this sector's output for new capital formation,
$M =$ imports into the economy of this sector's category of output.

The first term, aX, is shorthand for a row in the northwest quadrant of the economy's flow table; it will have as many non-zero row elements as there are producing sectors to which this sector makes deliveries.

The small cs specify the way a final-demand column total, (C), for household consumption is subdivided into deliveries from each producing sector.

The small s coefficients serve to allocate a small fraction of each sector's row total to a final use category, current inventory.

Deliveries to Government and for Exports are treated throughout as lump sums exogenously specified in the plan.

The N term represents this sector's deliveries (if any) to fixed capital formation; its details are spelled out below.

The M term, for imports, is divided into two parts: mX, for imports that may be required per unit of gross output in the sector, and M'', for optional imports that may be possible and desirable. The plan-specified exports finance imports which here go only to the Agriculture and Industry sectors. After their small import requirements are covered and plan-specified trade debts are paid, optional imports are sent to one sector or the other or both by the optimizing solution.

These uses-and-sources inequalities, one for each sector in each year, form a linear framework for the current flows of intermediate and final demand in the economy.

Next we have a set of relations covering capital stocks, their expansion, and their connections with current flows. Capital stocks grow under the following restrictions (again, a simplified version of Eckaus–Parikh):

$$K(t+1) \leqslant K(t) - d(t) K(t) + Z(t+1), \tag{2}$$

where $K(t)$ is the fixed capital capacity available in a sector at the beginning of period (t), the $d(t)$ are sector-specific and year-specific depreciation rates, derived from plan data, and $Z(t+1)$ is the new fixed capital that reaches completion by the beginning of the year $(t+1)$. This new capital is not, however, all built during year t. As the fourth section below makes clear, Soviet plan documents indicate a four-year gestation period for capital equipment and structures; slender evidence suggests a composite three-year gestation period for livestock. Buildings and structures are delivered here by the Construction sector; equipment is delivered by the Industry sector; and livestock grows in the Agricultural sector. The Z that is required by each sector at the beginning of year $(t+1)$ must therefore be delivered by the Construction and Industry sectors in years $(t-3)$, $(t-2)$, $(t-1)$, and (t), while livestock must grow in the Agriculture sector during years $(t-2)$, $(t-1)$, and (t). The capital requirements of each sector are divided between plant (buildings and structures) and equipment in proportions that vary from one sector to another. We need, therefore, four coefficient matrices, $\mathbf{p}$, that record these proportions and spread them over the capital gestation period. We can then relate: (a) the deliveries of new capital that are supplied in year t by the capital-producing sectors to (b) the new capital demands of all the sectors in years $t+1, t+2, t+3$, and $t+4$. Summing up these demands from the standpoint of the capital-producing sectors, we have, in matrix form:

$$\mathbf{N}(t) = \mathbf{p}^i \mathbf{Z}(t+1) + \mathbf{p}^{ii} \mathbf{Z}(t+2) + \mathbf{p}^{iii} \mathbf{Z}(t+3) + \mathbf{p}^{iv} \mathbf{Z}(t+4). \tag{3}$$

The capital stocks available in each sector at the beginning of the first plan year, $\overline{K(1)}$, are set forth in the 1929/30 *Control Figures* and the capital-in-progress can be roughly estimated and entered, sector by sector, as $\overline{Q(2)}$, $\overline{Q(3)}$, and $\overline{Q(4)}$. These amounts supplement $Z(2)$, $Z(3)$, and $Z(4)$.

Requirements for deliveries to new capital capacity in the last four years of the plan period depend on plan expectations for the post-terminal period. I follow the Eckaus and Parikh Target model assumption that the average growth rate specified in the plan for each sector's output over the plan period will apply to the growth of that sector's capital stock in years $T+1$, $T+2$, $T+3$, and $T+4$. The resulting Z terms are therefore reduced when the plan period is lengthened and annual growth rates decline.

Output ceilings for each sector in each year take the form:

$$bX \leqslant U, \tag{4}$$

where the bs are sector-specific and year-specific average capital–output ratios and the Us are the amounts of fixed capital capacity actually used. The Us, in turn, must be less than or equal to the capital capacity available for each sector at the beginning of each year. The distinction between U and K permits unused capacity to be carried forward for potential future use.

Within this framework of production possibilities, two alternative objective functions are designated. The first, following Eckaus and Parikh, is the sum of household consumption delivered by all sectors over all the years of the plan period. They found that use of a social discount rate had little effect on solutions. Consumption is constrained to grow each year by at least some specified rate, r, but the initial level is unconstrained in all but the first CTAR run.

The KTAR objective function is specified as total terminal-year capital stocks, in sectoral proportions laid down for 1933 in the 'optimal' variant of the first FYP. However, the IBM Mathematical Programming System package permits the expression of these shares in terms of upper or lower limits, so the shares of Industry and Construction are specified as lower limits, with the other four sector shares specified as upper limits. Household consumption is exogenously specified and and moved to the right-hand sides of the distribution inequalities.

In operational form these relationships are rearranged so that all inequalities are expressed in less-than-or-equal-to form, and so that all right-hand sides are either zero or an exogenously specified absolute amount. The tableau for this problem can be simplified through rearrangement and substitution. The N terms are eliminated. The E and G terms shift to right-hand sides as specified absolute numbers. Four matrices of specified coefficients can be added together. The general form of the output-flow inequalities then becomes:

$$(\mathbf{a}+\mathbf{s}-\mathbf{I}-\mathbf{m})\,\mathbf{X}+\mathbf{C}+\mathbf{Z}-\mathbf{M} \leqslant -\overline{\mathbf{E}}-\overline{\mathbf{G}}, \tag{5}$$

where $\mathbf{X}$, $\mathbf{C}$, $\mathbf{Z}$, and $\mathbf{M}$ are the unknowns to be solved for. The full CTAR model then appears as follows:

1. *Objective function*

Maximize:
$$W = \sum_{t=1}^{T} \frac{C(t)}{(1+w)^{t-1}}. \tag{1.0}$$

Subject to:

2. *Consumption growth constraints*
$$-C(1) \leqslant -(1+r)\,\overline{C(0)}, \tag{2.1}$$
$$-C(t) + (1+r)\,C(t-1) \leqslant 0 \quad \text{for} \quad t = 2, ..., T. \tag{2.2}$$

3. *Distribution relationships*
$$[\mathbf{a}(1) + \mathbf{s}(1) - \mathbf{I} - \mathbf{m}^i(1)]\,\mathbf{X}(1) + \mathbf{c}(1)\,C(1) - \mathbf{M}^{ii}(1) + \mathbf{p}^i\mathbf{Z}(2)$$
$$+ \mathbf{p}^{ii}\mathbf{Z}(3) + \mathbf{p}^{iii}\mathbf{Z}(4) + \mathbf{p}^{iv}\mathbf{Z}(5) \leqslant -\overline{\mathbf{E}(1)} - \overline{\mathbf{G}(1)}, \tag{3.1}$$
$$[\mathbf{a}(t) + \mathbf{s}(t) - \mathbf{I} - \mathbf{m}^i(t)]\,\mathbf{X}(t) + \mathbf{c}(t)\,C(t) - \mathbf{M}^{ii}(t) + \mathbf{p}^i\mathbf{Z}(t1)$$
$$+ \mathbf{p}^{ii}\mathbf{Z}(t2) + \mathbf{p}^{iii}\mathbf{Z}(t3) + \mathbf{p}^{iv}\mathbf{Z}(t4)$$
$$\leqslant -\overline{\mathbf{E}(t)} - \overline{\mathbf{G}(t)} \quad \text{for} \quad t = 2, ..., T-1, \tag{3.2}$$
$$[\mathbf{a}(T) + \mathbf{s}(T) - \mathbf{T} - \mathbf{m}^i(T)]\,\mathbf{X}(T) + \mathbf{c}(T)\,C(T) - \mathbf{M}^{ii}(T)$$
$$+ \mathbf{p}^i\mathbf{Z}(T1) + \mathbf{p}^{ii}\mathbf{Z}(T2) + \mathbf{p}^{iii}\mathbf{Z}(T3) + \mathbf{p}^{iv}\mathbf{Z}(T4)$$
$$\leqslant -\overline{\mathbf{E}(T)} - \overline{\mathbf{G}(T)}, \tag{3.3}$$

4. *Balance of payments constraints*
$$u\mathbf{m}^i(t)\,\mathbf{X}(t) + u\mathbf{M}^{ii}(t) \leqslant A(t) + u\mathbf{E}(t) \quad (t = 1, ..., T). \tag{4.1}$$

5. *Capital accounting relationships*
$$\mathbf{K}(2) \quad - \mathbf{Z}(2) \qquad\qquad\qquad \leqslant \overline{\mathbf{K}(1)} + \overline{\mathbf{Q}(2)}, \tag{5.1}$$
$$\mathbf{K}(3) \quad - \mathbf{Z}(3) \quad -[1-\mathbf{d}(2)]\,\mathbf{K}(2) \leqslant \overline{\mathbf{Q}(3)}, \tag{5.2}$$
$$\mathbf{K}(4) \quad - \mathbf{Z}(4) \quad -[1-\mathbf{d}(3)]\,\mathbf{K}(3) \leqslant \overline{\mathbf{Q}(4)}, \tag{5.3}$$
$$\mathbf{K}(t+1) - \mathbf{Z}(t+1) \quad -[1-\mathbf{d}(t)]\,\mathbf{K}(t) \leqslant 0, \tag{5.4}$$
$$\mathbf{Z}(T+1) - [1-\mathbf{d}(T)]\,\mathbf{K}(T) \leqslant (1+\alpha)\,\mathbf{K}(T), \tag{5.5}$$
$$- \mathbf{Z}(T+2) - \mathbf{Z}(T+1) - [1-\mathbf{d}(T)]\,\mathbf{K}(T) \leqslant (1+\alpha)^2\,\mathbf{K}(T), \tag{5.6}$$
$$- \mathbf{Z}(T+3) - \mathbf{Z}(T+2)$$
$$- \mathbf{Z}(T+1) - [1-\mathbf{d}(T)]\,\mathbf{K}(T) \leqslant (1+\alpha)^3\,\mathbf{K}(T), \tag{5.7}$$
$$- \mathbf{Z}(T+4) - \mathbf{Z}(T+3) - \mathbf{Z}(T+2)$$
$$- \mathbf{Z}(T+1) - [1-\mathbf{d}(T)]\,\mathbf{K}(T) \leqslant (1+\alpha)^4\,\mathbf{K}(T). \tag{5.8}$$

6. *Capacity Restraints*

$$\mathbf{b}(t)\,\mathbf{X}(t) \leqslant \mathbf{U}(t) \quad (t = 1, ..., T), \tag{6.1}$$

$$\mathbf{U}(1) \leqslant \mathbf{K}(1), \tag{6.2}$$

$$\mathbf{U}(t) - \mathbf{K}(t) \leqslant 0 \quad (t = 2, ..., T). \tag{6.3}$$

KTAR model constraints after substitutions (same as CTAR except for):

7. *Objective function*

Maximize: $\qquad P(\text{power}) = \sum_{1}^{6} \mathbf{K}(T). \tag{7.0}$

Subject to:

8. *Capital proportions constraints*

$$K(T)\,AG\,/u\,\mathbf{K}(T) \leqslant \overline{k(AG)}, \tag{8.0}$$

$$-K(T)\,IN/u\,\mathbf{K}(T) \leqslant -\overline{k(IN)}, \tag{8.1}$$

$$K(T)\,TR\,/u\,\mathbf{K}(T) \leqslant \overline{k(TR)}, \tag{8.2}$$

$$-K(T)\,CO\,/u\,\mathbf{K}(T) \leqslant -\overline{k(CO)}, \tag{8.3}$$

$$K(T)\,HO\,/u\,\mathbf{K}(T) \leqslant \overline{k(HO)}, \tag{8.4}$$

$$K(T)\,OT/u\,\mathbf{K}(T) \leqslant \overline{k(OT)}. \tag{8.5}$$

9. *Distribution accounting relationships*

$$\mathbf{J}(t) + \mathbf{N}(t) + \mathbf{S}(t) - \mathbf{M}(t) - \mathbf{X}(t)$$
$$\leqslant -\overline{\mathbf{F}(t)} - \overline{\mathbf{E}(t)} - \overline{\mathbf{G}(t)} \quad \text{for} \quad t = 1, ..., T, \tag{9.0}$$

$$\mathbf{F}(t) = (1 + \bar{\mathbf{r}})^{t}\,\overline{C(0)} \quad \text{for} \quad t = 1, ..., T. \tag{9.1}$$

DIMENSIONAL DECISIONS AND EMPIRICAL CHOICES

Several difficult decisions are required when one attempts to find or construct empirical estimates to fit this model. Perhaps the first that deserves discussion concerns Soviet prices. The ruble data in the first FYP are largely given in terms of the so-called '1926/7 prices' that became increasingly dubious in later years. For the base period, however, they seem quite acceptable as measures of the prevailing situation. The price level did not change by more than 3 or 4 % from 1926/7 to 1927/8. Data for capital stocks are given in 1925/6 prices but here too there was little change over the next two years. The first FYP was very optimistic about reductions in real costs of construction and production, so a great many terminal-year targets were estimated by Gosplan not only in terms of '1926/7 prices' but also in terms that would reflect these cost reductions. However, quite apart from their interpretability in relative terms, actual costs moved strongly in an upward rather than downward direction, which suggests that these targets in 'reduced cost' prices should be ignored.

For a comprehensive, economy-wide plan, *ex-ante* prices have to be employed. One might conceive of a set of relative prices emerging as the dual to a terminal-year solution for a vast linear programming problem incorporating all intervening real structural changes in the economy, but the concept itself was not explicitly available forty years ago, nor is the practical means of estimating such a set of prices available even today. If we intend to examine the economy's capacity to produce a new, intended bill of goods, there may be some analytic consolation in the Moorsteen point that base-period prices provide the best weights for aggregation.

For a manageable first application of this model to Soviet experience, we need principles of aggregation that can encompass the plan's enormous detail and throw light on the crucial policy alternatives in resource allocation. Here two points seem decisive. Since the stress is on capital stocks and planned changes in their structure, the choice of sectors should reflect the base-period capital situation. The 1928 Soviet capital stock, shaped by many decades of development, was dominated by very substantial amounts of residential, agricultural, and transport fixed capital. At a minimum, therefore, each of these categories requires recognition. The first Soviet plan concentrated, however, on nonagricultural, nonresidential capital construction, especially in industry. Plan data would permit isolation of fifteen or twenty industrial sectors, but industry is here treated as a single sector to preserve manageability and computability. A construction sector is separated out in view of its key role; all other activities are placed in a residual sector.

Large, highly aggregated sectors are opaque, but in the present context they have an important advantage. For linear programming purposes, resources within an aggregated sector are treated as though they are completely homogeneous. Intrasectoral flows are completely unconstrained. The effect is to make target achievement and structural transformation artificially easy, and easier than it would be if large sectors were disaggregated into finer detail. If we find, therefore, that crude tests with a highly aggregated model disclose sharp limits on feasibility, we know that a more realistically detailed analysis would narrow these limits still further. My six-sector results, that is to say, test the achievability of first FYP targets in a very generous way.

When linear constraints are permitted to shift at yearly intervals, short-run rigidity can be combined with structural evolution. This approach is both realistic and computationally manageable. Perhaps those economists who have found the proportionality assumptions of input–output economics highly objectionable will find this approach more acceptable. It is also true that changes in the economy's technology matrix were an important part of the first Soviet plan's intentions, as were changes in sectoral capital–output ratios and other parameters. In response to these considerations, it is entirely feasible to permit all these relationships to evolve smoothly during the plan period from their base year to their (intended) terminal-year levels. Plan documents would permit reconstruction of the original intentions for each year of the plan period, though this would be a time-consuming task. As a first approximation, I have instead let the computer move parametric values at uniform rates over the plan period, whatever its specified length.

Finally, there is the related question of a proper time horizon for planning and plan testing. Most of the powerful theory concerning economic development has had a long-run focus, proceeding along turnpikes toward a distant horizon, far above the short-run intersectoral rigidities of the real world. The answers to fundamental issues of optimality lie on this plane (for a powerful analysis see Chakravarty, 1969). But a great many practical planning problems have a relatively short-run focus, concerned with finite steps along a road whose immediate contours are decisive. Eckaus and Parikh argue persuasively for a planning horizon extending up to perhaps thirty years, and their Transit models deliberately shift attention toward this more extended framework. The USSR in practice has moved the other way, continuing to formulate five-year plans but putting major operational stress on annual plans. Ideally, annual plans should fit within five-year plans which should fit within longer-terms plans like a set of Russian dolls. The image is far too rigid, however, since humane and efficient resource use requires adaptive planning that can adjust short-run plans to take account of unanticipated opportunities and difficulties.[2]

The voluminous data of the first Soviet Five-Year Plan are not organized in an input–output format, nor is there a full presentation of the sectoral and commodity balances that had been worked on in Gosplan. Fortunately, however, the control figures for 1929/30 add useful base-period detail, and a separate plan document provides useful detail on the transportation sector. It has thus been possible to construct two comprehensive flow tables, covering the largest transaction elements in the economy. Their dimensions are roughly consistent with reconstructed national income and product accounts though it is clear that further work could greatly improve their precision. A detailed statement of sources used and adjustments carried out is available from the author.

Three major computational steps deserve notice. Official data for agriculture and industry in purchasers prices were reduced to values in producers prices by shifting transport charges to a row for the transportation and communication sector, and by shifting the trade markup to a row for the 'other and margin' sector. Imports into agriculture and industry (small in amount during 1928 and even smaller in 1933) were deducted from flow-table entries to make them show domestic production only. At four points it was necessary to add to these intersectoral deliveries some intrasectoral transactions not otherwise captured. Home-produced peasant consumption, as estimated in the plan, was added to the cell for agricultural deliveries to household consumption. The value of feed-and-seed deliveries was added to the diagonal cell for agriculture. The output of electric power was added to the diagonal cell for industry. Freight traffic hauled by one railroad for another ('company freight' in US terminology) was added to the diagonal cell for transport.

INVESTMENT AND THE CAPITAL GESTATION PROCESS

Annual outlays on fixed capital formation go into projects at various stages of completion. As we have seen, capital growth operates through a gestation process that typically involves several years. In the symbols employed above, $\mathbf{Z}(t) \neq \mathbf{N}(t-1)$, that is, the new fixed capital that is completed by the beginning of year t is not equal to the current output channeled into capital formation during year $t-1$. Only if the length of the gestation period remains constant and the rate of growth of the capital stock remains constant for the full length of the gestation period can one write

$$\mathbf{K}(t+1) = [1 - d(t)]\,\mathbf{K}(t) + \mathbf{N}(t).$$

This complication is very important for current planning. Where growth is rapid and projects require several years for completion, capital-in-process quickly becomes a large mass, tying up resources and spreading the impact of decision making over an extended period of time. The immediate past largely determines the immediate future, or at least decisions must fit into an ongoing process whose results emerge only with some delay. Changes in growth rates, sector by sector, whether intended or unanticipated, must be traced with some care over a several-year period while their impact works itself out.

In studying these phenomena for the first FYP period in the USSR, we are unusually fortunate in being able to benefit from the careful work of Gosplan. A supplement to volume III of the first FYP gives a detailed listing of new industrial construction projects, classifying them into twenty-seven regions of the USSR and eighteen industry groups, and noting the year of start and year of finish scheduled for each project, together with the anticipated total ruble outlay in 1926/7 prices and the amounts spent before the plan period began or assigned to the postplan period (if the project extended outside the years 1929–33). In order to obtain a detailed picture of gestation period patterns, some types of project must be excluded from the list. Mines, for example, whose construction and extension is a continuous process, do not have a neat 'construction period'. The list shows regional outlays for local fishing operations which group together numerous assets to be acquired serially over the whole plan period. Small brick works, turpentine stills and other small-scale projects are frequently lumped together in the list for each region. In some cases the dates for launching or completion are unspecified. After eliminating these entries, there remain some 1,166 specific projects, involving a total outlay of 7.1 billion rubles, whose gestation period patterns can be analyzed.

Though many aspects of these individual project plans involved rough estimates with wide margins of uncertainty, the list also reflected extensive communication between Moscow and regional plan offices. By the spring of 1930 the major projects, many of which had been initially proposed before World War I, had been re-examined in their current context and debated for as much as five years. The list was not, therefore, a hastily compiled piece of window dressing but rather a painstaking effort to set forth the time pattern and regional distribution of new construction outlays under way and anticipated in industry from 1926 through 1936.

Table 1 shows frequency distributions of these projects by size of project and length of construction period, indicating both the number of projects and the ruble amounts involved in each class. The anticipated construction period for almost half the projects was two years, and the three-year projects accounted for another quarter of the total. Projects requiring only one year numbered 177 out of 1,166, while those expected to require four or more years for completion made up another 165. The typical project was expected to cost between one and ten million rubles; those falling between 500,000 and one million rubles numbered 198, and the really small projects, costing less than 500,000 rubles, numbered 191. There were 129 projects in the ten to fifty million ruble class, nine costing between fifty and a hundred million, and eleven giants listed at over one hundred million rubles each. The giants were expected to absorb almost a quarter of all the funds allocated to new industrial construction and were also expected to require from four to seven years for their construction.

Table 2 shows how the projects were divided between heavy and light industry (Group A and Group B). The large projects and those with long construction periods were mainly in heavy industry, where most of the expenditures were concentrated, though there were thirty-nine light industry projects in the ten to fifty million ruble class, and forty-three light industry projects requiring four or more years for their construction. Regional details are not here examined, but the list clearly displays an intention to build new industry at least to some extent in every region of the USSR.

Table 1. *New industrial construction projects in the first FYP, classified by size of project and length of construction period*

Ruble size								Total number

| | Length of construction period (years) | | | | | | | Total |
Ruble size	1	2	3	4	5	6	7	number
	Number of projects							
Over 100,000				3	4	1	3	11
50,000–99,999			1	2	4	—	2	9
10,000–49,999		15	45	44	17	5	3	129
1,000–9,999	29	310	222	52	12	3	—	628
500–999	60	113	18	6	1	—	—	198
1–499	88	80	20	2	1	—	—	191
Totals	177	518	306	109	39	9	8	1166
	Rubles involved ('000)							
Over 100,000				462.0	520.0	180.0	496.0	1658.0
50,000–99,999			60.0	116.0	255.5	—	115.0	546.5
10,000–49,999		202.6	759.3	814.5	500.4	126.0	82.0	2484.8
1,000–9,999	58.8	881.7	977.1	239.8	52.1	20.7	—	2230.2
500–999	39.2	74.1	11.2	4.9	0.8	—	—	130.2
1–499	20.9	21.0	6.5	0.5	0.4	—	—	49.3
	118.9	1179.4	1814.1	1637.7	1329.2	326.7	693.0	7099.0

NOTE: dashes indicate zero entries.

Table 3 presents a matrix of annual outlays on new construction in industry, classified by year of start and year of completion. It shows how the great surge of investment spending was expected to spread over the decade from 1926 to 1936. One sees, for example, that 928 million rubles worth of four-year projects were to be launched in 1930 and completed in 1933. The one-year projects launched and finished in 1929, by contrast, totaled less than seven million rubles.

Diagonal entries in this matrix show the ruble volume of one-year projects, two-year projects, and so on up to seven-year projects. The impact of the giants is evident in the northeast cells of the matrix. One also sees that the volume of new construction activity reaches a peak and then declines along most of the diagonals. The list does not, that is to say, include a roster of the projects that would have had to be launched toward the end of the first FYP period in order to sustain the rate of new industrial construction during the next plan period.

For purposes of testing plan feasibility, one needs to modify the pattern here to record the planners' expectation that projects with long construction periods would begin to yield some output even before they were fully completed. Steel works with several blast furnaces and open hearths, electric power stations with several generators, and similar

A test of Five-Year Plan feasibility

Table 2. Industry projects in heavy and light industry

(a) Classified by size of project

Size of ruble outlay ('000)	Heavy industry		Light industry	
	Number of projects	Ruble amounts involved	Number of projects	Ruble amounts involved
Over 100,000	11	1658.0	—	—
50,000–99,999	9	546.5	—	—
10,000–49,999	90	1752.6	39	732.2
1,000–9,999	360	1249.2	268	977.8
500–999	121	78.2	77	52.0
1–499	132	33.9	59	15.4

(b) Classified by length of construction period

Length of construction period (years)	Number of projects	Ruble amounts involved	Number of projects	Ruble amounts involved
1	125	85.3	52	33.6
2	273	563.5	245	615.9
3	203	1143.2	103	670.9
4	75	1353.9	34	283.8
5	33	1199.4	6	129.8
6	7	297.7	2	29.0
7	7	678.6	1	14.4

Table 3. Total outlays on industry projects, classified
by year of start and year of completion

Year of start	Year of completion							
	1929	1930	1931	1932	1933	1934	1935	1936
1926	27.4	42.7	27.5	14.4	—	—	—	—
1927	52.5	71.1	113.0	45.2	365.6	—	—	—
1928	43.4	172.0	115.5	177.4	20.0	130.0	—	—
1929	6.7	107.5	193.2	124.0	451.0	—	—	—
1930	—	32.6	230.6	382.7	928.2	370.0	54.0	183.0
1931	—	—	19.5	251.0	637.9	186.0	175.0	180.0
1932	—	—	—	33.7	427.2	228.5	141.1	—
1933	—	—	—	—	26.3	119.8	147.4	44.4

installations with component units were all expected to come into operation serially. I have therefore subdivided each project requiring more than four years for construction into two, three, or four overlapping projects, each requiring four years. The results are shown in table 4 which shifts substantial ruble amounts away from the upper right-hand part

Table 4. *Adjusted total outlays on new construction projects in industry,*
classified by year of start and year of completion

Year of start	Year of completion							
	1929	1930	1931	1932	1933	1934	1935	1936
1926	59.1	—	—	—	—	—	—	—
1927	52.5	272.9	—	—	—	—	—	—
1928	43.4	172.0	414.1	—	—	—	—	—
1929	6.7	107.5	193.2	582.1	—	—	—	—
1930	—	32.6	230.6	382.7	1488.4	—	—	—
1931	—	—	19.5	251.0	637.9	571.4	—	—
1932	—	—	—	33.7	427.2	228.5	382.3	—
1933	—	—	—	—	26.3	119.8	147.4	202.7

of the preceding table and distributes them into cells along the four-year diagonal.

The underlying documentation for individual projects must have indicated how outlays were scheduled over each project's construction period, but the published list does not provide this detail. It does, however, show pre-plan or post-plan outlays on projects beginning or ending outside the Plan, and from the 228 cases of this kind it is possible to reconstruct general patterns, though they are by no means uniform. If a three-year project was slated to begin in 1928 and be completed in 1930, the list might show, for example, that two million of a six million ruble total outlay fell to the year 1928. Or a twelve million ruble project slated to start in 1932 and finish in 1935 might assign seven million rubles to the two years after the plan period ended. Assigning these pre- and post-plan outlays to appropriate cells, and comparing them with total project costs in each case, one obtains the fractions recorded in table 5 for two-year projects, three-year projects, and four-year projects considered separately. Pre-plan patterns differ appreciably from postplan patterns, so annual intervening transitional patterns have been inserted here by straight-line interpolation. The timing of outlays on individual projects differed quite widely from these weighted averages, but they can nevertheless serve well to express central tendencies.

These fractions in turn permit the reassignment of absolute amounts in the diagonal cells of table 4 into still another table, this one showing the actual outlays anticipated for each year on each component of projects with specified construction periods covering specified portions of the decade. For example one sees that 582.1 million rubles was to be spent on four-year projects maturing in 1932. Of this total, according to table 5, some 14.7 % would be spent in 1929, 22.6 % in 1930, 31.9 % in 1931, and 30.9 % in 1932. Table 6 presents the full results. It is arranged

Table 5. *Annual fractions of total project outlays scheduled for each year of four-year, three-year, and two-year projects*

| | Four-year projects | | | |
	1st year	2nd year	3rd year	4th year
Pre-plan projects	0.1824	0.2220	0.3255	0.2701
1929–32 projects	0.1466	0.2257	0.3185	0.3092
1930–3 projects	0.1108	0.2294	0.3116	0.3482
Post-plan projects	0.0750	0.2331	0.3046	0.3873

| | Three-year projects | | |
	1st year	2nd year	3rd year
Pre-plan projects	0.2115	0.6750	0.1135
1929–31 projects	0.2241	0.6039	0.1720
1930–2 projects	0.2367	0.5328	0.2305
1931–3 projects	0.2493	0.4616	0.2891
Post-plan projects	0.2619	0.3905	0.3476

| | Two-year projects | |
	1st year	2nd year
1928–9 projects	0.3083	0.6917
1929–30 projects	0.3438	0.6562
1930–1 projects	0.3793	0.6207
1931–2 projects	0.4147	0.5853
1932–3 projects	0.4502	0.5498
1933–4 projects	0.4857	0.5143

to show, for each of the five plan-period years, 1929 through 1933, the outlays attributable to projects maturing in that year but launched earlier, along with the outlays anticipated for that year on projects that would mature in each of the next three years. The lower portion of the table is incomplete because the published plan data do not extend full project estimates forward sufficiently into the post-plan period.

It will be seen that, for 1929 and 1930, each year displays ten components in its column. A column total is the amount of investment spending in that year on new construction. It is not ordinarily decomposed into these elements relating to the past and future. The totals in the final column on the right show the amount of new fixed capital in new projects expected to mature in each plan year. These row totals are, in conventional terms, the capital 'vintages' of 1929, 1930, ..., 1933, respectively. But each of these row totals on the right is a ten-element composite reflecting outlays made over the preceding four years on projects of different lengths. And they do not correspond at all to the

Table 6. *Components of annual planned construction outlays in industry, by length of construction period and by year, 1926–33, in millions of 1926/7 rubles*

Year of start	Year of completion								Totals
	1926	1927	1928	1929	1930	1931	1932	1933	
1926	10,793	13,137	19,261	15,983					
1927		11,110	35,457	5,962					
1928			13,369	29,993					
1929				6,719					
Total	10,793	24,247	68,087	58,657					161,784
% shares	6.67	14.99	42.08	36.26					
1927		49,770	60,575	88,816	73,700				
1928			36,380	116,106	19,523				
1929				36,944	70,514				
1930					32,643				
Total		49,770	96,955	241,866	196,380				584,971
% shares		8.51	16.57	41.35	33.57				
1928			75,537	91,936	134,799	111,856			
1929				43,298	116,680	33,232			
1930					87,461	143,124			
1931						19,545			
Total			75,537	135,234	338,940	307,757			857,468
% shares			8.81	15.77	39.53	35.89			
1929				85,339	131,385	185,407	179,993		
1930					90,580	203,890	88,207		
1931						104,100	146,925		
1932							33,690		
Total				85,339	221,965	493,397	448,815		1,249,516
% shares				6.83	17.76	39.49	35.92		
1930					164,914	341,439	463,785	518,260	
1931						159,023	294,444	184,410	
1932							192,315	234,862	
1933								26,332	
Total					164,914	500,462	950,544	963,864	2,579,784
% shares					6.39	19.40	36.85	37.36	
Totals				521,096	922,199	1,301,616	1,399,359	963,864	

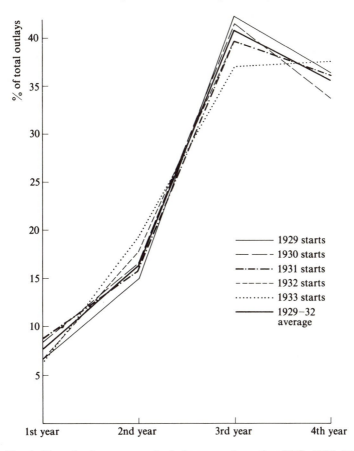

Fig. 1. Gestation leg patterns for industry projects, first FYP, 1929–33.
SOURCE: table 6.

annual outlay column totals for these same years, which involve another ten elements of which only four overlap. Unfortunately it is these total annual outlays on fixed capital that are normally reported in Soviet statistics.

For the first FYP period, however, we are now in a position to examine with precision the gestation patterns for each plan year that emerge from table 6.

The percent shares recorded in table 6 are an empirical reflection of the gestation period expectations embodied in the detailed project list of the first Soviet Five-Year Plan. Each plan year shows a slightly different pattern, as displayed in fig. 1. It will be noted, however, that only the terminal year of the plan period, 1933, deviates appreciably. The tendency to crowd completions into the final year raised fourth-year outlays for 1933 above the level of third-year outlays, which for the four other plan years was the peak year in the pattern. Had the planners placed ongoing intentions more fully into the project list, the pattern for 1933 would presumably have been more like that of the mid-plan years. In any case it is reassuring to find relatively modest differences among the five plan years in their gestation period patterns, and there seems no need to build annually changing gestation period patterns into the testing apparatus. The average percentage shares attributable to each year of a four-year gestation period, both including and excluding 1933, are shown in table 7.

Table 7

	4 years, 1929–32	5 years, 1929–33
1st year	0.0771	0.0744
2nd year	0.1627	0.1690
3rd year	0.4061	0.3986
4th year	0.3541	0.3580

The first FYP does not provide similar detail on expected gestation periods for fixed capital outlays on the reconstruction and enlargement of existing facilities in industry, nor is there similar detail for fixed capital in agriculture, transportation, housing, or other sectors. I have, however, applied this same pattern everywhere in the economy except to livestock. The pattern says that 35 % of the fixed capital maturing in a given year involves outlays made that year; another 41 % comes in the preceding year; and the fractions requiring initiation three years or four years before completion are put at 16 and 8 % respectively. These seem rather plausible for sectors other than industry. Some transport and housing projects involved extended construction periods, but portions of these large projects were probably expected to come into service before the full project was finished. Placing three-quarters of the claim on resources in the two years preceding project completion does not put an extreme burden on earlier years. As for livestock, I have arbitrarily assumed a gestation pattern allowing three years for most horses and one year for most hogs, but two years for most cattle and one year for poultry. The weighted result assigns 20% to the first year, 60% to the second year, and 20 % to the third year of a three-year gestation period for all livestock.

The project list for fixed capital outlays on new construction does not distinguish between outlays on equipment and outlays on buildings and structures. The distinction does appear in an early 1930 article by a Gosplan analyst who provides details on a large iron and steel plant at Krivoi Rog, a large machine-building works in the Urals, and the Stalingrad tractor plant. As one would expect, outlays on equipment

288

appear later than outlays on structures but these three examples are not sufficient to establish a secure distinction, so the standard pattern developed above is applied here to both forms of fixed capital.

SOME INITIAL TEST RESULTS AND ALTERNATIVE EXPANSION PATHS

Application of the modified Target model to the official data of the first FYP, reconstructed in this framework, shows that the 'optimal' targets, taken all together, were infeasible both algebraically and politically. With the original targets for consumption, and using all the other constraints and targets, no initial feasible solution to the linear programming problem can be found. We cannot get within the feasible space. The levels of household consumption called for by the plan, when combined with all the intended capital formation, lie outside the boundaries of the achievable, whether we try to maximize consumption or capital formation. Too much was called for, simultaneously, both in output increases and in transformation of the economy's structure. No allocation of resources among the six sectors and over the several plan years would enable the terminal-year levels of capital and output to be reached, along with the intended levels of household consumption and other final uses. Even with the plan period extended to six, seven, or eight years, the full set of official targets is unachievable.

If we ask instead how much could be delivered to households over the plan period, on the assumption that terminal-year capital stock requirements are met, we find that there is a feasible and optimal solution in five years. It is displayed in fig. 2, along with a number of alternative expansion paths. The five-year solution here incorporates a mild requirement that year-to-year increases in household consumption, after the first plan year, at least match the rate at which total population was expected to grow, namely, 2.26 % per year. The trouble with this solution, of course, is that it would have reduced household consumption from its 1928 level of 21.2 billion rubles to about 15.7 billion rubles in 1929; the level would have risen to 16.8 billion by 1932 and only in the last year would it have risen to the target level of 30.3 billion rubles. Though this path is algebraically optimal, it would not have been politically feasible. One thinks of the surgical operation which was technically successful, except that the patient died.

Fig. 2 shows how belt-tightening could have been reduced through extending the plan period to six, seven, or eight years. With eight years in which to achieve the capital stocks and output levels that were called for in the plan, some 21.1 billion rubles of consumption could have been delivered to households in 1929 and per capita consumption levels would have been very nearly maintained throughout the plan period.

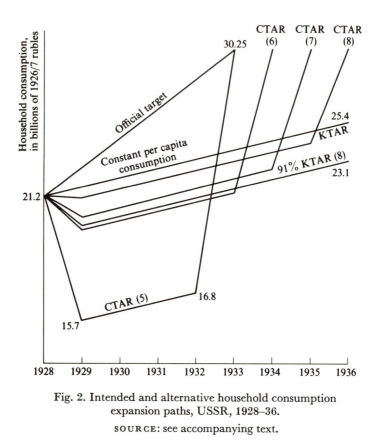

Fig. 2. Intended and alternative household consumption
expansion paths, USSR, 1928–36.

SOURCE: see accompanying text.

These alternatives retain the original targets, merely extending the
plan period and lowering the required mid-plan level of consumption.
It is instructive to examine a sterner approach, one that would require
household consumption only to keep pace with the expected growth of
total population, so that per capita consumption, while not permitted to
fall, would not be permitted to rise during the plan period. Letting the
composition of household consumption undergo structural change as
the plan intended, but constraining its expansion with this kind of floor,
amounts to requiring the consumption growth path marked KTAR
(for capital target).

It is obtained by restating the whole problem, placing the deliveries to
household consumption among the boundary conditions that have to be
met, and shifting the focus to fixed capital construction as the activity to
be maximized. Under this approach, the objective function contains
terminal-year capital stocks in each of the six sectors, in proportions laid
down by the original plan. We seek to push this function out as far as

possible. If we set a consumption floor that requires constant per capita household consumption, there is no feasible solution, even over an eight-year plan period. The Soviet economy was tightly constrained at the end of the 1920s, and there was no easy way to build an altered structure. Experiment indicates that roughly a 9 % cut in household consumption would have freed enough resources to set the growth model in motion, and the line marked 91 % KTAR (8) records an algebraically optimal path under these specifications. It would have kept household consumption standards at a mid-1920s level during the extended plan period from 1929 through 1936, while resources were channeled into capital formation. The first FYP called for raising the total completed capital stocks from 60.5 to 88.5 billion rubles by the beginning of 1933. The solution computed here would have brought capital stocks up to 83 billion rubles by the beginning of 1934 and about 150 billion rubles by the beginning of 1936. The precise details need not be taken literally but it is clear that a very substantial expansion of fixed capital stocks could have been obtained under such a policy.

These alternative expansion paths are deceptively easy. They greatly overstate the actual achievability of these activity levels. The reason is that, in linear programming, resources within a single sector are treated as though they are completely homogeneous. Intra-sectoral flows are completely unconstrained. With only six large, highly aggregated sectors in this model, target achievement and structural transformation are artificially easy, and a great deal easier than would be the case if these large sectors were disaggregated into finer detail.

Disaggregation would increase the number of constraints and restrict the feasible space within which solutions would have to be sought. Even the present simple model assures us, not only that the official targets lay outside the feasible space, but also that a more realistically detailed formulation would push computed solutions toward the origin. If the first five-year plan, that is, were reconstructed in fine detail, the computed feasible growth of consumption and/or capital stocks would not be as high as fig. 2 implies.

The grim fact is, to repeat, that there was no easy way to pursue the first plan's objectives. The economy was already strained at the beginning of the plan period. Quick structural changes were impossible because of the gestation process required to build the desired new fixed capital, drawing directly and indirectly on every part of the economy. The intended sectoral growth rates were extraordinarily high by contemporary standards and, seen in the perspective of a quarter century's development experience of dozens of countries, these rates appear even more obviously unrealistic today.

Our initial experiments which altered plan parameters have stayed very close to the plan's objectives. One hesitates to rewrite history, not least because it is hard to make non-arbitrary selections from among innumerable hypothetical alternatives. In due course some of the reasonable choices that were available in 1928, some of the alternative policies that might have been followed, can be embodied in a modified structure of plan targets and usefully tested for results. Such work, however, lies in the future.

Meanwhile, it should be stressed that the focus here has been on feasibility, not optimality in the economist's sense. Lacking any statistical basis for estimating consumers' preferences, or planners' preferences, or any other criterion of optimality, we have no yardstick against which to evaluate the plan's output targets. And given these targets, juggling of the constraints in search of improved growth paths does not constitute a systematic search for genuine 'optimality'.

Nevertheless, these paths suggest that, without altering the structure of the terminal-year targets in the first Soviet Five-Year Plan, and without changing their level except for introducing a stern no-growth, no-fall policy toward per capita consumption standards, the purposes embodied in the plan could have been sought through consistent and plausible programs. Lower growth rates and slower structural shifts might have brought the Soviet economy out of its strained situation by the middle 1930s, and done so fairly smoothly. A milder set of targets would still, of course, have required some difficult changes. The regime would have had to coax more off-farm output from the peasants, raising the level of 1928 procurements by perhaps 4 % per year. It would also have been necessary to divert a larger share of the national income away from consumer goods and into capital formation. In the face of difficulties arising from the world depression, poor harvests, or construction delays, the plan period might have had to be stretched out.

Additional difficult research is clearly needed to throw light on these possibilities. Moreover, the whole testing process should be extended to the second FYP period as well, though a new price structure will have to be dealt with and the second plan is considerably less detailed than the first. Analysis of the nine-year period, 1929 through 1937, will permit adequate recognition of the impressive results that flowered during the second FYP period after having been launched during the first plan period. Examination of the first plan period by itself truncates the record unfairly because economic growth processes take a good deal of time. The proper question is how some gradual alternatives for the 1928–37 period would compare with the actual performance of Stalin's economy. Readers of this paper are encouraged to join the search for answers.

APPENDIX

Table A1. *First Soviet Five-Year Plan, base-period flow table, 1927–8*
(in millions of rubles at 1925/7 prices)

	Output to						
Inputs from	Agriculture	Industry	Trans-port	Con-struction	Housing	Other sectors	Total inter-industry
Agriculture	1,818	1,382	—	—	—	—	3,200
Industry	528	5,685	750	711	110	217	8,001
Transport and communications	47	714	184	64	11	19	1,039
Construction	—	—	—	—	—	—	—
Housing	—	—	—	—	—	—	—
Other sectors	431	937	148	140	—	43	1,699
Total intermediate	2,824	8,718	1,082	915	121	279	13,939
Value added	10,783	4,705	1,024	2,973	1,573	6,919	27,977
Total inputs	13,607	13,423	2,106	3,888	1,694	7,198	

	Output to						
	Consump-tion	Govern-ment	Inventories	Fixed capital	Exports	Total final demand	Total domestic output
Agriculture	10,024	134	50	—	199	10,407	13,607
Industry	3,794	981	344	—	303	5,422	13,423
Transport and communications	824	178	32	—	33	1,067	2,106
Construction	—	—	—	3,888	—	3,888	3,888
Housing	1,694	—	—	—	—	1,694	1,694
Other sectors	4,882	297	107	—	213	5,499	7,198
Total intermediate							
Value added	21,218	1,590	533	3,888	748	27,977	
Total inputs							41,916

SOURCE: Derived by the author from Gosplan SSSR (1930).

Table A2. *First Soviet Five-Year Plan, terminal-year flow table, 1932–3,* '*optimal*' *targets* (*in millions of rubles at 1926/7 prices*)

	Output to						
Inputs from	Agri-culture	Industry	Trans-port	Con-struction	Housing	Other sectors	Total inter-industry
Agriculture	2,487	2,914	—	—	—	—	5,401
Industry	1,484	18,815	1,810	5,245	166	365	27,885
Transport and communications	137	1,248	388	480	17	34	2,304
Construction	—	—	—	—	—	—	—
Housing	—	—	—	—	—	—	—
Other sectors	916	1,368	300	863	—	60	3,507
Total intermediate	5,024	24,345	2,498	6,588	183	459	39,097
Value added	16,691	13,915	1,653	7,138	2,378	10,870	52,645
Total inputs	21,715	38,260	4,151	13,726	2,561	11,329	

	Output to						
Inputs from	Consump-tion	Govern-ment	Inventories	Fixed capital	Exports	Total final demand	Total domestic output
Agriculture	14,033	777	777	—	727	16,314	21,715
Industry	6,111	1,925	1,451	—	888	10,375	38,260
Transport and communications	1,263	329	154	—	101	1,847	4,151
Construction	—	—	—	13,726	—	13,726	13,726
Housing	2,561	—	—	—	—	2,561	2,561
Other sectors	6,282	603	524	—	413	7,822	11,329
Total intermediate Value added	30,250	3,634	2,906	13,726	2,129	52,645	
Total inputs							91,742

SOURCE: Derived by the author from Gosplan SSSR (1930).

NOTES

1 Along with gratitude to Eckaus and Parikh for showing the way, I want to pay my respects to the late Susan M. Kingsbury, distinguished member of the Bryn Mawr College faculty, who returned from a visit to the USSR in the early 1930s with a number of rare planning documents, including the annual control figures for 1928–9 and 1929–30, which provided much base period data for this study. The research was begun under grant No. GS-2609 from the National Science Foundation, whose support is greatly appreciated. Valuable guidance in programming was supplied by Helen M. Hunter and John S. Wylie. The Bryn Mawr–Swarthmore–Haverford Computer Center, and especially William Baker and Hazel Pugh, provided essential services with generosity and dispatch. Critical queries from Professors Leonard J. Kirsch and Michael R. Dohan have served to improve my analysis.

2 For much fuller analysis of adaptive planning see Dolan (1970) and Manove (1973). Some earlier discussion is in Hunter (1961).

REFERENCES

Chakravarty, Sukhamoy (1969). *Capital and Development Planning.* Cambridge, Mass.: MIT Press.

Dolan, Edwin G. (1970). The teleological period in Soviet economic planning. *Yale Economic Essays,* **10**, 3–41.

Eckaus, Richard S. and Kirit S. Parikh (1968). *Planning for Growth: Multisectoral, Intertemporal Models applied to India.* Cambridge, Mass.: MIT Press.

Gosplan SSSR (1930). *Piatiletnii plan narodno-khoziaistvennogo stroitel'stva,* 3rd edition.

Hunter, H. (1961). Optimal tautness in development planning. *Economic Development and Cultural Change,* **9**, 561–72.

Hunter, H. (1973). Overambitious first Soviet five-year plan (with replies by R. Campbell, S. F. Cohen, and M. Lewin and a rejoinder). *Slavic Review,* **32**, 237–91.

Manove, Michael (1973). Non-price rationing of intermediate goods in centrally-planned economies. *Econometrica,* **41**, 829–52.

2. Production Functions and Costs

Dynamic L-Shaped CES Functions in Eastern Europe

ALAN A. BROWN AND EGON NEUBERGER[1]

INTRODUCTION

This paper presents the initial stages of an attempt to analyze the rate and stability of economic growth in Eastern Europe, using the analytical apparatus of the CES (constant elasticity of substitution) production function. This approach enables us to study the pattern of growth as a function not only of the rate of change in labor and capital inputs and the rate of change in 'technology' or 'total factor productivity',[2] but also of the elasticity of factor substitution, σ. The emphasis on σ is particularly important in the many countries, including those in Eastern Europe, where the much more rapid relative growth rate of capital compared to labor raises the problem of the rate and pattern of factor substitution.[3]

Analysis of the growth experience of centrally planned economies (CPEs) by means of the CES production function is only at a beginning stage: a major study of Soviet growth, to be used as a starting point in our investigation, is an article by M. Weitzman (1970). He considered explicitly the possibility of explaining the postwar retardation in the Soviet growth rate by the difficulty of substituting capital for labor, i.e. a low σ.

The present paper compares the growth experience of the Soviet Union with that of Hungary. In this effect we have encountered a paradox, whose solution has, in turn, taken us to a virgin territory in production function analysis.

In the next section we present the basic analytical notions of the CES approach, adapted for analyzing effects of the growth of 'factor productivity' (g_A) and the elasticity of factor substitution (σ). The third section summarizes briefly the results of Weitzman's study of the Soviet experience, while the fourth section presents our analysis of the Hungarian experience. We compare the Soviet and Hungarian experiences, and discover an apparent paradox in the behavior of g_A, σ, and the other variables in the Hungarian case. Since preliminary statistical tests of g_A and σ do not enable us to solve the paradox, we are led to investigate the underlying functional relationship. The fifth section deals with the economic and econometric properties of short-run and long-run CES production functions, the latter consisting of a set of nearly Leontief-type, L-shaped segments. We also discuss the difficulties encountered in any

296

attempt to fit a continuous CES function to observations representing such discontinuous segments. The sixth section presents a hypothetical model of the investment cycle that could explain this type of production function. Finally, in the concluding remarks we discuss the significance of our results and suggest further avenues of investigation.

THE SIMPLE ANALYTICS OF CES PRODUCTION FUNCTION GROWTH ANALYSIS

In order to separate the effects of technical change from that of factor inputs in the growth process, Solow (1957, p. 312) presented a two-factor production function

$$V = Af(K, L), \tag{1}$$

where V, K, and L stand for the variables output, capital stock, and labor force; and A represents disembodied technical change. (Time subscripts are understood.) Following in Solow's footsteps, we differentiate equation (1) with respect to time and divide by V, and derive the relationship in terms of relative changes of the variables

$$g_V = g_A + \alpha g_K + \beta g_L, \tag{2}$$

where the relative rates of growth (say, annual percentage changes) of output, technical change, capital, and labor are shown as g_V, g_A, g_K, and g_L. The weights of g_K and g_L, α and β, are respectively the output elasticities (or imputed competitive shares)[4] of the two factors,

$$\alpha = \frac{\partial V/\partial K}{V/K} \quad \text{and} \beta = \frac{\partial V/\partial L}{V/L}.$$

If, as in Solow's original model, the weights or factor shares are constant (with respect to g_K and g_L), and assuming constant returns to scale ($\alpha + \beta = 1$), as shown by Domar (1961, p. 711), integration of equation (2) will yield an underlying production function of the Cobb–Douglas-type

$$V = AK^\alpha L^\beta. \tag{3}$$

The function implies that the elasticity of substitution is one. To avoid the unduly restrictive assumption of unitary elasticity and to 'provide a substantial generalization of the Cobb–Douglas function', Arrow–Chenery–Minhas–Solow (1961, p. 229) derived a family of production functions with constant elasticity of substitution, which they abbreviated to CES. In their time series analysis, ACNS assume that a (Hicks) neutral 'technological change proceeds at constant geometrical rate' (p. 244). Combining this assumption with their general formulation of the CES function (p. 230), we have

$$V = \gamma e^{\lambda t} [\delta K^{-\rho} + (1 - \delta) L^{-\rho}]^{-1/\rho}, \tag{4}$$

where V (output), K (capital), and L (labor) are variables with respect to time; and γ, λ, δ, and ρ are parameters to be estimated. Of particular interest are λ, which indicates the rate of growth of technological change, and ρ, which is a transform of the elasticity of substitution $\sigma = 1/(1+\rho)$ or $\rho = (1/\sigma) - 1$. As σ ranges from 0 to ∞, ρ goes from ∞ to -1.

The CES function can also be employed to show the relationship between the growth rates of the variables.

$$g_V = g_A + \eta_K g_K + \eta_L g_L, \tag{5}$$

where g denotes, as before, the relative (percentage) rates of growth of the variables; and η_K and η_L, like α and β in equation (2), are imputed factor shares. The change in notation signifies that these shares, or relative weights, are no longer assumed to be invariant with respect to g_K and g_L.

It will be of interest to consider two alternative formulations of equation (5). If there are constant returns to scale, the growth rate of labor productivity g_Y (where $Y = V/L$) can be shown as a function of the growth rate of the capital–labor ratio g_X (where $X = K/L$)

$$g_Y = g_A + \eta_K g_X. \tag{5a}$$

Or, we may write the rate of growth of technical change as a weighted average of the growth rates of the labor productivity ($Y = V/L$) and of the capital productivity ($Z = V/K$)

$$g_A = \eta_K g_Z + \eta_L g_Y. \tag{5b}$$

This formulation makes it explicit that g_A is a weighted sum, or total, of individual factor productivities, which helps to explain why this concept is often called total factor productivity.

There is an obvious similarity between equations (5) and (2). In fact, it can be shown that the latter is a special case of the former. This can be proven by showing the equation (3), the integrated form of (2), is a special case of equation (4), from which equation (5), was derived by differentiation. ACMS offer a choice of three rigorous proofs (1961, p. 231) demonstrating that the limiting form of the CES function is the Cobb–Douglas, and at $\rho = 0$ (i.e., $\sigma = 1$) equation (4) becomes $V = \gamma e^{\lambda t} K^\delta L^{1-\delta}$.

Another extreme case, which is of greater interest to our present investigation, occurs when the elasticity of substitution approaches zero, $\sigma \to 0$ or $\rho \to \infty$ (ACMS, 1961, p. 231). At this point equation (4) becomes

$$V = \gamma e^{\lambda t} \min (K, L) = \min \left[\frac{K}{(\gamma e^{\lambda t})^{-1}}, \frac{L}{(\gamma e^{\lambda t})^{-1}} \right]. \tag{6}$$

This may be represented by L-shaped Leontief-type isoquants with corners on a ray from the origin.

As indicated, the imputed shares of capital and labor will not be constant in equation (5), unless the elasticity of substitution is one. In his analysis of Soviet growth, Weitzman (1970) demonstrates that if the elasticity of substitution is less than one ($\sigma < 1$) and if capital grows faster than labor ($g_K > g_L$), this implies that η_K will decline and η_L will rise ($g_{\eta_K} < 0$ and $g_{\eta_L} > 0$).[5] As derived by Weitzman in an earlier paper (1968), the relationship is

$$\rho = \frac{1}{\sigma} - 1 = -\frac{g_{\eta_K} - g_{\eta_L}}{g_K - g_L} \tag{7}$$

as long as $g_K \neq g_L$.

To consider the determinants of changes in the growth rate of output (or changes in the growth rate of labor productivity) we differentiate equation (5) (or equation (5a)) with respect to time

$$\dot{g}_V = \dot{g}_A + \eta_K \dot{g}_K + g_{\eta_K} g_K + \eta_L \dot{g}_L + g_{\eta_L} g_L \tag{8}$$

$$\dot{g}_Y = \dot{g}_A + \eta_K \dot{g}_X + g_{\eta_K} g_X, \tag{8a}$$

where $\dot{g}$ represents change in growth rates.

If, for instance, there is a deceleration in the growth rate of output ($\dot{g}_V < 0$), this may be the result either of a decline of the rate of growth of total factor productivity ($\dot{g}_A < 0$) or, if the rate of growth of factor inputs does not decline ($\dot{g}_K \cong \dot{g}_L \cong 0$), of a gradual shift of factor weights ($g_{\eta_K} < 0$ and $g_{\eta_L} > 0$). Such a shift in factor weights implies, if capital grows faster than labor ($g_K > g_L$), that the elasticity of substitution is low ($\sigma < 1$).

In sum, a decline in the rate of growth of output may be explained by either or both of two hypotheses, $\dot{g}_A < 0$ and $\sigma < 1$. To test the first of these, we would have to reformulate equation (4). For example,

$$V = \gamma e^{\lambda t + \mu t^2} [\delta K^{-\rho} + (1 - \delta) L^{-\rho}]^{-1/\rho}, \tag{9}$$

where the growth rate of total factor productivity is $g_A = \lambda + 2\mu t$, and a systematic decline of factor productivity means that $\mu < 0$.

THE SOVIET GROWTH EXPERIENCE

We may summarize briefly the main points of Weitzman's argument.

1. During the postwar period there has been a retardation in the rate of growth of industrial output in the USSR, without a corresponding slowdown in the growth of factor inputs, i.e. in equation (8) $\dot{g}_V < 0$, $\dot{g}_K \cong \dot{g}_L \cong 0$. More precisely, the Soviet experience may be described in terms of declining labor productivity and no systematic decline in the capital–labor ratio, i.e. in equation (8a), $\dot{g}_Y < 0$ and $\dot{g}_X \cong 0$. At the same time, capital has grown at a much more rapid rate than labor, i.e. $g_K > g_L$ or $g_X > 0$.

2. Previous explanations of this growth retardation attributed it to a decline in factor productivity, i.e. $\dot{g}_A < 0$. It is clear from equation (5)

that g_V will decrease if g_A declines over time, even though the growth of capital and labor (g_K and g_L) show no systematic decline over time, providing factor shares (η_K and η_L) remain constant.

3. Weitzman presents statistical evidence that supports the alternative hypothesis that the observed slowdown could be explained by increasing difficulties of substituting more rapidly growing capital for less rapidly growing labor, i.e. $\sigma < 1$ may have caused $\dot{g}_V < 0$. This conclusion follows from equations (5) and (7). Equation (5) shows, assuming $g_K > g_L$, that g_V will decline if η_K declines over time (conversely η_L increases). Equation (7) shows that this will occur if $\sigma < 1$ (or $\rho < 0$).

4. Since the rate of growth of capital in the Soviet Union actually declined, Weitzman's conclusions should be rephrased in terms of declines in the rate of growth of labor productivity: $\dot{g}_Y < 0$ either as a result of a slowdown in the growth of factor productivity ($\dot{g}_A < 0$) or, given the fact that the growth rate of the capital–labor ratio does not change systematically (i.e. $\dot{g}_X \cong 0$), as a result of a decline in the imputed share of capital ($g_{\eta_K} < 0$) or both. Statistical evidence provided by Weitzman supports the hypothesis that $g_{\eta_K} < 0$ (and by implication $\sigma < 1$) is a sufficient explanation for the observed retardation in Soviet labor productivity.[6]

THE HUNGARIAN EXPERIENCE

Comparison with Soviet experience

Since 1949, when the Soviet model of central planning was adopted in Hungary, there have been important similarities between the patterns of growth in the two countries. In both cases, growth has been vigorously promoted by means of massive infusions of labor and capital, particularly in the industrial sectors. Capital has grown much faster than labor ($g_K > g_L$) between 1949 and 1967; for example, gross fixed capital stock in Hungarian industry increased at 8–10 % per annum, while industrial employment grew at less than half this rate. At least since the early 1950s, there has not been a systematic change in the rates of growth of either factor. Thus, just as in the Soviet case, the long-term growth rate of the capital–labor ratio (disregarding random fluctuations) has remained fairly constant ($\dot{g}_X \cong 0$).

There exist, however, important differences between the Hungarian and Soviet patterns of postwar growth. Two of these will be considered here. First, unlike the Soviet case, the Hungarian rates of growth of aggregate output and labor productivity have not declined systematically. This observation applies to national income and its main components, as well as to available industrial branch series. Second, while there is no evidence of overall growth retardation in Hungary, it has experienced a much higher degree of instability in output than the USSR. Since these fluctuations appear to be systematic, one may argue that they represent cyclical movements.[7]

How was Hungary, while pursuing the Soviet development strategy, able to avoid a gradual long-term decline in the rate of growth of labor productivity? Let us consider three sets of conditions consistent with the lack of systematic change in the growth rate of labor productivity.

As shown in equation $(8a)$, we can express the changes in the rate of growth of labor productivity $(\dot{g}_y)$ as a function of the changes in the rates of growth of the variables:

$$\dot{g}_y = \dot{g}_A + \eta_K \dot{g}_X + g_{\eta_K} \dot{g}_X. \tag{8a}$$

Since in Hungary $\dot{g}_y \cong 0$ and $\dot{g}_X \cong 0$, equation $(8a)$ collapses into

$$\dot{g}_A + g_{\eta_K} g_X = 0. \tag{8b}$$

Since $g_X > 0$ (or, $g_K > g_L$), we may satisfy equation $(8b)$ only with certain restrictions on $\dot{g}_A$ and g_{η_K}. Alternatively, we consider the following three sets of g_A and σ (because, as shown in equation (7), σ is a function of g_{η_K}). Sets S_1, S_2, and S_3 exhaust the possible relations between our two variables.

$$S_1 = \{\dot{g}_A = 0, \sigma = 1\}$$
$$S_2 = \{\dot{g}_A < 0, \sigma > 1\}$$
$$S_3 = \{\dot{g}_A > 0, \sigma < 1\}.$$

Is it possible to indicate which of these three sets fits the Hungarian case? Since the difference between the growth rates of labor and capital were even more pronounced in Hungary than the USSR, it would be surprising if Hungary had much less difficulty than the Soviet Union in substituting capital for labor. Thus, we would expect $\sigma < 1$, which is true only if S_3 holds, i.e. only if there existed an acceleration in the rate of growth of factor productivity $(\dot{g}_A > 0)$. There is, however, no reason to assume that Hungary was able to bring about such improvements in g_A. Indeed, the Hungarian literature is replete with suggestions of the opposite, with numerous complaints about slow technological progress, managerial rigidities, and worker apathy. Unless the Hungarians are completely wrong about the influence of these institutional factors preventing increases in the growth rate of total factor productivity, we may reasonably expect that g_A has not been rising, thus eliminating S_3. If we are correct in assuming that neither $\sigma \geq 1$ nor $\dot{g}_A > 0$ are compatible with actual Hungarian developments, and if $\dot{g}_y \cong 0$ is correct, we find that none of the sets S_1, S_2, or S_3 is feasible. Our attempt to deal with this apparent paradox by statistical measurement is presented in the following subsection, while a more fundamental questioning of the applicability of the CES model to explain the Hungarian experience is provided in the next section.

Alan A. Brown and Egon Neuberger

Statistical tests for factor productivity and factor substitution in Hungary

We start our statistical investigation by testing the null hypothesis that $\dot{g}_A \simeq 0$ and $\sigma = 1$ by fitting a CES production function to the Hungarian data on output, capital and labor for the years 1949–67. For these years, information is available for aggregate national income (i.e., net material product), broken down by major producing sectors (industry, agriculture, construction, transportation and communications, retail trade and catering); for various industrial branches within total state industry (e.g., heavy, light, and food industry), and for a number of specific industrial branches. In order to test the probability of a decline in the growth of factor productivity g_A, we used the initial estimating equation as specified by equation (9). From this equation $g_A = \lambda + 2\mu t$; thus a positive (negative) μ would indicate a systematic increase (decrease) over time of the growth of factor productivity. The null hypothesis of no systematic change in g_A cannot be rejected since μ was not significantly different from zero in any of our tests. The result of our test of g_A was not influenced by setting $\sigma = 1$, thus respecifying the CES function as a Cobb–Douglas.

The tests for the value of σ proved to be curiously inconclusive. Following the method used by Weitzman to estimate the production function for Soviet industry, we used equation (4). We employed the same nonlinear regression program which selects, by means of an iterative process, least squares estimates for all parameters directly by minimizing the statistic

$$\phi = \sum_{i=1}^{n} (V_i - \hat{V}_i)^2, \tag{10}$$

where V_i are observed values of output and $\hat{V}_i$ are the predicted values.[8] In every instance when data for the whole period 1950–67 were used, the confidence interval for σ was too wide to ascertain whether the elasticity of substitution was high or low (i.e., $\sigma \gtrless 1$). An alternative iterative least squares estimating program, which we have designed to map the distribution of ϕ, showed no significant increase in the error sum of squares as we reduced the elasticity of substitution from infinity to nearly zero.[9]

The results of our tests suggest that there was no acceleration or deceleration in the rate of growth of factor productivity, i.e. $\dot{g}_A \simeq 0$. To the extent that these tests are conclusive, we can eliminate sets S_2 and S_3. Our inability to obtain statistically significant results for the value of σ deprives us, however, of the possibility of resolving the paradox: we cannot ascertain whether the value of σ was really such as to make set S_1 feasible. Thus, we are left with our initial conjecture, based on the analogy of Soviet and other cases, that it is unlikely that $\sigma \simeq 1$, given $g_K > g_L$. Therefore, the paradox remains unexplained.

THE L-SHAPED PRODUCTION FUNCTION

Our inability to resolve the paradox by econometric manipulations of the CES production function model raised the obvious question of the applicability of this model to the Hungarian experience. We proceeded to take a closer look at the underlying functional relationship.

The nature of the function

Following Weitzman's diagrammatic presentation, we plotted the detrended capital–output and labor–output ratios to derive the 'implied production isoquant'.[10] Because of the 1956 Hungarian revolt and the changes in government policies and priorities we concentrate on the 1956–67 period, and find that a striking 'isoquant' emerges (see fig. 1). As indicated in equation (6), the usual CES specification collapses into a Leontief-type L-shaped isoquant when $\sigma = 0$. And this is exactly what our empirical evidence shows for the 1956–65 period.

If the L-shaped function of fig. 1 were merely one segment of a long-run function consisting of a series of such L-shapes, we could explain our inability to measure the elasticity of substitution with any degree of certainty and thereby resolve our paradox. In the next section we present a heuristic explanation why such a step function, shown in fig. 2, might be a realistic interpretation of the Hungarian experience.

The production function illustrated in fig. 2 is dynamic since, based on time series data, it illustrates the path over time; it is not merely a comparative static analysis of full-capacity-utilization equilibrium points. These points may be far part, and in this case comparative static analysis will not be very helpful if we want to explain how capital is being substituted for labor, or, in terms of linear programming, how increasingly capital-intensive processes are substituted for labor-intensive ones. An isoquant derived from linear programming is usually shown as a continuous line connecting the corner points of a series of Ls, each representing a different process. As Samuelson has shown, a smooth neoclassical production function could be approached by means of linear programming if the number of available processes approached infinity. If the number of processes is finite, however, the isoquant becomes a set of discontinuous points, or line segments if we assume that processes are perfectly divisible. In the economic development literature it has been emphasized that in real life there may be very few processes available. If, in addition, there exist indivisibilities, then the road to more and more capital-intensive processes will not be the shortest distance from the corner of one L to the corner of the next L, but through the seemingly inefficient path which will trace out the horizontal and vertical line segments of succeeding Ls. If our period of observation is long enough,

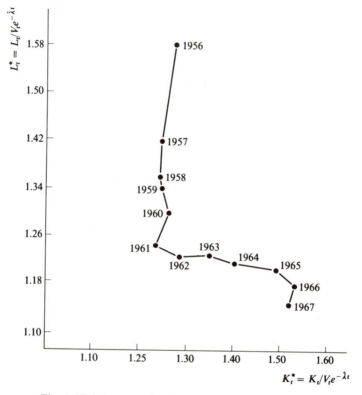

Fig. 1. Unit-isoquant for Hungarian industry, 1956–66.
SOURCE: table B.

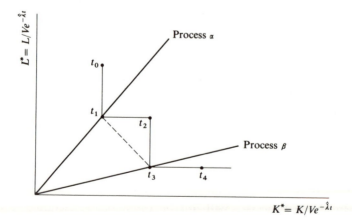

Fig. 2. Dynamic L-shaped production function and linear
programming (hypothetical).

the dynamic path may look like a step function. If the time span is too short, however, we may happen to find a puzzling inverted L, as between t_1 and t_3 in fig. 2. A dynamic production function should not be considered ill-behaved if from time to time its isoquant becomes concave to the origin; in fact, it is likely to have just as many concave as convex segments. The smaller these individual segments the better. Each inverted L represents, after all, an excursion below the production possibility surface.

Estimation problems

The possible existence of a long-run dynamic production function, consisting of a series of L-shaped segments, raises some thorny econometric problems. Taking each of the Leontief-type segments separately would show an elasticity of substitution of zero, or very close to zero. Moving from one L-shaped segment to the next, the elasticity of substitution could jump from zero to infinity, and back again to zero. Considering the function as a whole may yield a unitary elasticity.[11] If we look at one segment, and add a few observations at either end, the measured elasticity of substitution will appear much higher than the zero value for any one L-shape.

Weitzman's paper provides an example of this last problem. If he had omitted the observations after 1965, his σ for Soviet industry would have been much lower than the 0.40 reported in the article. Our own estimates indicate that between 1950 and 1965, σ in Soviet industry was no more than 0.25, and between 1956 and 1965 was only about 0.15, or very close to a Leontief-type L-shaped function. Even a visual inspection of Weitzman's 'Production Isoquant for Soviet Industry' (1970, fig. 1, p. 581) strongly suggests the possible existence of a subperiod with a much lower elasticity of substitution than the 0.40 for the whole period.

What can be done about these problems of estimating σ in a dynamic, segmented L-shaped production function? One solution is to ignore the nature of the long-run function and concentrate on the short- or medium-run and analyze solely each of the L-shaped segments individually. In this case, we must break the function into proper subperiods. This would probably require some exogenous information on key events, such as major systemic charges political disturbances, fundamental shifts in economic priorities or in technology, which would determine the appropriate periodization. This is not the optimal solution since it deprives us of the possibility of studying the long-term growth pattern. Thus, it is more desirable to attempt to deal with the whole long-run function and try to estimate both the long-run average σ and the cyclical movements in σ.[12] If the CES specification leads to difficulties, it may be necessary to replace it with a VES (variable elasticity of substitution) function where

σ itself becomes a variable. Alternatively we may have to specify a single equation with distributed lags or an underlying simultaneous equation system.[13].

If we assume the existence of the type of dynamic function presented in this paper, it would be a mistake to analyze only equilibrium points, e.g., full capacity utilization points, and argue that the function is simply a line joining these points. In any economy where investment decisions are either centralized or for any other reason bunched, such approximation is likely to lead to a serious distortion of reality. Our forecasts in the medium run (say, five to ten years) would be erroneous.[14]

Before launching on a difficult econometric Odyssey we should ask whether we can specify a reasonable hypothetical model of economic growth in centrally planned economics (CPEs) that could yield a long-run dynamic L-shaped production function. We now turn to this task.

HYPOTHETICAL INVESTMENT CYCLE MODEL

In this section we present a model of investment cycles that would generate a function consisting of L-shaped segments as presented in fig. 2, and *could* be used to explain the Hungarian growth experience since the war. The cycle model is a modified and simplified version of models presented by Eastern European economists, including Chelinski, Flek, Goldmann, Horvat, and Kouba.[15]

We start with the observation that, in the postwar development of Eastern European countries, decisions on new investment projects were highly interrelated and bunched, and that both the gestation period (the period between the initiation of a project and its completion) and the digestion period (the period from completion of a project until it is in full operation)[16] tend to be lengthy. This is partly due to the traditional emphasis in CPEs on large-scale projects in basic industries, and partly to other systemic features, e.g., poor coordination, supply bottlenecks, taut planning, etc. Given the combination of the bunching of investment decisions and the lengthy gestation and digestion periods, the process of substituting capital for labor will occur in a step-wise fashion and the resulting dynamic production function will be composed of a series of L-shaped segments. Such a process was illustrated in fig. 2 above, where we plotted the labor–output and capital–output ratios, each detrended by the growth of factor productivity.

For ease of exposition we shall refer to the hypothetical example presented in table 1, as well as to fig. 2. Suppose we start at a time when a CPE has just come out of a war and is entering a period of reconstruction. It suffers from disguised unemployment and has partly unutilized capital capacity, due to the lack of key equipment.

The capital can be brought quickly into production with new invest-

Table 1. *Cyclical growth path in a CPE (hypothetical).* % *per annum*

Time periods	g_V	g_A	g_K	g_L	$g_V - g_A$	g_{K^*}	g_{L^*}
$t_0 t_1$	11	3	8	4	8	0	-4
$t_1 t_2$	7	3	8	4	4	$+4$	0
$t_2 t_3$	11	3	8	4	8	0	-4
$t_3 t_4$	7	3	8	4	4	$+4$	0

NOTE: the dynamic L-shaped production function in fig. 2 illustrates this growth path. From $L^* = L/Ve^{-\lambda t} (= L/VA^{-1})$, we derive $g_{L^*} = g_L - (g_V - g_A)$; similarly, $g_{K^*} = g_K - (g_V - g_A)$.

ments and relatively small additions to the labor force. In this case, we would be moving from t_0 to t_1, and output would be growing at 11 % per annum, that is, proportionately with increases in capital of 8 % and increases of g_A of 3 %.

The additional capital and raw material supplies lead to full utilization of labor, showing up as a steady decline in the labor–output ratio (detrended), g_{L^*}, of 4 %, which means, of course, a corresponding increase of labor productivity. During this period, the similarly detrended capital–output ratio, g_{K^*}, is constant, i.e. there is no change in capital productivity.

At time t_1 the reconstruction is completed, and the government is ready to engage in a series of major new investment projects. Between t_1 and t_2, the period of investment boom, the capital stock is continuing to grow at 8 % and the labor force is still rising at the slower rate of 4 %. Due to the lags of gestation and digestion, the new capital is not yet contributing to a rise in output. Thus, growth of output is reduced to 7 %, constrained by the rate of growth of the labor force and the growth of factor productivity. The labor–output ratio, g_{L^*}, is unchanged, while the capital–output ratio, g_{K^*}, is increasing at 4 %.

At time t_2 there is a change in the nature of new investment. Instead of building large new capacities, investment is used to complete and bring into full operation the capacities constructed in the preceding period of investment boom. In this period of consolidation, output once again increases at the rate at 11 %, i.e. the rate at which capital and factor productivity are rising. This period is, of course, parallel to the reconstruction period, except for the causes behind the unutilized capacity at the beginning of the period. We again find that the capital–output ratio is constant, while the labor–output ratio is falling at 4 %.

By time t_3 the new investment projects are fully operational and the planners are ready to initiate the next set of investment projects; thus the cycle starts again.

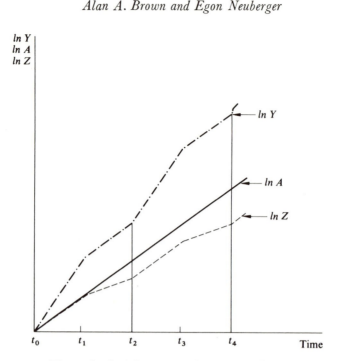

Fig. 3. Cyclical fluctuations in factor productivities
and stable growth in total productivity.

Over the entire period, from t_0 to t_4, there is a steady growth of capital and labor, as well as of factor productivity, and yet there is an observable cyclical movement in the growth of output and of labor and capital productivities.

This may help to explain the postwar experience in Hungary where the individual factor productivities of labor and capital moved cyclically, while, paradoxically, their weighted average, total factor productivity, was growing at a steady rate. This proposition is illustrated in fig. 3.

The key features of this investment cycle model are: an initial bunching of new investment projects; a gestation-cum-digestion period, long enough to cause the planners to become sufficiently concerned about the drop of capital productivity and the consequent drop in the rate of growth of output to introduce a consolidation period; and a gestation-cum-digestion period, sufficiently correlated in most sectors to prevent investment booms in some sectors being balanced by consolidation in other sectors.

One may argue whether our hypothetical cycles, which are essentially administrative cycles, should be considered endogenously determined. We have postulated above a possible endogenous, recursive model, with technological as well as institutional lags (see note 13). The parameters of this model indicate that if, say, the planners were to abandon taut planning and space investment projects more evenly over time, these cycles would be dampened. In this case, within the framework of our production function analysis, the L-shaped segments might become small enough and a long-run CES specification would be appropriate for the entire period.

CONCLUDING REMARKS

This paper represents a small first step in the application of CES production function analysis to the examination of East European growth patterns, and perhaps more generally of economies with supply determined growth cycles. It suggests a combination of two main avenues for further study: an exploration of the nature of an economic model that generates a production function consisting of a series of L-shaped segments and the econometric implications of such a model, and empirical extensions of this approach to investigations of growth patterns of other countries.

Our finding of the possible existence of a long-run production function with L-shaped segments in the medium run, raises the whole question of the econometric implications of such a model, and empirical extensions of this approach to investigations of growth patterns of other countries.

Our finding of the possible existence of a long-run production function with L-shaped segments in the medium run, raises the whole question of the applicability of the usual microeconomic approach in production and consumption theory. We generally show static production functions or indifference maps, the assumption being that technology, labor, and capital, or income and taste are constant. In comparative statics, of course, there is no possibility of exploring the time path of these variables. Very little has been done to examine their nature in the long run.

Our analysis indicates the need to investigate long-term dynamic production functions. A potentially illuminating approach in production theory would be to test the hypothesis that the long-run dynamic production functions in all economies consist of a series of L-shaped segments, but that the Ls are significantly larger in CPEs than in market economies. This hypothesis is based on the observation that more centralized decision-making leads to a bunching of investment decisions and that the planning system's rigidities lead to longer gestation-cum-digestion periods. The systemic, technological and other factors leading to steps of different size and nature should be examined in a cross-sectional comparison of CPEs (like the USSR, Poland, or Rumania) and market economies (like Japan, Canada, US, and UK) as well as by time series analysis of countries that have moved from one type of system to another (as, for example, Yugoslavia, Hungary, or prewar as against postwar France).

The long-run function explored in this paper may also have some implications for the theory of economic reforms. In a system that generates large L-shaped segments, the system's directors may not realize that a falling rate of growth and falling capital productivity, without substantial rise in labor productivity, are merely symptomatic of one leg of the L, and they may be periodically motivated to institute a flurry of reforms. This function also has obvious efficiency and welfare implications, since *ceteris paribus*, the larger the L-shaped segments the more cyclical and the less efficient is the growth pattern.

Much work remains to be done on the econometric problems raised by the analysis of this paper. There is the problem of deciding on the relative significance of the values of certain parameters in the long run as against their values in the short run, as well as the difficulty of measuring effectively values of the parameters when the long-run functions fail to display nice neoclassical properties. The first problem involves a basic question of research methodology and choice of hypotheses to be tested (short-run or long-run), while the second represents various technical econometric problems (e.g., the measurement of σ if there are discontinuities in the function).

Let us recapitulate the plot of our little 'detective story'. We applied Weitzman's methodology for analyzing Soviet growth to explain the Hungarian growth pattern. We ran into an apparent paradox and our attempt to resolve this paradox by econometric means was unsuccessful since we were unable to measure one key parameter, σ, with any degree of accuracy. This led us to a reconsideration of the underlying model. We discovered a most interesting hypothetical monster, a dynamic production function composed of Leontief-type L-shaped segments. Since a CES function collapses into an L-shaped function when the elasticity of factor substitution is zero and combinations of complete or partial L-shapes yield widely different estimates of σ, we suspect that the correct specification should utilize a variable rather than a constant elasticity of substitution formula. We provided an explanation for the failure of our econometric attempt to solve the paradox. Once a dynamic function is considered, our paradox vanishes, since it was based on the assumption that we were dealing with the usual continuous CES function.

APPENDIX

Table A. *Output, labor and capital in Hungarian state industry, 1949–67 (official)*

Year	Index (1959 = 100)			Annual growth rates (% per annum)					
	V	L	K	r_V	r_L	r_K	$r_{V/L} = r_Y$	$r_{V/K} = r_Z$	$r_{K/L} = r_X$
1949	34.0	52.9	44.1	30.2	17.2	8.0	11.1	20.5	−7.8
1950	44.2	62.0	47.7	33.4	15.8	10.1	15.2	21.2	−5.0
1951	59.0	71.8	52.5	19.2	13.2	11.2	5.3	7.2	−1.8
1952	70.3	81.3	58.4	7.8	9.8	10.2	−1.7	−2.2	0.4
1953	75.8	89.2	64.3	−0.9	3.2	7.9	−3.9	−8.2	4.6
1954	75.2	92.1	69.4	6.4	−0.9	7.9	7.3	−1.4	8.8
1955	80.0	91.3	74.9	−10.4	1.4	6.8	−11.6	−16.1	5.3
1956	71.7	92.6	80.0	13.0	−1.8	7.2	15.1	5.4	9.2
1957	81.0	90.9	85.8	12.0	4.0	8.3	7.7	3.4	4.1
1958	90.7	94.5	92.9	10.3	5.8	7.7	4.2	2.4	1.8
1959	100.0	100.0	100.0	13.2	6.3	11.6	6.6	1.4	5.0
1960	113.2	106.3	111.6	11.4	3.4	5.2	7.7	5.9	1.8
1961	126.0	109.9	117.4	8.4	3.6	9.4	4.6	−0.9	5.6
1962	136.6	113.8	128.5	6.9	4.1	9.0	2.7	−1.9	4.7
1963	146.1	118.5	140.0	7.8	3.4	8.3	4.3	−0.4	4.7
1964	157.5	122.5	151.6	4.3	0.4	7.5	3.9	−3.0	7.1
1965	164.2	123.0	163.0	6.4	0.9	5.8	5.5	0.5	4.9
1966	174.8	124.1	172.5	8.2	2.1	4.3	6.0	3.7	2.2
1967	189.0	126.7	179.9						

NOTES TO TABLE A. Relationship between annual growth rate (r) and continuous growth rate (g).

The annual growth rate (r) is derived from

$$V_1 = V_0(1+r)^t, \tag{1}$$

$$r = \ln^{-1}\left[\left(\frac{1}{t}\ln\frac{V_1}{V_0} - 1\right)\right]100. \tag{2}$$

Letting $t \to 0$ yields the continuous growth rate (g),

$$V_1 = V_0 e^{gt}, \tag{3}$$

$$g = \left[\frac{1}{t}\ln\left(\frac{V_1}{V_0}\right)\right]100. \tag{4}$$

Therefore,

$$g = \left[\ln\left(\frac{r}{100} - 1\right)\right]100, \tag{5}$$

$$r = [e^{g/100} - 1]100. \tag{6}$$

For example, if

$$r = 10\%, \quad g = 9.53\%,$$

$$9.53 = [\ln(0.1 + 1)]100,$$

$$10.00 = (e^{0.0953} - 1)100.$$

Table B. *Detrended labor–output and capital–output
ratios for Hungarian industry, 1949–67*

Year	$L_t^* = L_t/V_t e^{-\hat{\lambda}t}$	$K_t^* = K_t/V_t e^{-\hat{\lambda}t}$
1949	1.558	1.299
1950	1.451	1.115
1951	1.304	0.952
1952	1.280	0.919
1953	1.348	0.972
1954	1.451	1.095
1955	1.399	1.148
1956	1.638	1.416
1957	1.472	1.389
1958	1.414	1.390
1959	1.404	1.404
1960	1.363	1.432
1961	1.309	1.399
1962	1.295	1.461
1963	1.304	1.540
1964	1.294	1.600
1965	1.288	1.707
1966	1.264	1.757
1967	1.234	1.752

SOURCE: calculated from data in table A.
NOTE: $\hat{\lambda} = 0.03$.

NOTES

1 Without blaming them for our errors (since they are not likely to accept the blame, in any case), we are grateful to Edward Ames, William Gillen, Antonio Guccione, Estelle James, Mahmoud Sakbani, and George Stolnitz for their valuable comments and suggestions. The work on this study was performed as part of the Project on Economic Development and Systemic Change in Eastern Europe of IDRC, Indiana University.

2 The unexplained portion of growth has been called many names and these may be used interchangeably. Domar (1961), who introduced the term 'residual', presents a lucid summary of the literature and a list of the various terms used. 'Total factor productivity' was used by Kendrick (1956) and 'technical change' by Solow (1957), and, trying to keep us honest, Abramowitz (1956), referred to it as a 'measure of our ignorance'. For the most recent discussion of this issue, see Nadiri (1970).

3 As Nelson (1965) has shown, estimates of output, using a Cobb–Douglas specification in lieu of a CES, will only diverge widely if rates of growth of capital and labor are very different.

4 By imputed shares of capital and labor we do not mean that the two factors are necessarily paid according to marginal productivity theory; these shares need not be considered distributive shares; they may simply represent contributive shares, i.e. based on the factors' calculated marginal contributions to output.

5 The proposition is that, given a faster growth of capital than of labor ($g_K > g_L$), the imputed share of capital η_K will decline if $\sigma < 1$,increase if $\sigma > 1$, and remain the

same if $\sigma = 1$. Assuming constant returns to scale, which of course means that the shares of the two factors always add up to one, changes in the imputed share of capital will be accompanied by corresponding changes in the share of labor but in the opposite direction. (For proof of this proposition, see Weitzman, 1970, p. 679 n7.)

6 However, having run the nonlinear regression mentioned by Weitzman, using his data with capital and labor as independent variables, we have found strong evidence of multicollinearity among these independent variables. This suggests that the functional relationship ought to be respecified, relating labor productivities to the capital–output ratios instead of relating output to capital and labor separately. Therefore, in our explanation of retardation we should refer to equation (5a) above, rather than to equation (5). This would not vitiate Weitzman's main line of argument.

7 This has, in fact, been argued by A. Bródy in Bronfenbrenner (1969).

8 If we assume a logarithmic error sum of squares, as Weitzman did, we should minimize $\phi' = \sum_{i=1}^{n} (\log V_i - \log \hat{V}_i)^2$. In our calculations we experimented with both assumptions and found no difference in the results. We used the program cited by Weitzman, IBM Share Program No. 309401, Rev. 8-15-66 ('LSE of Nonlinear Parameters', based on an algorithm by D. W. Marquardt). Since this program can only estimate local optima (which may not be the global minimum ϕ), we also checked the results by means of another iterative program that was prepared at the International Development Research Center (IDRC, Indiana University) on the basis of a simpler algorithm of our own.

9 Calculation of confidence regions is discussed in the writeup of the IBM Share Program ('Exhibit B-1'), where it is stated that 'there is no general theory of confidence region estimation for nonlinear parameters, but useful estimation based on the nonlinear theory can be derived'. For a good summary of this discussion see Weitzman (1970, pp. 680–1 n11).

10 Unfortunately Weitzmann's interesting scatter diagram, 'Production Isoquant for Soviet Industry, 1950–1960', (1970, p. 681) is presented without much discussion of its derivation. Although the two axes are labelled K and L, respectively, they do not stand for capital and labor as in the text, but for capital per unit of detrended output ($K^* = K/Ve^{-\hat{\lambda}t}$) and labor per unit of detrended output ($L^* = L/Ve^{-\hat{\lambda}t}$). Output is detrended by $\hat{\lambda}$ (or $\hat{g}_A$), the rate of change in factor productivity, which had been estimated by means of a CES production function. We may contrast Weitzman's 'implied isoquant' with the usual static isoquant. A static isoquant tells us how many units of capital and labor are necessary to produce a given amount of output, in contrast, Weitzman's implied isoquant shows how much capital and labor per unit of detrended output is necessary to produce one unit of output. Therefore, we will call this a *unit-isoquant*.

11 In fig. 2, whenever the short-run elasticity of substitution is zero, the imputed share of capital (η_K) will drop from one to zero: i.e. as we move from $t_0 t_1$ to $t_1 t_2$, then again from $t_2 t_3$ to $t_3 t_4$. This means that η_K must have increased from zero to one between these two inelastic sub-periods, i.e. between $t_1 t_2$ and $t_2 t_3$, which implies that the elasticity of substitution in this range must have been infinite. In sum, the short-run elasticity of substitution changes from zero to infinity, and again to zero while the long-run elasticity, for the whole period $t_0 t_4$, can be equal to one.

12 The procedure of calculating our capital–output and labor–output ratios, after detrending output by the maximum likelihood estimate of the growth rate of the residual (the method used by Weitzman), should separate the systematic departures from the trend. Assuming that the trend is indeed linear (the likelihood that this is

not the case is examined separately), we are left with the cyclical component of the time series. Changes in the rate of capacity utilization constitute a key element in this cyclical pattern and these changes are due to both the cyclical nature of the technological process and to specific systemic factors. Thus, while it would be highly desirable for analytical purposes to isolate the effect of changing capacity utilization on the behavior of factor productivity, it would not be permissible to exclude altogether unfinished projects from the capital stock series, even if this were feasible. In other words, if the changing proportion of the nation's capital stock that is in the form of unfinished or underutilized capacities constitutes one of the key elements in explaining the pattern of economic growth, it would be a mistake to ignore this fact. Therefore, we have not attempted to exclude, as frequently attempted in estimations of the elasticity of substitution in the West, changes in capacity utilization.

13 We may test, for example, the following simple recursive model.

$$Y_t = f_1(R_{t-a}), \qquad \qquad \text{(i)}$$
$$R_t = f_2(Y_{t-b}). \qquad \qquad \text{(ii)}$$

Combining the two equations,

$$Y_t = f_1[f_2(Y_{t-b})]_{t-a} = f(Y_{t-a-b}), \qquad \qquad \text{(iii)}$$

where $Y_t = (V/L)_t =$ labor productivity at t; $R_t = (K'/K)_t =$ proportion of operational capital to total capital stock at t; $a =$ technological lags (e.g. indivisibilities); $b =$ institutional lags (e.g. bunching of large-scale investment projects). The model shows that Y_t may go through all sorts of cyclical movements, depending on the lags a and b (see equation iii).

14 For instance, one of the authors of this paper, unaware of the exceedingly low short-run elasticity of substitution, as distinct from the higher long-run elasticity, used an extrapolation of the past trend and considerably underestimated the rate of growth of the Hungarian economy during the second half of the 1960s. (See Brown, 1967, pp. 807–27.)

15 Alexander Bajt (1971) presents an excellent discussion of these and other theories of the investment cycle.

16 The gestation period for capital is analogous to the schooling period of labor, while the digestion period may be thought of as analogous to the apprenticeship period. Using the labor analogy, one would then wish to exclude capital invested in projects whose gestation period has not yet ended from the capital stock, while including capital that has not yet been fully digested. But, as we argued above in note 13, this is not always the appropriate approach, and there may be good reasons for including capital that has not yet entered into production in our calculation of the capital stock.

REFERENCES

Abramowitz, Moses (1956). Resource and output trends in the U.S. since 1870. *American Economic Review, Papers and Proceedings*, **46**, 5–23.

Arrow, K. J., H. B. Chenery, B. S. Minhas and R. M. Solow (1961). Capital–labor substitution and economic efficiency. *Review of Economics and Statistics*, **43**, 225–50.

Bajt, Alexander (1971). Investment cycles in European socialist economies. *Journal of Economic Literature*, **7**, 53–69.

Bronfenbrenner, Martin (ed.) (1969). *Is the Business Cycle Obsolete?* New York: Wiley-Interscience.

Brown, Alan A. (1967). L'économie Hongroise perspectives d'ici 1970. *Analyse & Prévision, Futuribles*, **4**, 807–27. Reprinted in *The Prediction of Communist Economic Performance*, ed. Peter J. D. Wiles, pp. 175–99. Cambridge University Press, 1971.

Brubaker, Earl R. (1970). Synthetic factor shares, the elasticity of substitution, and the residual in Soviet growth. *Review of Economics and Statistics*, **52**, 100–8.

Domar, Evsey D. (1961). On the measurement of technological change. *Economic Journal*, **71**, 709–29.

Kendrick, John W. (1956). Productivity trends: capital and labor. *Review of Economics and Statistics*, **37**, 248–57.

Nadiri, M. Ishaq (1970). Some approaches to the theory and measurement of total factor productivity: a survey. *Journal of Economic Literature*, **8**, 1137–77.

Nelson, Richard (1965). The CES production function and economic growth projections. *Review of Economics and Statistics*, **47**, 326–8.

Solow, Robert M. (1957). Technical change and the aggregate production function. *Review of Economics and Statistics*, **39**, 312–20.

Weitzman, Martin L. (1968). Soviet postwar growth: some econometric aspects. Presented to Annual Meeting of Econometric Society, Evanston, Illinois, 1968. As cited in Brubaker (1970).

Weitzman, Martin L. (1970). Soviet postwar economic growth and capital–labor substitution. *American Economic Review*, **60**, 672–92.

Wiles, Peter J. D. (ed.) (1971). *The Prediction of Communist Economic Performance*. Cambridge University Press.

Some Models of Technical Progress in the Soviet Nonagricultural Nonresidential Sector

EARL BRUBAKER

In macroeconomic planning for the intermediate or long term a reliable model of the relationships between outputs, inputs, and technical change is an essential ingredient. In the course of recent decades a multitude of more or less plausible and logically consistent models of production and technical progress have been elaborated. On the face of it they may be as useful for analyzing an economy developing under Soviet-style planning as they are for analyzing an economy developing under a system more heavily oriented toward coordination through the market mechanism.

In the present paper we shall be concerned with alternative hypotheses about the character of the shift in the production function relevant to the Soviet nonagricultural nonresidential economy. The hypotheses include the relative familiar Hicks, Harrod, and Solow varieties as well as a series of six additional *a priori* equally plausible types. For purposes of assessing their empirical relevance based on consistency with the historical record, it will be important to develop a precise statement of the hypothesized relationships. If such models are to contribute to under standing economic development, it is imperative also to recognize at the outset that: (1) the normal specification of a 'well behaved' production function has implications for the direction of relationships between certain strategic variables, and (2) many hypotheses about the character of neutral technical progress are mutually incompatible. The first section of this paper is devoted to a discussion of these matters. The second section deals with the source and meaning of data on the rate of return to tangible capital, which is used, and, in a sense, also is tested, in an examination of the hypotheses on neutrality. In the final section attention is focused on the results of tests designed to indicate which of the many available models seems to fit best the systematic historical record on Soviet growth. For purposes of evaluating the analysis of the Soviet case it will be useful to present the results of similar analyses of three major market economies, Germany, Japan, and the United States.

THE MODELS: IMPLICATIONS AND LOGICAL CONSISTENCY

In the context of the traditional, single-product, two-factor theory of production nine principal types of neutral technical progress may be described as generated from specific varieties of upward shift in the relationship between output per man and capital stock per man.[1] Namely, the shifts are restricted to maintain exact functional variation between certain pairs from among marginal productivities of the inputs, absolutely or in ratio, and either average products of the inputs or ratios of inputs themselves. Quite specifically, the pairs of variables[2] and names of the associated neutralities are as shown in table 1.

Table 1

Name	Generated from invariant relations between:
Hicks	r/w, L/K
Harrod	r, Y/K
Solow	w, Y/L
Labor-combining	w, Y/K
Capital-combining	r, W/L
Labor-decreasing	r/w, Y/K
Capital-decreasing	w/r, Y/L
Capital-additive	w, L/K
Labor-additive	r, K/L

where r = rate of return to tangible capital
w = wage rate
L = labor input
K = capital input
Y = output.

As an example of a specification of a unique relationship between the pair of variables involved in Hicks neutrality we may consider

$$r/w = a_1 + b_1 L/K, \qquad (1)$$

that is, a simple linear function with a_1 and b_1 parameters to be determined. Given the necessary quantitative evidence such determination might be accomplished by statistical analysis.

In order to test the uniqueness of the relationship between r/w and L/K over time, a proxy for technical progress, we may introduce time itself as a variable. Thus we could have written

$$r/w = a_1 + b_1 L/K + c_1 t. \qquad (1a)$$

If statistical analysis shows c_1 differs insignificantly from zero, it would

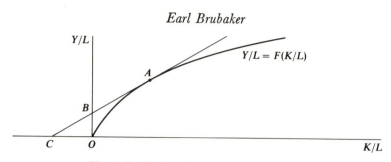

Fig. 1. Production function in *per capita* terms.

appear that the relationship between r/w and L/K is unaffected by the passage of time, and technical change would be, in this sense, neutral. Other specifications of unique relationships between the variables could be made while retaining the property of the indicated neutrality. Similar statements, with parameters a_i, b_i, c_i, about the remaining pairs of variables in our tabulation above would be appropriate.

Graphical representations of the production function in per-unit-labor terms can illustrate quite clearly the meaning of these hypotheses and the extent of their mutual compatibility. Likewise such representations can be used to derive the implications for the direction of the relationships anticipated in the absence of technical progress. That is, we can see immediately from the graph that 'good behaviour' of the production function, in the sense of positive marginal products declining with relative input abundance, has implications for the anticipated sign of b_1 in equation ($1a$) or of b_i in any similar linear specification necessary for one of the other types of neutrality.

Fig. 1 illustrates the 'well behaved' production function in per-unit-labor terms. Output per unit labor and capital per unit labor are measured directly on the ordinate and abscissa, respectively. The marginal productivity of capital at any point such as A is measured by the slope of the corresponding tangent to the curve. The corresponding marginal productivity of labor is measured by the height of the ordinate intercept at B. The ratio of factor marginal productivities is represented by the distance from the origin to point C, the tangent's abscissa intercept (see Allen, 1968, p. 47). Finally, the slopes of rays from the origin represent output to capital ratios.

Bearing these graphical representations in mind it will be clear from inspection of fig. 1 that the directions of relationships shown in table 2 are implied. The predicted directions of the relationships are also the predicted signs for b_i coefficients since they should indicate the relationship between the paired variables after the influence of time has been removed.

It is hypothesized that technology (a term used throughout merely as a convenient label for all forces affecting the functional relationship

Table 2

Pair of variables	Predicted direction of relationship
$r/w, L/K$	+
$r, Y/K$	+
$w, Y/L$	+
$w, Y/K$	−
$r, Y/L$	−
$r/w, Y/K$	+
$w/r, Y/L$	+
$w, L/K$	−
$r, K/L$	−

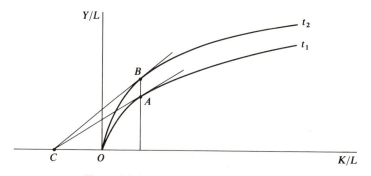

Fig. 2. Hicks neutral technical progress.

between Y/L and K/L) changes over time to permit higher average productivity of labor at any given capital to labor ratio. Thus in fig. 2 the curve shifts upward during the interval of time from t_1 to t_2. The hypotheses on neutrality described above constitute, in effect, a set of statements about logically possible ways in which the curvature of the function might have been affected by changes in technology.

In fig. 2 the shift is drawn to represent Hicks neutrality, at least so far as the movement from A to B is concerned. That is, the shift from A to B, involving no change in the capital to labor ratio, also does not affect the value of the corresponding ratio of marginal productivities measured by OC. Similar representations of the eight remaining hypotheses could be given.

From these graphical representations of the various types of neutrality it is possible to learn which are compatible and which are not. Inspection of fig. 3, for example, reveals that the pair of specifications $[r = f(K/L)]$ and $[w = g(Y/K)]$ is not compatible. The hypothesis that $r = f(K/L)$ requires parallel tangents at points A and B. The hypothesis that

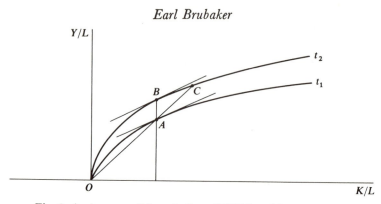

Fig. 3. An incompatible pair, $[r = f(K/L)]$ and $[w = g(Y/K)]$.

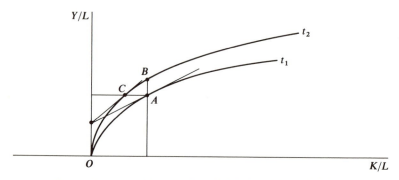

Fig. 4. A compatible pair, $[r = f(K/L)]$ and $[w = h(Y/L)]$.

$w = g(Y/K)$ requires the same ordinate intercept for tangents from A and C. Inspection of the graph shows that if the tangents at A and B are parallel, the ordinate intercept of the tangent at C must fall above that of the tangent at A. Fig. 4 illustrates a compatible pair. As in the previous case the tangents at A and B are parallel. There is no reason why the curvature of t_2 could not result in the same ordinate intercept for the tangents from A and C.

The results of a similar analysis of all thirty-six combinations of paired statements of neutrality are summarized in table 3. Of the thirty-six only nine are logically consistent. There is only one compatible triple combination, i.e., Hicks, Harrod, and Solow, and there are no compatible combinations of four or more.

As was suggested above, if one had sufficient sets of time series observations on the relevant variables, one could attempt a statistical estimation of the relationships. In fact there now is available a substantial body of data meticulously prepared by Western analysts on all the relevant variables but one, the rate of return to tangible capital. But where in the world shall we find data on it?

Table 3. *Compatibilities of hypotheses (plus-compatible; minus incompatible)*

	(r/w, L/K)	(r, Y/K)	(w, Y/L)	(w, Y/K)	(r, Y/L)	(r/w, Y/K)	(w/r, Y/L)	(w, L/K)
(r, Y/K)	+							
(w, Y/L)	+	+						
(w, Y/K)	−	−	−					
(r, Y/L)	−	−	−	−				
(r/w, Y/K)	−	−	+	−	−			
(w/r, Y/L)	−	+	−	−	−	−		
(w, L/K)	−	+	−	−	−	+	−	
(r, K/L)	−	−	+	−	−	−	+	−

RATE OF RETURN TO TANGIBLE CAPITAL

Fortunately, as we shall see, available time series on Soviet output, capital, labor, and wages as compiled by Western researchers apparently have implications for trends in the rate of return on tangible capital in the Soviet nonagricultural nonresidential sector.[3] At this stage of our investigation it will be especially interesting to explore the possible meaning and usefulness of rates of return computed from such data.

The strategy for computing the net rate of return on capital from Western accounts on Soviet economic variables is straightforward. For most years during the period 1932–66 we have, or are able to compute, statistics that might plausibly be regarded as approximations to 'true' values in real terms for remuneration to labor, depreciation charges (D), and net capital stock (K). Total value added less depreciation and labor earnings leaves value added attributable (in an accounting sense) to capital, and this residual taken as a ratio to the net capital stock provides a measure of the rate of return (r).

Patterns and procedure

The data on r as computed from time series essentially in 1937 prices appear in table 4 and the patterns of resulting variations in r are shown in fig. 5. To understand the meaning of these patterns, however, it will be necessary to probe deeper into the procedures used in compiling the ingredient time series. Why, for example, do we obtain several possible patterns? The answer, essentially, is that the procedures employed in obtaining data on output, capital stock, and depreciation make *variation* in r a function of the *level* arbitrarily chosen for some base year. Thus, in 1937 the sum of wage earnings, nominal profits, and depreciation in the nonagricultural nonresidential sector amounts to 143.3 billion rubles. Upon replacement of the nominal rate of return to capital with net

Table 4. *Rates of return in the Soviet nonagricultural nonresidential sector, 1932–66* (%)

	Assumed value for r in 1937		
Year	8	15	20
1932	5.0	13.5	19.6
1933	7.4	14.8	20.3
1934	10.4	17.5	22.6
1935	13.5	20.2	24.9
1936	13.3	20.1	25.0
1937	8.0	15.0	20.0
1938	3.6	10.8	16.0
1939	7.0	13.4	18.0
1940	7.3	13.2	17.4
1945	21.9	25.3	27.7
1948	15.5	19.7	22.7
1950	10.3	15.9	19.8
1951	8.9	14.7	18.8
1952	7.0	12.8	17.0
1953	3.5	9.8	14.2
1954	3.1	9.5	14.0
1955	5.5	11.5	15.8
1956	5.7	11.5	15.7
1957	6.0	11.5	15.5
1958	4.3	9.9	13.9
1959	4.3	9.6	13.4
1960	3.7	8.8	12.5
1961	2.9	8.0	11.6
1962	3.4	8.2	11.7
1963	4.0	8.6	11.9
1964	4.0	8.4	11.6
1965	2.3	6.8	10.1
1966	2.1	6.5	9.7

NOTE: see appendix A for a description of data and sources.

interest rates of 8 % and 20 %, the total value added becomes 151.0 billion rubles and 201.8 billion rubles respectively (Moorsteen and Powell 1966, pp. 371, 622).

The reasoning underlying the variation in the values of output with the interest rate is as follows.[4] Specification of alternative values for the return on capital, while leaving labor earnings unchanged, implies alternative values for the total costs of production. If the capital–labor ratio is the same in consumer goods and capital goods industries, the costs, and value, of output will be changed in the same proportion in both sectors. Thus output, capital stock, and depreciation charges will be revalued in the same proportion. Furthermore any such revaluation will

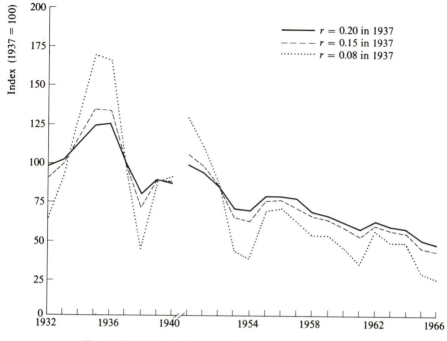

Fig. 5. Variation in the rate of return, 1932–40, 1950–66.

have to leave total product consistent with the new values of factor costs. In algebraic notation:

$$Y'/Y = K'/K = C'/C = D'/D, \qquad (2)$$

and

$$Y' = Lw + C', \qquad (3)$$

so that

$$Y' = Lw \frac{Y}{Y-C}. \qquad (4)$$

Primes indicate values for variables after adjustment, and C represents the sum of interest and depreciation charges.

Thus one can compute Y' from (4) given 'observations' on Lw and Y along with assumed values for r and estimates for C and D.

The revaluation as explained to this point pertains only to data for a single year. How might one obtain corresponding measures for other years in the time series? Moorsteen and Powell (1966, p. 265) perform a limited test from which they conclude that growth rates for output appear to be little affected by the revaluation especially in the non-agricultural nonresidential sector. Thus given revaluations for a single year, an appropriate corresponding time series can be generated through application of an index of unadjusted values for output, capital stock, and depreciation. It is from these along with the 'observations' on labor

Table 5

Assumed values for 1937 (%)	Range (excluding 1945 and 1948)	
	1932–66[a]	Postwar highs
8	2.1–13.5	10.3
15	6.5–20.2	15.9
20	9.7–25.0	19.8

[a] Minima were recorded for 1966; maxima for 1935 and 1936. Postwar maxima pertain to 1950.

income that one can compute rates of return on capital as a residual in the various years.

As is clear from fig. 5, the pattern of variation appears to depend substantially upon the arbitrary initial choice for r. Thus, as may be seen from table 5, the level and extent of the ranges of variation depend heavily on it. In all three series substantial fluctuations are superimposed on the general downward trend from the mid-1930s to the mid-1960s. The relative extent of the fluctuations varies inversely with the rate of return set for 1937. This result is a direct implication of the computational procedure. As the value for r is set higher, adjusted values of output and capital rise correspondingly relative to labor's income, and the residual income available for 'remuneration' of capital increases. Thus as r is raised the pattern of variation approaches the pattern of variation in the output to capital ratio.

What meaning can be attributed to rates of return computed in this fashion? What hypotheses about behavioral (including technological) relationships might be tested with reference to data of this sort? To answer such questions we need to delve deeper still into the possible meaning for data on r as computed.

Meaning of data on r

One of the important and interesting uses to which data on r generated from 'observing' predominately market economies has been put is to aid in tests of hypotheses about the character of technical change. For this purpose it often has been found useful to suppose that the accounting values for r serve as a reasonable approximation to the marginal productivity of capital. Under what conditions would the unit residual remuneration as calculated above correspond also to the marginal productivity of Soviet capital?

To provide a possible answer to this question it is useful to express the accounting computational procedure in algebraic notation and to compare it with a plausible behavioral hypothesis about the underlying production function.[5] In algebraic notation the computational procedure described in Section A may be written as an identity, (5), from which r was computed.

$$Y = LW + rK. \tag{5}$$

Now let us consider a plausible and widely employed behavioral hypothesis about the relationship between Y, L, and K, namely, that, as we have already supposed, the production function linking them is linear homogeneous. This means that in the absence of technical change we would expect proportional variation of inputs to be accompanied by a change in output of like proportion. Furthermore, and of immediate interest here, according to Euler's theorem the hypothesis implies

$$Y = \frac{\partial Y}{\partial L} L + \frac{\partial Y}{\partial K} K. \tag{6}$$

Consider now implications for the time series estimates of two alternative outcomes of the estimating procedure for 1937: (1) wages equal $\partial Y/\partial L$, and (2) wages deviate from $\partial Y/\partial L$ by a proportion, k.

The essence of the procedure of Western analysts in their attempts to approximate Y has been to accept basically the Soviet data on labor earnings as the appropriate labor contribution to value added and then to experiment with values for r, hoping thereby to bracket the 'true' contribution of capital. If the linear homogeneous production function accurately represents the underlying process, this procedure involves accepting average wages as equal to $\partial Y/\partial L$ and hoping to find rates of return representing the 'true' marginal products of capital.

Let us suppose now, that having followed the computational procedure outlined above, that we have successfully identified the 'true' value for r in 1937 and that labor earnings also in fact correspond to the sectoral marginal productivity of labor, Then the sum of labor earnings and capital 'remuneration' will amount to 'true' value added for that year. If the index of value added is accurate, an accurate series of absolute values may be generated. Under the circumstances the computed values for r can correspond to marginal productivities of capital only if labor earnings reflect marginal productivities of labor for remaining years as well.

We have, however, no guarantee, or even evidence to suggest it, that earnings of labor might correspond to aggregate marginal productivity. There would seem to be little or nothing in Soviet labor planning procedures to suggest any tendency toward setting the level of real wages to reflect the corresponding marginal productivity. It would appear rather that the general level of wages is set basically in consonance with the decisions by the systems' directors regarding the division of national product between consumers' and producers' goods, and such decisions need not be very closely related to the factor productivities.[6]

Thus under this interpretation it would seem that there is after all essential symmetry in the problem of determining 'appropriate' earnings for the factors. In each case we have little confidence that the accounting price accorded the factor necessarily represents its 'actual' aggregate marginal productivity. True, a zero price for capital does appear to be an especially clearcut case, but grievous errors also might be introduced by deviations of wages from aggregate marginal productivities.

Let us consider the consequences for computed values of r of a systematic deviation of wages from $\partial Y/\partial L$. Given the leadership's emphasis on additions to the physical capital stock, few Western analysts would doubt strongly that there may have been a tendency for Soviet labor's earnings to fall short of $\partial Y/\partial L$.[7] It would appear, however, with no firm foundation in facts about the 'true' $\partial Y/\partial L$, to be little more than a collective hunch.[8] Let us suppose that factors making for deviation, say understatement for ease in exposition and for consistency with our collective hunch, operate systematically through time so that a proportional understatement, $\widehat{\partial Y/\partial L} = k\,\partial Y/\partial L$, of w occurs throughout. If the assumed $\partial Y/\partial K$ amounts to the 'true' value for 1937, the corresponding value for Y will understate the 'true' Y by a proportion, say k', less than k. If the index of value added remained 'true', estimated values for G would understate 'reality' by a factor k'. Thus computed values for r would in no year be understated by as much as k.

If we were concerned with generating a series for r that would permit a 'true' relative factor productivity *ratio*, as we well might be, our objective in selecting r in 1937 would be to find the value understating it in the same proportion as $\partial Y/\partial L$ is understated by labor earnings. Given a value for Y in 1937 generated in this fashion, the 'true' index for Y, and wages systematically equal to $k\,\partial Y/\partial L$, our computed values for r would equal $k\,\partial Y/\partial K$, and the ratio, r/w, obtained in part from the accounts would amount to the 'true' $(\partial Y/\partial K)/(\partial Y/\partial L)$.

Of course, in the present state of our knowledge of the Soviet economy we can scarcely rule out other possible patterns of error. Clearly any user of the alternative series on r will do well to refrain from stating conclusions with especially great conviction. These series do, however, constitute one implication of a meticulously prepared body of data on output, capital stock, labor inputs, and wages. One might speculate, therefore, that the computed patterns are affected in some ways by the underlying 'true' variables. While remaining particularly wary of results based on the patterns of variation in r presented above, we can scarcely refrain entirely from attempting to shed any available empirical light on this strategic variable and to explore and test its possible meaning.

Suppose, for example, we were to use the available historical record on the Soviet nonagricultural nonresidential sector including the time series generated on r for purposes of testing the hypotheses about neutrality as elaborated in the first section of this paper. In view of the discussion immediately preceding we may wish to view what would nominally be regarded as tests of the hypotheses on neutrality as tests also of the meaningfulness of the data on r. That is, if the data on r are merely random numbers, tests of neutrality presumably would tend to give meaningless results. If, on the other hand, data on r reflect somehow the 'true' values, we would have some opportunity to make useful tests, however imperfect. The matter is complicated, of course, by the fact that even if the data measured reliably the underlying values for the conceptual variables, including r, the hypotheses themselves may not approximate the underlying 'reality' very closely.

THE TESTS

In any event then it may be of interest to compare the results of regressions using the Soviet data with what we might regard as standards set by the work of Professors Martin Beckmann and Ryuzo Sato (1969) who used similar data drawn from national accounting records of three major market economies, Germany, Japan, and the United States.

In examining the results of such a statistical analysis what pattern would we expect to see if the 'true' production function was 'well behaved', and if neutrality appeared only in a compatible sense? First we would expect *all* the b_i coefficients to be statistically significant and have the 'correct' sign. Secondly we would expect all c_i coefficients to be statistically significant (sign being of no special consequence) except, possibly, for compatible combinations. c_i coefficients not significantly different from zero in a pair of incompatible specifications for neutral technical progress would tend to raise doubts about the reliability of the data, about the specification of the model, or about the statistical estimating procedure.

With these expectations in mind let us set up our standard by considering the results of the statistical analyses pertaining to the market economies, the salient features of which are summarized in table 6. Inspection of table 6 reveals that with regard to Germany, Japan, and the United States the proposed test tends to cast considerable doubt on the 'good behavior' of the production function. About 40 % of the b_i coefficients either are not significantly different from zero or have signs different from those implied by good behavior. Nevertheless, there appears at least some tendency towards consistency with expectations since approximately 60 % of the b_i coefficients are statistically significant and have the predicted sign.

From the point of view of compatibility of apparent single neutralities

Table 6. *Summary interpretation of regression results with linear specification of single neutralities[a]*

Type of neutrality	'Good behavior'				Neutrality			
	Soviet Union	United States	Japan	Germany	Soviet Union	United States	Japan	Germany
1	$+$	$+$	$+$	$+$	N^{b}	N^{bc}	N^{bc}	B
2	$-^{b}$	$+$	$+$	$+$	B	N^{bc}	B	N^{bc}
3	$+$	$+$	$+$	$+$	N^{b}	B	B	B
4	$-$	$-$	$-$	$-$	B	B	B	B
5	$+^{b}$	$-^{bc}$	$-$		N^{bc}	N^{b}	B	B
6	$-$	$+$	$+$	$+$	B	B	B	B
7	$+$	$-^{b}$	$+$	$+$	N^{bc}	N^{bc}	B	B
8	$+^{b}$	$-^{bc}$	$-^{bc}$	$-$	N^{bc}	B	B	B
9	$+^{b}$	$+$	$+$	$-$	N^{bc}	B	N^{bc}	B

[a] Based on data in Beckmann and Sato (1969, pp. 96–100) and, for the Soviet Union, on data from the period 1932–66 with r assumed equal to 0.20 in 1937 as described in appendix B. Plus and minus signs indicate, respectively, b_i coefficients consistent with and inconsistent with anticipated directions of relationships. N and B stand for 'neutral' and 'biased' based on the statistical significance of the c_i coefficients. The superscripts b and c refer to statistical insignificance at the 1 % and 5 % levels respectively.

the results suggest the importance of simultaneously considering the several hypotheses. With respect to the US the data are consistent not only with Hicks and Harrod neutrality, a compatible pair, but also with capital-combining and with capital-decreasing neutralities, an incompatible combination of single types neither of which is consistent with the Hicks or Harrod variety. The data for Japan suggest only one pair of single neutralities, but they too appear on theoretical grounds to be incompatible. Only in the case of Germany do no inconsistent pairs appear.

Inspection of the data pertaining to the USSR, also appearing in table 6, reveals that with respect to the b_i coefficients the impression of the degree of consistency with our theoretical expectations is roughly similar to that in the West. The apparent tendency toward greater frequency of doubtful statistical significance of the coefficients disappears when only a slightly less stringent test is permitted. That is, in three of the four cases where doubt is raised, the coefficients are very close to being statistically significant at the 1 % level. In the fourth case, a plus sign, the coefficient is significant at about the 4 % level. With this in mind it appears that the degree of consistency is approximately the same as that for Japan, the market-oriented country whose data produced the set of coefficients perhaps most nearly consistent with expectations.

The Soviet data perform relatively poorly, however, with respect to generating incompatible neutralities. The indicated Hicks neutrality is not compatible with the four nontraditional varieties suggested. The Solow variety is not compatible with three of these same four. Capital-combining is compatible with no other, and so on. In this respect the interpretation of the Soviet results is somewhat more difficult than for those pertaining to the market-oriented economies, especially Germany, whose data generate no incompatibilities at all.

It seems important to note that similar conclusions seem appropriate no matter which of several experiments is tried. That is, the results presented here for the USSR were obtained by using data from the period 1932–66 generated under the assumption that the rate of return was 20 % in 1937 and by making simple linear specifications of the neutralities. Several experiments were tried using various combinations of data from the periods 1932–66 and 1950–66 with the assumptions that the rate of return was either 8 % or 20 % in 1937.[9]

In conclusion, an important test of the meaningfulness of the data would appear to be the consistency with expected signs of the b_i coefficients, and in this respect the Soviet data, including that on the rate of return, seems to perform as well as or better than that pertaining to the more heavily market-oriented economies. With respect to the character of the shift in the production function, one might tend toward the conclusion that the historical record is consistent with a number of hypotheses about neutrality of 'technical progress'.[10] An overall view, however, taking account of the logical incompatibility of many pairs of hypotheses seems to suggest the need for greater caution and further testing.

APPENDIX A: DESCRIPTION OF DATA AND SOURCES

Data used in the computation with $r = 0.20$ in 1937 are presented in table A1, and explanations of each series are presented in order of appearance therein.

The statistics on *value added* for 1937 (151.0 billion rubles with $r = 0.08$ and 201.8 billion rubles with $r = 0.20$) from Moorsteen and Powell (1966, p. 371) are extended forward and backward by an index obtained from data in Moorsteen and Powell (1966, pp. 361–2) and in Becker, Moorsteen and Powell (1938, p. 25). The value added for 1937 with an assumed $r = 0.15$ computed according to the same procedure amounts to 176.9 billion rubles.

Labor earnings are the product of estimated average annual real wages and man-years worked. Data on man-years worked are from Moorsteen and Powell (1966, p. 365) and Becker *et al.* (1968, p. 26). The basic procedure employed to obtain annual data on real wages is to apply an index based on Chapman's (1963) benchmarks along with inter-polations and extrapolations from data in Jasny (1961) and various official sources to the value implied by data for 1937 in Moorsteen and Powell (1966, pp. 256, 365).

Table A1. *Computation of rates of return*[a] ($r = 0.20$ in 1937)

Year	Value added	Labor earnings	Capital charges	Depreciation	Net remuneration to capital	Net capital stock	Net rate of return (%)
1932	125.20	83.8	41.4	3.1	37.8	192.3	19.6
1933	127.86	80.6	47.3	4.8	42.5	209.7	20.3
1934	142.79	84.8	58.0	5.5	52.5	232.1	22.6
1935	163.22	90.8	72.4	6.1	66.3	266.0	24.9
1936	190.96	107.2	83.8	7.2	76.6	307.0	25.0
1937	201.80	123.9	77.9	8.6	69.3	346.5	20.0
1938	213.50	142.1	71.4	9.8	61.6	386.2	16.0
1939	231.26	142.1	89.2	11.0	78.2	434.4	18.0
1940	243.98	145.9	98.1	13.4	84.7	486.4	17.4
1945	205.63	74.2	131.4	13.1	118.3	427.6	27.7
1948	241.96	110.0	132.0	16.1	115.9	510.2	22.7
1950	315.21	173.9	141.3	19.4	121.9	614.7	19.8
1951	351.33	202.1	149.2	21.1	128.1	679.8	18.8
1952	378.17	226.2	152.0	23.8	128.2	752.9	17.0
1953	405.21	262.2	143.0	26.0	117.0	824.3	14.2
1954	442.95	289.6	153.4	28.2	125.2	891.0	14.0
1955	481.29	297.7	183.6	31.1	152.5	964.7	15.8
1956	519.64	317.2	202.4	34.6	167.8	1,069.4	15.7
1957	561.00	337.2	223.8	39.4	184.4	1,190.3	15.5
1958	606.79	378.1	228.7	44.4	184.3	1,327.4	13.9
1959	653.83	402.9	250.9	51.2	199.7	1,490.2	13.4
1960	699.74	434.6	265.1	58.1	207.0	1,652.0	12.5
1961	748.62	472.3	276.3	66.0	210.3	1,813.5	11.6
1962	800.58	494.0	306.6	74.5	232.1	1,984.0	11.7
1963	849.15	507.9	341.3	83.2	258.1	2,167.8	11.9
1964	901.96	534.3	367.7	92.8	274.9	2,376.0	11.6
1965	965.05	601.2	263.8	102.7	261.1	2,584.1	10.1
1966	1,026.01	640.7	385.3	112.4	272.9	2,801.4	9.7

[a] Billions of adjusted (see text) 1937 rubles unless otherwise noted.

A comparison of Chapman's index with the implications of official data for 1952–4 suggests reasonably similar movements. Chapman's benchmarks are available for 1928, 1937, 1940, 1948, and 1952 (1963, p. 153). Estimates of variation in real wages are available as follows: 1932–6 (Jasny, 1961, pp. 172); 1938–9 (Jasny, 1961, pp. 225–6); and 1945 (Jasny, 1961, p. 417). Implications of official data for real wages are derived by deflating money wages with a weighted average of prices in state retail establishments with prices in collective farm markets.

Data on money wages for 1957–66 refer to the series on all non-agricultural workers in US Congress (1968, p. 67). An approximate extension for 1950–6 is obtained by moving this series backward with an index of money wages in the entire economy. A comparison of a similar forward extension for 1957–66 with the officially reported data for these years increases somewhat the author's confidence in the procedure.

The Soviet official index of state retail prices was obtained from the following sources: 1950–55 (TsSU, 1956, p. 131); 1956–7 (TsSU, 1962a, p. 771); 1958, 1964 (TsSU,

Table A2. *Man-hour inputs, wages, and capital stock adjusted for hours*

Year	Labor input[a] (billion man-hours)	Wages[b] (1937 rubles per man-hour)	Adjusted net[c] capital stock (billion rubles)
1932	48.77	1.72	193.03
1933	48.32	1.67	213.81
1934	50.79	1.67	236.42
1935	54.39	1.67	271.08
1936	55.58	1.93	308.50
1937	58.31	2.12	346.50
1938	62.50	2.27	386.20
1939	66.87	2.12	435.01
1940	81.10	1.80	508.87
1945	101.11	0.73	479.98
1948	89.51	1.23	555.86
1950	101.86	1.71	669.22
1951	107.15	1.89	739.21
1952	112.00	2.02	817.72
1953	114.20	2.30	896.67
1954	117.73	2.46	965.49
1955	118.90	2.51	1,045.54
1956	119.91	2.65	1,156.45
1957	120.03	2.81	1,278.02
1958	120.45	3.14	1,402.26
1959	119.25	3.38	1,542.95
1960	117.46	3.70	1,667.53
1961	120.80	3.91	1,814.77
1962	125.36	3.94	1,984.00
1963	129.74	3.91	2,180.16
1964	133.61	4.00	2,387.40
1965	139.13	4.32	2,595.99
1966	143.18	4.47	2,815.69

[a] Computed from data in Becker *et al.* (1968, p. 26) and Moorsteen and Powell (1966, p. 365).

[b] May be viewed, essentially, as computed from data on man-hour inputs presented in this table and from data on labor earnings presented in table A1.

[c] Sources are the same as in table A1 except for utilization adjustment (one-half the percentage deviation from 1937 hours implied in the Moorsteen–Powell 'prevailing man-year' and '1937 man-year' series; see Becker *et al.* (1968, p. 26) and Moorsteen and Powell (1966, p. 365)).

1967, p. 652); 1959–61 (TsSU, 1962b, p. 654); 1962 (TsSU, 1963, p. 532); 1963 (TsSU, 1964a, p. 539); 1965–6 (TsSU, 1968, p. 739).

The index of collective farm market prices was pieced together from the following sources: 1950–4 (TsSU, 1956, p. 182); 1955–7 (TsSU, 1962a, p. 789); 1958–63 (TsSU, 1964b, p. 266); 1964 (TsSU, 1966, p. 667); 1965–6 (TsSU, 1968, p. 763). The data for 1964–6 depend on the results of a 251-city sample, which sometimes moves quite differently from the index reflecting complete extra-village coverage. In any event, however, the weight accorded collective farm market prices in the overall index is quite small for the later years.

To obtain an overall index of retail prices a value-weighted average was computed. The shares in retail trade were obtained from the following sources: 1950, 1952–3, 1955–63 (TsSU, 1964b, p. 39); 1951, 1954, (TsSU, 1956, p. 19); 1946 (TsSU, 1966, p. 630); 1965–6 (TsSU, 1967, p. 251).

Capital charges were computed as the difference between gross product and labor earnings.

Depreciation was obtained as the difference between gross and net products (Moorsteen and Powell, 1966, pp. 261–2) and adjusted according to assumed values for *r* as described in the text.

Net remuneration to capital is the difference between capital charges and depreciation.

Data refer to *net* (straight-line depreciation) *capital stock* (Moorsteen and Powell, 1966, p. 348; Becker *et al.*, 1968, p. 20) adjusted: (1) to mid-year values (arithmetic means of year-end values), (2) for revaluations corresponding to assumed rates of return (see text), and (3) for hours worked (one-half the percentage deviation from 1937 hours implied in the Moorsteen–Powell alternative labor input series (1966, p. 365)).

The *net rate of return* is computed as the ratio of net remuneration to net capital stock.

APPENDIX B

Table B1. *USSR: Results of regressions with linear specifications of neutralities* [a]

Type of neutrality	a	b	c	R^2
1	− 0.35412	2.1645	0.0083296	
	(0.18519)	(0.75398)	(0.0045833)	0.5160
2	0.48547	− 0.37221	− 0.0071877	
	(0.096191)	(0.15120)	(0.0013105)	0.7576
3	− 0.29930	0.75045	− 0.01781	
	(0.09712)	(0.04608)	(0.007144)	0.9772
4	− 6.36430	11.34383	0.18249	
	(1.57352)	(2.47346)	(0.02144)	0.8560
5	0.27574	− 0.017353	− 0.0016741	
	(0.014919)	(0.0070788)	(0.0011434)	0.7572
6	1.00186	− 1.31002	− 0.01500	
	(0.16448)	(0.25855)	(0.00224)	0.6825
7	− 14.57097	7.95438	− 0.07519	0.9522
	(1.64417)	(0.78008)	(0.12600)	
8	4.9190	− 16.862	− 0.0083605	
	(1.7621)	(7.1745)	(0.043613)	0.7829
9	0.25255	− 0.0049987	− 0.0018324	
	(0.011248)	(0.0027813)	(0.0014162)	0.7333

[a] Data analyzed pertain to 1932–66 and reflect an assumed value of twenty percent for the rate of return in 1937.

Technical progress in the Soviet economy

NOTES

1 Note that we assume returns to scale are constant.
2 For convenience in exposition marginal productivities will be taken as equal to rates of factor remuneration. For a thorough and rigorous examination of relationships between factor prices and marginal productivities when inefficiency exists, see Bergson (1969).
3 See Thornton (1965) for an important analysis of nominal rates of return in Soviet industry.
4 This argument follows that presented in Moorsteen and Powell (1966, pp. 256–7).
5 This analysis ignores material inputs. A computation by Professor Raymond Powell (1963, p. 169) suggests that materials inputs and their prices were of considerable consequence for Soviet industry. Their share in total inputs amounted to something on the order of 35–40%, 25%, and 15% in 1928, 1937, and 1950 respectively. Presumably the impact of material inputs in the entire nonagricultural and nonresidential sector could scarcely be entirely inconsequential.
6 Relatively free operation of the labor market on the supply side and substantial room for maneuver by enterprise managers on the demand side may be cited as evidence of a tendency toward proportionality between average earnings of labor and marginal productivities among industries, occupations, and regions. Thus we may conclude that 'the principles of relative wages in the Soviet Union are also capitalist principles' (Bergson, 1944, p. 208). But clearly such proportionality would not ensure the quality that would be so useful for interpreting Soviet growth and especially the data on *r* as computed in this paper.
7 See Professor Robert W. Campbell, *Accounting in Soviet Planning and Management* (1963, pp. 31ff), for an elaboration of the proposition that 'The absolute level of wages, on the other hand, appears at first glance to be above the actual worth of labor.' The qualification, 'at first glance', is important, for Campbell goes on to explain how the fiscal system may operate to reverse the substance of this statement.
8 In fact one of the most sophisticated currently available attempts to estimate econometrically parameters for the Soviet production function suggests quite the reverse (Weitzman, 1960).
9 In a similar vein, the pattern of results pertaining to the market-oriented economies is little affected by specification of neutralities via log linear functions.
10 See Beckmann and Sato (1969) for an example of this conclusion with respect to the historical record on Germany, Japan, and the United States.

REFERENCES

Allen, R. G. D. (1968). *Macro-Economic Theory*. New York.
Becker, A. S., R. Moorsteen and R. P. Powell (1968). *Two Supplements to the Soviet Capital Stock, 1928–1942*. New Haven.
Beckmann, M. J. and R. Sato (1968). Neutral inventions and production functions. *Review of Economic Studies*, 35, 57–67.
Beckmann, M. J. and R. Sato (1969). *Two Supplements to the Soviet Capital Stock, 1928–62*. New Haven.
Bergson, A. (1944). *The Structure of Soviet Wages*. Cambridge, Mass.
Bergson, A. (1969). Comparative productivity and efficiency in the USSR. Mimeographed.
Brubaker, E. R. (1970). Aggregate production functions and types of technical progress: comment. Mimeographed.

Earl Brubaker

Campbell, R. W. (1963). *Accounting in Soviet Planning and Management.* Cambridge, Mass.

Chapman, J. G. (1963). *Real Wages in Soviet Russia Since 1928.* Cambridge, Mass.

Jasny, N. (1961). *Soviet Industrialization 1928–1952.* Chicago.

Moorsteen, R. and R. P. Powell (1966). *The Soviet Capital Stock, 1928–1962.* Homewood, Ill.

Powell, R. P. (1963). Industrial production. In *Economic Trends in the Soviet Union,* ed. A. Bergson and S. Kuznets. Cambridge, Mass.

Thornton, J. (1965). Estimation of value added and average returns to capital in Soviet industry from cross-section data. *Journal of Political Economy,* **73,** 620–35.

TsSU (1956). *Sovetskaia torgovlia.* Moscow.

TsSU (1962a). *Narodne khoziastvo v 1958 godu.* Moscow.

TsSU (1962b). *Narodne khoziastvo SSSR v 1961 godu.* Moscow.

TsSU (1963). *Narodne khoziastvo SSSR v 1962 godu.* Moscow.

TsSU (1964a). *Narodne khoziastvo SSSR v 1963 godu.* Moscow.

TsSU (1964b). *Sovetskaia torgovlia.* Moscow.

TsSU (1966). *Narodne khoziastvo SSSR v 1965 godu.* Moscow.

TsSU (1967). *Strana sovetov za 50 let.* Moscow.

TsSU (1968). *Narodne khoziastvo SSR v 1967 godu.* Moscow.

US Congress Joint Economic Committee (1968). *Soviet Economic Performance: 1966–67.* Washington.

Weitzman, M. L. (1960). Soviet postwar economic growth and capital–labor substitution. *American Economic Review,* **60,** 676–92.

Estimation of a cost function in the state of structural disequilibrium: the case of Soviet manufacturing industry, 1960–69

YASUSHI TODA[1]

INTRODUCTION

The major purpose of this paper is to study the effect of a structural disequilibrium on the estimation of the shares of factor incomes and the efficiency of an industry. By structural disequilibrium, we mean the situation in which factor prices fail to reflect the marginal productivities; in other words, the fact mix (the capital–labor ratio) is not an optimal one that reduces the production cost to a minimum.[2]

The next section discusses the environment in which the Soviet-type planning generates the structural disequilibrium. For our estimation purpose, the third section sets up a model which takes this phenomenon into account. The fourth section presents the results of our estimation. In the last section, our major findings are summarized.

GENERAL FRAMEWORK

We start with the general description of a system which will be the basis for a specific model to be estimated in the latter part.[3]

The level of output

The central organ such as the Gosplan assigns the output level annually to each industry. An individual industry, in turn, accepts this output level as given. Although the level is probably not an optimal one, that is outside the concern of individual industries. It is important and also rewarding for officials in charge of an industry to fulfill the assigned output target even at the sacrifice of the cost and the qualities of a product.

Quantities of factors of production

Generally, the output target is set at a high level, while the resources are in short supply. Although the raw materials and the equipment are not literally rationed, their availability to an industry is limited. The industry tends to purchase the unnecessarily large quantities of raw materials and equipment, whenever they are available, and to hoard them. The input point is often located in 'north-east' to the isoquant which corresponds to the assigned output. The industry may then be said to be technically inefficient.

Furthermore, even if the input point lies right on the isoquant, the industry may nevertheless be inefficient. Suppose it is unconcerned with the costs and uses a scarce factor to such an extent that the marginal productivity of that factor falls below its price. The industry uses the scarce factor wastefully and thus may be considered to lack the price efficiency.[4] Under these circumstances the production cost is not at minimum.

The price inefficiency may be due to the rigidity built in the Soviet-type economy. First is the rigidity of input prices. The prices are set by the central organ and remain at the same levels for years. Although the effort to achieve an ambitious output target often generates an excess demand for materials, an increase in prices does not ensue. Secondly, the input allocation also lacks flexibility. Suppose the price of one input is low (compared with its shadow price) and the price of another input is high (compared with its shadow price). Suppose further that the officials in charge of an industry know this, want to reduce a use of the high-priced input and realize that they will fail to achieve the output target unless this reduction is balanced by an increasing use of the low-priced input. But it is not the Soviet practice to obtain more allotment of the low-priced input while declining the allotment of the high-priced input.

Factor pricing

The central organ does not consider the rate of profit as a yard-stick in determining the allocation of investment funds. It is merely one of the means with which the central authorities control individual producing units. The principle of 'economic calculation' requires enterprises not to run in deficit, but to raise a normal profit. Thus the profit is looked upon as a rough indicator for the resource saving. But the primary concern for a gross output, the rigidity in prices and the limited availability of raw materials and equipment prevent the Soviet industry from pursuing the cost saving thoroughly to the effect that the capital service is priced according to the marginal productivity.

One of the characteristics of the Soviet price structure as compared with the structure of other countries is that the prices are high for consumer goods and low for producer goods. Since the prices affect little the quantities of products sold, the peculiar price structure contributes to the fact that a higher rate of profit accrues from the consumer good production than from the producer good production. As a result, the revenue of the State budget is derived to a considerable extent from the profits of the consumer good industries. For the purpose of raising the State revenue, it does not matter which industry contributes more. In the centralized planning scheme, it may be even convenient to rely on the consumer good industries, because a change in the State revenue will then be achieved by a variation in the consumer good prices without further changes in the prices of goods in 'earlier stages' of production. But this practice sets loose a link between the marginal productivity and the recorded rate of return to capital of individual industries.

Let us turn to wages. The Soviet authorities set up an elaborate scale of wages for the whole industry according to the workers' skills, the risks, the work intensities, and so on (Kirsch, 1972). One gains the impression that the wage rates reflect the productivities of workers fairly well. Once the wage rates are set, however, they remain fixed for years, despite the fact that the production technology and the workers' qualities are always changing. This time-lag may create the gap between the wage rate and the labour productivity.

With the ambitious output target and the scanty supply of raw materials and equipment, it is often difficult to find enough workers to achieve the output quota. The difficulty continues as long as the going wage rate is offered. Then the interpretation of the official wage scale which links the wage rate to the skill level becomes less strict. A worker may be offered the wage rate which is officially for those workers whose skills are one step above. This expediency, however, may widen the gap between the wage and the productivity.

Product price

As said earlier, the central organ uses the profit norm as an instrument to prevent the industries from wasting the assigned resources. Further, a part of profits retained within industry is spent for bonuses and other payments for workers' welfare. In addition to its role as a control device, the profits thus also serve as an incentive to work.

However, due to the limited substitutability between assigned inputs as discussed before, the changes in wage rates and prices of raw materials directly affect the cost. Therefore, although the profit margin is to some extent a result of the effort of an industry to save the cost, the margin also varies with the changes in wage rates and prices of raw materials.

The effect of a change in price to the quantity is also limited on the product side, because the quantity of a product is to a large extent predetermined in the plan. Thus the central organ can affect the amount of profits through the change in product price. In fact, the central organ occasionally finds it necessary to raise the product price of an industry

whose profit margin has been narrowed, not due to the fall in productivity, but due to the increase in wage rates and raw material prices.

In the next section, we hypothesize this relation by assuming a direct
correspondence between the ratio of the observed product price to the
shadow product price and the ratio of the observed wage rate to the
shadow wage rate. Suppose the wage rate is raised to attract workers.
The wage rate may then be set above the marginal productivity. If the
product price remains at the same level, the profit rate may well fall
below the marginal productivity of capital. This may lead to the situation
where the quality of a product deteriorates and thus the price rises
informally. Or alternatively, the Gosplan may finally approve the
increase in official price, as the industry presses a change in the product
price.

A MODEL FOR ESTIMATION

We use the following notations:

R is the rate of return to capital as a shadow price
R_a is the rate of return to capital as actually observed
W is the wage rate as a shadow price
W_a is the wage rate as actually observed
π is the price of a capital good
K is the quantity of capital good
L is the quantity of labour
Y is the net output
C is the average cost measured in shadow prices
C_a is the observed average cost
P is the observed price of a product
$\omega = \pi R/W$ is the ratio of shadow factor prices
$r = \pi R_a/W_a$ is the ratio of observed factor prices
$p = P/W_a$ is the ratio of the observed price to the observed wage rate
$\beta = \pi RK/CY$ is the share of profits in the factor cost measured in shadow prices
$\theta = \pi R_a K/C_a Y$ is the observed share of profits in the factor cost
t is time (the calendar year).

We assume that as the wage diverges from the labour productivity,
the price of a product will also diverge from the cost at equal pace. That
is to say,

$$W_a/W = \exp(\eta + \sigma t + \sigma' t^2) P/C, \tag{1}$$

where η, σ and σ' are constant.

Secondly, the observed factor prices may differ from the marginal
productivities. It is assumed that the ratio of shadow factor prices and

the ratio of observed factor prices are related as

$$\omega = \exp{(\gamma + \lambda t + \lambda' t^2)}\, r^\delta, \tag{2}$$

where γ, λ, λ', and δ are constant.

In the third place, we define the total cost as the aggregate of the capital cost and the labour cost. The capital cost is the product of the quantity of capital stock, the price of a capital stock and the rate of return to capital. The wage cost is the product of the number of workers and the wage rate. We thus define the total cost in shadow prices as

$$CY = R\pi K + WL. \tag{3}$$

By assuming that the total cost is minimized with factor prices and an output level as given, we obtain a cost function. Specifically, we choose a Cobb–Douglas form:

$$C = \exp{(\alpha - \rho t - \rho' t^2)}\,(R\pi)^\beta\, W^{1-\beta} Y^{-\mu}. \tag{4}$$

This function has a well-known property that the elasticities represent the shares of profits and wages,

$$\beta = R\pi K/CY \quad \text{and} \quad 1 - \beta = WL/CY. \tag{5}$$

Hence, the parameter β should be within the range

$$0 < \beta < 1. \tag{6}$$

The parameter μ, on the other hand, represents the returns to scale effect; the positive μ implies increasing returns, whereas the negative μ implies decreasing returns. However, in order for the marginal cost to be positive, the range for μ must be such as[5]

$$\mu < 1. \tag{7}$$

In order to estimate the cost function, we divide both sides of (4) by W and obtain $C/W = \exp{(\alpha - \rho t - \rho' t^2)}\,\omega^\beta Y^{-\mu}$. From (1), we find

$$C/W = \exp{(\eta + \sigma t + \sigma' t^2)}\, p.$$

From these two equations and (2), we eliminate C/W and ω, and obtain

$$p = \exp{[(\alpha - \eta + \beta\gamma) + (\beta\lambda - \rho - \sigma)\, t + (\beta\lambda' - \rho' - \sigma')\, t^2]}\, r^{\beta\delta} Y^{-\mu}. \tag{8}$$

From (5), the profit share in shadow prices is shown as $\beta = \omega K/(YC/W)$. With ω and C/W in the right-hand side substituted by (1) and (2), we derive

$$\beta = \exp{[\gamma - \eta + (\lambda - \sigma)\, t + (\lambda' - \sigma')\, t^2]}\, r^\delta K/(YP/W).$$

Hence, the capital–output ratio equals

$$K/Y = \beta \exp{[\eta - \sigma + (\sigma - \lambda)\, t + (\sigma' - \lambda')\, t^2]}\, r^{-\delta} p.$$

By substituting (8) into $p = P/W_a$ in the above equation, we obtain

$$K/Y = \beta \exp{\{\alpha - \gamma(1 - \beta) - [\rho + (1 - \beta)\, \lambda]\, t}$$
$$- [\rho' + (1 - \beta)\, \lambda']\, t^2\}\, r^{(\beta - 1)\delta}\, Y^{-\mu}. \tag{9}$$

Finally, we express (8) and (9) in a log-linear form and combine them. Then we have

$$\begin{pmatrix} \ln p \\ \ln (K/Y) \end{pmatrix} = a_1 \begin{pmatrix} 1 \\ 0 \end{pmatrix} + a_2 \begin{pmatrix} 0 \\ 1 \end{pmatrix} + a_3 \begin{pmatrix} t \\ 0 \end{pmatrix} + a_4 \begin{pmatrix} 0 \\ t \end{pmatrix} + a_5 \begin{pmatrix} t^2 \\ 0 \end{pmatrix} + a_6 \begin{pmatrix} 0 \\ t^2 \end{pmatrix}$$

$$+ a_7 \ln r \begin{pmatrix} 1 \\ 1 \end{pmatrix} + a_8 \ln r \begin{pmatrix} 0 \\ 1 \end{pmatrix} + a_9 \ln Y \begin{pmatrix} 1 \\ 1 \end{pmatrix} + \begin{pmatrix} u_1 \\ u_2 \end{pmatrix}, \qquad (10)$$

where

$$\left. \begin{aligned} a_3 &= \beta\lambda - \rho - \sigma \\ a_4 &= -\rho - (1-\beta)\,\lambda \\ a_5 &= \beta\lambda' - \rho' - \sigma' \\ a_6 &= -\rho' - (1-\beta)\,\lambda' \\ a_7 &= \beta\delta \\ a_8 &= -\delta \end{aligned} \right\} \qquad (11)$$

and

$$a_9 = -\mu.$$

In addition, u_1 and u_2 represent the random terms; a_1 and a_2 the intercepts.

The first objective of our estimation is to obtain the rate of technical change. The rate of technical change may be defined either as the rate of upward shift of a production function or as the rate of downward shift of a cost function. The two movements are different only by the degree of returns to scale.[6] From (4), the rate of a downward shift of the cost function is

$$- (\partial C/\partial t)/C = \rho + 2\rho't. \qquad (12)$$

Suppose, however, one assumes that the observed factor prices represent the values of marginal products and the observed commodity price equals the cost of production measured in shadow prices. Then one erroneously considers that the rate of technical change is estimated by the shift in equation (8),

$$- (\partial p/\partial t)/p = \rho + \sigma - \beta\lambda + 2(\rho' + \sigma' - \beta\lambda')\,t$$
$$= -a_3 - 2a_5 t. \qquad (13)$$

We further simplify the model and assume that the coefficients σ and σ' in (1) are both zero. With this simplification, ρ and ρ' can be identified as

$$\left. \begin{aligned} \rho &= -a_3(a_3 - a_4)\,a_7/a_8 \\ \rho' &= -a_5 - (a_5 - a_6)\,a_7/a_8 \end{aligned} \right\} \qquad (14)$$

and

with $\sigma = \sigma' = 0$.

Our second objective is to estimate the degree of price efficiency of an industry. First of all, we have to assume that the industry is technically efficient. Under this assumption, we propose the following method for estimating the price efficiency. The observed data may be interpreted as showing that an industry chooses the observed input-mix (K and L)

that entails the unit cost C_a under the given factor prices in order to attain the observed output. But these factor prices may be different from the marginal productivities at that factor-mix. Then the industry may choose another input-mix, say K_* and L_*, that entails the minimum cost C_* under the same factor prices and is still able to produce the observed output.

Let us compare the minimum cost C_* with the observed cost C_a. We may estimate the degree of price efficiency with the ratio C_*/C_a. In the Cobb–Douglas form, it turns out that this ratio is expressed in factor shares,

$$\frac{C_*}{C_a} = \left(\frac{\theta}{\beta}\right)^{\beta} \left(\frac{1-\theta}{1-\beta}\right)^{1-\beta},\tag{15}$$

where θ represents the observed profit share, and β the profit share at the optimal mix.[7] We estimate β from a_7 and a_8, because $\beta = -a_7/a_8$ in (11). If the observed share happens to be an optimal one, the cost ratio will equal unity. The more widely the observed share diverges from the optimal share, the lower will be the cost ratio. Indeed it can be shown that the cost ratio is maximal at $\theta = \beta$.[8]

RESULTS OF ESTIMATION

As shown in equation (10) in the preceding section, we estimate the cost function (8) and the demand for capital function (10) jointly. The estimations are made for seven industries and the results are presented in appendix B.

In regard to the factor shares, the rate of technical change and the degree of price efficiency, we also present the estimations for three aggregate sectors: the producer good industries, the consumer good industries and all the industries. They are the weighted means of seven individual estimations. The share of each industry in the total factor cost is used as a weight.

Before presenting the results of our estimation, an explanation of some statistical problems we encounter is in order. Suppose we estimate (10) by the ordinary least square. Although the two random terms should be unrelated in order for the estimation to be efficient, it is hardly likely that u_1 and u_2 are not correlated. We rely on the generalized least square (GLSQ) in order to eliminate this correlation (Zellner, 1962).

When a fairly high degree of autocorrelation is suspected, we follow a common procedure of Cochrane and Orcutt; the first-order auto-regressive scheme is assumed and the observations are transformed accordingly. This adjustment is made for the food industry.

The coefficient representing the returns to scale effect is subject to the restriction (7). The GLSQ estimation violates this condition for two industries (1, the electric power industry, and 7, the food industry, as seen in appendix B). In such time series data as we now have, it is extremely difficult to distinguish the economies of scale effect from the technical progress. Those two estimations are the extreme cases where the economies of scale overshoot and the marginal cost becomes a negative figure. In order to put back the estimate of μ in the permissible range, we rely on a prior information on μ and use the method of mixed estimation (Theil and Goldberger, 1960). The results of our estimation show that μ is positive for all industries. From this evidence, it seems very unlikely that two industries are subject to decreasing returns to scale. Together with equation (7), this implies that μ lies between zero and unity. We assume further that the mean of μ is 0.5. With these assumed mean and variance as a prior information, an estimation in the two industries is made by the iterative GLSQ.

A test of the structural disequilibrium

The observed factor price ratio (r) will be different from the shadow factor price ratio (ω) if the coefficient δ in equation (2) differs from unity. This coefficient is estimated by a_8 (see equation (11)). We test the null hypothesis that $a_8 = -1$ to find whether δ is significantly different from unity or not. The t-test in appendix B shows that all a_8s are significantly different from -1. Hence, we may conclude that the observed factor price ratio differs from the shadow factor price ratio.

Shares of profits and wages

The profit share β and the wage share $1-\beta$ expressed in shadow prices are obtained from the estimates of a_7 and a_8. The estimated βs for seven industries are presented in the first column of table 1. The second column of this table presents the averages of the observed profit shares over ten years.

Comparing the two columns, one notices that for producer good industries the share of profits is higher if it is measured in shadow prices than in observed prices. The contrary is the case for consumer good industries. In calculating the shares in shadow prices, we are using the observed quantities of capital and labour. Our findings thus indicate that for producer good industries the rental–wage ratio is higher in terms of shadow prices than in terms of observed prices. (However, our findings say nothing about the absolute levels of the capital rental rate and the wage rate.)[9]

Rate of technical changes

We contrasted the actual rate of technical change in equation (12) with the apparent rate in equation (13). However, in the actual estimation,

Table 1. *Two estimations of the share of profits*
(in %, on average of 10 years)

	In shadow prices	In observed prices
1. Electric power	89.99	68.78
2. Ferrous metals	84.50	47.80
3. Machine building and metal working	57.58	36.45
4. Timber, pulp and paper	86.95	26.66
5. Construction materials	71.46	28.09
6. Light industry	40.36	45.68
7. Food industry	50.50	61.23
8. All the industries	61.04	42.53
9. Producer good industries	68.27	37.68
10. Consumer good industries	45.22	53.14

we add the economies of scale effect $\mu(dY/dt)/Y$ to equation (12) and equation (13) and estimate

$$- (\partial C/\partial t)/C + \mu(dY/dt)/Y = \rho + 2\rho't + \mu G_Y, \qquad (16)$$

and
$$- (\partial p/\partial t)/p + \mu(dY/dt)/Y = -a_3 - 2a_5 t + \mu G_Y. \qquad (17)$$

To calculate the average rate of growth of net output G_Y, we simply run the regression $\ln Y = \text{constant} + G_Y t$ and interpret the estimated G_Y as the rate of growth. The middle year in our observation, 1965, is considered as representing t in $2\rho't$ and $2a_5 t$.

We present the result in table 2. The first column shows the actual rate in equation (16) and the second column the apparent rate in equation

Table 2. *The combined effect of technical change and*
economies of scale (% per year)

	Actual rate	Apparent rate	Average rate of growth of net output
1. Electric power	0.003	0.85	(11.21)
2. Ferrous metals	− 1.77	1.09	(6.65)
3. Machine building and metal working	3.97	5.09	(12.07)
4. Timber, pulp and paper	1.18	2.94	(5.22)
5. Construction materials	0.90	5.15	(8.56)
6. Light industry	2.72	3.10	(7.60)
7. Food industry	0.39	0.96	(6.53)
8. All the Industries	2.13	3.43	(9.15)
9. Producer good industries	2.38	4.05	(10.09)
10. Consumer good industries	1.60	2.07	(7.09)

Table 3. *Estimation of price efficiency* (%)

1. Electric power	87.98
2. Ferrous metals	74.58
3. Machine building and metal working	91.22
4. Timber, pulp and paper	44.82
5. Construction materials	66.80
6. Light industry	99.42
7. Food industry	97.66
8. All the industries	86.85
9. Producer good industries	81.49
10. Consumer good industries	98.58

(17). All the figures in the first column are smaller than the corresponding figures in the second column. It implies that the estimation under the equilibrium assumption overstates the actual rate of technical change.

The degree of price efficiency

In table 3 we present the degree of price efficiency for seven industries according to the formula (15). Our estimation is based on the factor shares β and θ which are already estimated in table 1. The figures for the last three aggregate sectors are weighted means of the first seven figures.

The efficiency of each industry varies considerably, from 44 % of the timber, paper and pulp industry to 99 % of the light industry. In general, this static efficiency is higher for consumer good sectors than for producer good sectors.

One should be cautioned, however, as to the limitations of our estimation. First, we estimate the efficiency in terms of the observed factor prices. Ideally, one should measure it in the overall equilibrium prices. Secondly, the price efficiency constitutes only a part of the static efficiency. We ignore the technical efficiency. Furthermore, the inter-industrial resource misallocation is also disregarded. In the third place, the static efficiency has no direct connection with the shift over time of the production function and the cost function.

CONCLUSIONS

Our interest focuses on the possibility that the prices of factors of production diverge from the shadow prices. This direction of our interest may be justified, as we are dealing with a socialist economy that lacks an institutional mechanism whereby the investment resources are allocated among contending claimants.

Specifically, our analysis is based on three hypotheses. First, the observed factor price ratio differs from the shadow factor price ratio. Second, in correspondence to the observed wage rate being pushed up above the value of the marginal product of labour, the observed commodity price is also set above the shadow price. Third, the production technology is represented by a Cobb–Douglas function. We maintain the latter two hypotheses and test only the first one.

We find that the ratio of shadow factor prices differs from the ratio of observed factor prices and that this difference is statistically significant.

The divergence of observed factor prices from shadow factor prices affects the calculation of factor shares. For all the industries taken as a whole, the share of profits turn out to be 61 % when the shadow prices are used. This offers a contrast to the observed profit share of 42 %. The finding that the profit share is higher in terms of shadow prices than in terms of observed prices is valid for producer goods industries. However, the contrary is found for consumer goods industries.

If one is interested in the rate of technical change of an industry, one may be tempted to estimate the shift overtime of a cost function by assuming that the industry is in such a long-run equilibrium that the factor prices equal the marginal productivities and the commodity price equals the average cost. But this estimation may be spurious if a structural disequilibrium exists and the divergence of observed factor prices from shadow factor prices varies over time.

We calculate the rates of technical change by adjusting the effect of the changes in the structural disequilibrium. We find that for all industries the rates after these adjustments turn out to be smaller than the rates estimated under the equilibrium assumption.

The divergence of observed factor prices from shadow factor prices implies that the observed cost of production is not a minimal one under the going factor prices. The ratio of the two costs may be viewed as an indicator for the degree of inefficiency. We find that consumer good industries are almost 100 % efficient, while producer good industries are only 81 % efficient. As a result, all the industries on average turn out to be 86 % efficient.

APPENDIX A. THE SOVIET DATA

We compiled the annual data of the Soviet industry from 1960 to 1969. Most of manufacturing industries are covered. They consist of seven sectors: (1) electric power, (2) ferrous metals, (3) machine building and metal working, (4) timber, pulp and paper, (5) construction materials, (6) light industry, and (7) food industry. The former five belong to the producer good industry ('the A sector' in the Soviet terminology), and the latter two to the consumer good industry ('the B sector'). We rely almost exclusively on the published official data.

Output

We make an approximate estimation of the net output by adding two figures in the Soviet cost accounting: the wage bills and the enterprise profits after the depreciation and before the payments to the Budgets. The revenue from turnover taxes is not included in the enterprise profits. In order to obtain the 'quantity' of net output (the variable we denote as Y), the value of net output is deflated by P, the enterprise whole-sale price index excluding the turnover tax.

Capital

We rely on the official data on the 'basic fund' and the 'circulation fund' in estimating the fixed capital and the material working capital, respectively. In order to estimate the fixed capital, we start with the value of basic fund at the beginning of the base year, add the increase in fund and subtract the physical depreciation for that year in order to obtain the value of capital at the beginning of the following year. The same calculation is repeated until the end year. The material working capital at the beginning of each year is also calculated in a similar way. We denote the series of capital stock in constant (1960) prices as K, indicating the 'quantities' of capital stock.

Profits

The enterprise profits in the official data consist of two parts: the payment to the State Budget and the sum retained in an enterprise. The manager of an enterprise is entitled to use the retained profit for the investment in fixed and working capitals, the bonus payments and the welfare of enterprise personnel. (The investment is thus financed either from the retained profit or from the outside sources such as the Budget and the Gosbank.)

These are the profits as defined in the industrial cost accountings. It is another matter whether or not they exactly correspond to the profits as a factor cost that we are interested in. The payment to the Budget is naturally interpreted as a capital cost, since it is the part of products accruing to the State which owns means of production. Likewise, that part of retained profits appropriated for investments may also be included in the capital cost. In the period when most policy decisions are made at the centre, the bulk of investments is financed from the Budget. On the other hand, the share of internal investments increases, when the central authorities relax the control over enterprises. The amount paid to the Budget and the amount of internal investment, if taken separately, rise or fall, depending on the political climate that has little to do with the productivity of capital. It makes more sense to lump them together and regard the sum of the two as rewards to the capital service.

The bonus payment and other expenditures for stimulating workers, though included in the accounting profits, have to be put aside, because it is not the payment to capital service. The amount of bonuses depends on the extent to which an enterprise fulfills various norms assigned by higher agencies. Only a part, if any, of this amount is attributable to an improvement in qualities of capital. Given the unsteadiness of this sum, we may simply consider it as a windfall gain or, alternatively, ascribe it to the entrepreneurship: the third factor which is not specified as an input in the production or cost function. In fact, this amount may very well be attributable to the managerial skill, the manager's ability to have access to raw materials and investment funds, his familiarity with higher planning and administrative agencies, etc. In short, we define the net output as consisting of the capital cost, the labour cost and the third part we have just discussed.

346

The cost function under structural disequilibrium

Employment and wages

Fairly accurate information is available for two groups of industrial personnel: workers and engineers–technical personnel. Those two groups constitute 92–3 % of total working force of the industry. With approximations our coverage is extended to other two groups: office workers and others.

The employment is measured in man-years. The wages include premiums paid to the personnel who fulfilled and overfulfilled the assigned norms.

The quantity of labour series is measured in the number of heads. We do not estimate it in terms of efficiency units by taking into account the skills, the intensity of work and so forth.

We rely on man-year figures and not on man-hour figures. Though the working hours had been reduced substantially in the 1950s, there was little change in the working hours for the following period under our present study.

APPENDIX B. ESTIMATED RESULTS OF EQUATION (10)

Industry	a_1	a_2	a_3	a_4	a_5	a_6	a_7	a_8	a_9	R^2	DW
1. Electric power											
GLSQ (20th round)	6.09130 (9.1855)	8.75509 (24.0342)	0.06958 (6.5304)	0.11481 (29.3388)	0.00452 (4.5339)	—	0.61334 (10.2558)	−0.66730 (−14.2040)	−1.01598 (−30.1665)	1.0000	1.6841
Mixed estimation	5.52049 (7.1687)	8.30411 (19.4433)	0.06063 (4.8299)	0.10950 (23.6133)	0.00493 (4.1628)	—	0.58861 (8.3502)	−0.65410 (−11.7902) (−6.2350)	−0.96898 (−24.3343)	1.0000	1.6684
2. Ferrous metals											
GLSQ	6.17026 (14.8466)	7.88551 (14.6216)	0.05397 (12.0087)	0.08779 (16.9843)	—	—	0.60522 (22.6988)	−0.71623 (−18.5635) (−7.3550)	−0.97487 (−18.1159)	1.0000	1.9553
3. Machine building and metal working											
GLSQ	4.21809 (2.1356)	5.90826 (2.9406)	0.05882 (4.0132)	0.09285 (6.2660)	−0.00128 (−2.8854)	−0.00311 (−6.3049)	0.39009 (4.6287)	−0.67743 (−5.7335) (−2.7301)	−0.82448 (−5.6727)	1.0000	2.1223
4. Timber, pulp and paper											
GLSQ	2.8066 (6.8550)	7.3234 (16.4385)	0.01565 (7.8699)	0.03593 (14.8862)	—	—	0.29453 (20.1926)	−0.33875 (−10.5913) (−20.6748)	−0.86380 (−22.1379)	0.9999	2.2958
5. Construction materials											
GLSQ	3.94667 (2.0735)	6.51827 (3.6958)	0.02818 (1.7098)	0.12569 (8.3246)	—	−0.00476 (−5.5374)	0.39485 (5.0343)	−0.55257 (−7.1686) (−5.8046)	−0.93062 (−4.6522)	1.0000	1.5509
6. Light industry											
GLSQ	0.57149 (0.4313)	2.32782 (1.3085)	0.01384 (1.8006)	0.02323 (2.6683)	—	—	0.27045 (2.5849)	−0.67017 (−5.2523) (−2.5850)	−0.59067 (−7.4604)	1.0000	2.1660
7. Food industry											
GLSQ	5.88053 (2.1525)	8.31170 (3.0462)	0.07651 (6.1107)	0.10255 (8.4132)	−0.00169 (−1.4794)	−0.00349 (−3.2155)	0.50255 (4.6409)	−0.63302 (−5.11536)	−1.00348 (−4.5737)	1.0000	2.7492
Adjustment for autocorrelation	6.13203 (2.4416)	8.56521 (3.4177)	0.08029 (7.8859)	0.10632 (10.5404)	−0.00182 (−1.7474)	−0.00364 (−3.5938)	0.50664 (5.1102)	−0.63242 (−76.2652)	−1.02969 (−5.1362)	1.0000	2.3692
Mixed estimation	1.25981 (0.7813)	3.68396 (2.2982)	0.06121 (8.2927)	0.08669 (12.2992)	−0.00364 (−4.5675)	−0.00542 (−7.2317)	0.32005 (3.8158)	−0.63382 (−62.2142) (−35.9431)	−0.63753 (−4.9812)	1.0000	2.7483

The numbers within parentheses are t-values. As to two t-values for the coefficient a_8, the first one is for testing the null hypothesis $a_8 = 0$, and the second one is for testing the null hypothesis $a_8 = -1$.

The DW test statistics are adjusted for two gaps in the mixed estimation. They are adjusted for one gap in other estimations.

The GLSQ and the mixed estimation show the results at the 10th round of iteration, unless otherwise indicated.

348

NOTES

1 An earlier version of this paper was presented to the Winter Meeting of the Econometric Society in Toronto. The author was much benefited from the written comments by Gregory Grossman and the conversations with Hajime Oniki, though of course he retains the sole responsibility for remaining errors.

2 Throughout this paper, we are concerned only with misallocation within individual industries. It is true, even under the situation where individual industries attain the minimum cost, the allocation will still not be optimal if the factor prices vary between industries. But we leave the question of the misallocation between industries untouched. Thornton (1971) explores this problem.

3 Our purpose in estimating a function from the actual Soviet data precludes us from making our model as intricate as the one of a command economy (Grossman, 1963), although we try to make our model reflect some aspects of the Soviet-type economy.

4 The technical efficiency and the price efficiency are first defined by Farrell (1957). The difference between the two terms is conceptually clear, but practically it is very difficult to distribute the actually observed inefficiency at the industry level into the two categories.

5 From equation (4), it may be seen that the marginal cost is derived as

$$\partial(CY)/\partial Y = (1-\mu)\,C.$$

6 The two rates of shift over time are the same, if the returns to scale are constant.

7 We prove equation (15) in the following way. From the Cobb–Douglas form, the share of wages at (K_*, L_*) equals $1-\beta$, that is, $1-\beta = W_a L_*/C_* Y$. Then the ratio of (15) is

$$C_*/C_a = W_a L_*/[(1-\beta)\,C_a Y]. \tag{i}$$

Since the two input-mixes, (K_*, L_*) and (K, L), are on the same isoquant, they are related as

$$K_*^\beta L_*^{1-\beta} = K^\beta L^{1-\beta}. \tag{ii}$$

Furthermore, at the optimal input-mix K_* and L_*, the ratio of profits to wage earnings $\pi R_a K_*/W_a L_*$ is equal to $\beta/(1-\beta)$. Therefore, one finds

$$K_*/L_* = [W_a/(\pi R_a)]\,[\beta/(1-\beta)]. \tag{iii}$$

Let L_* in (ii) be expressed in terms of L, K/L and K_*/L_*, and substitute (iii) into (ii). After this, substitute L_* into (i). We thus obtain equation (15).

8 We estimated the two input-mixes with the observed factor prices, R_a and W_a. Ideally, however, one should use the factor prices in the overall equilibrium situation. In order to arrive at this equilibrium, it is not enough to eliminate the intra-industrial misallocation we are now concerned with. One should also eliminate the interindustrial misallocation caused by the factor price differential between industries, the gap between the production cost and the consumers' buying price, and so on. Needless to say, what we called the optimal factor-mix $(K_*$ and $L_*)$ is in fact only a second best point and is different from the factor-mix under this overall equilibrium.

9 The observed rate of return to capital of the Soviet industry is high not only for consumer good industries but also for producer good industries. In view of this fact, our result may sound strange.

But this high rate of return may well be due to the undervaluation of the capital stocks. And the undervaluation, in turn, is caused by the underpricing of producer goods as compared with consumer goods.

Suppose all the fixed and working capitals in the base year 1960 were underestimated by the same rate. The capital stocks in all subsequent years are assessed with these 1960 prices, if they are put as a variable of the production function. There-fore, the underestimation persists throughout the period. In view of the double-log form of the Cobb–Douglas production function, however, the underestimation will not alter the estimate of the elasticity β as long as it affects the capital stocks at the same rate.

REFERENCES

Farrell, M. J. (1957). The measurement of productive efficiency. *Journal of the Royal Statistical Society*, Series A (General), **120**, 253–81.

Grossman, Gregory (1963). Notes for a theory of the command economy. *Soviet Studies*, **15**, 101–23.

Kirsch, Leonard J. (1972). *Soviet Wages: Changes in Structure and Administration Since 1956*. MIT Press.

Theil, H. and A. S. Goldberger (1960). On pure and mixed statistical estimation in economics. *International Economic Review*, **2**, 65–78.

Thornton, Judith (1971). Differential capital charges and resource allocation in Soviet industry. *Journal of Political Economy*, **79**, 545–61.

Zellner, A. (1962). An efficient method of estimating seemingly unrelated regressions and tests for aggregation bias. *Journal of American Statistical Association*, **57**, 348–68.

3. Elasticity of Supply

Crop response to price in the Soviet Union

ELIZABETH CLAYTON

Observation of agriculture in the Soviet Union during the 1953–9 period provides an opportunity to compare a socialist producer's response to price changes under three different forms of economic organization: (1) the collective farm (*kolkhoz*); (2) the state farm (*sovkhoz*); (3) the private subsidiary plot ('private market'). This study is concerned with the specification of supply functions for agricultural crops in the Soviet Union in each of these three forms of organization. While prices often are considered to be effective incentives in a planned agricultural economy, this undertakes the empirical specification and test of this conclusion.

Economists have taken an ambivalent view toward price increases in the Soviet economy. On one hand, prices may be incentives which allocate inputs (particularly labor) and change output. On the other hand, prices simply may redistribute income between the state budget and the producer, leaving inputs and outputs unchanged.[1] This study tests the hypothesis that Soviet output responds to price changes through input response. Economic theory demonstrates that if the production function is given and the supplies of all inputs wholly determined in quantitative terms by the planners, then there can be no output response to price. The institutional feasibility of input response to price in each of the three sectors is examined in the first section.

One must further distinguish between the aggregate supply elasticity of all crops and individual supply elasticity of a single crop. This study focuses on the response of specific crops to price changes in each sector. The dependent and independent variables are defined in the second section where supply functions are specified which are logical for each form of organization and comparable to each other. The dependent variable is yield, the output per unit of land. The price independent variable reflects the alternative employment of labor. Price in the socialized sectors is the price paid by the state for its purchase from the socialized sectors relative to the price paid in the private market sector. Price of the crop in the private sector also is defined logically as a relative price. The supply functions are tested empirically using Soviet data modified for this purpose in the third section.

FEASIBILITY OF POSITIVE INPUT RESPONSE TO PRICE: INSTITUTIONAL BACKGROUND

If we are to consider that the supply functions in each of the three forms of agricultural organization may be different, then the differences lie in the institutions which constrain the responses of input suppliers to price. For the purposes of this study, inputs for each crop ideally should be divided into two classes: those which may respond to price and those which may not. As is common in economic investigations, however, the numerical data to make this classification precisely are unattainable in the desired form. Some substitute measures and theoretical assumptions are employed to fill this void.

The three Soviet agricultural sectors do not share a common economic environment with regard to inputs, outputs, or price mechanisms. In the socialized sectors, the planning of material inputs and the procurement of output by the state were administered by separate agencies during most of the 1953–9 period. There is no *a priori* reason to expect that the procurement prices of outputs and the quantitative allocation of inputs were systematically coordinated. In the private sector, the quantity of land was constrained by fiat, but land use and the choice of other inputs and output apparently could have been made by the producer. Prices were regulated very little in the private sector but wholly fixed in the socialized sectors.

Observation shows that the composition of crops reflects the input endowments of each sector. Table 1 summarizes some comparative input and output characteristics. The socialized sectors specialize in the production of land-extensive crops such as grain; land-intensive crops such as vegetables predominate in the private sector. While land regulations may limit the class of products which may be feasibly produced in a sector, the allocation of labor to specific crops within that class may be induced by price changes. The institutional feasibility of such an input response to price is examined below.

Land

Socialized ownership requires that land in all sectors is 'free'. Rents, taxes and regulations imposed on the land may constrain land use patterns, but use of the land is not determined wholly by the state. Correlation between the price increases of the 1950s and the increase in the total quantity of land under cultivation is well known; there is, however, no correlation between the price increases for any specific crop in socialized sector and the land input to that crop. Aggregate land in the private sector also did not respond to price increase. Although one might expect that the land–price relationship for specific crops would be positive

Table 1. *Relative share of the state and private sectors in
selected inputs and outputs USSR, 1950–8*

	State sector			Private sector (%)
	Kolkhoz	Sovkhoz	Total state	
Inputs				
Sown area				
1950	83	12	95	5
1958	67	29	96	4
Employment (man-days)				
1950	59	5	64	36
1958	53	11	64	36
Crops				
Quantity marketed				
1950 grain	87	11	98	2
1958 grain	63	37	100	0
1950 cotton	96	4	100	0
1958 cotton	87	13	100	0
1950 potatoes	34	5	39	61
1958 potatoes	41	10	51	49
1950 vegetables	—	—	76	24
1958 vegetables	—	—	85	15
Quantity produced				
1950 grain	—	—	93	7
1958 grain	68	25	93	7
1950 cotton	96	4	100	0
1958 cotton	87	13	100	0
1950 potatoes	23	4	27	73
1958 potatoes	29	5	34	66
1950 vegetables	45	11	56	44
1958 vegetables	39	16	55	45

SOURCES: Narkhoz (1965, p. 288); Nimitz (1967, p. 192); Selkhoz (1960, pp. 48, 202 ff).

in the private sector, this is not verified, surprisingly, by examination of the data in the crop sector.[2] However, about 80 % of the output of the private sector is consumed in the household and the average plot size is small, only 0.25 hectare; the large component of non-marketable product apparently constrains the land use response to price and limits the significance (or elasticity) of price incentives in this sector to effects on other inputs.

Labor

This study assumes by hypothesis that quantitative planning which was wholly binding was not imposed on this input in any sector. There was no observable correlation between the aggregate quantity of labor employed in the socialized sectors and the level of agricultural prices.[3] Alternative employments were available: both the state farmer and the collective farmer might choose to work on their private plots; and all sectors' workers faced the classic option described by Domar (1966) as 'lying on the stove', i.e., leisure. Restrictions were placed on the ability to respond to alternatives; collective farmers faced minimum work-day requirements and state farmers faced the national minimum work-week also imposed on industrial workers. By making the assumption that labor might respond to price in some positive fashion, it is necessary only to assume that the negative economic effects of coercion and restriction are of lesser impact than the positive economic effects of price increases.

The institutional arrangements linking output, and labor income differed in each form of organization. Collective farm workers were paid a share of the residual of farm revenues after taxes and insurance payments were disbursed. State farm workers were paid a centrally determined wage which correlated with time rather than with output. Private market producers received the entire net receipts from the sale of their output.

Labor response to income incentives in the state farm and private sectors is logical by ordinary economic assumptions and familiar models. The labor response to output price changes in the collective farm sector is less clear. Ward's model (1957) implies a negative response, but Oi and Clayton (1968), following Domar (1966, appendix), show that introduction of opportunity cost reverses this relationship in a model. Oi and Clayton consider the private sector explicitly as an alternative use of labor; Domar considers alternative socialized sector uses of labor. The presence of either alternative reverses the negative labor supply response of the single crop co-op model where no alternative uses of labor are available. Oi and Clayton further show that labor responds positively to price changes where land inputs are exogenously determined and that these conclusions hold when output quotas and work-day minimums are introduced.

The state farm worker's wages were not related directly to the sales of product from the state farm, but the quantity of labor was predetermined partially by central determination of wages and wage bills. While the response of the individual supplier to labor price (wage) may be positive in such an environment, the aggregate state farm demand for labor may not be responsive to changes in output price. Since aggregate labor input is planned in quantitative terms, the demand may be perfectly inelastic and labor supply response irrelevant for predicting output. Proceeds from the sale of state farm output affect the income of the state farm worker least of all agricultural workers and we can expect that the labor response to price would be least in this sector.

The labor response to price in the private market sector is similar to the labor response to price in a market economy. Proceeds from the sale of farm products affect the income of the producer–laborer directly and there is pecuniary motivation to respond to price changes. The collective farm model suggests that this price also should be defined as a relative price to indicate the opportunity cost of such labor in other activities foregone.

Fertilizer and raw material inputs

Production and deliveries of fertilizer during this period were correlated positively with an aggregate index of agricultural prices. Any measure of positive price response for a specific product would include the effects of fertilizer applications to that crop. There are no data relating the quantity of fertilizer applied to any specific crop or delivered to any specific form of organization.[4]

Capital

Capital inputs in the Soviet Union during the 1950–9 period were allocated directly in quantitative terms. Machine Tractor Stations (MTS) determined the flow of capital services to the collective farms until 1958. Stocks of capital inputs were allocated directly to the state farms and MTS through independent state agencies. Capital inputs were negligible in the private market sector. Data are available for the sectoral stocks of tractors for the period under consideration; there is no clear correlation between even the aggregate stocks of this input and the level of an aggregated crop price index, though the data are so few as to be only suggestive.

Soil and weather

Weather is obviously unresponsive to price changes but adequate specification of Soviet agricultural supply functions requires that its effects be considered. Soviet climate lacks the weather-modifying effects of large bodies of water and is classed as 'continental'. Continentality effects may be subdidivded into two major components: extremes of temperature which are broadly correlated with latitude, and annual rainfall which is determined by factors other than latitude.

Soil variations also are not price responsive in the short run. Modification of soil conditions may take place over longer periods of time, but there is no indication that the Soviet efforts were either coordinated with prices or well-endowed with resources from the public sector. Regional soil variations form a rough basis for the system of differential prices paid after 1958 by the Soviet agricultural procurement agencies, indicating that Soviets consider the differences to be subject to long-run stability.

MEASUREMENT OF THE PRICE–OUTPUT RELATIONSHIP

Western economists have estimated market price–output response by specifying land as the dependent variable rather than output. This procedure effectively separated the farmers' *ex-ante* response to expected prices from their *ex-post* price response which included unanticipated price change and exogenous weather variables. In the Soviet economy, land use does not respond to price incentives, because of either central planning or household subsistence needs. As previously demonstrated, only labor and perhaps raw materials feasibly may respond to price incentives.

Procurement prices in the socialized sectors are paid by the state to the collective and state farms. Price premiums are granted for quantities above a quota level. These premiums are fractional multiples of the basic price. Prices are announced in advance in the socialized sector, and price expectations do not play an important role in the Soviet state farm and collective farm sectors. Prices received in the socialized sector are f.o.b. the socialized producing unit.

Market-clearing, fluctuating prices are paid in the private sector markets; random samples are taken to derive an annual average. The absolute level of prices in the private sector markets is several times higher than the socialized sector, but prices in the private sector are c.i.f. the producing unit and part of the difference in absolute price levels thus includes transportation charges, transit losses, storage, and preliminary processing. Quota minima to be sold at socialized prices to state procurement agencies were required in the socialized sectors during all years studied but were abolished in the private sector after 1957. Table 2 compares relative price changes in the socialized and private sectors between 1953 and 1959. State procurement prices increased rapidly during this period but ever attained the absolute level of the collective farm market prices.

Non-price incentive policies accompanied price incentives. In market studies of price elasticity, producer income and price are very closely correlated. In the Soviet environment, non-money income, as well as money income, played an important role. Not all of the socialized sector income was pecuniary during this period; table 3 indicates that the share of money in labor payments even in 1958 was relatively small. While the share of money in total income increased during the 1950s a significant

Table 2. *Agricultural prices*

State procurement prices (1952 = 100)

Year	All agriculture	Crop	Grain	Technical	Vegetables and fruits	Potatoes	Meat	Cotton	Sugar beets	Corn	Wheat
1953	154	132	236	122	119	316	214	105	144	207	245
1954	207	171	739	125	135	369	307	102	111	564	752
1955	209	169	553	137	138	368	319	96	130	685	524
1956	251	207	634	163	192	814	371	114	229	572	647
1957	266	209	617	166	188	859	420	115	243	738	603
1958	296	203	695	155	179	789	546	106	219	819	621
1959	302	206	743	154	169	834	561	107	217	1008	656

Collective farm market prices (1940 = 100)

Year	Grain	Potatoes	Vegetables	Milk	Meat	Eggs	Six-product group
1953	93	88	136	96	100	95	96
1954	109	109	134	110	105	101	110
1955	114	102	123	109	111	98	111
1956	91	93	105	98	98	99	97
1957	89	79	122	89	99	98	94
1958	89	97	132	92	102	102	100
1959	78	92	147	96	96	101	97

SOURCES: Selkhoz (1960, p. 117), and Karcz (1964, appendix).

Table 3. *Share of money in payment of one man-day, RFSFR, 1958*

Less than 50 % money	28 *kolkhozy*
50–60 %	24
60–70 %	11
70–80 %	3
80–90 %	—
Higher than 90 %	—

SOURCE: Morozov (1965, p. 98).

proportion of income remained a share of farm product, feed grain from the socialized sector, or the opportunity to buy scarce consumer goods which could not be obtained otherwise. Labor response has two components: the response to the price incentive and the response to the non-money incentive. Insofar as the price incentive replaced the non-money incentive, the measured response to price will be understated.

Since land does not respond to price incentives, the dependent variable in the estimating equation becomes yield, output per unit of land.[5] Labor and raw material response to price, regional soil differences, and inter-temporal weather variations become the independent variables. The estimating equation is:

$$\frac{X_{it}}{T_{it}} + a_0 + b\frac{P_{xt}}{P_{yt}} + cD_i + dR_{it} + eC_{it} + u_{it}, \tag{1}$$

where

$\dfrac{X_{it}}{T_{it}}$ = yield of crop X in the ith region and ith time period;

$\dfrac{P_{xt}}{P_{yt}}$ = relative price of sector crop X and alternative sector crop Y in ith time period;

D_i = dummy variable for the ith region;

R_{it} = index of average annual rainfull in the ith time period and ith region (10-year average = 100);

C_{it} = index of continentality in the ith time period and ith region[6]

and

u_{it} = error term for the ith region in the ith time period.

Proposing by hypothesis that labor rather than non-human inputs may respond to crop price incentives is a vastly different economic environ-

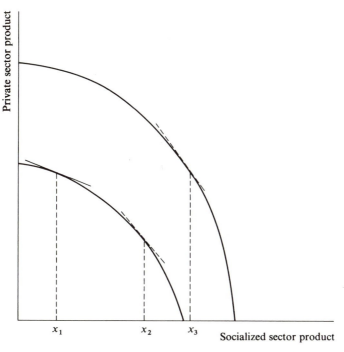

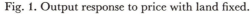

Fig. 1. Output response to price with land fixed.

See Oi and Clayton (1968) for further discussion of this concept.

ment than that of a market economy where all inputs (including land use) are mobile. Labor mobility in response to price changes may be divided into short-run and long-run effects; both are constrained by the institutional rigidities governing the use of land. In the short run, a fixed labor stock may be reallocated between crops. This is illustrated in fig. 1 where an increase in the price of crop X will motivate labor to produce X, and output will rise from X_1 to X_2, decreasing the output of crop Y. In adding labor to a fixed stock of land, the marginal physical product of labor in that use will diminish, thus effectively limiting the output response to price which may occur. In the long run, the stock of the variable input labor may increase in response to price changes. The production frontier will move outward, increasing output to X_3 as in fig. 1, but diminishing product will continue to limit the effectiveness of the response in increasing output.

The possibility of diminishing returns implies that the form of the estimating equation could be logarithmic or semi-logarithmic.[7] Accordingly, each form of the estimation was tested.

Table 4. *Estimates of crop supply elasticity, USSR*[a]

Crop (yield)	Price coefficient (a)	Elasticity[b]	R^2	F ratio
Kolkhoz				
Grain ($N = 125$)	0.0576*	0.41	0.82	16.23*
	(0.0083)			
Potatoes ($N = 90$)	0.3124*	0.38	0.65	6.35*
	(0.0650)			
Cotton ($N = 49$)	0.4495	0.23	0.68	9.23*
	(0.3646)			
Sovkhoz				
Grain ($N = 125$)	0.0593*	0.86	0.22	1.08
	(0.0216)			
Potatoes ($N = 90$)	− 0.2574*	− 0.30	0.71	8.63*
	(0.0835)			
Private sector				
Grain ($N = 100$)	0.0310*	0.02	0.70	6.42*
	(0.0083)			
Potatoes ($N = 90$)	0.4975	0.50	0.81	14.76*
	(0.4208)			

[a] Estimates are straight-line except for the private sector where potatoes are logarithmic and grain is semi-logarithmic.

[b] Calculated from price coefficient (a) and the means of yield and price except for the logarithmic coefficients which are transferred directly and the semi-logarithmic coefficients evaluated at mean of yield.

* Significant at level of 95 %.

DATA SOURCES: output, *Sel'skoe Khoziaistvo* (1960); land, *Sel'skoe Khoziaistvo* (1960) and *Posevnye Ploshchadi* (1957); prices, Karcz (1964, Appendix) and *Sel'skoe Khoziaistvo*; rain and temperature, *World Weather Records*, 'Asia' and 'Europe' (USDC, 1964).

STATISTICAL RESULTS FOR THE USSR AND INTERNATIONAL COMPARISONS

USSR estimates

Estimates of the Soviet producers' responsiveness to prices are summarized in table 4, for three crops (potatoes, grain and cotton) in three sectors. Collective farm sector behavior is the most price responsive of the three. The most widespread crops, potatoes and grain, are significantly price responsive, the yield elasticity is high and the regression equation valid statistically. Price elasticity of collective farm cotton is lower and not significant. The narrow geographic limits on cotton production in the Soviet Union suggest that an all-Union aggregate price index is not an appropriate deflator to indicate alternative uses of labor; using alternative-sector meat prices increases the measured effectiveness of price response in this sector significantly.[8]

Producers' response to price in the state farm sector is insignificant or negative. Despite the high elasticity coefficient for grain in this sector, the correlation is suspect for the regression equation itself does not account for a significant part of the variance in yield and is not significant statistically. State farm labor may participate in the private sector market, but the prices in that market do not affect the performance of this variable input in the state farm sector in a statistically significant manner.

Producer response to price incentives is not unequivocal in the private sector. While prices account for some of the variation in yield, it is not clear that they play a major role. The price elasticity of grain is significant but low; the price elasticity of potatoes is high but not significant statistically. The logarithmic and semi-logarithmic forms of the relationship were more reliable predictors of yield than the straight-line estimates of the other sectors. Diminishing marginal physical product of variable (non-land) inputs would explain this idiosyncrasy plausibly. The relative prices of the socialized and private sectors is hypothesized to affect the behavior of labor and yield in both sectors; this conclusion can be supported by collective farm behavior but cannot be supported from the price coefficients and elasticities in the private sector.

This paper has tested the hypothesis that the relationship between prices in the market and prices in the socialized sectors determines the allocation of labor (and other variable inputs) in the absence of exogenous and binding constraints. Collective farm sector behavior supports such a hypothesis positively; state farm behavior does not deny such a hypothesis due to known constraints. Behavior of the private market sector does not support this hypothesis nor are there exogenous constraints which would explain the observed behavior. In order to pursue the elusive behavior of the private sector, the following aggregated regression relationships were tested in each sector.[9]

$$Y_t = a + bP_t + u_t, \tag{2}$$

where Y_t = yield of the sector in year t;[10]

P_t = prices of the sector deflated by prices in the alternative sector in year t;

u_t = error term for year t.

Results are shown in table 5. Collective farm and state farm conclusions are unchanged by this new test: the collective farm responds to price incentives and the state farm does not. As price-responsive inputs were mobile in the first sector and immobile in the second, both would tend to verify the hypothesis proposed. The negative price elasticity of yield of the private sector is statistically significant. Constraints known to elicit such a response have not been considered in the behavioral model; the statistical hypothesis should be rejected for this sector. As relative prices increase, private producers respond in the aggregate by reducing yield.

Elizabeth Clayton

Table 5. *Elasticity of aggregate agricultural supply, USSR*

	Price coefficient	Elasticity	R^2	F ratio
Collective farm ($N = 7$)	0.2691* (0.0383)	0.53	0.91	49.23*
State farm ($N = 7$)	-0.04 (0.07)	0.11	0.07	0.38
Private ($N = 7$)	-0.5971* (0.1241)	0.25	0.82	23.14*

* Significant at level of 95 %.
SOURCES: output and land; Clayton (1970); prices; see table 4.

Predicting market sector behavior through an aggregate income-maximizing model is not supported by the results obtained here. Intra-sectoral comparisons of price elasticities in the private sector suggest that traditional market behavior is an appropriate model within the sector, but the market model loses validity as one considers inter-sectoral price relatives.[11] Inter-sectoral price relatives do not have symmetrical effects; producer response to price relatives is positive in the collective farm sector and negative in the market sector.

Prices in the private sector were higher than prices in the socialized sector during the period studied. However, crop prices in the private sector diminished relative to both the rapidly rising prices of the socialized sector and private sector meat prices. The significant cross-elasticity of private sector crop yields and meat product prices suggests that intra-sectoral price differentials are more significant in predicting private producer behavior than inter-sectoral. In graphic terms, the private sector experienced shifts of the crop supply curve upward and to the right in response to alternative product opportunities. Until 1958, this shift to meat products was encouraged by fodder allocations from the socialized sector. The private sector has allocated its resources from crops to meat increasingly, with some diminution in the early 1960s.

However, the aggregated yield of the private sector does not demonstrate that the shifts into meat production offset the shifts from crop production. Indeed, diminishing productivity in the private sector cannot be dismissed. Variable inputs have been injected into the private sector despite a fall in relative price and constant absolute price. The share of variable inputs in the production function is fractional and thus their elasticity of supply is greater than yield elasticity.[12] The role of complementary variable inputs and their price (labor and fodder, for example) becomes crucial in this context and warrants further study.

Table 6. *Elasticity of crop supply, USSR and other countries*

Crop	Nation	Dependent variable	Elasticity of supply
Cotton	USSR (kolkhoz)	Yield	0.23
	USA	Acreage	0.7
	India	Acreage	0.59
	Pakistan	Acreage	0.41
	Greece	Acreage	0.70
Grain	USSR (kolkhoz)	Yield	0.41
	(sovkhoz)	Yield	0.86
	(private)	Yield	0.02
	USA*	Acreage	0.48
	India*	Acreage	0.08
	Pakistan*	Acreage	0.20
	Greece	Acreage	0.43
	Greece*	Acreage	0.37
Potatoes	USSR (kolkhoz)	Yield	0.38
	(sovkhoz)	Yield	−0.30
	(private)	Yield	0.50
	USA	Acreage	0.08
	Greece	Acreage	0.32

* Wheat only.

SOURCES: USSR, text, table 4; USA; cotton and grain; Nerlove (1958); potatoes; Kohls Paarlberg cited in Nerlove (1958); India, Krishna (1963); Pakistan, Falcon (1964); Greece, Paulopoulou (1967).

International comparisons

Price elasticity measures are devoid of units of measurement to facilitate comparison across boundaries and between crops. International comparisons are not uniformly devised, however. Market economy studies commonly use acreage as a dependent variable (in order to analyze the *ex-ante* response of producers to prices before the *ex-post* effects of non-price variables such as weather have intervened. Price elasticity measurement of USSR crops included the effects of rainfall and continentality in order to facilitate an international comparison between market acreage elasticity and non-market yield elasticity. The only market study of yield (Falcon, 1964) had statistically insignificant response to price results. Comparisons are summarized in table 6. The elasticity of all crops lies within the inelastic range $(0 < \eta < 1)$, suggesting that there might be common production function or behavioral limits to price responsiveness. Price elasticity in the USSR is not appreciably different from the price elasticity of market economies, measured by rank correlation. The margin of error is relatively large in any price coefficient, but the uniformity between nations with different economic institutions suggests a similarity in price responsiveness which transcends national boundaries.

SUMMARY AND CONCLUSIONS

This study of price response in Soviet agriculture has demonstrated the complex role of money incentives under physical planning. While one may observe that prices and income induced certain behavioral responses on the part of producers, production constraints from physical planning may affect the observation. Price incentives in the state farm sector have been purely an income reallocation from the state budget to the state farms; in effect, they have changed the line title on budget grants. Price increases in the collective farm sector have increased income and output as well. Price decreases in the private sector have not had similar effects; the behavioral response in this sector suggests that input planning and production function characteristics play a more influential role than prices in determining output in this sector as they do in the state farm sector.

The shift from production intended for domestic use to market-oriented production requires specialization and dependency upon the socialized sectors both for complementary inputs and domestic consumption products. Private sector producers have accepted the opportunity offered by increasing meat prices; they have not responded in aggregate production to relative price incentives. This suggests that, at present, labor flows from the private sector to either socialized sector or leisure are negligible. Concurrently, complementary inputs exogenously supplied to the private sector are more critical in production expansion than is commonly assumed. The constraints on land and labor-complementary inputs ensure that the observed diminishing returns to variable inputs limit the feasibility of expanding private sector agriculture in the Soviet Union. Diminishing returns and centralized planning, by circumscribing the price response of the private sector, place a boundary on increased output.

NOTES

1 For a comprehensive survey of Soviet arguments surrounding the mid-1950s price increases, see Millar (1965).

2 Land utilization shifted from crops into livestock during this period, however. Prices in the livestock markets and feed allocations from the socialized sectors abetted this shift.

3 Independent estimates from several competent observers to not agree on the direction (let alone the magnitude) of labor supply changes in the socialized sector during the 1950 period. See Nimitz (1967) and Diamond (1966).

4 Conklin (1969) suggests that production and delivery data of fertilizers should not be correlated with output due to transportation and application bottlenecks.

5 The relationship between the yield response to price and the output response to price may be shown by the following comparison of supply elasticities:

$$X = L^a T^b, \text{ a Cobb–Douglas production function where}$$
$$X = \text{output},$$
$$L = \text{price-responsive inputs},$$
$$T = \text{land}. \tag{1}$$

Changes in output (%) are shown by:

$$\frac{dX}{X} = a\frac{dL}{L} + b\frac{dT}{T}. \tag{2}$$

Transforming to elasticities:

$$\eta_{x,P_x} = a\frac{dL}{dP_x}\frac{P_x}{L} + b\frac{dT}{dP_x}\frac{P_x}{T}. \tag{2a}$$

The yield (Y) response to price, where $Y = X/T$, is:

$$\frac{dY}{dP_x}\frac{P_x}{Y} = \frac{dX}{dP_x}\frac{P_x}{X} - \frac{dT}{dP_x}\frac{P_x}{T} = \eta_{Y,P_x}. \tag{3}$$

Substituting (2a) into (3):

$$\eta_{Y,P_x} = a\eta_{L,P_x} + (b-1)\eta_{T,P_x}, \tag{4}$$

or,

$$\eta_{Y,P_x} = a\eta_{L,P_x},$$

when

$$\eta_{T,P_x} = 0. \tag{4a}$$

Yield response to price always will be less than output response to price with all inputs variable due to diminishing returns.

6 An index of continentality measures the variation in temperature extremes experienced during a given year in relation to the latitude. The following form of the index (C), following Johansson was used:

$$C = 1.6\frac{\text{annual high–annual low}}{\sin\phi\text{ latitude}} - 14.$$

Several forms of the continentality index have been developed by climatologists, but the index form (0–100 range) of this formulation permits direct comparison with the index form of the other variables in the regression equation. (Using growing season extremal temperature does not change the results.) See Conrod and Pollack (1950, pp. 296 ff.) for discussion.

7 In logarithmic form $0 < b < 1$, diminishing returns to the variable factor of production are present. Soviet farms may not operate in this region, although profit maximizing firms will.

8 Price elasticity is 0.34 and significant using private sector meat prices as an alternative price deflator. See Clayton (1968, table 3).

9 This regression differs from (1) in two respects: output is a 9-product series and prices are the only independent variable.

10 Yield was obtained by dividing an index of output by an index of sown hectares. An output index was composed of nine products: grain, cotton, sugar beets, potatoes, vegetables, milk, meat, eggs and wool; collective farm market prices (1959) were used to aggregate the series.

11 Meat prices rose rapidly during this period and other restrictions on meat production were reduced. When intra-sector meat prices are used to deflate the own-price, price elasticity is positive and significant (Clayton, 1968).

12 See note 5.

Elizabeth Clayton

REFERENCES

Clayton, Elizabeth (1968). The impact of economic organization on the supply elasticity of some Soviet agricultural products. Unpublished doctoral dissertation, University of Washington.

Clayton, Elizabeth (1971). Productivity in Soviet agriculture: a sectoral comparison. *Jahrbuch der Wirtschaft Osteuropas*, Band 2, Günter Olzog Verlay München: Vienna, 1971, pp. 315–28.

Conklin, D. W. (1969). Barriers to technological change in the USSR: a study of chemical fertilizers. *Soviet Studies*, **20**, 353–65.

Conrod, V. and L. W. Pollack (1950). *Methods in Climatology*, 2nd edition. Cambridge, Mass.: Harvard University Press.

Diamond, D. B. (1966). Trends in output, inputs, and factor productivity in Soviet agriculture. In *New Directions in the Soviet Economy*, Joint Economic Committee, Washington.

Domar, Evsey (1966). The Soviet collective farm as a producer cooperative. *American Economic Review*, **56**, 734–57.

Falcon, Walter P. (1964). Farmer response to price in a subsistence economy: the case of West Pakistan. *American Economic Review*, **54**, 580–91.

Karcz, Jerzy (1964). Quantitative analysis of the collective farm market. *American Economic Review*, **54**, 315–34.

Krishna, Raj. (1963). Farm supply response in India and Pakistan. *Economic Journal*, **73**, 477–87.

Millar, James (1965). Price and income formation in the Soviet collective farm sector since 1953. Unpublished doctoral dissertation, Cornell.

Morozov, V. A. (1965). *Trudoden' den'gi i torgovlia na sele*. Moscow: Izdat.

Nerlove, Marc (1958). *Dynamics of Supply: Estimation of Farmers Response to Price*. Baltimore.

Nimitz, Nancy (1967). Farm employment in the Soviet Union. *In Soviet and East European Agriculture*, ed. J. Karcz. Berkeley.

Oi, W. Y. and E. M. Clayton (1968). A peasant's view of a Soviet collective farm. *American Economic Review*, **58**, 37–59.

Paulopoulou, Pan. G. (1967). *Synartiseis Prosforas Agrotikon Proyuonton*. Athens.

Tsentral'noe Statisticheskoe upravleniye pri Sovete Ministrov, *Narodnoe Khoziaistvo* (abbreviated *Narkhoz*); *Selskoe Khoziaistvo* (abbreviated *Selkhoz*); *Posevnye Ploshchadi*. Statistical handbooks, Moscow.

US Department of Commerce (1964). *World Weather Records*. Washington.

Ward, Benjamin (1958). The firm in Illyria: market syndicalism. *American Economic Review*, **48**, 566–89.

Author Index

Author Index

Subject Index

369